Collective Action, Philosophy and Law

I0891214

Collective Action, Philosophy and Law brings together two important strands of philosophical analysis. It combines general philosophical inquiry into collective agency with analyses of specific questions about plural entities and activities in the legal domain. These are issues of growing interest in areas of philosophy like action theory and social ontology, as well as in philosophy of law.

The book contains 13 original chapters written by an international team of leading philosophers and legal theorists and is divided into 4 parts:

- The nature of law and of legislative intention
- Practical reasoning and duties
- Causality, blameworthiness and responsibility
- Citizens, states and institutions.

These sections cut across, and build on, different accounts to advance the debate on classical and new issues in collective agency. Each part also features legal-philosophical analyses that draw on general accounts of collective agency to cast new light on the law, descriptive as well as normatively.

Collective Action, Philosophy and Law is the first major interdisciplinary and multi-authored work bridging legal and philosophical approaches to collective agency. As such, it is essential reading for students and researchers of philosophy of law, ethics, political philosophy, jurisprudence and legal theory.

Teresa Marques is Profesora Agregada (Associate Professor) in the Philosophy Department at the University of Barcelona, Spain. She is also a member of the LOGOS Group and of the Barcelona Institute of Analytic Philosophy. With Åsa Wikforss she is editor of *Shifting Concepts: The Philosophy and Psychology of Conceptual Variability* (2020). She has published in journals like *Philosophical Studies*, *The Australasian Journal of Philosophy*, *Synthese*, *Erkenntnis*, *Inquiry*, *Thought*, *Ratio*, *Philosophia* and *Metaphilosophy*.

Chiara Valentini is Senior Researcher in Philosophy of Law at the University of Bologna Law Department, Italy. With Bongiovanni, Postema, Rotolo, Sartor and Walton, she is editor of the *Handbook of Legal Reasoning and Argumentation* (2018). Her work has been published in journals like *Law and Philosophy*, *The American Journal of Jurisprudence*, *Ratio Juris* and *Jurisprudence*.

Collective Action, Philosophy and Law

Edited by
Teresa Marques and Chiara Valentini

Routledge
Taylor & Francis Group
LONDON AND NEW YORK

First published 2022
by Routledge
2 Park Square, Milton Park, Abingdon, Oxon OX14 4RN

and by Routledge
605 Third Avenue, New York, NY 10158

Routledge is an imprint of the Taylor & Francis Group, an informa business

© 2022 selection and editorial matter Teresa Marques and Chiara Valentini; individual chapters, the contributors

The right of Teresa Marques and Chiara Valentini to be identified as the author of the editorial material, and of the authors for their individual chapters, has been asserted in accordance with sections 77 and 78 of the Copyright, Designs and Patents Act 1988.

All rights reserved. No part of this book may be reprinted or reproduced or utilised in any form or by any electronic, mechanical, or other means, now known or hereafter invented, including photocopying and recording, or in any information storage or retrieval system, without permission in writing from the publishers.

Trademark notice: Product or corporate names may be trademarks or registered trademarks, and are used only for identification and explanation without intent to infringe.

British Library Cataloguing-in-Publication Data
A catalogue record for this book is available from the British Library

Library of Congress Cataloging-in-Publication Data
A catalog record has been requested for this book

ISBN: 978-0-367-65102-2 (hbk)
ISBN: 978-1-032-15083-3 (pbk)
ISBN: 978-1-003-24245-1 (ebk)

DOI: 10.4324/9781003242451

Typeset in Bembo
by KnowledgeWorks Global Ltd.

To Agata and Miranda, who grew with this project

Contents

Contributors

Nicholas Almendares is Associate Professor of Law at the Maurer School of Law, Indiana University Bloomington and previously served as the program director for the Karsh Center for Law and Democracy at the University of Virginia School of Law. His research focuses on accountability and democracy, especially relating to collective action, joint intention and aggregate litigation.

Caroline T. Arruda is Associate Professor of Philosophy at the University of Texas at El Paso. Her work focuses on issues at the intersection of philosophy of action and meta-ethics and has appeared in venues such as the *Australasian Journal of Philosophy*, *Analysis*, *Mind & Language*, *The Journal of the American Philosophical Association*, among others. She has been a Visiting Researcher at the Center for the Study of Mind in Nature at the University of Oslo and an Academic Visitor at the Australian National University. She is currently at work on a monograph entitled *Enriching Practical Reason*.

Carla Bagnoli is Professor of Theoretical Philosophy at the University of Modena & Reggio Emilia. She specializes in the theory of rational agency and practical rationality, meta-ethics. Recently, she was Professorial Fellow (Professor II) at the University of Oslo and has held visiting posts at the universities of Paris 1 Panthéon-Sorbonne, ENS Lyon, Ludwig-Maximilians-Universität München, and Oxford. Her articles appear in journals such as *Oxford Studies in Normative Ethics, Oxford Studies in Agency and Responsibility, Ethical Theory and Moral Practice, Synthese, Theoria, Philosophia*, and *The Canadian Journal of Philosophy*. She edited *Morality and the Emotions* (Oxford UP, 2011), and *Constructivism in Ethics* (Cambridge UP, 2013). Her most recent monograph in Italian defends a theory of responsibility (Il Mulino, 2019).

Sara Bernstein is Thomas J. and Robert T. Rolfs Associate Professor of Philosophy at the University of Notre Dame. She specializes in metaphysics, with publications on causation, counterfactuals, ontology, fundamentality, time travel and feminist philosophy. She has held the Philip L. Quinn

Fellowship at the National Humanities Center, the Andrew W. Mellon Assistant Professorship, been a visitor at Arché at the University of St. Andrews, and is a frequent visitor at the Australian National University. Prior to her current position, she was assistant professor of philosophy at Duke University.

Damiano Canale is Professor of Philosophy of Law and Critical Thinking at Bocconi University, Milan. He studied Political Science and Philosophy at the University of Padua. His areas of research include philosophy of language, legal interpretation, legal argumentation, the history of legal and political concepts. He is co-editor of *A History of Philosophy of Law in the Civil Law World, 1600–1900* (Springer, 2009); *The Rules of Inference. Inferentialism in Law and Philosophy* (EGEA, 2010); *The Planning Theory of Law. A Critical Reading* (Springer, 2013). His papers on legal theory and legal argumentation have been published in *Law and Philosophy*, *Ratio Juris*, *Rechtstheorie*, *Informal Logic*, *Argumentation*.

Sara Rachel Chant is currently a visiting scholar at Purdue University, formerly Associate Professor of Philosophy at the University of Missouri. Chant has worked in the areas of Applied Ethics, Philosophy of the Social Sciences, Social Ontology, Metaphysics and the Philosophy of Mind. However, Chant's main contribution has been to the Philosophy of Collective Action. There she has argued against the traditional approaches to questions arising from collective action, especially questions concerning collective intentionality and group-level moral responsibility.

Brian Flanagan is an Associate Professor at the Department of Law, Maynooth University. His research focuses on the nature of institutional agency and its implications for legal and political theory and on topics in experimental jurisprudence. His work has been published in outlets including the *Australasian Journal of Philosophy*, *Philosophical Studies*, *Journal of Moral Philosophy*, *International & Comparative Law Quarterly* and *Oxford Journal of Legal Studies*.

Natalie Gold is Visiting Professor in Practice in the Centre for Philosophy of Natural and Social Science, at the London School of Economics and Political Science; and Senior Director in the Behavioural Practice at Kantar Public UK. She studied Philosophy, Politics and Economics and has an MPhil and a DPhil from the University of Oxford. After postdoctoral fellowships at the University of Konstanz and Duke University, she was appointed as Lecturer in Mind, Reason and Decision in the Philosophy Department at the University of Edinburgh. Prior to coming to PHE, she was Senior Research Fellow at King's College London, where she was Principal Investigator on the project "Self-Control and the Person: An Inter-Disciplinary Account", funded by the European Research Council. She has also had funding from the Arts and Humanities Research Council (UK), the Economic and Social Research Council (UK), the British

Academy, and the Carnegie Trust (Scotland). Since 2015, Natalie has also been an Associate at the Political Economy of Financial Markets programme (PEFM) in St. Anthony's College, Oxford University. She has previously held visiting positions at Hong Kong University, the University of Pittsburgh, the London School of Economics, the Institute of Cognitive Sciences and Technologies—Consiglio Nazionale delle Ricerche Rome, and the Australian National University. Natalie has published on topics including framing, moral judgements and decision making, cooperation and coordination, trust, self-control, nudge, health improvement and financial regulation

Dimitrios Kyritsis is Reader in Law at the University of Essex. Prior to that, he was Associate Professor at the University of Reading (2014–2020), Lecturer at the University of Sheffield (2007–2014), and Hauser Global Law Fellow at New York University (2006–2007). His main research interests are in legal and political philosophy, constitutional theory and human rights law. He is the author of *Shared Authority: Courts and Legislatures in Legal Theory* (Hart, 2015) and *Where Our Protection Lies: Separation of Powers and Constitutional Review* (OUP, 2017).

Teresa Marques is "Profesora Agregada" (Associate Professor) at the Philosophy Department of the University of Barcelona. She is also a member of the LOGOS Group and of the Barcelona Institute of Analytic Philosophy. Before joining the University of Barcelona in 2017, she was a Marie Curie Fellow with a grant from the European Commission with the Law & Philosophy Group of Pompeu Fabra University. Teresa Marques specializes in philosophy of language, in particular on speech acts, evaluative discourse, and on social and political philosophy of language. She has additional interests in meta-ethics, feminist philosophy, and social and legal philosophy. She has published in journals like *Philosophical Studies, The Australasian Journal of Philosophy, Synthese, Erkenntnis, Inquiry, Thought, Ratio, Philosophia, Metaphilosophy,* and edited *Shifting Concepts: The Philosophy and Psychology of Conceptual Variability* (OUP, 2020), with Åsa Wikforss.

Maggie O'Brien is an Assistant Professor at the Philosophy Department of the University of York, Toronto. Formerly she was a Lecturer in Legal Theory at the University of Edinburgh. Her research focuses on the nature and conditions of authoritative pronouncements, whether in the context of a judicial voice in a court decision or in more general questions of public standing to speak. Her research is interdisciplinary crossing legal theory, moral philosophy, gender studies and political theory.

Abraham Sesshu Roth is Professor of Philosophy at Ohio State University. He has taught at UCLA and at the University of Illinois at Chicago and received his PhD from Princeton. He works mainly in the philosophy of action, focusing on issues concerning intentions, practical reasoning, reasons explanation, shared agency, and related issues in epistemology and moral psychology. He has published in *The Philosophical Review*, *Noûs*, *Ethics*, *Oxford Studies in Agency and Responsibility*, *Philosophy and Phenomenological Research*, *Stanford Encyclopedia of Philosophy* and *Philosophical Studies*.

Kevin Toh is Professor of Philosophy of Law at University College London. He has published a number of articles in philosophy of law (or jurisprudence), and has also made forays into moral philosophy and constitutional theory. His work in philosophy of law addresses the nature of legal thought, discourse, and practice by exploiting certain theoretical resources from contemporary meta-ethics, aesthetics, and philosophy of action.

Chiara Valentini is Senior Researcher and Lecturer in Philosophy of Law at the University of Bologna Law Department. Previously, she was a Ramon y Cajal Researcher with the Law & Philosophy Group of the Pompeu Fabra University and a Max Weber Fellow at the European University Institute. Chiara Valentini specializes in philosophy of law, with a focus on legal reasoning, constitutionalism, judicial review and deliberative democracy. She also has research interests in social ontology and political theory. Her works have been published in journals like *Law and Philosophy*, *The American Journal of Jurisprudence*, *Ratio Juris*, *Jurisprudence*, and she edited the *Handbook of Legal Reasoning and Argumentation* (Springer, 2018) with Bongiovanni, Postema, Rotolo, Sartor and Walton.

Bill Wringe is Associate Professor of Philosophy at Bilkent University, Ankara. He is the author of *An Expressive Theory of Punishment* (Palgrave MacMillan, 2016) and has published elsewhere on collective agency and collective responsibility, on philosophy of emotion, and on a variety of non-paradigmatic forms of punishment, including the punishment of collective agents and of non-citizens.

Introduction

Teresa Marques and Chiara Valentini

This book brings together two important strands of philosophical analysis. It combines general philosophical inquiry into collective agency with analyses of specific questions about plural entities and activities in the legal domain. These are issues of growing interest in areas of philosophy like action theory and social ontology, as well as in the philosophy of law.

In the past two decades, the philosophical debate on collective agency in the social world has been flourishing, with a focus on the nature of activities shared by individuals, and on their mental states. According to some authors, collective actions require collective intentions, where the notion is sometimes understood as *we-intentions* – intentions with the content that *we* do certain things – or *participatory intention* – intentions of individual group members to do their part of a joint action. It has also been argued that "team reasoning" is a distinctive form of strategic practical reasoning, and that understanding it is necessary to address the difficulties that standard game theory has in accounting for the rationality of selecting *cooperative* options in strategic scenarios such as the Prisoner's Dilemma.

However, the notion of a *collective attitude* is a complex one, whether by "attitudes" we understand intentions, beliefs, or emotions. Christian List (2014), for example, distinguishes between three things that can be meant by the phrase "collective attitude". First, a "collective attitude" could just be an attitude that is common among a group of people, and such that this fact is common knowledge. As List puts it, in this sense, it is an attitude "held by all individual members of the collective, where their holding it is a matter of common awareness" (List 2014a, 1609). Cases of common attitudes are, for instance, those where there is unanimity in a group deciding what to do, or where there is common knowledge among all the group members. Second, the phrase "collective attitude" is sometimes used to describe aggregate attitudes in cooperative situations where team reasoning can produce a belief or a decision *of the group*. An aggregate attitude would be "an aggregate or summary of the attitudes of the individual members of the collective, produced by some aggregation rule or statistical criterion" (List 2014a, 1603). In this case, it is not necessary that each individual in the collective has that attitude

DOI: 10.4324/9781003242451-1

or agrees with the decision. An example of an aggregate attitude is the voting process (ranked-choice vote) in the Eurovision song contest. The winner is not the preferred candidate of each person who voted, and perhaps also not the first choice of the majority. Third, List considers that by "collective attitude" we can mean a *corporate attitude*, "an attitude held by the collective as an intentional agent" and that it is possible that "the collective is an agent in its own right, which holds that belief or desire". (List 2014a, 1615). Cases of corporate collective attitudes would be, for instance, the European Union's intention to impose sanctions on Belarus. In saying this, we seem to assign to the European Union a collective attitude, although most citizens of the EU have *no* opinion about the sanctions, nor was there any calculation on the basis of the aggregate of their attitudes. The decision was made entirely by relevant European Union leaders. Corporate attitudes, then, are attitudes of a collective entity that, say, may be common only to particular designated people who have the power to act on behalf of the collective or may be the result of the team reasoning of a small group of those representatives.

As the distinctions above show, collective actions and attitudes of a group need not be identical to the actions and attitudes of individual members of a collective or a plural entity. Collective agency is, it is often said, irreducibly collective. It is not clear, however, whether this irreducibility requires treating plural entities as intentional agents in their own right. In other words, it is not clear whether this irreducibility requires treating, for example, the European Union as an intentional agent.

In very general terms, the debate has been marked by a contrast between eliminativist and non-eliminativist views. The former is the view that there are no group agents but only individual agents. Individuals may do something together but, nonetheless, they do not constitute "collective" entities with actions and attitudes of their own. The latter is the view that a plurality of individuals doing something together forms an entity acting over and above the individuals involved. What characterizes the agency of such an entity is not a mere convergence of individual actions and behaviors but rather the collective's own agential status.

In these terms, the issue of collective agency raises controversial questions about the intentionality that underlies joint action, conceived as "the power of minds to be directed at objects, matters of fact, states of affairs, goals, or values". (Schweikard and Schmid 2020). First, it is highly disputed whether we can ascribe to *groups* of individuals "collective" intentional states, that is, a distinctive kind of state that cannot be reduced to the intentional states held by individual people, as eliminativist views purport to show. For example, it is disputed whether the explanation of corporate actions requires assigning *intentions* and *beliefs* to large organizations like nations (see, for instance, Ludwig 2015, 2017, Quinton 1976). Second, it is also controversial what form collective intentional states may take among the various possible forms, such as intention, belief, acceptance, or emotion. (On collective emotions, see, for instance, Gilbert 2002, 2013, 2014, Salmela 2012, Salmela and Nagatsu 2017,

Salmela and von Scheve 2017. For different perspectives on collective cognition, see, for example, Bird 2010, Fallis 2007, Povich 2018, Rupert 2014.)

Making sense of forms of intentionality with regard to groups requires us to address a fundamental tension between, on the one hand, the idea that collective intentionality is different from individual intentionality and, on the other, the idea that the only real intentionality in the world is that of individual minds. Some accounts are eliminativist, and solve this tension by reducing collective intentionality to the intentions of the individuals involved in joint actions, that is, to individual mental states *concerning* collective actions. These would correspond to accounts of collective agency in terms of the two first notions of collective attitudes in List's (2014) characterization, namely, common attitudes and aggregate attitudes. Other accounts are non-elimininativist and solve this tension by rejecting the idea that only individuals can have intentionality.

The distinction between eliminativist and non-eliminativist theories is complicated by how some authors present their own views. Non-eliminativist accounts present collective intentionality as a distinctive kind of intentionality that cannot be reduced to the attitudes of individuals and include the work of Margaret Gilbert (2009, 2014), John Searle (1990, 1995, 2010), Raimo Tuomela (2006), Philip Pettit (2001, 2007), or Christian List and Philip Pettit (2011), for instance. But authors don't agree on what non-eliminativism requires. Margaret Gilbert has argued that collective agency is based on a joint commitment that derives from the readiness of *each member* of the group to be jointly committed in doing something as *a body*. To have a shared activity, thus, it is necessary that each member of the group openly expresses the readiness to be jointly committed in a certain way with others. For Tuomela, collective agency depends on collective intentionality conceived as a *we-attitude*. More precisely, an individual has this attitude with respect to a certain joint action if she "has a respective individual intention regarding her contribution and certain beliefs about the actions and beliefs of the other agents involved" (Schweikard and Schmid 2020). The we-intention consists of a group member's intention to carry out their part of a joint action, alongside other members while believing that the group upholds a mutual belief about this action (see also Tuomela and Miller 1988). The group member views their contributory action as helping to realize the group's aim and believes that other members will do likewise. A member cannot we-intend to carry out their part of the action without also intending to bring about the aim of the joint action.

These are accounts of collective intentionality that nonetheless rely on assigning attitudes to individuals participating in a group activity. What is irreducibly collective in these accounts is *the content* of the individual mental states (Tuomela characterizes these attitudes as attitudes held in the we-mode rather than the I-mode, see Tuomela 2007, p. 46; it is not clear if this is a characteristic that is not part of content). Moreover, these views are limited to group activities where individual members of a group have beliefs and intentions about what the group as a whole is doing, and knowledge of the mental states of others.

For John Searle (1995, 2010), collective intentionality cannot be understood as the mere interconnection of individual intentional states oriented toward collective activities. Rather, the collective intentionality that underlies cooperative action exists when each individual involved has an individual intention in a collective form and the belief that the other individuals involved have the same intention. In order for the intention to be "collective", this belief is sufficient, beyond the actual intention on the part of others as well.

Nonetheless, activities of groups with a hierarchical structure, or of very large unstructured collectives, do not appear to fit easily in accounts like Gilbert's, Tuomela's, or Searle's, since many group members in those settings can do their part of collective activities without intending to bring about the aims of the joint action. Moreover, there are cases of collective activities that do not require a participant in the activity to believe that other participants have the same intentions or beliefs. As Kutz (2000) points out, a pacifist who takes a job at a nuclear weapons plant sees himself as contributing toward a collective end though he does not intend to realize that collective end (Kutz 2000, p. 26). A small variation of Kutz's example of the pacifist also shows that his colleagues need not assume that he has the same intentions or beliefs about the collective end of the activity. This kind of theoretical limitation is also a limitation for the application of these theories in the legal domain.

These accounts differ radically from Pettit's view that groups have minds of their own, where "minds" are understood in explanatorily functional terms (Pettit 2007; see also the development of in List and Pettit's works, cited earlier). If Pettit were right, collective group agency would recognize that groups can have collective attitudes, understood as corporate attitudes, as discussed earlier. This is a fundamental assumption in the argument supporting the decision in *Citizens United v. Federal Election Commission* which grants corporations personhood status.

The interconnection of individual intentions has been characterized in strong terms in Michael Bratman's theory of collective agency as a shared cooperative activity (Bratman 1992, 1999, 2009). According to him, collective action requires the individuals involved to *share* their intention to act together. To this end, there must be a coordination of the individual intentions that refer to the formulation of plans and the actions required to realize those plans. Such individual "plan states" are interconnected so as to form an interpersonal structure of related intentions that serves to coordinate joint actions. Furthermore, there must be an interconnection between the beliefs of the individuals involved and common knowledge with respect to the intentions and the beliefs connected in these terms.

This view has had a great impact on the legal-philosophical debate. With regard to the law, two types of intentional states are particularly relevant. First, the state of acceptance, that is, the state of assent and recognition with respect to a certain situation. Understanding the terms in which this attitude can be shared by those who, in a legal community, identify valid legal norms and apply them as such (see Hart 2012) is crucially relevant for our understanding of the law. The second important state is the state of intention, representing a commitment to perform a certain action. Understanding how this state can be shared by a plurality of individuals with respect to their acting together in enacting a law or adjudicating a legal case is extremely relevant. In fact, the practice of legal interpretation significantly relies on such intentions to ascribe meaning to laws and judicial precedents.

Scott Shapiro has adapted Bratman's idea of a shared cooperative activity to the legal domain, arguing that this kind of activity, in the law, does not require shared intentions but rather a shared acceptance (Shapiro 2002, 2011). In fact, the latter state is compatible with the possibility that legal officials, while not sharing intentions with respect to the realization of the basic values of the system, share an acceptance of its overall "plan" with common knowledge of this and of the plan. From this perspective, legal officials can recognize and apply the law of a certain system while not sharing an active commitment to cooperate, based on the intention to achieve the ultimate aim of that system. On the moral nature of this aim and the extent to which it determines the content of valid law, there are, as we will see in the first part of this volume, several open and controversial questions, to which positivism and anti-positivism offer different solutions. Another legal theorist that relies on Bratman's model of cooperation is Jules Coleman, who proposes that the social practice that is constitutive of the rule of recognition is a Bratmanian style shared activity (Coleman 2003).

In contrast with these authors, Christopher Kutz (2000, 2001) offers a minimalist account which is reductivist, and that tries to explain collective action without relying on *group-intentions*, i.e., "ordinary, instrumental individual intentions whose subject is the individual agent and whose object is a collective act or outcome" (Kutz 2000, p. 21). Theories that rely on group intentions make common knowledge requirements on the group's members. By rejecting the need for group-intentions, Kutz departs from theories like Gilbert's, Tuomela's, Searle's, or Bratman's, and those based on Bratman's theories like Shapiro's or Coleman's. Kutz argues that collective activities and goals can be explained instead in terms of the *participatory intentions* of the individuals involved in the action. Individuals may have the intention to do their part in collective acts, and perform the task that is given to them in order to realize the goal shared with the other individuals involved. A goal is shared among two or more individuals if the intentions of those involved would be satisfied by performing or realizing a particular action or outcome. Such a view is "minimalist" insofar as it presents collective intentionality as an overlap of participatory intentions held by individuals. This overlap does not involve the mutual responsiveness of the participants, but only an also minimal common knowledge condition about intentions, such that each participant is willing that his or her intention be known to the others and hope that the others will do their parts in realizing the appropriate outcome or "collective end" (Kutz 2000). Kutz's model of the judicial community also differs from Bratmanian models, and, as he puts it, "is an account of collective behavior capacious enough to encompass the Scalias and the Brennans, the lone rangers and the coalition builders, an account that makes the constitutive institutional norms matters of contingent emergence, not conceptual necessity" (Kutz 2001, p. 461).

The different views illustrated so far provide arguments and theses that are extremely helpful to shed light on the agency of plural entities in the law. The theoretical inquiry into the nature of collective agents, and their modes of action and intentional states, is crucial for the ontological and conceptual analysis of law. In fact, there are many different types of plural entities that operate in the legal domain. Legal officials and institutional actors producing and applying the law – from the legislature to courts – are plural entities. The addressees of legal norms can form plural entities as well. From the citizenry to corporations, firms, and associations, there are many collectives that are regulated by the law. And many forms of action, in the law, involve individuals who do not act independently, but jointly. These include members of judicial bodies deliberating on cases brought before them, members of legislatures discussing and passing a law, citizens acting together in accordance with legal norms, firms and corporations coordinating on the market, groups and masses striking, protesting, deliberating, and so on.

On the one hand, all these entities and forms of agency have a bearing on the validity, content, and application of the law, in different ways and to varying extents. It is crucial, thus, to inquire into the terms in which individuals may act together and what kind of intentionality underlies their joint actions. In descriptive terms, this inquiry may provide the resources needed to capture and describe appropriately the many aspects of the law that involve groups and forms of joint action. In fact, the collective nature of subjects and forms of agency is decisive for the attribution of legal rights and obligations, for the ascription of legal responsibilities, and for the reconstruction of the intent with which laws and other acts have been produced. In normative terms, the inquiry into collective agency and intentionality provides important elements to reflect upon the legitimacy of laws and how such legitimacy depends on the production and application of laws via collective agency based on shared attitudes.

On the other hand, the specific questions raised by collective agency in the law offer new resources to the philosophical analysis of group action. The legal practice, in fact, presents some features that are especially relevant for our understanding of collective agency in the social world, for instance, the convergent behaviors and attitudes of legal officials as well as disagreements among them, the coercive interactions among institutional and non-institutional subjects, the ascription of responsibility and the infliction of sanctions, or the constraints and procedural rules for joint actions and decision-making. Reflection about the responsibility of corporations or other large collectives can help philosophers elucidate notions like that of an individual's participatory intentions, or the difference between distributive and non-distributive responsibility. Corporate activities can also help us to better appreciate contested epistemic and metaphysical claims, such as the claim that the action of a collective entity requires assigning an agential status to that collective similar to that assigned to individuals, including beliefs, intentions, goals, and minds of their own. A thorough philosophical analysis of collective responsibility can recommend caution in regarding collectives as full-blown intentional agents. Reflection about the law can also provide clues about the nature of duties and obligations in contexts of shared agency. For instance, the contrast between torts and directed duties can help shed light on the source of the obligations in directed duties, i.e., duties that are owed to a friend, one's child or parent, as opposed to duties that are owed to others *qua* people in general. These and many other aspects of the law prompt new approaches to general questions about collective entities and shared agency, about norms and obligations in joint action, and a better understanding of collective responsibility.

We believe that there is growing interest in these issues in areas of philosophy like action theory and social ontology, as well as in legal theory, and that this is the right time to bring together leading philosophers and legal theorists working on the various theoretical challenges that arise from collective action. The inspiration for the volume came from a jointly organized conference on collective action, philosophy, and law organized at the University Pompeu Fabra, with the support of a Marie Curie grant funded by the European Commission, and a Ramon y Cajal grant funded by the Spanish Ministry for Science and Innovation.

The chapters in this book are organized into four parts. This division is somewhat artificial since there are common threads running through them. Nonetheless, the division brings to the fore common themes that are central both for law and for collective action theory. These four parts cut across, and build on, different accounts to advance the debate on classical and new issues in collective agency. Each part also features legal-philosophical analyses that draw on general accounts of collective agency to cast new light on the law, descriptive as well as normatively. This volume is the first major interdisciplinary and multi-authored work bridging legal and philosophical approaches to collective agency.

The chapters in the first part focus on general themes related to the nature of law and legislative intention: on the relation between law and coercion, the attitude of acceptance, legal disagreements, and the moral aim characterizing the practice of legal officials, the nature of legislative intent and legal interpretation.

The second part focuses on team reasoning and on individual and collective duties. One chapter in this section offers alternative accounts of team reasoning that dispense with common knowledge conditions for collective action. Other chapters focus on the obligations and rationality of individuals deciding whether to join a group to carry out further obligations, and on how shared intentionality can help explain the source of directed duties while making a contrast with contract law and tort law.

The chapters in the third part are devoted to questions about causality, blameworthiness, liability, and responsibility. While one chapter in this section argues that assigning collective moral responsibility to a group does not require regarding collectives as groups with "minds of their own", the remaining chapters address two different problems for the law that arise from the determination of an agent's causal contribution to criminal outcomes, namely, the problem of assessing liability in cases of deviant causal processes, and the problem of assessing complicity given the causal contribution to a crime.

Finally, the fourth and last part of the book collects chapters that develop perspectives on broader issues about citizens, nations, and institutions. The section addresses the issue of legal punishment as the expression of a collective attitude, the nature of constitutional communities as collective moral agents, the extent to which masses can count as collective entities, and the degree of alienation that these entities can tolerate. In the remainder of the introduction, we offer a more detailed summary of the chapters in each section.

PART I – The nature of law and legislative intention

A classical, central theme in the legal-philosophical literature is the attitude with which individuals – especially legal officials – converge in the identification and application of legal norms in a certain legal system. The first part of this volume is organized around questions related, precisely, with the nature of law and legislative intentions. According to the command theory of law (Austin 1832, Bentham 1970), individuals ultimately converge in obeying the law because of their fear of sanctions. This view, however, does not fully capture the internal point of view with which legal officials identify and apply valid legal norms (Hart 2012). In fact, as argued by H. L. A. Hart, "the external point of view of social rules is that of an observer of their practice, and the internal point of view is that of a participant in such practice who *accepts* the rules as guides to conduct and as standards of criticism" (Hart 2012, p. 255). Such acceptance amounts to a person's "standing disposition" to take the patterns of conduct mostly followed by the members of a group "both as guides to their own future conduct and as standards of criticism which may legitimate demands and various forms of pressure for conformity" (Hart 2012, p. 255).

Relevant questions arise with regard to the terms in which a plurality of individuals – the members of a legal community – may share this disposition in acting together, and how this bears on the existence and application of the law. It is controversial whether the shared acceptance of legal norms is a condition of their validity and how the relation between acceptance and legal validity is compatible with some features of the legal practice. On the one hand, there is the occurrence of legal disagreements. As Dworkin notes

(Dworkin 1986), legal officials can disagree about the identification and content of the law, which challenges the view of the law as a joint activity emerging from the officials' convergent behaviors and attitudes of acceptance. On the other hand, the legal practice is characterized by coercive interactions, and it is controversial how coercion can coexist with convergent attitudes of acceptance as required by this view of the law.

Kevin Toh's contribution to this volume, "Collectivity and law", presents and addresses these questions in new terms. He focuses, first, on the possibility of combining the idea of a joint acceptance of legal norms – and the conventional nature of law – with the possibility of disagreements and legal judgments that go against established legal trends. Second, he accounts for the relation between law and coercion within the legal practice. In addressing both issues, Toh's chapter relies on a view of legal judgments as aimed at instigating, and maintaining, a *shared* acceptance of legal norms. According to this view, the acceptance of norms need not be motivated by the same motivations for each member of the community. Members' acceptance can be motivated in different ways so that each member can be motivated by his own considerations and disregard the other members' motivations. Nonetheless, they can eventually converge in accepting the same norm "as their rule of recognition".

The second and related issue in Toh's analysis regards the compatibility of a collective attitude of acceptance with coercive interactions. Coercion characterizes, to a certain extent, the relations among individuals within the legal practice. Nonetheless, this practice can have the aim of a shared acceptance of norms. Indeed, the fact that such aim is not fully realized or regulative in the actual legal practice does not undermine the thesis that such practice is characterized by psychological attitudes with that particular aim. Toh argues that there can be coercion among individuals interacting with the aim of realizing a shared acceptance of norms, given the tension between this aim and the individual aim of normative correctness.

The nature of acceptance as a collective attitude held by members of a legal community is not the only issue that is relevant for our understanding of the nature of the law and the activities jointly realized by the members of a legal community. A related and traditionally central issue in the legal-philosophical debate concerns the moral dimension of the joint action of legal officials and how this dimension bears on the validity and content of the law.

The contribution of Dimitrios Kyritsis, "The two lives of law's moral aim", addresses this issue, comparing the different ways in which anti-positivist and positivist theories of the law account for the joint activity of legal officials and the moral aim of this activity. On the one hand, the focus here is on the anti-positivist account provided by "robust" natural law theory, according to which moral considerations are crucially relevant for our understanding of the nature of law and figure among the truth conditions of propositions of law. On the other hand, attention is also paid to the positivist account as provided by Scott Shapiro's planning theory of the law, according to which moral considerations do not necessarily determine the validity and content of the law.

Kyritsis points out that, in the positivist view, the idea of a joint activity of legal officials plays an explanatory role. It represents the legal practice emerging from the intentions and actions of the plurality of officials operating in the legal system. In Shapiro's account, this practice has a moral aim, but this does not entail that the aim is realized and that the content of the law is determined by morality. In robust natural law theory, the idea of a joint activity of legal officials plays a justificatory role. Lying at the core of a "moralized understanding of institutional cooperation", this idea captures the moral worth of collective action: under certain conditions, the cooperation of legal officials makes a moral difference, by placing them under a duty to be responsive toward others and to rely on what others say. In these terms, collective agency is structured by moral considerations and contributes to the legitimacy of State power.

With the contributions of Canale and Flanagan, the first part's focus shifts from the officials' acceptance to the officials' intentions and, in particular, to the ascription of collective intentions to institutional, plural, subjects such as the legislature. In fact, a highly disputed issue in the legal-philosophical debate on collective agency concerns the nature of legislative bodies and their attitude in making the law. It is controversial whether they are collective entities with their own agency and intentionality or how this bears upon the existence and application of legal norms. In particular, understanding the nature of the intentions held by lawmakers is especially relevant for the theory and practice of legal interpretation. Legal interpreters frequently refer to legislative intent in order to ascribe a meaning to statutes. They ascribe to legislatures an intention and then use this as a basis for determining the content of the law as a product of what the legislature "intended" to say with the norms enacted.

Skeptics argue that legislative assemblies, as plural entities, cannot hold intentions of their own. Ultimately, only the members of such institutions can hold intentions. Therefore, there is no legislative intent as such, and it cannot guide the interpretation of the norms enacted by legislative bodies. This approach, however, leads to counterintuitive consequences, as Damiano Canale argues in his contribution, "Legislative intent, collective intentionality and fictionalism". In fact, the idea that interpretative practices referring to legislative intent ultimately rest on a metaphysical mistake is "at odds with the traditional way of thinking of the legal community" that greatly relies on legislative intent. Canale's paper, thus, refines the concept of legal intent to produce a convincing account of the legislative and interpretative practice so as "to accommodate the skeptical standpoint to the common view that legislatures have communicative intentions".

From this perspective, Canale argues that individual legislators share collective participatory intentions when they legislate. These intentions do not determine the content of the law, nor do the individual legislators necessarily share communicative intentions when they take part in law-making. When legal interpreters refer to legislative intent, they refer to a fictional entity that, nonetheless, plays an important role in a legal system. In fact, it guides the interpretation of the law and thereby serves as a "tool of coordination" in the practice of legal officials.

In different terms, Brian Flanagan's chapter, "Legal disagreement as disagreement about the collectively intended meaning", also addresses the questions posed by the use of legislative intent as a source of meaning in the interpretation of the law. He starts from a critical analysis of the challenge posed to legal positivism by legal disagreements and argues that positivists should address this challenge by endorsing the view that the meaning of a legal text is "a function of its intended meaning". From this perspective, Flanagan reviews the main doubts about the possibility of ascribing collective intentions to legislatures in light of two rival conceptions of collective agency. He concludes that "any positivist accommodation of legal disagreement that invokes authorial meaning will appeal to the meaning intended, not the meaning received". In seeking to secure legal intentionalism, such alternatives open up a way for positivism to make room for the entire range of legal disagreement, and in doing so, they can match anti-positivist approaches in avoiding "the need for any error theory of accepted legal phenomena".

PART II – Practical reasoning and duties

The papers included in the second part develop accounts and puzzles about practical team reasoning, joint commitments in shared activities, and the kinds of duties to act that are owed to other agents in cases of collective action. It is necessary to account for these foundational problems for the deployment of collective action theories in the law. As mentioned earlier, Scott Shapiro modified Michael Bratman's theory of shared cooperative action to account for legal positivist views of the law as a social practice. Bratman's theory applies mainly to small-scale sociality, and Shapiro's modification purports to account for two features of collective agency that may appear challenging from a Bratmanian point of view: the social activity of large groups, and activities involving the exercise of authority. Shapiro purported to accommodate the fact that agents can do their part in shared activities even when there is no communication among them. This solution still required certain common knowledge assumptions. Moreover, when authority is involved in collective agency, some group members may not be invested in the intended outcome. In these cases, what is at stake are causal mechanisms and team mechanisms ensuring that the authority is part of the best plan for the group.

Natalie Gold defends an alternative solution to Shapiro's in her chapter, "The judicial community and team reasoning", where she deploys a decision-theoretic account of team reasoning. Her aim is to show how recent developments in theories of rational decision-making can help legal philosophers. Gold points out that an individual can identify with a team but that the individual can be a member of both structured and unstructured massively large groups. This poses a challenge to views like Shapiro's. Natalie Gold argues that her account of team reasoning allows her to explain how individuals can form a group which can be an intentional agent in its own right, and whose decisions and actions are not identical or reducible to those of the individual members. For instance, there is no need to rely on the mutual responsiveness of individual group members on her account. Objections like Dworkin's disagreement-based argument that challenges the view of the law as a joint activity emerging from convergent behaviors and attitudes (Dworkin 1986) may not apply to decision-theoretic models of social activities. Gold can hence also relax the common knowledge condition. She illustrates her proposal with group agents like courts, explaining their collective agency with an extension of standard game theory, which allows the court, understood as a team of individuals, to count as an agent and solve problems of cooperation and coordination.

Nonetheless, theories of team reasoning may still not solve all puzzles related to group action and collective duties. Caroline Arruda considers some of these puzzles in her paper, "'I thought we were on the same team!' Collective duties and individual moral orientation", where she raises an unexpected and puzzling problem for extant accounts of team reasoning. The problem concerns agents who consider whether to take part in joint activities as a collective, depending on whether or not others share similar kinds of reasons for doing that action. Specifically, Arruda's paper addresses the question: does *a person's moral orientation affect how she deliberates about forming a group agent with others to fulfil what she judges is their collective moral obligations*? Decision theoretic considerations can't solve these cases since no group or a team is yet formed. In Arruda's cases, the question is whether the fact that an individual cares about the moral orientation of the other agents informs and affects the way in which she deliberates as to whether to join the group. None of the standard solutions in collective action theory, such as theories of *judgement aggregation* or theories of *team reasoning*, can handle these cases well. The cases also cannot be fully described by explaining how each person practically deliberates, and the people in these cases are not yet a collective agent. Moreover, the cases do not just depend on the reasoning that an end can be attained instrumentally.

We could be tempted to think that there is some parallel between this idea of the moral orientation of various members of a possible collective, on the one hand, and the ways in which we should be invested in the law for it to have any purchase on us, on the other. This would relate to what Hart calls the *internal perspective* on the law (Hart 2012). Our ability to understand and take seriously rebukes for failing to adhere to the law (as well as the price for conforming to it as grounded in a pattern of good reasoning and good reasons) could illustrate how we care about others' legal orientation. However, Arruda notes that the parallels with Hart's view are superficial. According to her, our concern for acting for the right reasons is related to how we care about how others act, but it is not a necessary condition for a genuinely collective enterprise. Joseph Raz notably pointed out that it does not seem to be necessary that agents in fact act for the same reasons when they act in conformity with the law (Raz 2009). If that's right, it suggests that we can separate the questions of the *investment* in moral and legal duties from the question of how to establish the grounds *for mutual conformity* to legal duties.

There are further problems related to duties in contexts of collective action. As citizens, we are subject to the law of our countries, we are under various obligations incurred via the contracts and agreements we enter into, as well. These are distinct kinds of obligations. The former duties are monadic obligations. They apply to a person, individually, simply for being a member of a society or a national of a country, and for being a moral agent with obligations to not infringe other people's rights. In contrast, the latter kinds of duties are dyadic. These are duties that are *directed* or owed to the other persons with whom we have entered into a contractual relation. Promises are another example of such duties, as are duties of care of parents toward their children. Understanding the directedness of duties is relevant in private law, as some of these examples above make clear. Tort law is a specific aspect of the law where directed duties have been thought to be of special interest. If an agent wrongs another person, it seems that the agent owes compensation to the wronged person. Torts differ from cases where the agent breaks the law but where the penalty is owed to the state, not to another person.

In his paper, "Directed duties, practical intimacy, and legal wronging", Abraham Roth starts by giving reasons to reject other accounts of directed duties. Extant accounts of the directedness of duties may have two shortcomings: either they fail to distinguish monadic duties from directed duties, or they offer a circular account which presupposes the directedness of duties. Some accounts point to the fact that at least some cases of directed duties seem to involve a special relationship between parties, as is the case, for instance, of promises, agreements, contracts, or friendships. In these cases, *the normative nature* of these relationships seems to ground the directedness of the duties owed to others. Here, Roth contends that the very notion of normative relationships seems to presuppose directedness. Other accounts offer an explanation in terms of *relational wrongings*. Yet, connecting relationships with directedness doesn't yet tell us what is special about some relations; and the directedness seems again to be presupposed. A further attempt is to account for directedness in terms of *accountability*. The person to whom an agent owes an obligation is the one who has the relevant standing to demand that the agent is held accountable. But, Roth argues, this risks not distinguishing monadic obligations from directed ones. Anyone can object to moral wronging, either the participant involved in an action, or a third-party observer. Moreover, one may suspect that this difference between the participant and third-party accountability also presupposes the directedness of some attitudes. Finally, one could explain directed duties in terms of *normative power*. The directedness of a duty would be a matter of the power exercised by the individual to whom the duty is directed. The problem with this explanation is that we may have duties owed to someone who is in no position to exercise their normative power. Moreover, it may well be, again, that what explains this normative power is the underlying directedness of obligation and not the other way round.

Roth argues that directed duties have similar features to shared agency, and that this similarity indicates that directed duties can be explained in terms of shared agency. To this end, he develops the idea that directed duties involve the same kind of practical intimacy that exists between individuals when they act together. In Roth's view, the notion of *contralateral commitments* and the notion of *intentions to act* underpin shared agency. First, contralateral commitments are intention-based commitments to fellow participants to do one's part in a joint activity. Second, in joint actions, other agents figure not only in the content of the commitment but also, as Roth claims, in the "willing of the committing itself". In Roth's theory, this means that the intentions of fellow participants have "practical intimacy". When one makes a decision and forms an intention, one then acts directly on that earlier intention. Likewise, in shared activities, one can act directly on the content of others' intentions, which here serve as "fixed-points". This theory is not circular, Roth argues. Moreover, it can help understand the appealing features of accounts of directed duties in terms of wronging, accountability, and normative power. Roth concludes with some considerations to the effect that torts can occur outside the substantive relationships underlying directed duty, and that perhaps torts and wrongs can be understood in terms of monadic duties against the harming of others, and, once a civil law proceeding is initiated, in terms of the shared agency there involved: "The directed duties would be to do one's part in a collective act of reconciliation".

PART III – Causality, blameworthiness, and responsibility

If groups can act together as an agent, then arguably groups are responsible for their actions. To conceive of groups as agents with responsibility invites assigning them other metaphysical properties that we assign to individual responsible agents. In other words, recognizing group agency invites the recognition of group intentions, of group rights and group duties, and ultimately personhood status. The assumption that groups can have these features is an essential assumption, for example, in the argument supporting the decision in *Citizens United v. Federal Election Commission* which grants corporations personhood status, and hence some of the same rights that individuals enjoy, such as the right to free speech.

The responsibility and the rights of collectives raise a series of questions that demand attention. Authors like Philip Pettit have argued that the moral responsibility of a group action depends on group agents with minds of their own. However, in her contribution to this volume, "Responsibility

*Un*incorporated: Group agents and corporate persons", Sara Rachel Chant argues that this idea is a consequence of a methodological mistake, and that that mistake is the same one at the root of the Citizens United decision. Chant argues that this error is based on a bad analogy with standard explanations of individual agency. The consideration of an individual *as an agent* is a necessary condition to attach individual responsibility to that person. Other similar first-personal singular principles concern free will; for instance, that it is necessary that the person have individual free will if she is to be responsible for her actions. Now, we talk of groups acting together, and of their responsibility for their actions. By analogy with the individual case, we could infer that for groups to be responsible for their actions, it is also a necessary condition that groups be proper agents. Sara Rachel Chant presents a series of cases that challenge the idea that we can make the same assumptions about the metaphysically necessary conditions for group action and responsibility as we make about individual action and responsibility.

The explanatory options that are normally considered pose an apparent dilemma: if we do not regard groups as agents, we cannot attach collective responsibility to groups; but if we want to recognize that groups can be responsible for what they do, then we must be committed to collective agency or collective free will. In other words, either we reject collective responsibility, or we accept that groups can be agents. Sara Chant shows, with a series of examples, that this is a false dilemma and that it is possible to decouple collective moral responsibility from collective agency and collective free will. She concludes that facts about the metaphysics of groups are less important than is often thought. As Chant says, what matters are empirical facts about a group's structure, its decision-making processes, and the informational dynamics. And this means that the ontological categories of groups "have no extra explanatory power". Her conclusions apply to legal decisions such as the *Citizens United* case in the United States. The group was to release a documentary about Hilary Clinton during an electoral campaign, but that intention was in conflict with the Bipartisan Campaign Reform Act (BCRA), which prohibited corporations from expressing advocacy within 30 days of an election. It was argued before the Supreme Court that BCRA violated Citizens United's free speech rights. The argument in favor of Citizens United is a straightforward case of *modus ponens*. Corporations have long been recognized by the court as "persons" under the law. If persons have certain constitutional rights, corporations have the same rights. Therefore, Citizen United has the same constitutional rights as individuals, including the right to free speech. Sara Chant claims that it is a distraction to focus exclusively on the question of whether corporations are "persons", as it is a distraction to focus exclusively on the question of whether the moral responsibility of groups requires that we look at them as agents. Instead, she argues that each case should be assessed by looking at the structure of the organization, the flow of information, and power dynamics, in order to assess if a group has moral responsibility, and whether an organization ought to have constitutional rights. Ultimately, the responsibility and rights of a collective depend on the structure and dynamics of the group.

Legal responsibility for criminal actions, i.e., liability, is typically determined on the basis of assessing the *intentions* of the person who realizes a specific *action*. Liability thus depends on the *actus reus* – the criminal act – and on the *mens rea* – the ill intention. Attempts to commit certain criminal acts that are unsuccessful may go unpunished, or at least, they are not normally punished as they would have been if the attempts had been successful. On the other hand, an accidental and unintended bad consequence of some action is also not punished as gravely as the same action would have been if there had been criminal intent. This is complicated by the fact that some unsuccessful attempts are serious and punishable – an attempted terrorist attack, for instance –, as are some non-intentional acts, say manslaughter.

Intended actions and their results contrast with unintended effects in further respects. Someone may be liable for unintended consequences if she ought to have avoided those consequences. Cases of negligence fall under the category of action with unintended consequences. These cases can fall outside the range of criminal law. Two contributions to this volume show that some of these central legal concepts in criminal and in tort law are ambiguous: attempts and completed crimes, attempts, and preparations, what makes someone an accomplice in a criminal act, the notion of foreseeability, and. crucially, causation for legal responsibility. This underdetermination of legal concepts, the authors argue, leads to arbitrary judicial decisions.

In her chapter, "Deviant causation and the law", Sara Bernstein argues that deviant causal chains pose problems to most of the legal concepts here in question. A deviant causal chain is a causal chain where the result intended by the agent does not occur in the way the agent intended but in a "deviant" way. Bernstein provides several examples to illustrate deviant causation. She further provides examples where the outcome differs from the one planned, although part of the planned course of action is as intended. What these cases show, Bernstein argues, is that deviant causal processes demonstrate that legal concepts are underspecified. Although the cases fulfill some of the conditions for criminal and tortious liability, they do not easily or correctly fit into existing legal taxonomies of crimes. First, deviant causal chains pose a problem for the distinction between attempts and completed crimes. An attempt involves an intention to commit an act and taking action toward the completion of the act. In some deviant cases, the intended outcome is caused by the agent, but the means toward that outcome are not the intended ones and thus the agent doesn't consider that he *did* the action in question. Second, and for similar reasons, deviant causal chains pose problems for the distinction between attempts and preparations. Moreover, deviant causal chains also pose problems for the notion of negligence since foreseeability is required for negligence torts, but the agent cannot be expected to foresee an unexpected outcome that results from deviant causation. Finally, and in general, although deviant causal chains meet the "but-for" constraint (had a person not formed an intention and initiated actions motivated by that intention, the consequence would not have happened), people are not in general liable for unforeseeable consequences. The law is ambiguous about these cases. In some deviant cases, what we ordinarily think of as merely preparing to attempt a crime could count instead as a full-blooded attempt, or as a completed crime, due to the presence of *mens rea*, *actus rea*, and the intended outcome. The lesson we should draw from these cases, as Bernstein argues, is that although the law is ambiguous about the role of deviant causal processes in legal culpability, the law should provide as detailed principles as possible for applying rules of liability and avoid arbitrary rulings.

Nicholas Almendares's chapter, "Forceability, causation, and guilt", tackles the problem of causation in the law from a different perspective. He considers conflicting standards in law about complicity, and controversial doctrines about the nature of complicity in a criminal act or outcome. The lack of clarity in the law about the nature of complicity stems, as he argues, from a lack of clarity of complicit liability. The problem is common in causal theories that typically define complicity as aiding and abetting with *causal* contribution. Almendares shows that the definition of complicity on the basis of causal contribution to an outcome results in the overgeneration of criminal guilt. Anyone who may have causally contributed to a criminal outcome would be, implausible, an accomplice of that outcome. Almendares considers John Gardner's (2006) limitation on causal contribution as determinant of criminal complicity, namely the idea that one's complicity depends on one's "rational attention". Others consider that one's causal contribution makes one a liable accomplice only if it is reasonably foreseeable that one's action causally contributes to the criminal outcome. However, the foreseeability doctrine still counts people who are not blameworthy as accomplices.

Almendares's positive proposal offers an alternative explanation in terms of the joint intentions of criminals and their accomplices. By adopting this kind of definition for complicity, he rectifies what causal theories were lacking, namely the accommodation of the joint participatory intentions of accomplices in a crime: "Given that complicity is an inherently joint offense, an accomplice should be defined as someone with the proper joint intention in relation to the substantive offense. This approach can yield an account of complicity with the proper scope and that better captures the critical assessments of blameworthiness and proportionality".

PART IV – Citizens, states, and institutions

The fourth part of the volume explores relevant issues that have been relatively overlooked by the legal-philosophical debate on collective agency, such as the ascription of emotions to collective political agents; the status of constitutional communities as collective moral agents; the conditions under which masses can be conceived as collective agents. The section draws on the philosophical literature on collective agency to advance our understanding of these issues and to point out their relevance for our conception of the law and constitutionalized legal systems. In this regard, the section makes a twofold contribution to the legal-philosophical debate. It contributes to ongoing disputes about important legal institutions, such as punishment, constitutional bill of rights, and judicial review. Furthermore, it raises and addresses new issues concerning the subject of penal expression, the action of masses, the relation between constitutional charters and collective moral agency.

At the same time, the final part of the book contributes to the broader philosophical debate on collective agency in the social world beyond the legal domain. First, by advancing our understanding of vast plural entities – such as the State, the citizenry and masses – that play a central role in the social world. Second, by providing some elements to reflect upon the applicability of dominant philosophical paradigms of collective agency to very large collective entities.

Bill Wringe's contribution, "Expressive theories of punishment", opens the fourth part. It draws on philosophical accounts of collective agency to elucidate a crucial aspect of the expressivist account of legal punishment, according to which punishment conveys reprobation and resentment toward the offender (Feinberg). Expressivist accounts mostly focus on two aspects. On the one hand, "what" is expressed through punishment. That is, the emotions expressed by punishment. On the other hand, "how" punishment conveys such emotions. Wringe calls our attention to a third, often overlooked, aspect: the "subject" of penal expression. He argues that such subject is the State, conceived of as a collective agent. On this basis, Wringe argues that an expressivist theory should conceive of the imposition of punishment as the way in which the State, as a collective agent, communicates messages of reprobation. The addressee of this message, according to Wringe's "denunciatory" version of expressivism, is not the offender. Rather, it is the society as a whole and, therefore, a collective agent: the political community in which the State is ultimately embodied. Wringe, in these terms, contributes to the expressivist theory of legal punishment by elucidating the collective nature of the agents involved in penal communication. On the other hand, he also contributes to the general philosophical inquiry into collective agency, by shedding light on the State and the political community as collective entities holding, and expressing, their own attitudes.

From a different perspective, the nature of political communities as collective agents is also addressed by Maggie O'Brien. Her chapter, "There's no I in team: Judicial review and community moral agents", observes that the notion of collective agency is necessary in order to understand group activities, and she applies this notion to political communities in constitutionalized legal systems. O'Brien builds on Ronald Dworkin's view of the political community as "deeply personified", (Dworkin 1986: 167–175) to claim that, as such, a political community is a collective subject capable of moral agency and responsibility. And it becomes a "better" moral agent if entrusted with a bill or charter of rights. In fact, according to O'Brien, a nation's citizenry can exercise a form of collective agency that she describes as "sincere artificial agency". Sincerity, here, is the citizens' commitment to the political and moral ideals that are established by charters of rights. These ideals serve as bonds among citizens who identify themselves with – and strive for – them. O'Brien draws on John Gardner's view of teamwork (Gardner 2002) to argue that it is necessary to undercut the doubts that individuals may have with regard to the other individuals so as to work *with* them. What makes a team a "better" one is not just the skills of its members. Rather, it is a feeling of trust among the individuals who are part of the team. They must feel that they are on a team and, then, they must act accordingly. Charters allow the members of a political community to feel and act in such terms, since they are "declarations of faith which remind everyone of what they are committed to", prompting solidarity and the pursuit of the common good. By this, they make a political community a "better moral agent". With her contribution, O'Brien connects and contributes to two separate strands of philosophical literature: one concerning collective agency and intentionality, and the other concerning the value of charters and judicial review in constitutionalized legal systems.

In different terms, Carla Bagnoli's contribution, "One among many: self-governance and alienation in mass action", is also centered on a relevant but overlooked form of collective agency. She focuses on massive pluralities, such as digital masses, flash-mobs, financial crowds, and the nature of their actions. In the literature on collective agency, masses have been mostly conceived of as large aggregations of individuals that cannot count as collective agents. The underlying view is that masses lack the forms of normative organization that characterize collective agents, such as shared attitudes, joint commitments, coordinative and cooperative regulatory schemes. Bagnoli challenges this view, which sets normative conditions that are too demanding to be generalized and thereby captures only some forms of collective agency and fails to account for other important forms such as those involving masses of individuals.

In fact, the agency of masses does not fulfill the normative requirements that collective action theory sets in contrast to alienation understood as "a defective condition of agency", characterized by a "lack of authority, self-control, self-understanding, and self-knowledge". Bagnoli puts forward and explores the hypothesis that different forms of collective agency tolerate different forms of alienation, drawing a differentiated map of the ways in which individual agents can take responsibility for collective action.[1]

Note

1. Financial support was provided by a Marie Sklodowska-Curie Grant (622114), *Collective Attitudes and Normative Disagreement*, funded by the European Commission, by a Ramon y Cajal Fellowship (RYC-2012- 12175), by the project *Shifting Concepts and Hybrid Dispositionalism* (FFI2015-73767-JIN), both funded by the Spanish Ministry for Science, Innovation and Universities. The book project took form after the

Conference *Collective Action & the Law*, also sponsored by the Law Department at the Universitat Pompeu Fabra, by the Research Group Law & Philosophy, funded by AGAUR (2014 SGR 626), and by the project *Global Constitutionalism: Legal and Philosophical Foundations*, MINECO research project (DER2013-48066- C2-1- R). We thank all the authors who contributed to the volume, and the participants at the conference *Collective Action & the Law*. Special thanks to Josejuan Moreso and to José Luis Martí, Luís Duarte de Almeida, Manuel García-Carpintero, and two referees for Routledge.

References

Austin, J. (1832): *Province of Jurisprudence Determined*. London: John Murray.

Bentham, J. (1970): *Of Laws in General* (ed. H. L. A. Hart). London: The Athlone Press.

Bird, A. (2010): "Social knowing: The social sense of 'scientific knowledge'". *Philosophical Perspectives* 24(1):23–56.

Bratman, M. (1992): "Shared cooperative activity". *The Philosophical Review* 101:327–341.

Bratman, M. (1999): *Faces of Intention*. Cambridge: Cambridge University Press.

Bratman, M. (2009): "Shared Agency". In: C. Mantzavinos (Ed.), *Philosophy of the Social Sciences: Philosophical Theory and Scientific Practice*. Cambridge: Cambridge University Press, pp. 41–59.

Coleman, J. (2003): The Practice of Principle: *Defence of a Pragmatist Approach to Legal Theory*. Oxford: Oxford University Press.

Dworkin, R. (1986): *Law's Empire*. London: Belknap.

Fallis, D. (2007): "Collective epistemic goals". *Social Epistemology* 21(3):267–280.

Gardner, J. (2002): "Reasons for teamwork". *Legal Theory* 8:495–509.

Gardner, J. (2006): "Complicity and causality". *Criminal Law and Philosophy* 1:127–141.

Gilbert, M. (2002): "Collective guilt and collective guilt feelings". *Journal of Ethics* 6:115–143.

Gilbert, M. (2009): "Shared intentions and personal intentions". *Philosophical Studies* 144 (1):167–187.

Gilbert, M. (2014): "How we feel: Understanding everyday collective emotion ascription". In: C. von Scheve and M. Salmela (Eds.), *Collective Emotions*. Oxford: Oxford University Press, pp. 17–31.

Hart, H. L. A. (2012): *The Concept of Law*. Oxford: Oxford University Press.

Kutz, C. (2000): "Acting together". *Philosophy and Phenomenological Research*, 61:1.

Kutz, C. (2001): "The judicial community". *Noûs* 35(s1):442–469.

List, C. (2014): "Three kinds of collective attitudes". *Erkenntnis*, 79(9): 1601–1622.

List, C., & Pettit, P. (2011). *Group Agency: The Possibility, Design, and Status of Corporate Agents*. Oxford: Oxford University Press.

Ludwig, K. (2015): "Is distributed cognition group level cognition?" *Journal of Social Ontology* 1(2):189–224. doi:10.1515/jso-2015-0001

Ludwig, K. (2017): "Do corporations have minds of their own?" *Philosophical Psychology* 30(3):265–297. doi:10.1080/09515089.2017.1295636

Pettit, P. (2007). "Responsibility incorporated". *Ethics*, 117(2), 171–201.

Pettit, P. (2001). "Collective intentions". In: *Intention in Law and Philosophy*. Burlington: Ashgate. pp. 241–254.

Povich, Mark (2018): "Social knowledge and supervenience revisited". *Erkenntnis* 83(5): 1033–1043.

Quinton, A. (1976): "The presidential address: Social objects". *Proceedings of the Aristotelian Society* 76:1–8

Raz, J. (2009): "Legal validity". In: *The Authority of Law*, 2nd Edition. Oxford: Oxford University Press.

Rupert, R. D. (2014): "Against group cognitive states". In: S. R. Chant, F. Hindriks, and G. Preyer (Eds.), *From Individual to Collective Intentionality.* Oxford: Oxford University Press, pp. 97–111.

Salmela, M. (2012): "Shared emotions". *Philosophical Explorations* 15(1):33–46.

Salmela, M. and Nagatsu, M. (2017): "How does it really feel to act together? Shared emotions and the phenomenology of we-agency". *Phenomenology and the Cognitive Sciences* 16(3):449–470.

Salmela, M. and von Scheve, C. (2017): "Emotional roots of right-wing political populism". *Social Science Information* 56(4):567–595.

Schweikard, D. P. and Schmid, H. B. (2020): "Collective Intentionality". In: E. N. Zalta (Ed.), *The Stanford Encyclopedia of Philosophy*, <https://plato.stanford.edu/archives/win2020/entries/collective-intentionality/>

Shapiro, S. (2002): "Law, plans and practical reason". *Legal Theory* 8:417–437.

Shapiro, S. (2011): *Legality.* Cambridge, MA: Harvard University Press.

Searle, J. R. (1990): "Collective Intentions and Action". In: P. Cohen, M. Morgan, and M. Pollack (Eds.), *Intentions in Communication.* Cambridge, MA: MIT Press, pp. 401–415.

Searle, J. R. (1995): *The Construction of Social Reality.* New York: The Free Press.

Searle, J. R. (2010): *Making the Social World: The Structure of Human Civilization.* Oxford: Oxford

Tuomela, R. (2006): "Joint intention, we-mode and I-mode". *Midwest Studies in Philosophy* 30 (1): 35–58.

Tuomela, R. (2007): *The Philosophy of Sociality.* New York: Oxford University Press.

Tuomela, R. & Miller, K. (1988): "We-Intentions". *Philosophical Studies* 53 (3):367–389.

Part I

The nature of law and legislative intention

1 Collectivity and law

Kevin Toh

1.1 Introduction

This chapter sketches a way to deploy some resources from recent philosophical thinking about collective agency to address some longstanding problems in theorizing about the nature of law. One problem has to do with reconciling the conventional nature of law with the apparent possibility of legal judgments that consciously buck established legal trends. A second problem has to do with delineating the appropriate place of coercion in legal goings-on. In addressing these two problems, I argue that we should conceive legal judgments as aimed at instigating and maintaining shared acceptance of norms.

1.2 The Hartian conception of law

What has to be true of a community of people for that community to have laws or a legal system? In other words, what possible facts about a community amount to or constitute its having laws or a legal system? In my opinion, somewhat embarrassingly for legal philosophers, the answer to this question that H.L.A. Hart provided in his 1961 book *The Concept of Law* (1961/94, chs. 5–6) is still the best answer available in the philosophical literature.

Hart's answer can be introduced intuitively by a bit of natural history.[1] Imagine a community of people governed in their behavior and practical thought by a set of customary norms. Such a community likely suffers from certain significant and recurrent problems. First, the members would often be uncertain about which norms are the applicable norms. Second, the members would be unable to change their norms deliberately to adjust to changing circumstances. And third, they would lack the means to adjudicate disputes about what the norms require in ways that are conclusive and authoritative. We can imagine the community adopting to address these problems a set of second- and higher-order norms – i.e. (i) a norm that enumerates the characteristics of the applicable norms; (ii) norms that specify ways to change existing norms (including ways to introduce new norms and to extinguish old ones); and (iii) norms that specify ways to adjudicate authoritatively disputes about what the norms call for. Hart's names for these norms are "the rule of

DOI: 10.4324/9781003242451-3

recognition", "rules of change", and "rules of adjudication", respectively. His proposal is that the transition from the prelegal to the legal stage of a community's development is accomplished by its adoption of such higher-order norms. In the latter stage, the community has laws, and even a legal system.

It is widely acknowledged that this Hartian conception of law is far superior to the older, so-called command theories of law, proposed by Jeremy Bentham and John Austin among others, according to which a community of people has laws or a legal system if a member (or a body of members) of the community, who is habitually obeyed by other members, issues general commands to those other members, which commands are backed by threats of sanctions.[2] Hart argued that such a characterization of laws fails to capture some of the roles that laws actually play in our lives. Commands backed by threats of sanctions are likely to be treated by the members of a community as providing reasons to act as commanded. But the crucial difference is that where laws exist, according to Hart, at least some members of the community treat laws as *appropriately* or *properly* regulating their conduct and practical thought. That is certainly not necessarily the case when commands and the attendant threats of sanctions are involved. Hart's point was that the central basic psychological phenomenon that we should zero in on to explain legal goings-on is neither the community members' fear of a superior's sanctions nor their habit of obedience induced by such fear, as Bentham and Austin supposed, but instead a distinctive conative psychological attitude on the part of the members that he calls "acceptances" of norms. An acceptance of a norm by a person, according to Hart (1961/94, pp. 57, 140, 255), consists of that person's dispositions to regulate his conduct in accordance with the norm, to justify his own and others' conduct by appeals to that norm, and to criticize his own and others' noncompliance by appeals to that norm. A norm exists or prevails in a community insofar as the bulk of that community accept the relevant norm in the sense just described and follow the norm as a result. What distinguishes laws (or *legal* norms) from other norms, according to Hart, is that laws of any single community come in a package of systematized norms with the higher-order norms of the sort described above. And their existence or prevalence in a community is accomplished by a division of labor among the members of the community as follows. A legal system exists or prevails in a community if some powerful subset of the members of the community (call them the "officials" of that community) accept the higher-order norms in the sense indicated, and the rest of the community at least follow the norms that are valid according to the rule of recognition of that community – i.e. the highest-order norm governing identification of the norms of the system.[3]

1.3 Recognitional disputes

Again, in my opinion, Hart's is still the most plausible conception of law or legal system in the philosophical literature. That is not to say that it is without some serious defects. As said in the preceding section, according to

Hart, a community that has laws is one in which its officials commonly or jointly accept a set of higher-order norms, including a rule of recognition. But as Ronald Dworkin (e.g. 1967, 1986, ch. 1) has forcefully argued over the years, some actual communities with laws do not appear to have commonly accepted rules of recognition.[4] Actual communities, including those with flourishing legal systems, are often sites of persistent disagreements and controversies among officials and others about their most fundamental laws. For example, a number of present-day communities with written constitutions have ongoing controversies as to whether the literal meanings of constitutional provisions are among the most fundamental determinants of legal validity in their communities. To put the point another way, using an example, an originalist like the late Justice Antonin Scalia of the U.S. Supreme Court often relied on originalism about constitutional interpretation and advocated it, while knowing full well that his position was not commonly accepted by his fellow judges. And while many have thought that originalism is legally wrong, no one has considered Scalia's actions and thoughts legally inappropriate or out of bounds – i.e. no one has thought that he was failing even to play the legal game, so to speak.

Now, although such phenomena clash with Hart's official legal theory, there are some indications in his discussion that give us hints as to how he would have handled them. In his discussion of international law in the little discussed Chapter 10 of *The Concept of Law*, Hart provides us some guidance as to how we could go about addressing the problem about the existence of laws in the absence of a jointly accepted rule of recognition. Despite the fact that the norms of international law are not held together by a commonly accepted rule of recognition, Hart insists on the genuinely legal nature of such norms because they display other salient features of law. In particular, a set of commonly accepted higher-order norms of international law, including a rule of recognition, though they are currently nonexistent, would not be absurd if they were to exist (1961/94, pp. 230, 236–237). In comparison, such higher-order norms of morality, for example, would be absurd. For morality, unlike law, is not the type of thing for which there are rules of change, rule of adjudication, and a rule of recognition. Following Hart's lead, we may take the position that a legal system, or at least a legal *regime*, exists or prevails in a community if: (i) its members regulate their conduct by a set of norms; and (ii) modifications of such norms, authoritative resolutions of disputes about contents of such norms, and identification of such norms are all treated by the members as *amenable* to being carried out by appeals to a set of jointly accepted higher-order norms. The important point here is that (ii) can obtain even when there is no current joint acceptance in the relevant community of any higher-order norms. The case for attribution of a legal system to the relevant community would be strengthened considerably if we were to observe the following further fact: (iii) despite continuously disagreeing about the content of their rule of recognition, the members of the community or their officials carry on deliberations and other activities aimed at discovery and maintenance of a jointly accepted rule of recognition. Arguably, that is what is going on in many communities in which there are persistent recognitional disputes – i.e. disagreements about the content of the most fundamental laws.

1.4 What kind of disputes?

It appears then that Hart's original or official conception of legal systems can be revised to account for communities in which there are ongoing disputes about the rule of recognition. We are not quite out of the woods yet, however. For there is a worry about the nature of such recognitional disputes.

If Hart's original conception of legal systems, with its picture of joint acceptances by officials of rules of recognition, could be maintained, then we would have a pretty clear idea of what a recognitional dispute is all about. Disputants would be arguing about which norm, if any, is the norm that officials jointly accept as enumerating the ultimate criteria of legal validity in the relevant community. In effect, such disputes would essentially be sociological disputes and would be relatively easy to carry out and settle. The problematic nature of Hart's original conception is made obvious by the fact that many recognitional disputes in actual legal systems are persistent and ongoing. Moreover, the way lawyers and others go about advocating their respective positions rarely approaches the way social scientists go about arguing for their sociological hypotheses. In any case, if we abandon Hart's original conception in favor of the revised conception outlined at the end of the preceding section, it is not clear what lawyers and others are arguing about when they take part in recognitional disputes.

According to one prominent tradition in legal philosophy, the so-called natural law tradition, what the law is invariably constrained by what morality requires; and one way of developing this tradition for the issue at hand is to say that when legal norms that are jointly accepted by legal officials run out, so to speak, thereafter disputes about what the law is turns into a moral dispute. This is no place to assess this approach in a systematic way, but we can get a feel for its shortcomings by examining the most influential version of it in recent years – namely, Dworkin's. According to Dworkin, a community's law consists of an explicit part and an implicit part. The *explicit law* consists of the legal norms that the community's officials jointly accept and include statutes and widely recognized judicial precedents, whereas the *implicit law* consists of the morally correct principles that justify the explicit law. This conception of law is meant to imply that judges are to appeal to and draw inferences from the moral principles that fit and justify the explicit law when they decide difficult cases that cannot be decided merely by deploying the explicit law. This picture of adjudication captures well the way that many judges decided some actual cases and the way that many trained in the law think that judges ought to decide some imaginary cases that Dworkin outlined. In *Riggs v. Palmer*,[5] the most famous example that Dworkin has relied on, it was decided that a grandson who poisoned his grandfather could not inherit the grandfather's estate despite a valid will clearly designating him as the beneficiary, and in so deciding the court relied on the moral principle that no wrongdoer shall benefit from his wrongdoing. Cases like *Riggs*, both actual and hypothetical ones, provide counter-examples to Hart's original conception of legal systems and also motivate Dworkin's own alternative conception according to which unwritten and hitherto unrecognized moral principles form a crucial part of the law that pick up the slack, so to speak, when a community's explicit law runs out.

While Dworkin's alternative conception matches our intuitions in cases like *Riggs*, it runs into trouble when dealing with some other cases. Dworkin's conception implies that even when morally dubious aspects clearly dominate a community's explicit law (or the part of the explicit law that is relevant to the issue at hand), judges would seek out morally correct principles that fit and justify that explicit law, instead of settling on a set of morally *incorrect* standards that would much better fit and justify the relevant explicit law. In such cases, Dworkin's conception has implications that clearly diverge from our considered judgments about what judges legally ought to conclude, a divergence that is put into a very sharp relief in Dworkin's review of Robert Cover's book *Justice Accused* (1975). Cover chronicled the story of judges sitting in the Northern states of the United States who had to decide antebellum cases involving the Fugitive Slave Acts. Almost without exception, despite their very strong moral objections to what the Fugitive Slave Acts required of them, as well as some heavy political and personal costs in some instances, these judges decided to return runaway slaves caught in the Northern states to their masters in the South. In his review, Dworkin (1975) puzzles over these cases and eventually concludes that these judges behaved as they did because they made the mistake of overlooking a very compelling legal theory – namely, one like his own – that would have enabled them to be true to both their moral convictions and their legal scruples. This is less than persuasive and is especially troublesome for Dworkin given that the central part of his case for his legal theory is that it better describes or explains how judges actually decide legal cases like *Riggs* than Hart's theory. Dworkin himself seems to have been less than satisfied with this reasoning, as indicated by his repeated later returns to the same issue.[6]

In sum, both Hart's original conception of law and Dworkin's natural law-inspired conception appear to struggle in portraying accurately actual legal goings-on. If legal disputes, including recognitional disputes (i.e. disputes about the content of the most fundamental laws), are not about what norms are commonly accepted by the officials of the community, and if they are also not a species of moral disputes, then we are left with no attractive conception of such disputes. We may be left with the uncomfortable possibility that such disputes are mere political disputes in which participants try to push or manipulate each other to adopt positions that they favor, respectively.

1.5 The political conception

Let me call this last conception of persistent recognitional disputes simply "the political conception". Some legal philosophers (e.g. Leiter 2009) appear quite unsqueamish about adopting the political conception. Yet, this conception is quite at variance with our common everyday conception of what goes on in the most consequential cases at the highest rungs of our judicial systems, or in public debates about such cases in our learned publications. In fact, it seems to me, it is not merely that the political conception is not in tension with our pre-theoretical intuitions. The implications of the conception are more dire than that. The conception is, in a significant way, a return to command theories of law of the sort that we had very good reasons to leave behind. Let me explain.

Notice that the move from Bentham and Austin's command theories to Hart's acceptance-based theory involved a fundamental shift in the psychological phenomenon that is at the center of our attempt to explain legal goings-on. Whereas command theories take fear of sanctions and habits induced by such fear as the central psychological phenomena, Hart's theory takes acceptance of norms as the central phenomenon. An acceptance of a norm is a particular kind of conative psychological state, and consists of a person's dispositions to regulate his conduct in accordance with the norm, to justify his own and others' conduct by appeals to that norm, and to criticize his own and others' noncompliance by appeals to that norm. And the shift to focusing on such a psychological phenomenon was motivated by the view that where a community of people has and is governed by laws, at least some members of the community treat laws as *appropriately* or *properly* regulating conduct and evaluation. Once again, according to Hart, a legal system exists or prevails in a community if some powerful subset of the members of the community (call them the "officials" of that community) *accept* certain higher-order norms – namely, those governing changes in the norms, adjudication of disputes about the norms, and identification of the applicable norms – and follow them as a result, and the rest of the community at least follow the norms that are valid according to the rule of recognition of that community – i.e. the higher-order norm governing identification of the norms of the system.

Now, the question is whether we can maintain acceptances of norms at the center of our explanation of law while adopting the political conception of persistent recognitional disputes. A person who accepts a norm is not only disposed to behave and think as the norm says, but is also disposed to justify his own and others' behavior and thought that conform to the norm, and also to criticize his own and others' behavior and thought that flout the norm. Such a person thinks that the normative position that he accepts is both justified and justifiable. Could he maintain such thinking while also thinking, as the political conception implies, that at the most fundamental level his own position – i.e. the rule of recognition, or the version of it, that he accepts – is neither justified nor justifiable to his interlocutors, and that in advocating his most fundamental position he is trying merely to push or manipulate his interlocutors? Sure enough, there would not be much difficulty in maintaining acceptances of norms in good faith if one were ignorant or confused about the nature of the political conception. But if one were clear-eyed about that conception, then one's commitments to the relevant norms would no longer have the functional profile that characterizes acceptances of norms. A person's commitment to a rule of recognition, or the version of it that he favors, would no longer be characterized by his thinking that that norm, or the favored version, is justified or justifiable; and that lack of justification or justifiability would infect his commitments to other, less fundamental norms of the legal system as well.

In a significant way, the resulting psychology of participants in legal goings-on would resemble more the one sketched by command theories than the one posited by Hart's theory. Of course, what is involved would not be a coercer–coercee relationship of the sort posited by command theories. But the relationship among disputants about the most fundamental legal matters would be non-rational or non-normative in the way that the coercer–coercee relationship is likely to be.

We thus end up with an unpalatable choice among three options: (i) the original Hartian conception of law according to which there is always a common or joint acceptance of a rule of recognition among the officials of a community, which rules out the possibility of genuine disagreements about the rule of recognition; (ii) the natural law-inspired Dworkinian conception according to which the law of a community consists of the norms that are commonly accepted by officials, and the moral principles that fit and justify those commonly accepted norms, which conception implies that recognitional disputes are a species of moral disputes; and (iii) the revised Hartian conception that implies that recognitional disputes are mere political disputes in which disputants try to push or manipulate each other to get their own respective ways. It is difficult to maintain that intractable recognitional disputes are about what norm is commonly accepted as the rule of recognition of a community.[7] The very existence of such disputes in actual legal settings indicates that in the relevant communities there is no such commonly accepted rule of recognition that the original Hartian conception of law requires. We should then seriously consider the possibility that what the law is not a social factual matter, as the original Hartian conception implies, but instead a normative matter. This is the line of thinking that tempts us to adopt the Dworkinian conception. But for the reasons indicated above, it is difficult to maintain that intractable recognitional disputes are invariably moral disputes as the Dworkinian conception implies. We may in reaction consider the view that recognitional disputes are not genuine normative disputes at all but instead instances of mutual pushing and manipulation. But that appears a rather drastic step which involves abandoning wholesale the seeming progress we had made moving away from command theories of law, and we should avoid it if we can find a different alternative.

1.6 Shared acceptances of norms

The dialectic of the preceding sections indicates that we want to portray persistent recognitional disputes as normative disputes, yet not as necessarily moral disputes. At the end of Section 1.3 above, following some suggestions that may be inferred from Chapter 10 of Hart's *The Concept of Law*, I argued that the case for attribution of a legal system to a community of people would be quite compelling if, despite continuously disagreeing about the content of their rule of recognition, the members or their officials carry on deliberations and disputes aimed at discovery and maintenance of a jointly accepted rule of recognition. But if neither social facts nor moral principles provide the correctness conditions for members' or officials' recognitional judgments, it is not clear what it would mean for them to be trying to discover the correct rule of recognition.

Here, I want to sidestep that issue by making the following move. Instead of thinking that any member is motivated in his acceptance of some norm as the rule of recognition by some one set of considerations – be they social facts, moral principles, or something else – and expecting his interlocutors to be motivated by the same considerations, we can think of the member as motivated by some considerations of his own and not caring what his interlocutors are motivated by as long as they can converge in their acceptance of the same norm as their rule of recognition. Furthermore, we can think of each member as being disposed to withdraw his commitment to a particular norm in favor of a neighboring norm insofar as the neighboring norm is more likely to elicit commitments from other members, and other members are similarly disposed to modify their commitments with the aim of achieving a common acceptance of a single norm. Given that each member has his own ideas about what justifies his recognitional commitments, he is quite unlikely to go with just any option in the hope of achieving a joint acceptance of a norm as the rule of recognition of the community. But in recognition of the possible and even likely persistence of recognitional disputes, each member is disposed in his recognitional commitments to allow for some flexibility. We can think of such dispositions as constituting a psychological infrastructure that we have developed to deal with persistent fundamental normative disagreements.

The resulting conception of law could be construed as a particular hybrid of the original Hartian conception and the natural-law inspired Dworkinian conception. Unlike the Hartian conception, and like the Dworkinian conception, the new conception characterizes recognitional disputes as normative disputes. At the same time, it retains the Hartian concern for common or joint acceptances of a particular norm as the rule of recognition. What members or officials are after, when they make recognitional judgments, according to the new conception, is not so much to get any existing social facts right, but instead to create or instigate a new social fact – namely, a joint acceptance of some norm as the community's rule of recognition.

Let me, at this juncture, take advantage of Michael Bratman's influential recent conception of joint or shared intentions to flesh out some aspects of the new conception of law that I have in mind. According to Bratman (esp. 1992, 1993, 1997a, 1997b), certain conditional individual intentions, in the context of common knowledge among the relevant group of people, add up to or constitute a shared intention. According to an approximation that he outlines at one point (1993, p. 121), such a shared intention could be characterized as follows:

(1) We jointly intend to *J* if and only if:
 (a) (i) I intend that we *J* and (ii) you intend that we *J*.
 (b) I intend that we *J* in accordance with and because of (a)(i), (a)(ii), and meshing subplans of (a)(i) and (a)(ii); you intend that we *J* in accordance with and because of (a)(i), (a)(ii), and meshing subplans of (a)(i) and (a)(ii).
 (c) (a) and (b) are common knowledge between us.

We can model a joint or shared *acceptance of a norm* (as opposed to an intention) along a similar line:

(2) We jointly accept *N* if and only if:
 (a) (i) I accept *N* and (ii) you accept *N*.
 (b) I accept *N* partly because of (a)(i), (a)(ii), and meshing subordinate norms that are validated by *N*; you accept *N* because of (a)(i), (a)(ii), and meshing subordinate norms that are validated by *N*.
 (c) (a) and (b) are common knowledge between us.

Of course, when the relevant *N* is the rule of recognition of a legal system, it will not be a shared acceptance merely between two people. Instead, any joint acceptance would be among very many members or officials.

What is more important to point out for my purposes here is that what participants in a recognitional dispute are trying to do is not so much to *represent* accurately something like (2), or a many-party version of (2),[8] but instead to *create* or *instigate* something like it. Assuming that *N* calls for ϕ-ing, the psychological attitude of someone making a judgment that is aimed at realizing such a goal would have a content that resembles the following:

(3) Let us ϕ, on the assumption that you will come to think likewise, partly as the result of your becoming aware of this attitude on my part.

One significance of such an attitude is that a person may make a normative judgment, and thereby express his acceptance of *N*, even in the absence of a shared acceptance of a norm – i.e. a state of affairs sketched by (2) – already existing. Of course, a person can join in on an already existing shared acceptance of a norm by having an attitude like (3). So such an attitude need not be aimed at *creating* or *instigating* a new, hitherto unrealized shared acceptance of a norm but instead at *maintaining* an existing one. But the possibility of rejecting an existing shared acceptance of a norm and pitching a focal point for a new and even conflicting shared acceptance of a norm is what enables the new conception of law based on (3) to get around the problem that the original Hartian conception incurred. At the same time, (3) is not plausibly construed as an account of moral judgments. Or, more accurately, moral judgments do not necessarily have contents like (3). It may be the case that some moral judgments actually do; that may very well be the case for judgments of some kinds of moral obligations, for example.[9] But not all moral judgments involve commitments that are dependent on like commitments on the parts of others, as (3) would have it. By adopting a conception of law based on (3), we thus also escape problems that the Dworkinian conception incurs by characterizing recognitional judgments as invariably moral judgments.[10]

1.7 The place of coercion in law

It may be thought that the conception of law that I have just outlined implies an excessively idealized picture of legal practice. Certainly, any real legal practice is replete with coercive and quasi-coercive interactions, and the characterization of legal interactions as conducted through normative attempts at instigating or maintaining shared acceptances of norms could be thought to overlook that fact.

Notice first, however, that the new conception of legal goings-on is quite compatible with the fact that that practice contains many instances of people failing to interact with each other on the basis of norms that are jointly accepted or through normative attempts at inducing such joint acceptances. According to an influential conception of beliefs, beliefs necessarily aim at truth.[11] And this thesis about the nature of beliefs is quite compatible with, and not undermined by, the fact that people very often have false beliefs and even beliefs that they implicitly recognize to be false (in cases of self-deception). Analogously, the fact that the aim of joint acceptances of norms is not perfectly realized or perfectly regulative in actual legal practices does not (at least not by itself) undermine the thesis that legal practice is conducted through expressions of psychological attitudes with that particular aim.

Second, some amount of coercive and quasi-coercive pushing and manipulating can be expected among people who interact with each other with the aim of realizing shared acceptances of norms given the complex interplay between the individual aim of normative correctness on the one hand, and the aim of shared acceptances of norms on the other. If a person's normative judgment on a particular normative issue were at odds with that of the majority of his peers, then others may opt to forgo finding common ground with him in particular so that they can maintain a joint acceptance of a norm among themselves. A person's normative judgments may be ignored also when he is thought to be uncaring about interacting with others based on jointly accepted norms.[12] In these types of cases, the relevant person may be subject to coercive and quasi-coercive pushing and manipulation. But it is one thing to think, as Bentham and Austin did, that coercive interactions are paradigmatic, or at the heart, of legal practice; and it is quite another to think, as I do, that at times the interactions of people who aim to find common normative grounds with each other fall short of that ideal, and that in such cases they may resort to coercive and quasi-coercive measures.

Perhaps this is not an inopportune moment to address, albeit briefly, Frederick Schauer's (2010, 2015) recent attempt to revive command theories of law. Reacting to the Hartian line of thinking that de-emphasizes the place of sanctions in legal goings-on, for the presence of sanctions is neither necessary nor sufficient for the existence of legal obligations, Schauer insists that such an "essentialist" approach to theorizing about the nature of law overlooks the sheer ubiquity of sanctions in the workings of legal systems, especially contemporary regulatory legal systems. Schauer argues that people are in actuality vastly more prone to follow laws out of fear of sanctions than out of their acceptances of the norms that make up the law; and that in putting the latter phenomenon at the center of theorizing about the nature of law, the Hartian approach ultimately distorts the legal phenomenon that it is seeking to explain.

Schauer, however, appears to be working with a false choice and likely also an indefensible conception of empirical theorizing. Our choice is hardly between explaining people's motivation solely or primarily out of fear of sanctions on the one hand and explaining their motivation solely or primarily out of acceptances of norms on the other. And for this reason, the relative frequencies of the two kinds of motivation are not decisive for our purposes. Instead, our choice hangs on the relative explanatory powers or efficacies of the two explantia in accounting for both phenomena. The Hartian thought, which I followed above, is that by placing acceptances of norms at the center of theorizing about the nature of law, we can explain as much of the coercive aspects of law as we need to, whereas going in the other direction is unlikely to be as productive. Similarly, by conceiving water as H_2O, we can explain water's liquidity, clarity, potability, and much else at certain temperatures; whereas the opposite explanatory direction will not be as theoretically productive. This, despite the fact that the water we encounter most frequently in life is clear, potable liquid. I cannot help thinking that Schauer's position on theorizing about the nature of law is analogous to that of an eccentric chemist who insists that we should think of water as clear, potable liquid and that we should not give in to the "essentialist" trap of thinking of water as H_2O. At one point, Schauer says: "Coercion may be to law what flying is to birds: not strictly necessary but so ubiquitous that a full understanding of the phenomenon requires that we consider it" (2015, p. 40). I am here reminded of a quip by David Hills in a conversation about another matter: There is a difference between bird-watching and real ornithology.[13]

1.8 Assessings or optings?

As indicated above, my conception of shared acceptances of norms is modeled on Bratman's conception of shared intentions. And given this debt to Bratman's work, it may be wondered why I have chosen to construe the individual psychological attitudes that add up to a shared attitude as acceptances of norms, a species of normative judgments, rather than as intentions, a species of volitional commitments. Scott Shapiro (2002, 2011), for one, has gone in a different direction in exploiting Bratman's work in his characterization of laws as plans or plan-like volitional commitments. The fundamental question here is whether legal judgments or more specifically recognitional judgments are best characterized as volitional commitments or as normative judgments – i.e. whether they should be characterized as "optings" or as "assessings", to borrow T.M. Scanlon's (2002, pp. 168–169) useful terminology. While both conceptions of legal judgments would have considerable explanatory powers,[14] I believe that a conception of legal judgments as a species of assessings, albeit a fairly peculiar kind, would have some advantages over any conceptions of them as a species of optings.

First, intentions and other volitional commitments – i.e. commitments of the opting variety – are usually thought to *settle* practical issues so that once a person adopts an intention to do something, further deliberation about that issue is foreclosed.[15] But legal or recognitional judgments do not seem to have the same settling function. I can come to a legal or recognitional conclusion but still (without confusion) consider the issue unsettled. I may, for example, still want to consider moral or etiquette implications of doing what the law clearly requires before making up my mind as to what to do.[16] And presumably, the same would be the case for a group's legal or recognitional conclusion.

Second, as I have been emphasizing above, a person may be cognizant of an existing shared acceptance of a norm as the rule of recognition of his community and still make a pitch for a shared acceptance of an alternative norm in an attempt to instigate a new recognitional consensus. I believe that this characterization of legal and recognitional disputes is true to the constant normative negotiation and reconsideration, both piecemeal and occasionally wholesale, that occur in actual legal settings.[17] It is not clear to me that the conception of legal judgments as volitional commitments is as adept at capturing this dynamic aspect of our legal practice. Bratman characterizes intentions in general and shared intentions more particularly as providing *background frameworks* within which the relevant people's further practical deliberations take place. The conception of our commitments to laws as constituting such deliberative background frameworks appears to me to entail too great a degree of stability or rigidity of our commitments to laws for an accurate characterization of our legal practice.

1.9 Shared deliberation

In a chapter of a book that consolidates his recent thinking about shared agency, Bratman (2014, ch. 7) considers two conceptions of shared deliberation – or more specifically, of shared commitments to give certain weights to particular considerations – before he goes on to deem one of them clearly superior to the other. It is an assumption of the preceding discussion that there is a third option that Bratman is overlooking and which may actually provide a better model of at least some of the phenomena that he is seeking to explain.

The kind of social phenomena that Bratman seeks to explain are those in which two or more people treat some considerations as having a certain weight in their deliberations about what to do. For example, we may decide to give much weight to minimizing biofootprints when we plan our camping trip. And a jury may be prompted by a judge's instructions to give no weight to some hearsay evidence when they deliberate about the guilt of a criminal defendant.

Bratman (2014, pp. 136–137) considers two competing models of what is going on when two or more people share a commitment to weigh some considerations in a certain way. First, such commitments could be construed as converging normative judgments[18] in the context of common knowledge. Second, such commitments could be taken as shared intentions or policies to treat some considerations as having a certain kind of weight, where policies are general intentions, again in the context of common knowledge. Bratman ends up decisively favoring the second option by arguing that a convergence in normative judgments is neither necessary nor sufficient for a shared commitment to give a certain weight to some considerations. While agreeing with his comparative assessments, however, we need not embrace his conclusion that the second model is the correct one. For Bratman ignores a third option – i.e. the option of construing the relevant phenomena as involving *shared* normative judgments. Such shared judgments would differ from shared intentions or policies in that the individual attitudes that would make up a shared judgment would be normative judgments rather than volitional commitments like intentions or policies. Such individual normative judgments would have contents – something like (3) above – that make them mesh with each other in contexts of common knowledge the way that the individual intentions that make up a shared intention do.

Perhaps "overlooking" is too strong a word. For Bratman at one point considers the possibility of characterizing shared commitments about weights as made up of normative judgments that are conditioned by the difficulty of reaching normative consensus, and hence could depart to some degrees from the normative judgments that each person would be disposed to make in other, non-collective contexts. He does not find this view plausible and argues:

> In response to characteristic practical pressures, then, we might go beyond what consensus in evaluative [or normative] judgment there is and reach a more extensive policy-like convergence concerning weights for our shared deliberation. This would be puzzling if we thought that what we would be directly arriving at is a belief or judgment about which weights are the correct weights. We do not normally think of belief or judgment as rationally responding directly to these kinds of practical pressures: the formation of belief for these kinds of practical reasons is, normally, wishful thinking. But in participating in a shared policy about weights despite our prior evaluative differences, I need not be directly changing my beliefs or judgments about these weights. I need only be guided by a relevant policy in certain social contexts.
>
> (2014, p. 140)

A thorough answer to Bratman's point here would require delving into much deeper issues – e.g. about the nature of beliefs, judgments, and epistemic warrant[19] – than I can in this paper. But I think we can bring up some considerations that point us in a different direction.

For one thing, there are certain judgments (aside from legal or recognitional judgments of the sort that I have been talking about) that appear to be counter-examples to Bratman's view. A very important species of moral judgments are the judgments of public political justification that John Rawls sought to delineate in his later writings. Rawls argues that citizens of modern democratic societies, who could not realistically expect to converge in their comprehensive moral doctrines, "should be ready to explain the basis of their actions to one another in terms each could reasonably expect that others might endorse as consistent with their freedom and equality" (1993, p. 218). What is left unstated, but is very much implicit in Rawls's discussion, I believe, is that even when a citizen thinks that a particular political conception of justice is the most reasonable one available, he does not insist upon political proposals based on it should others not take them up. Instead, he would be disposed to withdraw them and come to accept other proposals that another citizen proposes based on another reasonable political conception of justice if those proposals have a greater prospect of joint acceptance. This ideal or aim of deliberating and settling on answers according to terms that are acceptable to others, so long as those others are similarly disposed, is required by what Rawls calls "the criterion of reciprocity" (1993, p. 49; 1996, p. xliv; 1997, p. 578). Bratman actually takes up these Rawlsian themes at one point in a footnote (2014, p. 191, n.22), but suggests that the kinds of commitments that Rawls is talking about could be construed along the lines of shared intentions or policies about weights that he favors. But such a diagnosis goes directly against Rawls's explicit conception of commitments regulated by the criterion of reciprocity as moral judgments.[20]

Second, it is not clear to me that normative judgments that are regulated by the aim of achieving shared acceptances of norms in ways that I have sketched are conditioned by "practical pressures" as Bratman says in the above-quoted passage if by that term Bratman means some "reasons of the wrong sort" as he seems to when he talks about wishful thinking in the same passage. A political liberal who refrains from making judgments of political justice based on a particular comprehensive doctrine (e.g. Catholicism) that he himself favors is making moral judgments that depart from the judgments that he would make in non-collective contexts, but he is not being motivated by illicit considerations that make the former judgments ones of wishful thinking or the like. Instead, his judgments of political justice appear to be motivated by the thoroughly appropriate kinds of moral considerations. In fact, at one point, Bratman himself seems to come very close to recognizing the possibility of normative judgments (as opposed to intentions or policies) that are appropriately regulated by the aim of shared acceptance of norms. After observing that any shared intentions or policies are likely to be instrumentally valuable, he says:

> [T]here is also, potentially, further support for these shared policies, a support that may be shared despite the divergence in relevant specific judgments of the right and the good. Once the shared policies are in place, their functioning can help realize relevant forms of sociality. And the participants may converge in their positive evaluation of those forms of sociality, despite their more specific evaluative differences. So these shared policies can sometimes involve a sensible reflexivity: they can sometimes sensibly say to give weight to *X* in part because of the acknowledged value of the forms of sociality that are partly constituted by this social role of those policies.
>
> (2014, pp. 141–142)

It does not seem strange to think that the kind of "sensible reflexivity" that Bratman is here talking about could turn what initially were shared intentions or policies into shared normative judgments. Judgments of public political justice that, according to Rawls, political liberals would be disposed to make may very well fit that model.

Third and finally, there appears to me a pretty good case to be made for loosening up the picture of shared deliberation that Bratman sketches in a way that favors the conception involving shared acceptances of norms over the one involving only shared intentions or policies. And here, I repeat a point I discussed in the last section. Strictly speaking, Bratman (2014, p. 189, n. 3) is concerned solely with group deliberations *from* shared commitments rather than group deliberations *towards* shared commitments. But when a group of people deliberate together, and even if they are working with a framework provided by shared commitments to weights as Bratman characterizes them, they will invariably need to deal with issues about which they currently do not have shared commitments. They will then need to deliberate *towards* shared commitments about those further issues. In shared deliberations, I would think, participants are always deliberating from some shared commitments and deliberating to some further shared commitments, and that a satisfactory conception of shared deliberation should provide a picture in which both of these activities dot the process of shared deliberation throughout. Now, if I am right about that, then it seems that we should wonder what kind of shared commitments – i.e. shared intentions or policies on the one hand and shared normative judgments on the other – would be better candidates to play the roles of bases and goals of shared deliberation as people seek out more and more shared commitments. I would think that as people seek out more and more shared commitments, often they would have occasions to reconsider prior shared commitments. In deliberating together, they would be disposed to constantly reconsider the contents of their prior shared commitments (unless there are some special reasons to classify certain matters as off limits for reconsideration). And to repeat a point I made in the last section, I believe that frequent reconsiderations of prior shared commitments would be incompatible (or at least in tension with) the settling function of volitional commitments like intentions or policies. It seems to me that the functional profile of normative judgments makes such judgments more suitable to serve in the role of making up shared commitments that dot the process of any shared deliberations.

1.10 Conclusion

For the reasons I outlined in the preceding section, the phenomenon of shared acceptances of norms – as opposed to convergences in normative judgments on the one hand and shared intentions or policies on the other – should be taken as a live possibility. And for the reasons that I outlined in the rest of the paper, I believe that the notion of shared acceptances of norms could play a crucial role in our devising a plausible philosophical conception of the nature of law.[21]

Notes

1. For some recent work relying on the genealogical method to extend the Hartian line of thinking about the nature of law, see Pettit (2019); Toh (2019, esp. §§ 9–11). See also Pettit (2018).
2. A notable recent detractor is Frederick Schauer (2010, 2015), whose views will be taken up briefly at the end of Section 1.7.
3. Recently, Peter Railton (2019) has questioned the adequacy of Hart's conception of norm-acceptance in a way that warrants serious consideration. See also Railton (2006). The alternative conception of regulation by norms that Railton sketches motivates a different picture of the existence of legal systems as well. Toh (2021) contains my preliminary reactions to these proposals.

4. Unfortunately, Dworkin's discussions are often marred by conflations of this point with several others that are not of similar merit. I am focusing only on the point that I am outlining in the text.
5. 115 N.Y. 506 (1889).
6. Dworkin's legal theory also implies that if a community's explicit laws were morally bad enough, then there would not be genuine laws in that community. Some like Hart (1966/82, p. 150; 1987, pp. 40–42) have taken this as a reductio of Dworkin's theory of law, and Dworkin himself has struggled to minimize the damage caused by this implication (1986, pp. 111–113; 1987, p. 20) without much success.
7. Another option, which likely overlaps in complicated ways with the three enumerated in the text, might be to portray recognitional disputes as what David Plunkett and Tim Sundell (2013b) call "metalinguistic negotiations". See also Plunkett & Sundell (2013a, 2021). A skeptical assessment of this proposal is outlined in Schroeter, Schroeter & Toh (unpublished manuscript).
8. For ease of exposition, I will hereinafter dispense with this tag.
9. Some philosophers (e.g. Hume 1738-40, bk III, part ii, § 5; Rawls 1971, § 52) have argued for the so-called "practice theories" of promissory obligations, according to which existence of moral obligations to keep promises depends on the existence of some ongoing practice of promise-keeping. Judgments of promissory obligations that fit such theories are arguably amenable to an analysis like the one of legal judgments that I offer in the text.
10. Toh (2011) provides a fuller picture of the conception of law that I have just sketched in this section.
11. See e.g. Williams (1970); Velleman (2000); Shah (2003). I am not here endorsing this view of beliefs.
12. I benefited from Philippa Foot's observation about an analogous issue. Foot argues that *approval* and *disapproval*, unlike mere liking and disliking, can properly take place only against a background of implicit agreement that certain people will have a *say* on what shall be done. Only those with a say can properly approve or disapprove of what gets decided to be done, whereas even those without such a say can like or dislike the decisions. Foot says:

    > And if this is not obvious it is because the presumption that account [of certain people's opinions] will be taken is only a presumption, and may be destroyed in an individual case. What may destroy it is for instance the fact that some individual forfeits our respect by his habitually foolish opinions. (1977, p. 199)

    Analogously, some people may forfeit our deference, and thereby warrant our exclusion of him from a circle of co-deference, by their habitual failure to defer to the rest of us.
13. Also, worth taking note here perhaps is the need to be more careful and scrupulous than Schauer is in deploying the notions of essence and necessity. Not all necessary features of something amount to parts of its essence, and there are a variety of necessities to keep apart in our theorizing. For influential treatments of these issues, see Fine (1994, 2002). In discussing the coercive aspects that would invariably attend the workings of legal systems that are constituted by the aim of shared acceptances of norms, I am in effect discussing what could be deemed natural or nomic necessities that follow from certain psychological and other facts about human beings. My discussion is in keeping with Hart's nuanced discussion of a number of "truisms" about human beings and their environments that call for certain principles that are necessary for human survival. Hart (1961/94, ch. 9) argues that such principles amount to what could be called "the minimum content of natural law". And he in fact at one point calls the need for use of sanctions in human societies a "natural necessity" (p. 199). A similarly careful treatment

of the relevant issues, it seems to me, would dissolve much of Schauer's line of thinking.

14. For example, both conceptions would enable us to explain the fact that legal judgments often facilitate interpersonal coordination, and the related fact that people have tendencies to adhere to established legal doctrines. And both conceptions can capture the fact that people often make legal judgments in the face of normative underdetermination – i.e. when the options a person needs to choose among are normatively on a par, when he lacks adequate information to compare options, and when options are incomparable.
15. See e.g. Bratman (1987, p. 16).
16. The relevant difference should not be obscured by the fact that legal statements often have contents, expressible in deontic terms such as "obligation" and "right", that purport to assert reasons that override or exclude other reasons. In a way, normative statements with such deontic contents have a settling function of their own. But what gets settled by such judgments is quite different from what gets settled by intentions and other volitional commitments. An intention or an intention-like volitional commitment forecloses further *deliberation* about the relevant practical issue. This is explained by its functional role of enabling creatures like us, with limited resources to attend to practical problems, to control and coordinate conduct without thereby expending too much of their resources. What a deontic normative judgment purports to exclude on the other hand is not further deliberation per se, but instead *reasons* that are contrary to what the normative judgment asserts. Unlike intentions and other volitional commitments, deontic normative judgments are not driven by the goal of resource-conservation, and that is reflected in their lacking the kind of *stability* or *inertia* that volitional commitments characteristically have. See Bratman (1987, pp. 16, 72–73).
17. As I have discussed above, highlighting this aspect of our legal practice has been one of the signal contributions of Dworkin's work.
18. Whereas Bratman uses the term "judgments of value", I use "normative judgments" for the sake of consistency with my foregoing discussion.
19. See e.g. van Fraassen (1984, 1989, ch. 7); Stanley (2005).
20. And no doubt there are other normative judgments – including some aesthetic judgments (e.g. judgments of fashionableness) – that are amenable to a construal like the one I am recommending for legal or recognitional judgments.
21. For their helpful feedback, I thank the participants at the Workshop on Collective Action and the Law, organized by Teresa Marques and Chiara Valentini, and held at Universitat Pompeu Fabra in September 2016.

References

Bratman, M. (1987). *Intention, Plans, and Practical Reason*. Cambridge: Harvard University Press.

Bratman, M. (1992). Shared Cooperative Activity. Reprinted in: Bratman (1999), pp. 93–108.

Bratman, M. (1993). Shared Intention. Reprinted in: Bratman (1999), pp. 109–129.

Bratman, M. (1997a). Shared Intention and Mutual Obligation. Reprinted in: Bratman (1999), pp. 130–141.

Bratman, M. (1997b). I Intend that We *J*. Reprinted in: Bratman (1999), pp. 142–161.

Bratman, M. (1999). *Faces of Intention*. Cambridge: Cambridge University Press.

Bratman, M. (2014). *Shared Agency*. Oxford: Oxford University Press.

Cover, R. (1975). *Justice Accused*. New Haven: Yale University Press.

Dworkin, R. (1967). The Model of Rules I. Reprinted in: R. Dworkin (1977), *Taking Rights Seriously*. Cambridge: Harvard University Press, pp. 14–45.

Dworkin, R. (1975). The Law of the Slave-Catchers. In: *The Times Literary Supplement* (December 15), p. 1437.

Dworkin, R. (1986). *Law's Empire*. Cambridge: Harvard University Press.

Dworkin, R. (1987). Legal Theory and the Problem of Sense. In: Gavison (1987), pp. 9–20.

Fine, K. (1994). Essence and Modality. *Philosophical Perspectives*, 8 (Logic and Language), pp. 1–16.

Fine, K. (2002). The Varieties of Necessity. Reprinted in: K. Fine (2005), *Modality and Tense*. Oxford: Oxford University Press, pp. 235–260.

Foot, P. (1977). Approval and Disapproval. Reprinted in: P. Foot (1978), *Virtues and Vices*. Berkeley & Los Angeles: University of California Press, pp. 189–207.

Gavison, R. (Ed.) (1987). *Issues in Contemporary Legal Philosophy: The Influence of H.L.A. Hart*. Oxford: Clarendon Press.

Hart, H.L.A. (1961/94). *The Concept of Law*, 2nd ed. Oxford: Clarendon Press.

Hart, H.L.A. (1966/82). Legal Duty and Obligation. Revised and reprinted in: H.L.A. Hart (1982), *Essays on Bentham*. Oxford: Clarendon Press, pp. 127–161.

Hart, H.L.A. (1987). Comment. In: Gavison (1987), pp. 35–42.

Hume, D. (1738–40). *A Treatise of Human Nature* In: L.A. Selby-Bigge and P.H. Nidditch, Eds., 2nd ed., 1888/1978). Oxford: Clarendon Press.

Leiter, B. (2009). Explaining Theoretical Disagreements. *University of Chicago Law Review*, 76(3), pp. 1215–1250.

Pettit, P. (2018). *The Birth of Ethics: Reconstructing the Role and Nature of Morality*. Oxford: Oxford University Press.

Pettit, P. (2019). Social Norms and the Internal Point of View: An Elaboration of Hart's Genealogy of Law. *Oxford Journal of Legal Studies*, 39(2), pp. 229–258.

Plunkett, D. and T. Sundell (2013a). Disagreement and the Semantics of Normative and Evaluative Terms. *Philosophers' Imprint* 13(23): 1–37.

Plunkett, D. and T. Sundell (2013b). Dworkin's Interpretivism and the Pragmatics of Legal Disputes. *Legal Theory* 19: 242–281.

Plunkett, D. and T. Sundell (2021). Metalinguistic Negotiation and Speaker Error. *Inquiry* 64: 142–167.

Railton, P. (2006). Normative Guidance. In: R. Shafer-Landau (Ed.), *Oxford Studies in Metaethics*, vol. 1. Oxford: Oxford University Press.

Railton, P. (2019). "We'll see you in court!": The Rule of Law as an Explanatory and Normative Kind. In: D. Plunkett, S. Shapiro, and K. Toh (Eds.), *Dimensions of Normativity: New Essays on Metaethics and Jurisprudence*. Oxford: Oxford University Press, pp. 1–22.

Rawls, J. (1971). *A Theory of Justice*. Cambridge: Harvard University Press.

Rawls, J. (1993). *Political Liberalism*. New York: Columbia University Press.

Rawls, J. (1996). Introduction to the Paperback Edition. In: J. Rawls (1993/96), *Political Liberalism*, paperback ed. New York: Columbia University Press, pp. xxxv–lx.

Rawls, J. (1997). The Idea of Public Reason Revisited. Reprinted in: J. Rawls (1999), *Collected Papers* (Samuel Freeman ed.). Cambridge: Harvard University Press, pp. 573–615.

Scanlon, T.M. (2002). Reasons and Passions. In: S. Buss and L. Overton (Eds.), *Contours of Agency: Essays on Themes from Harry Frankfurt*. Cambridge: MIT Press, pp. 165–188.

Schauer, F. (2010). Was Austin Right After All? On the Role of Sanctions in a Theory of Law. *Ratio Juris*, 23(1), pp. 1–21.

Schauer, F. (2015). *The Force of Law*. Cambridge: Harvard University Press.

Schroeter, F., L. Schroeter and K. Toh (unpublished manuscript). Metalinguistic Negotiation and Normative Inquiry.

Shah, N. (2003). How Truth Governs Belief. *The Philosophical Review*, 112(4), pp. 447–482.

Shapiro, S. (2002). Law, Plans, and Practical Reason. *Legal Theory*, 8(4), pp. 387–441.

Shapiro, S. (2011). *Legality*. Cambridge: Harvard University Press.

Stanley, J. (2005). *Knowledge and Practical Interests*. Oxford: Oxford University Press.

Toh, K. (2011). Legal Judgements as Plural Acceptances of Norms. In: L. Green and B. Leiter (Eds.), *Oxford Studies in Philosophy of Law*, vol. 1. Oxford: Oxford University Press, pp. 107–137.

Toh, K. (2019). Authenticity, Ontology and Natural History: Some Reflections on Musical and Legal Interpretations. In: L. Burton Crawford, P. Emerton and D. Smith (Eds.), *Law Under a Democratic Constitution: Essays in Honour of Jeffrey Goldsworthy*. Oxford: Hart Publishing, pp. 145–174.

Toh, K. (2021). Legal Positivism and Meta-ethics. In: T. Spaak and P. Mindus (Eds.), *The Cambridge Companion to Legal Positivism*. Cambridge: Cambridge University Press, pp. 561–584.

van Fraassen, B. (1984). Belief and the Will. *Journal of Philosophy*, 81(5), pp. 235–256.

van Fraassen, B. (1989). *Laws and Symmetry*. Oxford: Clarendon Press.

Velleman, J.D. (2000). On the Aim of Belief. In: J.D. Velleman, *The Possibility of Practical Reason*. Oxford: Oxford University Press, pp. 244–281.

Williams, B. (1970). Deciding to Believe. Reprinted in: B. Williams (1978), *Problems of the Self*. Cambridge: Cambridge University Press, pp. 136–151.

2 Legislative intent, collective intentionality and fictionalism

Damiano Canale

2.1 Introduction

It is commonly taken for granted that legislatures form intentions and act on them. When a legislature passes a law, it comes naturally to think that this is the law that the legislature intended to make. Furthermore, legal officials often claim that they interpret statutes according to the legislature's intention or on the basis of the ends that the legislature intended to pursue. These ways of thinking are not surprising. Legislatures are institutional entities that act in the world bringing about statutes, and any action is commonly understood as the result of an intentional attitude which plays a causal role in determining the behavior of the agent. In other words, we cannot explain an action whatsoever without assuming that the agent is able to entertain an intentional relation to the world. Now the question is: If that holds true for human agents, can we ascribe intentional attitudes to institutional entities such as legislatures? According to some writers, the answer is negative. Legislatures do not have a mind, therefore they are not capable of forming genuine intentions. Legislative intentions can obviously be attributed to the members of a legislative body, but individual intentions do not matter with regard to the content of a statute. This standpoint is puzzling, however. As a matter of political theory, it seems meaningless to give a legislative body law-making power unless the law that the members of this body make is the law they intended to make.

As Josef Raz has put forward,

> [T]o assume that the law made by legislation is not the one intended by the legislator, we must assume that he cannot predict what law he is making when the legislature passes any piece of legislation. But if so, why does it matter who the members of the legislature are, whether they are democratically elected or not, whether they represent different regions in the country, or classes in the population, whether they are adults or children, sane or insane? Since the law they will end by making does not represent their intentions, the fact that their intentions

DOI: 10.4324/9781003242451-4

> are foolish or wise, partial or impartial, self-serving or public spirited, makes no difference.
>
> (Raz, 2009, 274)

Furthermore, any conception of judging rooted in the principle of legislative supremacy appears unintelligible without a conception of legislative intent. If a statute is not the result of the lawmaker's intention, which determines the contribution of the statute to the law of the case, it is implausible that legislatures have some bearing on the way in which statutes govern social life. Once a statute is enacted, it would be completely removed from the legislature's control.

This is the reason why a number of legal scholars defend the common view that legislatures do have intentions and act on them. To vindicate this view, however, one is to show that intentional attitudes can be attributed to legislative bodies and that such intentions can be known. An obvious way to address these issues is to rely on collective intentionality. The general idea is that legislative intent is not a simple summation (or distributive aggregation) of the intentions of individual legislators. Legislative intent is something that individual legislators join together that allows them to act in a coordinative and cooperative fashion and to achieve collective goals.

Based on all this, I will defend four claims in this chapter. (1) Individual legislators necessarily share a collective participatory intention when they legislate. A legislature is able to legislate only if individual legislators intend that the legislature enacts a statute. (2) However, participatory intentions do not determine statutory contents, nor individual legislators necessarily share any form of communicative intention when they participate in the legislative activity. (3) When legal officials resort to legislative intent in legal interpretation, they actually make reference to a fictional entity. Legislatures are looked at as if they had collective communicative intentions, even though real legislatures do not have any. (4) Yet, legislative intent qua fictional entity serves important functions in current legal systems. It is the cornerstone of a set of interpretive methods that provide guidance to legal interpretation, contributes to align individual expectations with regard to statutory contents, puts constraints on how litigants and courts pursue their goals, helps identifying the practice legal officials are engaged in. In short, legislative intent serves as an important tool of coordination in the practice of legal officials.

This chapter proceeds as follows: I will first examine the skeptical standpoint according to which legislatures do not have intentions. Then I will consider three accounts of legislative intent based on different forms of collective intentionality: participatory intentions, joint intentions and group intentions. My aim is to show that participatory intentions are a necessary feature of legislative activity, whereas legislative bodies are not the sort of social entities that makes the other two accounts true. Finally, I will come back to the skeptical standpoint and try to accommodate it to the common view that legislatures do have communicative intentions. As a matter of fact, legislatures can be considered as both social entities and fictional entities, the properties of which depend on the narrative they are embedded in. In the latter case, legislatures can convey their intentions via statutes and we can reasonably know which intentions they have. This idea accounts for the fact that legal officials have been referring to the intentions of the legislature for centuries building a well-establish practice among the relevant linguistic community. Furthermore, fictionalism shows that this practice can be explained without assuming demanding ontological commitments with regard to the existence of collective intentions. We should be aware, however, that such intentions are not real in the same sense in which individual or collective intentions are supposed to be. Furthermore, fictionalism calls attention to the fact that when judges interpret statuses according to legislative intent, they actually employ various interpretive methods that are grounded on concurrent principles of political morality.

2.2 Ontological eliminativism on legislative intent

In the case *United Steelworkers of America v. Weber* (henceforth *Weber*), the U.S. Supreme Court was asked whether Title VII of the *Civil Rights Act* of 1964 permits employers and unions to adopt voluntary affirmative actions to eliminate racial imbalances in the skilled workforce. In 1974, the United Steelworkers of America and Kaiser Aluminum Chemical Corp. entered into a collective agreement including an affirmative action plan. The plan reserved for Afro-American employees 50% of the training programs until the percentage of skilled workers would have been commensurate with the percentage of the white ones. The litigation arose when Mr. Weber, a senior white employee at Kaiser Corp., instituted a class action in Federal District Court, alleging that, as a result of the affirmative action plan, white employees had been discriminated against. According to Weber, the action plan was in violation of §§ 703(a) and (d) of Title VII of the *Civil Rights Act* that made it unlawful to "discriminate … because of … race" in the selection of apprentices for training programs. The case was finally brought to the U.S. Supreme Court. The Court claimed that the statutory provision should not be constructed literally, as suggested by Weber, for literal meaning did not correspond to legislative intent. The provision "must be read against the background of the legislative history of Title VII and the historical context from which the Act arose".[1] According to the majority of the judges, the examination of those sources made it clear that an interpretation of the provisions that forbids all race-based affirmative actions would bring about an end completely at variance with the one intended by the lawmaker. The prohibition against racial discrimination was intended to open opportunities for Afro-American people in occupations which have been traditionally closed to them.[2] Therefore, the Court concluded that the adoption of the affirmative action plan was not in violation of the *Civil Rights Act*.

I spite of our evaluation of the decision, we might wonder whether the Court's reasoning was sound and if its conclusion was legally justified. Did

Title VIII of the *Civil Right Act* actually communicate the intent of Congress? And if it was so, was the intentional content of the statute correctly identified by the Court? Let us first consider the answers that the skeptics would give to these questions.

As mentioned before, the skeptic line of thought traditionally starts from the assumption that legislatures are not able to form intentions. Therefore, it is a metaphysical mistake to consider legislative intent as a matter of what the legislative body intends to communicate via a statutory provision. But it is also mistaken to look at the legislative intent as representative of the unified intentions of the individual legislators. First, even if an individual legislator does not even know what the statute is all about or does not form any intention whatsoever with regard to the ends that the statute is meant to achieve, her or his vote counts nevertheless. So, legislative outputs may be independent of the intentional attitudes of individual lawmakers. Second, in democratic political systems, legislative assemblies are "gathering[s] of persons who disagree with one another and who represent a divided community" (Waldron, 1999, 121). Legislative bodies comprise a large number of individuals with different aims, interests, backgrounds, even if they belong to the same majority. Hence, a specific statutory provision is usually the result of a compromise. The wording of the statute is not meant to express the specific intention of the group nor the intention of one single legislator. The language of the statute must rather be vague or ambiguous enough to make each member of the majority to believe that the statute may convey her or his intention. Third, even if the intentions of the individual legislators were uniform, we have no means of knowing their content except by the utterances and behavior of the members of the legislative body, which are recorded in floor debates, committee reports and hearings, and in other materials included in the legislative history. But these external acts can be reasonably explained in different ways, i.e., as the result of different intentional attitudes. Any action performed in reality may result from a different intentional attitude under a different description (Davidson, 1963, 685–686). If we were to consider the reasons that each individual legislator might have for doing what she or he did in the legislative process, therefore, we would come to the conclusion that a univocal legislative intent cannot be known, even though the individual legislators had in fact uniform legislative intents.

If all that is true, we are given two options. The first one is to get rid of the idea of legislation as an activity performed by a single law-making author. Statutory provisions are the outcome of an institutional process which aggregates votes on texts, not intentions or reasons. Legislators may obviously have coherent intentions and plans about what should be done, and the legislative process is intentionally designed to achieve certain political ends. But the legislature acts as a "voting machine", the outputs of which do not reflect or convey the intentional content associated by the actual legislators to their vote (Waldron, 1999, ch. 6). The second option is to recognize that legislative intent is a "theoretical construction" (Dworkin, 1984, 315). When legal officials search for legislative intent, they do not actually look for what a single agent had in mind and meant to communicate through a statute. They rather consolidate the intentions of the individual legislators into a collective, fictional intention, or even construct a fictional legislature, the characteristics of which mirror the principles of the legal system or the fundamental values of the political community. In a nutshell, 'legislative intent' is just a label for what emerges from the interpretive process rather than an intentional content that exists prior to judicial intervention.

The standpoint just outlined entails the following two philosophical assumptions that are worth being emphasized.

From an ontological point of view, legislatures are social artifacts the properties of which depend on constitutive rules. These rules determine the identity conditions, modalities of action, powers and prerogatives of the legislature and impose status function on the outcome of the legislative procedures. For instance, the constitutive rule according to which a group of people counts as the legislature makes it the case that the text enacted by those people is a valid legal provision. Moreover, the existence of legislatures depends on the intentional attitudes of their creators and on those of the people who take part in the legislative process. Legislatures are social artifacts intentionally designed to achieve a certain goal, i.e., to change the law in a given legal system, and a legislature is able to legislate because the members of the legislative body have some sort of intentional attitude. Yet, it is ontologically mistaken to attribute intentional properties to collective bodies. Social artifacts do not bear mental states, nor do they include structural features based on constitutive rules that exhibit the aboutness or directness characterizing intentionality. In other words, legislatures qua collective bodies cannot instantiate the property of representing something or directing human behavior. These properties are actually the result of an intellectual construction which is typically employed to justify a judicial outcome.

From an linguistic point of view, furthermore, the skeptics claim that legislation is not a form of conversational communication (Poggi, 2020). In other words, the linguistic content of a statutory provision cannot be seen as the content that the legislature intended to communicate, which may differ from the semantic content encoded in the statute. Therefore, any speaker-based theory of communication is not well suited to account for statutory interpretation. If the skeptic upholds a form of semantic minimalism, she or he claims that statutes have a minimal propositional content that does not depend on the speaker's intention nor on pragmatic/contextual processing. In the case of interpretation, syntax and semantics are all we need to decode a statutory text. On the contrary, those skeptics who believe that statutory contents depend on the background assumptions of linguistic practitioners (plus an open set of contextual constraints) claim that the understanding of a statute implies a form of constructive interpretation. It is so because linguistic contents are always under- or over-determined by the syntactical and semantic rules. Therefore, the interpreter is to make up the statutory meaning on the basis of the relevant context of communication, which determines what a piece of legislation is supposed to bring about in society. And the relevance condition is a matter of political choice and not of linguistic decoding. Be as it may, what matters is that in both cases, legislative intent does not serve any relevant role in legal communication and interpretation.

In the light of these remarks, the U.S. Supreme Court's decision in *Weber* rises a number of concerns for the skeptic. Given that statutory provisions do not convey the speaker's meaning, the Court was not justified in interpreting the statute according to the legislature's intent. Legislatures simply do not have intentions, and even if the individual legislators had uniform intentional attitudes as they voted for the *Civil Rights Act* in 1964, their unified intentions could not be univocally inferred from the information available to the Court. As a consequence, the semantic minimalist would argue that statutory provisions must be read according to their literal meaning.[3] On the basis of this interpretive method, the provisions that make it unlawful "to discriminate … because of … race" forbid discrimination against white people as well as against Afro-American people,[4] and since the Kaiser affirmative action plan operates to discriminate against white employees solely because they are white, it follows that the Kaiser plan was in breach of §§ 703(a) and (d), Title VII, of the *Civil Rights Act*. On the contrary, the contextualist might agree on the conclusion reached by the Supreme Court but on a different interpretive basis. A literal reading of §§ 703(a) and (d) is simply illusory. The interpretation of a statutory provision always depends on background assumptions and contextual factors that fix the semantic content in a specific communicative process. Therefore, legal officials are necessarily engaged in constructive interpretation, which depends not only on the text and its historical background but also on its subsequent interpretational history, related statutory developments, other provisions included in the legal systems, general principles of law, current social facts, etc. In *Weber*, the argumentative articulation of these elements may justify the consideration that "to discriminate because of race" does not mean "to prevent any and every differential treatment on racial grounds", as argued by Mr. Weber. It rather means "to prevent *de facto* inequality of opportunities for minorities".[5] At the time in which the case was decided, Afro-American people were strongly underrepresented in the skilled workforce and affirmative measures were needed to afford any chance for a color-blind society (Eskridge, 1987, 1488). So, as stated by the majority opinion, the purpose of the statute was to obtain more jobs for Afro-Americans, and the Kaiser affirmative action plan mirrored the purpose of the statute. On the basis of that, the plan was not in violation of the *Civil Right Act*.

Note that this line of reasoning starts from the assumption that textual interpretation is inconclusive and legislative history is merely one of the contextual factors that may be considered in the interpretive process. Legislature's intent is a fictional entity that merely acts as a "catalyst" for those contextual factors that justify the interpretation of a legal text.

2.3 Legislative intent as collective intention

As mentioned at the beginning of this chapter, however, the skeptical viewpoint brings about counterintuitive consequences. According to the skeptic, ordinary legal language takes it for granted that legislature's intentions belong to the inventory of the world, but in fact, such entities do not exist at all. Hence, interpretive practices are founded on a metaphysical mistake, or judges are systematically insincere when they claim that the law that they apply corresponds to the intention of the law-giver.[6] But this is at odds with the traditional way of thinking of the legal community, which is used to making reference to the intention of the legislature in statutory interpretation. In most cases, so it is argued, legislative intent is easily detectable by looking at legislative history and statements. Therefore, the idea that the legal community is systematically mistaken in making reference to legislative intent, or that most judges are liars, appears highly implausible. What we all need is a refinement of the concept of legislative intent in order to give a convincing account of contemporary legislation, to defend legislative supremacy in democratic legal systems, and to put legal interpretation under control according to the principles of the rule of law.

These are the reasons why legal scholars have recently tried to restate the traditional account of the legislature's intent in an updated theoretical context, taking into account the philosophical debate in the field of social ontology and collective intentionality. The general idea is that collective entities such as legislatures exist because their members are able to intend and to act in a we-referential fashion (Sellars, 1980, 98). A legislature is able to legislate because the members of the legislative body represent and direct their action as the action of the legislature. However, the we-referential attitude of individual legislators can be of different sorts. It may be referred to the connection between the members of the group *qua* legislators, to the content of the statute that the collective action brings about, or to the institutional setting of the legislative process. We will here briefly consider three influential conceptions of collective intentionality which seem well suited to account for these different aspects of legislation: Christopher Kutz's notion of participatory intention, Michael Bratman's theory of shared cooperative activity, and Philip Pettit's theory of group agency.

2.3.1 Overlapping participatory intentions

It goes without saying that there are many kinds of collective intentional activities. Their characteristics vary depending on the complexity of the task to be accomplished, the cooperative spirit animating the members of the group, the way in which the group is internally organized, and so forth. According to Kutz, however, it is possible to identify the minimal conditions for a collective intentional activity to obtain. These conditions are minimal in the sense that they are both necessary and sufficient conditions. When they are satisfied, a form of collective intentionality emerges, even though there are several complex activities in which such conditions are supplemented by further requirements. In Kutz's view, it is the minimal case of an intentional collective activity when the members of a group act on the basis of overlapping participatory intentions. A participatory intention is the intention to do one's part in a collective activity. An attitude of this sort has two main representational components: individual role and collective end. The act performed by the agent is mentally represented as the contribution to an end, the realization of which depends on several agents acting together. So, individual legislators have a participatory intention if they intend to do their part in the legislative process, for instance, by voting in favor or against the enactment of a statute. However, a minimal collective activity takes place only if participatory intentions overlap. This happens when the individual intentions to do one's part refer to the same activity or outcome, and "there is a nonempty intersection of the sets of states of affairs satisfying those collective ends" (Kutz, 2000, 94). For instance, recalling *Weber*, individual legislators may intend to pass the statutory provision "it is unlawful to discriminate because of race" in order to communicate different legal directives or to achieve different ends. Legislator L1 may intend that the statute prohibits any form of affirmative action based on race, legislator L2 may intend that the same statute permits affirmative actions in favor of Afro-American workers, and legislator L3 may intend to pass the statute because the head of the political party said to do so, even though L3 has no intention at all with regard to racial discrimination. What matters is that the participatory intention of the individual legislators overlap, making it the case that they intentionally enact the statute in question. In other words, a legislative body is able to legislate if the individual legislators intend to participate in the legislative activity and believe that the others do the same.[7] This viewpoint has some relevant implications. Assuming that P is an outcome of the legislative process (i.e., a text which counts as a valid statutory provision in a given legal system) and X is the intentional content of P, a statement such as

(1) The legislature intends that X[8]

is systematically false or, at least, not truth-up. All we can say about the legislative intent is the following:

(2) The individual legislators have the overlapping participatory intentions that P.

This makes it apparent that the intentions of the individual legislators do not determine X. Furthermore, the communicative relationship between P and X, if any, does not depend on the intentional attitudes of the lawmakers. Individual legislators simply make it possible that the "voting machine" does the work that is supposed to do.

2.3.2 Shared cooperative activity

In Bratman's view, groups are associations of individuals who are brought together by joint intentions, i.e., psychological states that allow individuals to act in a coordinative and cooperative fashion over time. A joint intention is a complex entity made up by four elements: (1) a set of interlocking individual intentions; (2) a certain amount of common knowledge among the group's members; (3) the coordinate pursuit of a common goal and (4) the adoption of a plan by the group's members as a means to achieve the common goal.

Here is the classical scheme proposed by Bratman (1993, 106):

We intend to J if, and only if:

1 (a) I intend that we J and (b) you intend that we J;
2 I intend that we J in accordance with and because of 1a, 1b, and the meshing subplans for 1a and 1b; you intend that we J in accordance with and because of 1a, 1b, and the meshing subplans for 1a and 1b;
3 1 and 2 are common knowledge between us.

This scheme permits to restate the very idea of legislative intent. The existence and activity of a legislature obviously depend on the participatory intention of its members. Without individual legislators forming overlapping participatory intentions, no legislative activity is even possible. Still, individual legislators may also form and act on joint intentions that determine statutory contents, and this typically occurs when their attitudes are connected in the way described above.[9] So, in the context of legal interpretation, the statement 'The legislature intends that X' is actually elliptical for

(3) The legislature intends that X via P iff when enacting P,
1 each individual legislator intends that (we the legislature intend that X),
2 each individual legislator intends that (we the legislature intend that X) because each other individual legislator intends that (we the legislature intend that X), under the meshing subplans for intending that X, and
3 1 and 2 are common knowledge between the individual legislators.

It is apparent that under this description, the intentional communicative content of P depends on a complex nexus of interdependent individual attitudes. Furthermore, the formation of X requires that individual legislators be mutually responsive, i.e., that each seeks to respond to the others' intentions and actions in a coordinated way, and that each seeks to guide her or his own behavior with an eye to the behavior of the others. This does not imply that all the individual legislators have the same intentional attitudes or pursue the same goal. Turning back to *Weber*, it might be that the subplan of legislator L1 is to be reelected for one additional term, the subplan of L2 is to protect the interests of Afro-American workers, and the subplan of L3 is not to impose constraints on employers in the organization of their economic activities. However, if these subplans mesh with one another, in the sense that each individual legislator belonging to the majority realizes her or his subplan under a master plan intentionally attributed to the collective body, then a joint communicative intention takes place. According to the master plan in question, the legislature, when enacting the statutory provision "it is unlawful to discriminate because of race", intends that it is permitted to adopt private affirmative actions in favor of Afro-American workers. If this is common knowledge among individual legislators, and they coordinate their action over time so that their individual subplans mesh under the master plan, then the communicative intention just mentioned can be attributed to the legislative body. In other words, each individual legislator may vote in favor of P for different reasons. What matters is that what they think and do brings about a joint intention according to which the intentional content of P is X.

2.3.3 Group agency

Philip Pettit rejects the eliminativist view according to which groups can be described as intentional subjects "only by figment, and for the sake of brevity of discussion" (Austin, 1880, 18). Social artifacts such as legislatures count as personal subjects having intentions if they fulfill the general conditions of agency, i.e., if the legislative activity instantiates a specific kind of rationality. It is so when the legislature (1) is an "integration of individuals" with a shared purpose, (2) performs those actions that are rationally required by the pursuit of that purpose; (3) collectivizes reasons in forming judgments, preferences, intentions (Pettit, 2001b, 243; 2002, 443 ff.). In other words, the legislature intends that X if, and only if, the law-making process makes it the case that the majority performs those actions that are rationally required for P to mean that X. It is apparent that a complex form of social organization and control is needed to fulfill this condition, given that legislative assemblies are usually composed by a large number of individuals having different beliefs, desires and intentions. Pettit shows that the majority principle is not sufficient to this effect. Based on this principle, it is not possible to ensure that the aggregation of consistent votes on interconnected issues is itself consistent. It may well be that the outcome of majoritarian legislation is not the one that conveys the intentional attitudes of the majority members.[10] To avoid this problem, the law-making process shall be designed so as to impose constraints on the formation of the individual legislators' attitudes. Besides, it shall include a reliable mechanism to aggregate such attitudes, and procedures for translating them into statutory provisions. A legislature satisfies such desiderata if the legislative process (a) is based on true information (individual legislators do not form their beliefs on the basis of a misrepresentation of reality), (b) is "incentive-compatible" (individual legislators have incentives to pursue the interests of the group rather than their own interests), (c) aggregates the preferences of the individual legislators so as to avoid any inconsistency between what they voted for and the legislature's aggregated intention,[11] (d) includes a control mechanism that ensures a match between the individual's attitude on a given statute and that of the group (List and Pettit, 2011, 131–132). On the basis of this theoretical framework, it follows that the statement 'The legislature intends that X' is elliptical for

(4) The legislature intends that X via P iff when enacting P, the legislative procedures and settings make it the case that
  1 each individual legislator forms true belief about X,
  2 individual legislators' preferences are incentive-compatible, and their aggregation avoids inconsistencies,
  3 the resulting aggregation of individual preferences is that X, which is conveyed via P,
  4 each individual legislator keeps control over P, i.e., may refuse to vote for P if she or he does not believe that P conveys X.

Contrary to the shared agency approach, the group agent approach maintains that a legislature, under certain circumstances, counts as a plural subject and bears intentional attitudes. This occurs when the legislative assembly implements a particular mechanism for decision-making that forces the individual legislators to "collectivize reasons" by means of a sequence of majority votes which are each treated as the group's view on the respective question (Pettit, 2001a, 110). This does not imply that the legislature's intention is the summation of individual intentions. Collective attitudes may be discontinuous with individual attitudes, as stated by Bratman, but for a different reason. The connection between individual intentions is here external to the agents' psychology. It is a form of procedural organization that ensures the reliability, consistency and coherence of the law-making process over time.

2.3.4 Some critical remarks

We might wonder whether the conceptions of collective intentionality just outlined provide a suitable account of legislative intent, an account that is able to vindicate the traditional understanding of it in legal thinking and practice. The first conception identifies a necessary feature of the legislative activity that is actually presupposed by the current debate on legislative intent. A legislature is able to legislate only if the individual legislators intend to do their part in this activity, and their participatory intentions overlap. It is worth underling that this claim is consistent with both the skeptical and the anti-skeptical standpoint on legislative intent. The members of a legislative body need to bear a minimal form of collective intentionality, based on social acceptance and mutual beliefs, in order to carry out the legislative process, irrespective of whether they have further shared intentional attitudes. However, participatory intentions do not convey any propositional content. They allow the legislature to make a law without determining which law was actually made. The theoretical frameworks of shared cooperative activity and group agency are much richer in this respect since they establish the conditions under which collective communicative intentions obtain. Our question here is: are these conceptions of collective intentionality well suited to a peculiar institutional activity such as legislation? There are reasons to doubt this.

As for Bratman's joint intentions, a shared activity is typically tailored to small groups of people in which responsiveness and common knowledge may take place (Bratman, 2014). From this perspective, the legislature's intent would be the result of a cooperative activity in which each individual legislator does her or his part in coordination with the others, forms her or his attitudes in the light of what the others legislators do, and comes to share the intentional content conveyed through the statutory provision enacted by the assembly. But contemporary legislatures are typically made up by a large number of individuals who represent competing interests, disagree on the goals to be achieved and on the means to achieve a certain goal, who are not responsive to others and may be easily alienated from the group. In other words, the legislative process is non-cooperative and does not permit the formation of the collective we-intentions described by Bratman. Apart from that, courts would be justified in making reference to the legislature's intention only in those occasions in which a statutory provision is the result of a shared cooperative activity. But contemporary legislation does not satisfy this condition. The account of the legislature's intention just outlines is not made true by current institutional reality. Furthermore, even though the legislation had the form of a shared cooperative activity, it would be impossible to identify a *univocal* intentional content conveyed by the statutory provision. As I have argued elsewhere (Canale and Poggi, 2019), the speaker's meaning depends on a set of contextual variables which determine what is conversationally implicated by a statute, i.e., its intentional content. As far as legislation and statutory interpretation are concerned, however, the context of communication is constitutively opaque. As Richard Ekins has pointed out, it is made up by legislative history, the previous state of the law, general legal principles, the rest of the statutory scheme, the ends that the statute seeks to realize, etc. However, we do not know which contextual elements are salient, and this makes the intentional content of the statute (if any) constitutively indeterminate. The communicative intent of the legislature can be plausibly reconstructed in many different ways, and each of them may lead the interpreter to attribute a different intentional content to the same statutory provision. Therefore, joint communicative intentions in legislation are either implausible or indeterminate.

At first sight, Pettit's theory of group agency does not face the difficulty just outlined. The group agent approach applies to large gatherings of individuals who are not responsive to one another and do not form shared intentional attitudes. Furthermore, the deliberation process described by Pettit permits to identify those contextual aspects that are salient in the communication of statutory contents. To act as a personal subject, however, a legislature must be internally organized so as to guarantee the truthfulness of individual beliefs, the consistency of legislative deliberations over time, the selection of the relevant reasons, the drafting of statutory provisions that convey the selected collective intention. To satisfy these conditions institutional settings, procedures, division of labor and hierarchies are needed. This gives rise to three concerns. First, not each legislature can be seen as a group agent but only those legislatures having specific institutional features. But these features are usually not present in contemporary legislative bodies, nor are they likely to be adopted since they would make the legislative procedure rigid and impose heavy constraints on the activity of parliamentary representatives. Second, the institutional setting indicated by Pettit is hardly compatible with the idea that each individual legislator keeps control on the legislature's intent. Although group agents supervene on individual agents, the intentional content conveyed by a statutory provision can be easily at variance with the actual intentions of the individual legislatures. To put it differently, this approach admits that the legislative intent does not match the intentions of the actual lawmakers. Therefore, the desiderata of the individual legislators' control on legislative outcomes cannot be easily reconciliated with the requirements of group rationality and democracy. Pettit admits that in large groups such as legislatures the individual control on collective decision-making has to be relaxed (List and Pettit, 2011, 144 ff.). This seems at odds, however, with the idea of legislation in a democratic institutional setting. Third, the deliberative procedure described by Pettit is supposed to determine the intentional attitude of the group via an ordered series of majority votes, the outcome of which is a statutory text. Consequently, it is the literal meaning of this text that truly conveys the legislature's intention. In this way, however, the intention of the legislature qua group agent is equated to literal meaning, a move that just makes legislative intent irrelevant in legal interpretation.[12]

To conclude, we could say that the idea of legislation as shared joint activity underestimates the non-cooperative, agonistic character of the legislative process and its institutional complexity. On the contrary, the idea of legislatures as group agents leads to overestimate the capacity of legislative procedures to collectivize reasons and to univocally determine the content of statutory texts.

In *Weber,* all these concerns are clearly exemplified. Although the Court claimed that the univocal legislature's intention was to bring about more jobs for Afro-American people, the legislative history of the *Civil Rights Act* tells us quite a different story. The legislative history simply shows that there was a great deal of discussion of quotas for Afro-Americans in the legislative debates. Supporters of the *Civil Right Act* repeatedly assured opponents and undecided legislators that the statute would not mandate racial quotas of any sort. The dissenting opinion in *Weber* meticulously recounted these debates and argued that the statutory deal was that there would be no mandatory or voluntary actions in favor of minorities.[13] This is far from clear, however, because nowhere in the legislative history does any member of Congress explicitly state opposition to both voluntary and mandatory affirmative action programs. The *Weber* situation was not discussed on the public record and most likely was not anticipated. As a matter of fact, the legislature did not form any shared collective intention on the matter discussed in *Weber*, nor acted as a group agent in the process of law-making. If this was the case, the legislative's intention was actually indeterminate.

2.4 Legislative intent in a game of make-believe

The analysis developed so far presents us with a dilemma, neither horn of which is attractive. If we take the legislature's intention be a form of collective intentionality, we come to the conclusion that legislative intent is either absent or indeterminate. However, if we assume that legislatures do not have intentions of any sort, we threaten to convict judges and lawyers of massive, widespread error. In this section, we will elaborate on the second horn of this opposition in order to show that it amounts to a false dilemma.

As mentioned before, the skeptic typically claims that legislatures cannot hold intentions, and even if they could, the intentional content of a statute would not be univocally identifiable. It is so because when judges and lawyers use this interpretive methodology, they actually engage in counterfactual reasoning. This is to say that the statement 'The legislature intends that X' is elliptical for the counterfactual statement

(5) If P conveyed the legislature intent, P would mean that X.

The interpreter imagines a fictitious situation in which legislatures do have intentions and communicate them via statutory provisions. Then the interpreter figures out what the intentional content of the statute could be on the basis of textual and contextual information, which include the wording of the statute, legislative history, the purpose of the law, etc.[14] Now, the antecedent of (5) is false in the actual world since legislatures do not form communicative intentions. When judges and lawyers say 'The legislature intends that X', they believe to make reference to a real entity, but this expression does not succeed in referring to anything (cf. Walton, 1985; Szabó, 2001). In this sense, the skeptic believes that the legislature's intention is a fictional entities that does not exist in reality. Still, making reference to legislative intent in the context of adjudication is rhetorically effective. In our legal cultures, legislative intent is widely recognized as an interpretive method that justifies the content ascribed to a statutory provision, even though this content has nothing to do with the alleged intention of the legislative body. But how can it be the case that a statement that does not refer to anything may justify a judicial outcome?

The skeptical antirealist about legislative intentions could provide the following explanation. When judges and lawyers utter (5), they imagine some possible worlds in which legislatures do have intentions and the antecedent of (5) is true. If they envisage some definite contextual reasons for the consequent's being true, i.e., a pertinent connection between the antecedent and the consequent, they are entitled to claim that (5) is true. This is why the pretense that the legislature has a certain intention can be reasonably accepted in an exchange of reasons. When making reference to legislative intent, however, legal officials are faced with the problem of ontological and linguistic indeterminacy. There is more than one possible world, equally close to the actual one, in which the legislature forms intentions about a certain legal issue, but these worlds may be crucially different in some respect. Which content is to be chosen? There seems to be no principled way of deciding[15]. This is why the skeptic claims that legal officials make up the legislature's intent according to their own preferences and needs. They actually pick and choose the possible world that makes their own reconstruction of legislative intent true and pretend that this reconstruction justifies the content they attribute to statutes in the actual world. This makes legislative intent, as Max Radin famously argued, an "absurd fiction" that we should get rid of (Radin, 1930, 863).

But couldn't we provide a different explanation of the legislative intent qua fictional entity, an explanation which is consistent with our linguistic practices, does not boil down to error theory, and justifies the recourse to legislative intent in legal interpretation? In the last part of this chapter, I will explore an alternative scenario.

As a matter of fact, when judges write their decisions, they articulate a narrative which is supposed to justify the decision they make. In this sense, the statement

(1) The legislature intends that X

is a fictional statement that may also occurs in narratives such as a roman, a short tail or a legal drama. Now, when we talk both within of about a narrative, "with" in these narratives, it seems that semantic phenomena such as meaning, reference and truth take place as they actually do in everyday, nonfictional language. Consider the following fictional sentences:

(6) Gandalf is a wise wizard
(7) Gollum was a gloomy sort of character
(8) Gandalf is a character from fiction
(9) According to *The Lord of Rings*, Gandalf was one of the five Istari sent to Middle-earth by the Valar of the Third Age.

It is beyond doubt that (6) and (7) are meaningful and that (8) and (9) are true. Furthermore, some fictional names appear to name the same individual and hence to be co-referential ("Gandalf", "The Wise", "Olórin"). The same consideration holds for collective fictional entities and properties:

(10) When the Council of Elrond ordered Frodo Baggins to keep the One Ring, the Council intended that Frodo should cast the Ring into the Crack of Doom.

According to J.R.R. Tolkien's novel, (10) is straightforwardly true, although the Council of Elrond is a fictional institutional entity and the intention that Frodo should cast the Ring into the Crack of Doom is a fictional property of this entity. Within the novel, no ontological and linguistic indeterminacy takes place, and the intention of the lawmaker is univocally detectable either on the basis of lawmaking procedure followed by the Council, or in the light of what the Council's members declared and did. Why is it so? Kendall Walton provides the following explanation. Imagine a children's game. In one such game, corks may be regarded as rabbits and a rope put around the cork may mean that the rabbit has been lassoed, or pointing the index finger at someone and saying "bang" may mean that the person has been shot. In games like these, corks, ropes, or saying "bag" when pointing at someone prompt our imagination and encourage us to engage in a game of make-believe (Walton, 1990, 11). Who is involved in this game engages in a rule governed imaginative activity in which it is pretended that corks are rabbits or that the legislature intends that X according to the rules of the game. So, sentences such as (1) and (10) represent the world as it needs to be in order to make these sentences fictionally true.

Under this description, legal officials engage in a fictional game of make-believe when they interpret a statute according to legislative intent, although they are often not fully aware of that. For instance, when the U.S. Supreme Court claimed that the Congress, through the *Civil Right Act*, intended to create more jobs for Afro-Americans, the Court represented the features of the world so as to make it true that bringing about more jobs for Afro-Americans was the intentional content of the statute, even though legislatures do not have communicative intentions in the real world. Hence, the intentional content of a statute has fictional truth conditions, i.e., it is true or false from the point of view of the narrative it is embedded in. This can be made explicit by means of an 'according to fiction F'-operator:

(11) According to fiction F, the legislature intends that X.

This is meant to show that judges and lawyers actually make reference to legislative intent in fictional contexts where statements of the form 'The legislature intends that X' have fictional truth-conditions and fictional truth-values, such as in (11). Furthermore, the singular term 'legislature' and the predicate 'intending that X' do refer to things and properties in F. Outside F, however, they are empty. So, (11) is truth-up in the fictional context F, whereas it has neither truth-conditions nor truth-values in the context of reality. It is so because who utters (11) in F does not pretend to describe the real world nor undertakes ontological commitments with regard to how the world actually is. At the same time, however, (11) may be truth-up also in a meta-fictional context of communication. If an external observer claims that, according to the ruling of the U.S. Supreme Court, the Congress intended to create more jobs for Afro-Americans by means of the *Civil Rights Act*, this claim is true even though legislatures do not have intentions of any sort.[16]

This kind of analysis shows that judges and lawyers are not systematically mistaken in making reference to legislative intent. They use this expression within an institutional, fictional context in which statements having the form 'The legislature intends that X' are meaningful, have truth-values and succeed to refer to entities and properties. The fact that the legislature conveys a certain intentional content through a statute depends here both on the narrative in which this fictional event occurs and on the pretense attitude of the speakers. Therefore, legislatures may have collective intentions in F, either as group agents or because they engage in a shared cooperative activity, even though this does not occur in the real world. As a consequence, the legislature's dilemma presented above turns out to be a false dilemma.

As *Weber* clearly shows, however, there may be different, competing narratives regarding the legislature's intention. According to the majority opinion in *Weber*, the legislature intended the statutory provision to bring about more jobs for Afro-American people in fictional context F_M, which makes the pretense of the court true. According to Justice Blackmun's dissenting opinion, on the contrary, the same provision was intended to prohibit racial discriminations in the workforce, a claim that the fictional context F_m makes equally true. So,

(12) According to fiction F_M, the legislature intends that X.
(13) According to fiction F_m, the legislature intends that Y.

Now, X and Y are incompatible with each other. Which fictional story is to be preferred? The story told by the majority opinion or that of the dissenting opinion? Aren't we facing the same indeterminacy problem highlighted by the skeptic?

This question admits different answers depending on the characteristics of the fictional context in which legislatures communicate their intentions through statutes.

2.5 Three sorts of fictional legislative intent

In current legal systems, there are at least three different narratives in which legislatures form intentions. The features of these narratives depend on what the term 'legislature' is referred to. Judges and lawyers employ this term to refer to:

(a) The *historical* legislature (the collective body that actually enacted the statute).
(b) The *coherent* legislature (the fictional legislature that takes care of the consistency and coherence of the legal system).
(c) The *good* legislature (the fictional legislature that rules the case so as to avoid unfair, unjust, or absurd consequences).[17]

Each sort of legislature typically acts in a specific narrative context. As to the historical legislature, the fictional context is constituted by the judicial reconstruction of the social and political circumstances that lead the legislative body to enact a certain statutory provision.[18] With regard to the coherent legislature, the fictional context is composed by the other legal provisions, precedents and principles belonging to the legal system, and the rational requirements of consistency and coherence. As far as the good legislature is concerned, the fictional context is constituted by the current or expected consequences of the ruling, plus their assessment as good/bad, fair/unfair, just/unjust, reasonable/absurd. Note that in the case of the historical legislature, the narrative elaborated by legal officials is about a real institutional entity with the fictional property of forming intentional attitudes. Ontologically speaking, therefore, to say that the historical legislature intended that X is like saying that the Eiffel Tower is flying to the moon. Unlike Gandalf, the Council of Elrod and the Crack of Doom, the historical legislature and the Eiffel Tower are real entities. Within a fictional narrative, however, they can take on fictional properties that they do not have in the real world, such as having intentions or flying to the moon. On the contrary, the coherent legislator and the good legislature are fictional or ideal entities with no counterpart in reality.

The difference between these sorts of legislatures is worth considering in more detail. If I say that Boris Johnson lives in London, for instance, I employ an *external* mode of predication. The property of living in London is predicated of Boris Johnson externally, in the sense that he exemplifies this property at a certain time. On the contrary, if I say that Sherlock Holmes lives in London, the same property is predicated internally. Sherlock Holmes encodes the property of living in London, in the sense that he has it as a constituent since there is no counterpart of Sherlock Holmes in reality that could not have such a property.[19] Similarly, the historical legislature exemplifies the property of having a certain communicative intention, whereas the coherent legislature and the good legislature encode that property.[20] The intention to preserve the coherence and consistency of the legal system, or to legislate for the common good, is what makes these fictional legislatures what they actually are within their own narrative.

The distinctions just outlined provide a criterion of evaluation for the competing narratives on legislative intent. Legislatures (a), (b) and (c) prompt different games of make-believe governed by different rules, which determine under what conditions the statements having the form 'The legislature intends that X' are true. The fictional context in which the historical legislature is embedded is "world-bound" since it is made up by events that occurred in reality.[21] As a result, if a court infers the original legislative intent from events that did not have a counterpart in reality or from irrelevant aspects of legislative history, the court violates the rules of the game and the proposed interpretation is not justified. At the same time, a narrative about original legislative intent can be easily challenged when courts avoid mentioning social or political factors that could have prompted the legislature to pass the statute being interpreted. In *Weber*, for instance, it was apparent that the majority opinion omitted mentioning those aspects of the legislative history that would have made the proposed reconstruction of legislative intent implausible, as clearly showed by Justice Blackmun in his dissenting opinion. So, within the game of make-believe the majority decided to engaged in, it was false that the legislature intended to bring about more jobs for Afro-Americans, whereas it was true that the Congress avoided taking a position on the matter. The majority did not satisfy the narrative commitments undertaken in the justification of the decision, and P cannot be taken to communicate the intentional content indicated by the majority opinion.

The fictional context of the coherent legislature has different characteristics. Legislative intent is here inferred from legal materials such as other statutory sections, related statuses, precedents and general principles of law that are relevant to the case to be decided. Starting from that, the court figures out which intentional content of P fits best with these materials so as to ensure the consistency and coherence of the law in the field in which the interpretive issue arises. As a consequence, if a court incorporates into the narrative a source of law that is not pertinent to the case, or the alleged intentional content X of P does not fit in with the other relevant legal materials, then the court is not justified in claiming that the legislature intended that X.

The same holds true with regard to the good legislator, the fictional legislative body that legislates for the common good. The context in which this fictional legislature operates is composed by principles of social and political morality, and the game of make-believe is successful if the court shows that the interpretation achieves a relevant moral end. Obviously, competing narratives are possible or even unescapable in this respect. Moral disagreement does not make whatever intention of the good legislature systematically untrue, however. The game of make-believe requires the court to engage in moral reasoning in order to identify the moral facts that make the legislature's intention true. To our purpose, what matters is that the (fictional) fact that the legislature intends that X depends on the discursive commitments that the legal officials take up in legal reasoning, not on the alleged collective intention of the lawmaker.

It is worth emphasizing that the three fictional legislatures just outlined do not come out of the blue. They are grounded on the fundamental principles and values of a given legal culture. In our legal systems, the historical legislator qua fictional entity embodies the value of democracy, the fact that the content of legal provisions should convey the intentions of the representatives of the people. The coherent legislature embodies the internal values of a legal system that is supposed, among other things, to provide consistent and coherent answers to the legal questions that come before courts over time. Finally, the good legislature personifies the values of justice or fairness. These three narratives, furthermore, represent the purpose of legal interpretation differently. In the fictional narrative of the historical legislature, courts are conceived as faithful agents of the legislature that are bound to preserve its original intent. On the contrary, the fictional narrative of the coherent legislature represents the judiciary as a branch of the government which takes care of the legal system in evolutive perspective. The task for legal interpretation is here to reconciliate statutory law with case law, the content of a statutory provision with the content of other statutory provisions, the original setting of the regulation with its subsequent development. Based on this perspective, judges act as faithful agents of the legal system who are called upon to protect the intrinsic features of the law. In the narrative of the good legislature, finally, courts are the keepers of the moral principles on which the political community is grounded. The task of the judiciary is to protect and realize those principles and to cooperate with the legislative branch of the government to make up the law according to them. And judges accomplish with this task if they avoid that the application of legal norms brings about absurd or unjust consequences, or cannot be recognized as means of realizing the core values of the political community.

2.6 Conclusion

Is the law made by legislation the one that the legislature intended to make? In this chapter, I have provided an articulated answer to this question. Given the characteristics of legislative bodies, legislatures do not actually communicate any collective intention through the statutes that they enact. It is so because legislative bodies do not comply with the requirements of group agents, nor can hold joint intentions. The only form of collective intentionality which characterizes legislation is the individual legislators' intention to participate in the lawmaking process. However, this does not imply that attributing communicative intentions to legislatures is absurd. When courts interpret a statute according to legislative intent, they actually engage in a game of make-believe in which judges pretend that legislatures have intentions and act on them. According to the rules of the game, legislatures qua fictional entities do convey their intentions through statutes and we can identify such intentions on the basis of the narrative the legislature is embedded in. As a consequence, statutes convey as many intentional contents as the sorts of narratives in which fictional legislatures act.

It has to be emphasized that the account just proposed does not aim to disqualify legislative intent but merely to shed some light on its distinguishing features in legal interpretation. Furthermore, assuming that legislative intent is a fictional entity does not imply "that judges could not be misunderstand or be mistaken about legislative intentions" (Ekins and Goldsworthy, 2014, 42), nor that the search for legislative intent opens the door to unbounded judicial lawmaking. First, the idea that legal interpretation involves a search of this sort makes legal interpretation intelligible. As mentioned in the opening, most people understand interpretation as an activity aimed at detecting the speaker's intention. Thinking of legal interpretation differently, therefore, would make interpretive practices in law obscure and inexplicable to the law addresses. Second, the idea of legislative intent is the cornerstone on which influential interpretive methodologies have been built over time in our legal culture. The doctrines of the historical legislature, coherent legislature and good legislature are an example of that. These interpretive methods provide a set of background assumptions as for the means and purpose of legal interpretation, allow legal officials to reason with others about the content of legal texts, put argumentative constraints on how litigants and courts pursue their goals, and generate expectations with regard to the ruling in similar cases. In short, legislative intent serves a coordination function in judicial decision-making. Third, the various doctrines of legislative intent, and their fictional narratives, are grounded on competing principles and values of the legal system. This is to say that any interpretive doctrine is ultimately defended on normative grounds. Choosing one doctrine over the others depends on the claim that this choice will make legal interpretation better rather than worse. This is one of the reasons why the nature of legislative intent is still an open question in jurisprudence and legal practice.

Notes

1. *United Steelworkers of America v. Weber* [1979] 443 U.S. 193 (Supreme Court of the United States); 205
2. "In view of legislative history" – so the Court continued – "the very statutory words intended as a spur or catalyst to cause employers and unions to self-examine and to self-evaluate their employment practices and to endeavor to eliminate, so far as possible, the last vestiges of an unfortunate and ignominious page in this country's history". *United Steelworkers of America v. Weber* [1979] 443 U.S. 193 (Supreme Court of the United States); 194.
3. Waldron justifies this claim as follows: "[the legislators] share an expectation about how the machine's output –whatever it is – will be understood by those to whom it is sent: they will read it as a set of English sentences" (Waldron 1999, 127).
4. This literal reading of the *Civil Rights Act* had been previously adopted by the Court in *McDonald v. Santa Fe Trail Transp. Co.,* [1976] 427 U.S. 273 (Supreme Court of the United State); 281.
5. *United Steelworkers of America v. Weber* [1979] 443 U.S. 193 (Supreme Court of the United States); 205
6. For a critical discussion of this claim see Kirby (2004) and Shapiro (1994).

7. Therefore, participatory intentions are based on collective acceptance and mutual beliefs. See Kutz (2000, ch. 3). Similarly, according to Tuomela and Miller an individual has a participatory intention with respect to X if she intends to do her part in X, believes that the conditions for success of X obtain, and believes that the members of the group mutually believe that the conditions for success obtain. See on this Tuomela and Miller (1988).
8. In this chapter, 'The legislature intends that X' makes reference to the intention of the voting majority of a legislative body operating in a democratic political system. However, it is disputed whether voting minorities have a role in determining legislative intent. See Dworkin (1984, 320), MacCallum (1993, 17–18), and Ekins (2012, 13).
9. Cf. Ekins (2012, 219). Ekins actually characterizes the participatory intention of the legislature in teleological terms. It is the intention "to adopt the procedures that characterize the legislative process as the means by which [the assembly] will act towards its defining purpose", i.e., the common good. For a discussion of this standpoint see Canale and Poggi (2019).
10. This is the so called "doctrinal paradox" or "discursive dilemma". See Pettit (2002) and List (2012).
11. Pettit claims that such a result can be reached via a "straw-vote procedure". To determine the intentional attitudes of a group, one is required to roughly follow these steps: "(1) Consider the propositions on the agenda one by one in a sequence, which may reflect either a temporal order or some other order of priority. (2) Take a majority vote on each proposition considered. (2.1) If the attitude formed is consistent with attitudes already formed, let it stand as the group attitude. (2.1) If the attitude formed is not consistent with these attitudes, consider all the different possible ways in which previously formed attitudes or the new attitude could be revised so as to restore consistency. Take a vote under a suitable procedure, or deliberate, on which of the possible revisions to make. (3) Assign suitable members or deputies to enact the resulting group attitudes" (List and Pettit 2011, 62).
12. The straw-vote procedure elaborated by Pettit (see footnote 10) seems to presuppose a form of semantic minimalism. The intentional attitudes of the legislature correspond to the minimal propositional content of a statute, which depends on syntax and semantics only.
13. *United Steelworkers of America v. Weber* [1979] 443 U.S. 193 (Supreme Court of the United States); 216.
14. According to Marmor, for instance, "an interpretative statement is either a statement on the communicative intentions of the actual speaker, or else it must be a counterfactual statement, characterizing the communication intentions of a stipulated hypothetical speaker, whose identity and nature are either explicitly defined or, as is more often the case, presupposed by the particular interpretation offered" (Marmor, 2005, 23). See also Stoljar (2001).
15. The realist could here come to the conclusion that none of these possible entities is the legislature's intention. Cf. Kripke (1980, 156–158). *Contra*, however, Lewis (1983, 276–278).
16. This is a typical example of "non-conniving" use of fictional sentences. Cf. G. Evans (1982).
17. Note that both (b) and (c) are fictional legislatures because there is no actual legislative body ruling the matter. The difference between them is that (b) operates on the basis of the present legal materials, while (c) operates on the basis of substantive evaluations. Moreover, both legislatures can be said to be "rational" in the corresponding narrative. Legislature (b) is rational insofar as it avoids legal antinomies and gaps, legislature (c) is rational because it matches what practical rationality dictates in moral reasoning. See Canale and Tuzet (2010).

18. In this chapter, it is not possible to examine the various ways in which original legislative intent is conceived in the current jurisprudential debate. An articulated analysis of this debate is provided by Goldsworthy (2019).
19. On the distinction between internal mode of predication and external mode of predication, see Castañeda (1989, 200). A similar distinction is drawn by Zalta (1983).
20. The intention of the historical legislature exemplifies a property in the sense that it is usually inferred through a generalization of the intention expressed by, or attributed to, one or more individual legislators.
21. On the notion of "world-boundness", see Lewis (1978).

References

Austin, J. (1880). *Lectures on Jurisprudence, or the Philosophy of Positive Law.* London: J. Murray.

Bratman, M. (1993). Shared Intention. *Ethics*, 104(1), pp. 97–113.

Bratman, M. (2014). *Shared Agency: A Planning Theory of Acting Together.* Oxford: Oxford University Press.

Canale, D. and Poggi, F. (2019). Pragmatic Aspects of Legislative Intent. *American Journal of Jurisprudence*, 64(1), pp. 125–138.

Canale, D. and Tuzet, G. (2010). Inferring the Intention. Or, What Law the Legislature Could Have Intended to Make. *Dignitas*, 47, pp. 254–272.

Castañeda, H.-N. (1989). *Thinking, Language, and Experience.* Minneapolis: University of Minnesota Press.

Davidson, D. (1963). Actions, Reasons, and Causes. *The Journal of Philosophy*, 60, pp. 685–700.

Dworkin, R. (1984). *Law's Empire.* Cambridge, MA: Harvard University Press.

Ekins, R. (2012). *The Nature of Legislative Intent.* Oxford: Oxford University Press.

Ekins, R. and Goldsworthy, G. (2014). The Reality and Indispensability of Legislative Intentions. *The Sydney Law Review*, 36, pp. 39–68.

Eskridge, W.N. (1987). Dynamic Statutory Interpretation. *University of Pennsylvania Law Review*, 135, pp. 1479–1555.

Evans, G. (1982). *The Varieties of Reference.* Oxford: Clarendon Press.

Goldsworthy, G. (2019). The Real Standard Picture, and How Facts Make Law: A Response to Mark Greenberg. *American Journal of Jurisprudence*, 64(2), pp. 163–211.

Kirby, M. (2004). *Judicial Activism: Authority, Principle and Policy in the Judicial Method.* London: Sweet & Maxwell.

Kripke, S. (1980). *Naming and Necessity.* 2nd ed. Oxford: Blackwell.

Kutz, C. (2000). *Complicity. Ethics and Law for a Collective Age.* Cambridge: Cambridge University Press.

Lewis, D. (1978). Truth in Fiction. *American Philosophical Quarterly*, 15, pp. 37–46.

Lewis, D., (1983). *Philosophical Papers.* Volume 1. Oxford: Oxford University Press.

List, C. (2012). The Theory of Judgement Aggregation: An Introductory Review. *Synthese*, 187, pp. 179–207.

List, C. and Pettit, P. (2011). *Group Agency. The Possibility, Design, and Status of Corporate Agents.* Oxford: Oxford University Press.

MacCallum, G. (1993). *Legislative Intent and Other Essays on Law, Politics, and Morality.* Madison: University of Wisconsin Press.

Marmor, A. (2005). *Interpretation and Legal Theory.* 2nd ed. Oxford: Hart.

Pettit, P. (2001a). *A Theory of Freedom: From the Psychology to the Politics of Agency*. Oxford: Oxford University Press.

Pettit, P. (2001b). Collective Intentions. In: N. Naffine, R.J. Owens and J. Williams (Eds.), *Intention in Law and Philosophy*. Aldershot: Ashgate, pp. 241–254.

Pettit, P. (2002). Collective Persons and Powers. *Legal Theory*, 8, pp. 443–470.

Poggi, F. (2020). Against the Conversational Model of Legal Interpretation. On the Difference Between Legislative Intent and Speaker's Intention. *Revus*, 40, pp. 9–26.

Radin, M. (1930). Statutory Interpretation. *Harvard Law Review*, 43(6), pp. 863–885.

Raz, J. (2009). *Between Authority and Interpretation*. Oxford: Oxford University Press.

Sellars, W. (1980). On Reasoning about Values. *American Philosophical Quarterly*, 17(2), pp. 81–101.

Shapiro, M. (1994). Judges as Liars. *Harvard Journal of Law & Public Policy*, 17, pp. 155–165.

Stoljar, N. (2001). Vagueness, Counterfactual Intentions, and Legal Interpretation. *Legal Theory*, 7, pp. 447–465.

Szabó, Z. (2001). Fictionalism and Moore's Paradox. *Canadian Journal of Philosophy*, 31, pp. 36–71.

Tuomela, R. and Miller, K. (1988). We-intentions. *Philosophical Studies*, 53, pp. 367–389.

Waldron, J. (1999). *Law and Disagreement*. Oxford: Oxford University Press.

Walton, K.L. (1985). Fictional Entities. In: P. McCormick (Ed.), *The Reasons of Art/L'art et ses raisons*. Ottawa: University of Ottawa Press, pp. 403–413.

Walton, K.L. (1990). *Mimesis as Make-Believe. On the Foundations of the Representational Arts*. Cambridge, MA: Harvard University Press.

Zalta, E.N. (1983). *Abstract Objects: An Introduction to Axiomatic Metaphysics*. Dordrecht: Reidel.

3 Legal disagreement as disagreement about the collectively intended meaning

Brian Flanagan

Our routine reference to legal concepts in everyday life is replicated in the work of lawyers, legal scholars and social scientists. A theory of the nature of law that takes this practice at face value has the merit of obviating any need for a further set of theories that can explain away such references as category errors. Accordingly, although some deny that law is a distinct order of social organization (e.g., Fish 1989; Tushnet 1998; Patterson 2011), for most philosophers, a theory's accommodation of legal concepts' accepted range of application is an important virtue. One leading school, positivism, not only recognizes law as distinct from politics tout court but also holds, further, that 'the existence and content of the law [is] a matter of social fact whose connection with moral or any other values is contingent and precarious' (Raz 1994, 210). This basic position is consistent both with the strong thesis that legal facts are determined by social facts alone (e.g., Gardner 2001) and with the weak thesis that, depending on the social facts, certain legal facts might be partly determined by the moral facts (e.g., Hart 2016 [1979]). Anti-positivists also recognize the existence of a legal realm but hold, to the contrary, that the legal facts are always partly determined by the moral facts (e.g., Finnis 1980; Dworkin 1986; Greenberg 2011). The major anti-positivist objection to positivism, due to Ronald Dworkin, is that it cannot always explain the perception that both sides in a legal case may be intelligibly invoking the law.[1] This objection has generated an array of sometimes-conflicting critical responses. So far, however, positivists have failed to show how it may be successfully resisted. This paper suggests a way forward.

On presenting a model of legal disagreement, Part I provides a brief overview of two actual disputes concerning constitutional and statute law respectively, which Dworkin famously challenged positivists to explain. Part II identifies Scott Shapiro's planning theory of law as the positivist's most promising existing explanatory strategy. It then proceeds to describe features of Dworkin's exemplar disputes for which even the potential to disagree over the content of social plans cannot account. Part III introduces an alternative explanation that does accommodate these features by appealing to the possible elusiveness of a legal provision's historically intended meaning. Crucially,

DOI: 10.4324/9781003242451-5

such an approach appears to commit positivists to a rejection of contemporary skepticism about collective legislative agency. Part IV outlines the application to legislative assemblies of two contrasting, non-majoritarian conceptions of group agency. The scope for such alternatives suggests that skepticism about collective legislation may be premature and, hence, that the prospect of a successful positivist account of legal disagreement remains in reach.

3.1 The objection to positivism from disagreement

A legal dispute occurs where there is a debate as to whether some entity ought, legally, to be allowed to realize some interest or other, in which participants offer arguments that refer not merely to prudence or morality but to the entity's existing legal entitlements. Not all legal disputes comprise a genuine legal disagreement. David Plunkett and Timothy Sundell distinguish the latter as occurring where 'speakers persist in engaging in a dispute about what to count as "the law" despite full agreement on the relevant empirical facts and awareness of that background agreement' (Plunkett and Sundell 2013, 267–268). It seems that ultimately the positivist will wish to recognize as genuine any disagreement that satisfies something like Plunkett and Sundell's definition.

To deny that a persistent dispute about what to count as 'the law' is truly legal in nature is to suppose that disputants are not actually motivated by 'lawyerly preconceptions' and thereby fail to really take part in legal practice (Shapiro 2007, 43). The disagreement-skeptic holds that the purportedly legal concept that prompts the dispute is simply incorrect. She then proposes a psychological theory that explains the lawyers' category error (e.g., Segal and Spaeth 1994; Epstein and King 2002; Posner 2008). It is true that explaining away certain accepted applications of legal concepts need not preclude positivism's overall superiority on the dimension of consistency with legal discourse. Thus, the cost of skepticism about disagreement is sometimes thought to be straightforwardly outweighed by the comparatively massive volume of legal questions on whose answers there is no disagreement whatever, and for which, presumably, positivism faces no difficulty in accounting: [Legal disagreements] … are no[t] numerous enough to cast doubt on [positivism] (Himma 2002 183; similarly, Kramer 2008; Leiter 2009; Marmor 2009). Notice, however, that anti-positivist theories claim to explain both legal disagreement and agreement. It follows that, pending some successful challenge to the latter claim, positivism's superiority might indeed turn on its accommodation of hard cases. Where both parties to a dispute are widely perceived to be intelligibly invoking the relevant legal facts, skepticism is the positivist's last resort.

Accordingly, we adopt Plunkett and Sundell's definition of legal disagreement subject to one important qualification, namely, that the 'empirical' facts on which those in legal disagreement must be taken to agree refer solely to the identity of the relevant legal texts and the attributes of the parties to the pertinent litigation, notably, their conduct and intentions, rather than to all relevant social facts. This qualification has two effects. First, it avoids precluding by stipulation the possibility of legal disagreement that stems from disagreement over a moral fact. Second, it does not unnecessarily constrict theory evaluation by making the question of the scope of legal disputes a test of positivism simpliciter. Rather, it allows us to distinguish different types of non-verbal legal disputes that alternative positivist theories may be found to have greater or lesser success in explaining. Let us now review some proposed historical candidates.

Starting with the examples described in Dworkin (1986), a range of actual legal disputes have been said to reveal positivism's inability to take our applications of legal concepts seriously (see also Dworkin 2006; Lakin 2008; Waldron 2009). Of these, the two disputes that appear to place perhaps the greatest pressure on positivism concern the right of convicted murderers to escape capital punishment under the US Constitution and the right of a murderer to inherit his victim's estate under New York's 1830 Statute of Wills. We will introduce them in turn.

> There is now a lively debate in the United States about whether capital punishment is constitutional. The argument hinges on whether the Eighth Amendment to the Constitution, which prohibits 'cruel and unusual punishments', incorporates some moral standard for appropriate punishments, which capital punishment might well be thought to fail, or whether, on the contrary, it incorporates no moral standard but instead prohibits only punishments that the statesmen and politicians who made the amendment – or the general public to which it was addressed – thought cruel. If we assume that capital punishment is in fact unacceptably cruel, but that almost no one thought it so in the 18th Century, then lawyers who accept the first of these interpretations will think that constitutional law prohibits capital punishment and those who accept the second will think that it permits capital punishment.
>
> (Dworkin 2006, 167)

Some positivists respond by insisting that those who believe that the constitutionality of capital punishment is independent of its moral status are correct: It is always the official's determination of the immorality, not the immorality itself, that bears on the action's legality … Cruel punishments … do not per se violate the Eighth Amendment (Gardner 2010, 71; similarly, Murphy 2008, 1094). By implication, holding the contrary view is either eccentric (e.g., Himma 2002, 168; Kramer 2008, 243) or duplicitous (Leiter 2009, 1224–1125). Nevertheless, prominent jurists[2] and academics alike have defended the conclusion that, in view of its cruelty, capital punishment is indeed unconstitutional (e.g., Ledewitz 1993; Bedau 1996; Smith 2011).

Accordingly, the dispute satisfies our proposed criterion for legal disagreement: participants persist in arguing about the legality of capital punishment despite full agreement on the identity of the pertinent legal texts (the Bill of Rights and the relevant criminal statute) and on the attributes of the parties (conviction for a relevant crime), and an awareness of that agreement.

The second dispute involves statute law. Elmer Palmer had been due to inherit the bulk of his grandfather's estate under the latter's will. Since making his will, Francis Palmer had remarried on the basis of a prenuptial agreement that required him to amend the will to make some provision for his new wife. Two months later, Elmer, fearing diminution of his inheritance in favor of his stepgrandmother, murdered Francis so as 'to inherit while the inheriting was good' (Scheppele 1990, 45). Elmer was duly convicted of the murder, and his aunts, as his grandfather's residuary legatees, sought to contest his inheritance on the basis that it was contrary to New York's law of succession that a testator's murderer should benefit under the former's will. New York's lower courts ruled in Elmer's favor, but the Court of Appeal overturned these decisions. The latter divided on the question: a majority held that Elmer was disqualified from inheriting, whereas the minority insisted that, notwithstanding the immorality of such succession, Elmer was legally entitled to his grandfather's estate (Riggs v. Palmer 115 NY 506 (1889)).

Some positivists respond to this example by insisting that those who recognize the testator-murderer's legal right to inherit are correct (e.g., Schauer 2009, 42–43); others characterize the legal position as indeterminate (e.g., MacCormick 1978; Coyle 2006; Toh 2011). But, again, this dispute extends on both sides from the judges who actually voted on the outcome to prominent members of the legal academy (e.g., Pound 1907; Hart and Sacks 1994 [1958]; Posner 1998). Accordingly, Elmer's case also satisfies our criterion for legal disagreement: participants persist in arguing about whether Elmer's inheritance is legally justified despite full agreement on the identity of the pertinent legal texts (the 1830 statute of wills) and on the attributes of the parties (Francis' proposed distributions of his estate and Elmer's conviction for the latter's murder), and awareness of that agreement.

Naturally, it is open to the positivist to try to accommodate genuine legal disagreements such as these. To this end, many seek to attribute legal disagreement to disagreement either over the content of the relevant social facts or over the content of moral facts that the social facts invoke. The worry is whether any treatment of the law as depending ultimately on social facts alone will be commensurate with the full scope of disagreement.

3.2 Disagreement over the original plan

The positivist who seeks to accommodate the existence of a legal disagreement must identify its ultimate source in some eligible social fact. In principle, there could be genuine debate, on which some legal issue might turn, over particular entities' historic acts and attitudes. Equally, the positivist might invoke the opacity of some moral fact that such social facts make relevant.

Taking care not to presuppose that legal facts always depend on moral facts, positivists have pressed the possibility of a social convention that the legal facts pertaining to a particular jurisdiction are determined by both social facts and substantive moral facts: In some legal systems, as in the United States, the ultimate criteria of legal validity explicitly incorporate principles of justice or substantive moral values ... (Hart 1994, 204; similarly, Lyons 1993; Waluchow 1994; Coleman 2001). In light of the possibility of genuine moral debate, such a convention would introduce a range of legal disagreement that is consistent with the law's ultimate dependence on social facts (e.g., Rodriguez-Blanco 2003). Critically, this range would not extend to encompass the disputes described in Part I.

Consider that some of the participants in the disagreements on which we have focused agree on the substantive moral facts. Thus, it can scarcely be doubted that some lawyers who believe that capital punishment is consistent with the Eighth Amendment also believe that the death penalty is immoral. Equally, in the case of the succession rights of the murderer-testator, all disputants agree that any such inheritance would be immoral. Accordingly, the case does not present a dispute whose participants all 'take the grounds of law to be moral in nature' but who differ simply because, 'figuring out whether such grounds obtain in a particular case is a demanding question about which reasonable people may disagree' (Shapiro 2011, 289). On the contrary, in holding, in dissent, that Elmer was legally entitled to inherit, Judge Gray noted the immorality of that outcome:

> [I]f I believed that... the question could be affected by considerations of an equitable nature, I should not hesitate to assent to views which commend themselves to the conscience. But the matter does not lie within the domain of conscience. (515)

Disagreement about neither the constitutionality of capital punishment nor the succession rights of testator-murderers can be explained by the opacity of any substantive moral value to which the disputants generally advert. Any positivist accommodation of these disagreements must therefore posit debate about the content of some relevant social fact. Having already conceded general agreement about the relevant legal texts (and, implicitly, their literal meanings), the only candidate sources of legal disagreement are facts about enactors' attitudes.

In the most prominent recent addition to the positivist literature, Scott Shapiro proposes that legislation consists in the activity of social planning. Building on Michael Bratman's work on shared cooperative intentions, the planning theory of law holds that the objective of legal interpretation is to identify the plan enacted by the relevant provision in the context of the structure of the legal system as a whole. The plan in question might affirmatively regulate the particular domain, or alternatively, delegate such regulation to some further set of officials:

> [In] exercis[ing] … legal authority … [one] plan[s] for the communities over whom [one] claim[s] authority, both by telling their members what they may or may not do and by authorizing some of these members to plan for others.
>
> (Shapiro 2011, 195)

In principle, the question of whether the legislated plan tells people what they may or may not do or instead authorizes some selection of officials to so decide may be a matter of social fact that is possessed of a determinate yet elusive answer. Thus, lawyers may genuinely disagree how the system's 'distribution of trust and distrust' between judges and other actors determines 'whose role it is to settle such matters and … whose … it is to implement such settlements' (Shapiro 2011, 383; similarly, Shapiro 2007, 47). For instance, it may be an open question whether the institutional framework established under the process of popular ratification, i.e., the Congress, the Supreme Court, etc., mandates the judiciary to exercise moral judgement. Disagreement over the relevance of morality in the interpretation of the contemporaneously enacted Bill of Rights can duly be understood as a product of interpreters' inquiry into this question. Thus, Shapiro explains the death penalty dispute as a genuine disagreement as to whether the 'degree of trust placed in the courts relative to legislatures … suggest[s] … that courts should be permitted a fair degree of discretion when enforcing constitutional rights' (Shapiro 2011, 385).

The planning theory succeeds in its goal of expanding the scope of positivist accommodation. It explains the potential for disagreement over the legal relevance of the moral and policy views of a text's enactors in deciding a particular case, namely, that it arises from disagreement on whether the plan enacted by the text affirmatively regulates or merely delegates the matter at issue. Accordingly, the positivist can account for disagreement over the legal relevance of the acceptance by enactors of the Eighth Amendment of capital punishment's constitutionality. Critically, however, this latter disagreement is just one aspect of the broader disagreement over the punishment's legality.

The disagreement about capital punishment extends to the issue of its constitutionality per se. One side objects, not merely to a particular legal argument for constitutionality, but to the wider notion that it might be legally open to the Court to hold the punishment constitutional. The objection is to *any* decision holding the punishment to be constitutional, even one reached on the basis of judges' independent moral judgement. Those contending that, in view of its agreed immorality, courts are legally *required* to forbid the death penalty are not merely debating whose role it is to decide that question. It follows that, insofar as the dispute is the product of a disagreement over the content of some historical event, this event must place the salience of the moral facts themselves at issue and not merely officials' judgements thereof.

Crucially, a legal interpreter's invocation of moral facts is rendered unintelligible by the notion of a legislated plan, which consists, after all, in an effort to authoritatively guide conduct. Conduct can scarcely be guided by references to concepts which prompt the very differences whose resolution demanded the formulation of an authoritative plan. Accordingly, planning theory holds that laws can only decide matters or delegate them; the moral facts lack any role of their own:

> The logic of planning requires that plans be ascertainable by a method that does not resurrect the very questions that plans are designed to settle. Only social facts, not moral ones, can serve this function.
>
> (Shapiro 2011, 177)

Planning theory thereby 'denies that normative premises can appear in a valid scheme of legal justification' (Shapiro 2011, 239). By thus precluding the possible salience of the moral facts themselves, the theory's accommodation of legal disagreement about the death penalty is significantly incomplete. The theory's ability to explain the disagreement over the inheritance of testator-murderers is more limited still.

Whereas those who settled on the plan enacted by the Eighth Amendment might, in principle, have taken the abstract term 'cruel' to refer to a specific set of punishments with which they were familiar, no equivalent term arose in the New York statutory provisions applicable to Elmer Palmer's inheritance. In the 1830 statute's enumeration of specific grounds for the revocation of wills, there was no term that could have been imagined to refer to any additional specific ground of revocation. Together with the general inability of plans to advert to moral facts, it follows that the statute, qua plan, cannot support the argument that, notwithstanding a will's failure to satisfy any enumerated ground of revocation, the only outcome legally open to a court is to deny inheritance due to the satisfaction of some unenumerated ground, e.g., the stated heir's murder of the testator. Accordingly, on characterizing the enactment of the relevant legislation as the establishment of a plan settling the matter of succession, it becomes mysterious why the view that the court was not legally required to deny Elmer's claim might prompt the disagreement that it did. Moreover, just as no term in the New York statutory provisions applicable to the revocation of Francis Palmer's will could have been supposed to refer to an additional ground of revocation, neither could any term have been thought to delegate the issue of revocation to the courts:

> [T]he designer's judgments of competence and character might be revealed simply by voting for a certain measure … Thus, drafting or voting for a bill that is extremely comprehensive and detailed, containing

> directives with few moral concepts and whose violation is met with severe sanctions, would bespeak a distrustful attitude on the part of legislators. (Shapiro 2011, 362)

On the logic of planning theory, the structure of the revocation provisions of the 1830 statue of wills, in thus bespeaking an attitude of legislative distrust, affirmatively settled the matter of the testator-murderer's right to inherit in Elmer's favor. Accordingly, these provisions can offer no basis on which to object even to the argument that Elmer must inherit due to the absence of any applicable specific ground of revocation to which enactors had adverted. Any such objection would instead have to invoke some broader footing for 'the relative priority [over statute] of … common law equitable principles' (Silver 1987, 385) in the determination of succession law. But acknowledgement of any far-reaching legislative delegation would overlook the broad range of legal questions about which, conversely, genuine disagreement is, in fact, inconceivable. Thus, such a delegation would imply that it would be legally open to a judge to reject as invalid all wills signed by fewer than three witnesses, rather than the minimum of two mentioned in the statute, on the basis that this would better prevent the possibility of fraud. Such an outcome would, however, be absurd.

In the following section, I suggest that the social fact most likely to prompt the full scope of legal disagreement is not a social plan but, rather, the text's intended meaning.

3.3 Disagreement over the intended meaning

Legal intentionalism is the theory that 'the proper way to interpret the Constitution (and statutes, regulations, and judicial orders as well) is to seek its authors' intended meanings' (Alexander 2011, 87). Intentionalism must be distinguished from its close relation, public meaning originalism, a theory associated most prominently with Justice Antonin Scalia of the US Supreme Court (e.g., Scalia 1997). Whereas the intentionalist privileges the attitudes of the enacting legislature, the originalist privileges the perceptions thereof of enactment contemporaries, that is, 'the content that a rational hearer, knowing the relevant conversational background and context, would be warranted in taking the speaker to be intending to assert' (Asgeirsson 2015, 1108). In this section, I assess the scope for intentionalist disagreement over capital punishment and inheritance. As we proceed, we will see that any positivist accommodation of legal disagreement that invokes authorial meaning will appeal to the meaning intended, not the meaning received.

We have seen that any effort to explain disagreement over the constitutionality of capital punishment as disagreement over the content of some historic event must suppose that the posited type of event is eligible to invoke the moral facts. Unlike the notion of a plan, that of an author's intended meaning presents no impediment here; it is perfectly intelligible for someone to produce a text whose intended meaning is that a particular domain of activity ought, on the authority of the text's production, to proceed in accordance with the moral facts. There remains the question, nevertheless, of whether the production of such a text constitutes an intelligible act of *legislation*, that is, of whether legislation is an activity that might legitimately summon moral facts. Not all conceptions of law-making admit this possibility; of those that do, not all are consistent with legal positivism.

The possibility of legislation invoking a moral fact depends, in part, on law's relationship to morality. On many anti-positivist analyses, all central examples of lawmaking secure some aspect of the common good: [A rule that is deficient in justice] is ... law only in a sense that should be judged ... to be a distorted and secondary, non-central sense (Finnis 2015). On this conception, the possibility of legislative reference to moral facts seems assured. Conversely, positivist theories that exclude *any* dependence of legal facts on moral facts appear to imply that legislation consists solely in the guidance of conduct, e.g., that 'law's function is to settle what ought to be done' (Alexander 2009, 228); these theories preclude any legislative invocation of morality. An alternative approach is to treat legislation as having a constitutive moral purpose, in something like the way that the formation of a belief and the making of an assertion have been thought to constitutively aim at truth:

> [T]he law's task, put abstractly, is to secure a situation whereby moral goals which, given the current social situation in the country whose law it is, would be unlikely to be achieved without it, and whose achievement by the law is not counter-productive, are realized.
>
> (Raz 2003, 11)

If all legislation has a moral aim, then an authoritative pronouncement that a particular domain of activity ought to proceed in accordance with the moral facts will duly qualify as an intelligible act of lawmaking. Equally, paradigmatic examples of legislation may fail to achieve their constitutive aim just as paradigmatic beliefs and assertions may fail to achieve their aim of representing the truth. However, it seems that rules whose amorality is openly acknowledged by their makers cannot intelligibly be treated as having a moral aim (Plunkett 2013, 604). In that case, the moral-aim view implies that such rules are not truly legal, and, hence, that the obtaining of relatively morally desirable states of social organization is a measure of the performance of an act of legislation. Consequently, it might be questioned whether such a view can ultimately be reconciled with the positivist insistence on the contingent morality of law.

Significantly, a conception of legislation that licenses the invocation of moral facts need not treat morality as either a condition or a necessary aim. Suppose that the activity of legislation consisted simply in the authoritative organization of society. On this account, a given act of legislation authoritatively organizes social conduct through *either* the provision of guidance *or* the prioritization of the common good:

> Perhaps law is less like Aquinas' saw than it is like a Swiss-Army knife: a multipurpose tool handy for lots of ends, but not necessarily an all-purpose tool.
>
> (Green 2010, 184)

A minimalist conception of legislation that derives from the disjunction of the moral-aim and guidance-of-conduct accounts has the advantage of eschewing, on the one hand, any recognition of moral desirability as a general measure of the performance of an act of legislation, and, on the other, any reduction of legislation solely to the provision of guidance. Thus, like the guidance-of-conduct conception, it clearly adheres to the core positivist insistence on the contingent morality of law, allowing even for openly amoral law-making. Equally, like the moral-aim conception, it appears to readily admit of the possibility of a legislative invocation of moral facts.

We shall take it, then, that a positivist conception of legislation is plausibly available that permits reference to morality. It follows that the enactors of the Bill of Rights, in producing a text whose intended meaning summoned the moral facts about cruelty, might intelligibly be thought to legislate on the admissibility of punishment.

The question of whether the intended meaning of the Eighth Amendment is indeed that objectively cruel punishments are prohibited is one about which there is a fact of the matter that is potentially elusive. The possibility of genuine disagreement on this question implies that, unlike planning theory, intentionalism succeeds in accounting for disagreement over whether it is legally open to a court to hold, contrary to the agreed moral fact of capital punishment's cruelty, that the punishment's imposition is constitutional. Intentionalism does so, crucially, without disturbing the basic positivist claim that the morality of the law is contingent on social fact, namely, the social fact of the legislature's intended meaning. A further advantage is that the explanation is not contingent on agreement among contemporaries of the enactors of the Eighth Amendment as to the relevance of morality to its interpretation. In contrast to that of its public meaning counterpart, the intentionalist object of interpretation is the legislature's intention itself rather than its perceived intention. Consequently, a disagreement as to the content of the relevant social fact, and, with it, disagreement over the legal fact that depends thereon, might legitimately emerge in the immediate aftermath of enactment.[3] For this reason, intentionalism also offers a better explanation of legal disagreement over the rights of murderous heirs.

We noted that in the New York statute of wills' enumeration of specific grounds of revocation, there was no term that could have been imagined to refer to any additional specific ground, and, hence, to indicate enactors' establishment of a plan that denied an inheritance otherwise due to a testator-murderer. The absence of such a term is consistent with the possibility that enactors commonly believed that it went without saying that the statute did not permit a will to confer property on the testator's murderer. As Dworkin himself observed:

> It is a perfectly familiar speech practice not to include, even in quite specific instructions, all the qualifications one would accept or insist on: all the qualifications, as one might put it, that 'go without saying'.
>
> (Dworkin 1997b, 1816)

Equally, the question of whether the statute's intended meaning did, in fact, exclude a right to inherit for murderous heirs is open to debate. One might acknowledge that it was not the purpose of the statute to provide for the enrichment of murderers and yet still regard the conclusion that the legislature intended to exclude testator murderers as 'somewhat strained' (e.g., Goldsworthy 2005, 502–503). It might instead have been an occasion in which the policy that enactors had in mind simply failed to fully serve their purpose. In the legislature's intended meaning, then, it seems that we have a fact that is sufficiently elusive that it might plausibly prompt the described disagreement about Elmer's inheritance. Disputants can be characterized as disagreeing over whether the legislature had decided on a defective but wholly explicit policy or on a non-defective but partly implicit policy.[4] Accordingly, intentionalism accommodates the existence of the disagreement consistently with the claim that the morality of the legal rights of testator-murderers is contingent on a social fact. In contrast, its public meaning counterpart again falls short.

Suppose that the disagreement over Elmer's inheritance was confined to, say, today's generation of lawyers. Suppose, further, that there had been a determinate original understanding of the legislature's intended meaning in respect of testator-murders. On these assumptions, the disagreement might be attributed to disagreement over the historic perception of that meaning. As it happened, however, the disagreement over Elmer's inheritance arose among the very audience to which the relevant statutory provisions were originally addressed. Whereas the overall statute of wills had been enacted in 1830, its grounds for revocation, on which Elmer's rights turned, had been the subject of subsequent revision. At least as recently as 1869, the clause attaching qualifications, 'except as hereinafter provided…', to the conferral of property according to a will had been amended to express a new meaning (both literal and intended).[5] When the disagreement over Elmer's inheritance emerged in New York's courts in the 1880s, it was between contemporaries of the legislature's enactment of the relevant text. Accordingly, the disagreement exposes the basic inadequacy of public meaning accounts of legal disagreement more starkly than the dispute over capital punishment. In Elmer's case, the dispute is itself original; consequently, it cannot revolve around the identification of a common original understanding of the legislature's intended meaning. The scope for disagreement over the statute's public meaning is not equal to the scope for disagreement over Elmer's inheritance: any accommodation of the latter's legal character must appeal to debate over the legislature's intention itself rather than merely to debate over its image in popular understanding.

Speaking of its ability to accommodate the contrasting phenomenon of legal *agreement*, Jeffrey Goldsworthy has observed that positivism's 'plausibility depends partly on that of intentionalism' (Goldsworthy 2005, 496). Part III's analysis suggests that, equally, if the positivist is to identify a fact that is sufficiently elusive to prompt disagreements commensurate with the described legal disagreements, it is to the legislatures' intentions that she must look. Unlike its public meaning or planning theory counterparts, however, it is generally supposed that an intentionalist interpretation must attribute to a text's enactors an exercise of collective agency. It would be prudent to assume, therefore, that the prospects for intentionalism and, by extension, legal positivism are contingent on whether the theory of group agency is hospitable to legislatures.

Among lawyers and judges, legal interpretation, both statutory and constitutional, has traditionally been thought to comprise an inquiry into a text's intended meaning (e.g., MacCormick and Summers 1991 522–524; Sinclair 1997, 1331; Kavanagh 2002, 256). Among theorists, in contrast, skepticism about the propensity of legal texts to convey a collective will is commonplace. Even prominent intentionalists concede that such doubts are potentially serious:

> The puzzle is to explain how the action of the legislators, plural, constitutes the action of the legislature singular.
>
> (Ekins 2012, 7; similarly, Knapp and Michaels 2005, 664–665; Alexander 2011, 91)

The puzzle is driven by a commitment to majoritarianism. In Part IV, I sketch two alternative, non-majoritarian theories of group agency, both of which offer possible positivist bases for realism about collective legislation.

3.4 Collective legislative intentionality?

Part III indicated that to succeed in accommodating legal disagreement, the positivist must appeal to the legislature's intentions. Part IV addresses whether this strategy is consistent with what we know about collective agency.

For many legal theorists, a group of legislators may be said to collectively decide on a particular alternative only if that alternative is majority preferred. The resultant objection to legal intentionalism is that the policy that a statute is intended to express is rarely majority preferred to every possible policy alternative. For one thing, many legislators will have not weighed each of a statute's provisions (e.g., Hart 1961, 26, 287; Brest 1980, 212–215; Dworkin

1981, 487–488); for another, the concentration of procedural control means that a legislative voting agenda is liable to have excluded some majority preferred amendment (e.g., Easterbrook 1983; Shepsle 1992; Waldron 1995). But the theory of group agency includes two radical alternatives to majoritarianism whose application to collective legislatures might undercut this concern. One alternative extends the base of relevant individual attitudes from member preferences over substance to preferences over procedure; the other holds that group attitudes may defy systematic determination by member attitudes altogether.

Groups that exhibit internal disagreement, such as collegiate courts and corporate boards, prompt both thin and thick conceptions of group agency (List and Pettit 2011, 7–10). A thin conception is one that aims to explain a group's decision as just a systematic function of the attitudes of group members, e.g., as a function of the majority attitude. Thick conceptions, in contrast, propose that what happens at group level cannot be reduced to what happens at the level of individual members. Thin and thick conceptions are not necessarily mutually exclusive; it may be allowed that some groups exhibit thick agency, whereas others qualify as thinly agential only. In the latter half of the 20th Century, however, many scholars rejected thick group agency as incurring an onerous metaphysical commitment to the existence of independent group minds (e.g., Searle 1990). Responding to this concern, theorists have lately sought to elucidate a form of thick group agency that eschews the introduction of any 'psychologically mysterious forces' (List and Pettit 2011, 6). On this account, group agency might wholly depend on the attitudes of group members but resist reduction nevertheless. To demonstrate the importance of this form of agency, Christian List and Philip Pettit have presented an influential argument that, granted certain conditions, a group's agency will defy derivation from member attitudes by way of a rule.

List and Pettit's case for thick group agents begins with the assumption that agency consists in a particular function defined by certain minimal conditions of rationality which, in principle, might be performed by an entity comprised of any sort of material, including, notably, individual agents. The argument then draws on technical results in the theory of attitude aggregation that show that these conditions of rationality cannot always be met where group acts are derived through the application to member attitudes of a rule of aggregation, such as, e.g., majority rule. On further supposing that, notwithstanding this constraint, both ordinary and social scientific discourse routinely ascribe agency to groups, List and Pettit conclude that some groups are possessed of minds that are not reducible to those of their members: [W]e must think of group agents as relatively autonomous entities – … groups with minds of their own (List and Pettit 2011, 77–78).

The debate about the implications of irreducible group agency has largely focused on the possession by groups of moral responsibilities over and above those of their members (e.g., Hindriks 2014; List 2016; Smith 2018). But there are implications, too, for the theory of legal interpretation, specifically, for the defense of intentionalism. As observed by Richard Ekins, the fact that a statute is not majority preferred is not decisive of its expression of the will of a legislature that possesses a mind of its own (Ekins 2012). In such a group, the process by which a proposal is considered need not be equally responsive to the policy preferences of all members. Rather, different members might hold greater responsibility in respect of different areas of concern and certain members might exercise special responsibility for deciding how to ensure coherence in group-wide attitudes. The result may be that the legislature's decision, and by extension, the meaning it intends its enactment of a statute to express, might legitimately depart from the majority preference.

Crucial to this reasoning, evidently, is that the relevant legislature actually qualifies as an agent. On List and Pettit's analysis, this assumption depends on the existence of an expectation that the group exhibit rationality, together with the group's satisfaction of the conditions that are constitutive of the type of act that it is empowered to perform i.e., legislating. For Ekins, one condition that constitutes the act of legislation is the achievement of the common good: The central case of legislative action … is a response … to the reasons that bear on whether, and if so how, the law should be changed (Ekins 2012, 127). It follows that, even without majority support, a legislature can collectively legislate through its enactment of a text, and thereby form a meaning that it intends the text to convey, by rationally pursuing the community interest. In principle, this analysis should extend to the act of making constitutional law, both through ratification and amendment.

Not every response to the objection to intentionalism from majoritarianism will be motivated by the defense of legal positivism. On Ekins' conception, legislation is an activity that paradigmatically accords with the moral facts. But there is nothing about the application of List and Pettit's argument to collective legislatures that requires such an account of the constitutive conditions of legislating. On the contrary, a group may be expected to exhibit rationality simply in acting to authoritatively organize social conduct. Accordingly, a non-moralistic conception of legislation seems available that permits equally the adoption of List and Pettit's logic in recognizing non-majoritarian collective agency, and hence, a defense of intentionalism that is consistent with positivism.

Conversely, a thick conception of the collective legislature's agency might not ultimately admit of a complete intentionalist accommodation of legal disagreement. We might find, for instance, that the scope of legal disagreement is not restricted to the interpretation of texts enacted by collective legislatures that actually exhibit basic rationality. Ex hypothesi, disagreements about texts enacted by non-rational legislatures would not concern legislative intentions that are irreducible to the attitudes of legislators. Accordingly, any account of such disagreement that invoked the relevant text's intended meaning might seem to remain vulnerable to majoritarian doubts about the existence of such a meaning. Whether texts enacted by non-rational legislatures may, in fact, generate legal disagreement is a question that cannot be considered here. But an alternative response to such doubts promises to avoid this question altogether: a non-majoritarian conception of *thin* group agency.

The attitudes of thin group agents are determined by the aggregate of those of their members. The dominant approach to thin group agency, strongly associated with Arrovian political economy, is to posit a rule of attitude aggregation that derives group acts from members' substantive preferences, that is, from their preferences over the set of alternative acts that the group might perform. Majoritarianism, which drives skepticism about collective legislative intentions, is the most prominent example of substantivism (e.g., Levine and Plott 1977; Riker 1980; Arrow et al. 2011) (closely comparable rules, including, notably, the Borda count, are also defended [e.g., Dummett 1984; Saari 2006]). As well as substantive preferences, group members have also been attributed 'procedural' preferences, that is, preferences over possible rule alternatives whose application to conflicting substantive preferences produces a ranking of the act alternatives. Where all group members share an identical procedural preference, it may be treated as generating in each a 'conditional' intention to decide on a particular alternative if it satisfies the pertinent rule for aggregating substantive preferences. The exercise of the function assigned to the group might then be explained through the operation of such a rule (Copp 1995; Tuomela 1995; Ludwig 2007; Bratman 2017). Notice that, on such an account, the identity of the majority preferred act alternative is material only if the commonly preferred procedure is majority rule.

Understood as just another sort of conditional intention, such as, e.g., the intention to buy a mansion if one inherits a fortune, a procedural preference is a routine facet of individual agency. But there is no reason why, in principle, they might not offer the basis for an alternative, thin conception of group agency. Just like their substantive preferences, group members' procedural preferences might be theorized to determine the group's attitudes. Notably, a group's attitudes might be attributed to the application to members' substantive preferences of the most popular rule of aggregation. In view of its radical contrast with the familiar substantivist alternatives, such a conception might even be thought to form a focal point of the theory of thin group agency's 'hypothesis space', to be explored expeditiously (Alfano and Loeb 2014). A possible example is Robert Dahl's model of 'procedural democracy' (Dahl 1979).

Taking the demos or people as its primary subject, Dahl develops a notion of group agency that allows for a group's will to be determined either by all members' substantive preferences equally or just by those of a subset, whichever procedure is the more popular (Dahl 1979, 101–107). As it stands, this notion would admit of decisions that are not majority preferred but would exclude rules that assigned unequal weights to members' substantive preferences. It is just these sorts of rules that are hypothesized by political scientists to determine the enactment of statutes, specifically, rules that concentrate control of the voting agenda. More significant, though, is that in a procedural democracy, the relative popularity of the act alternatives is secondary to that of the procedural alternatives. From this point of departure, an alternative conception of thin group agency that encompassed both peoples and institutional groups might be developed that allowed for a broader range of determining procedures. Such an account might admit of procedures that refer to the substantive preferences of ordinary members only as between the status quo and the text preferred by certain procedurally privileged members. Accordingly, it might accommodate the collective intentionality of statutes that fail, in light of legislator ignorance and voting agenda controls, to represent an alternative preferred by a majority to every other.

Together, Parts II and III suggest that any full accommodation of legal disagreement commits the positivist to identifying texts' legal meanings with their historically intended meanings. In this context, the potential attraction of a proceduralist theory of thinly collective legislative agency is that it allows that a provision that is not majority preferred may nevertheless possess an intended meaning. Like the described appeal to the irreducibility of legislative intentions, it does so without invoking any moral facts. Moreover, unlike that appeal, its application to the legislature is not conditional on the body's collective rationality.

Given a majoritarian account of collective agency, legal intentionalism is vulnerable to the criticism that the circumstances of enactment tend to inhibit the expression of any truly collective decision. We have just described two alternatives to that account: one which treats legislatures as thick group agents and another which reconceives them as thin group agents whose will depends ultimately on members' procedural rather than substantive preferences. In promising to secure legal intentionalism, these alternatives offer an avenue for positivism to accommodate the full range of hard cases and, by extension, to match the anti-positivist claim to avert an error theory of accepted legal phenomena.

3.5 Conclusion

Positivism can claim to explain the full scope of legal disagreement only by identifying a source of such disagreement in disputes over the substance of some relevant sort of historical attitude. On comparing the possible candidates, namely, the plan that leading legislators sought to enact and the policy that the legislature sought to convey, we concluded that the scope for disagreement over the former failed to encompass two actual legal disagreements. We then revisited the assumption on which the meaningfulness of any debate about a provision's intended meaning appears to depend, to wit, the existence of a collective legislative intention. Doubts about the occurrence of such intentions are common. But broader debates about group agency present possible alternatives to the majoritarianism on which such doubts rest. To match the capacity of rival approaches to take seriously our applications of legal concepts, positivists may ultimately be obliged to explore the prospects of defending the application to the legislature of some such alternative.

Notes

1. Recent empirical work suggests a further possible objection: that positivism fails to accommodate our intuition about the diminished legal status of wicked statutes (Flanagan and Hannikainen 2020).
2. See the concurring opinions of Justices Marshall, Brennan and Stewart of the US Supreme Court in Furman v. Georgia (1972) 408 U.S. 238.
3. Notably, on occasions in which Dworkin himself argued that the constitutionality of capital punishment depends on its morality, he chose to invoke the social fact of the Eighth Amendment's intended meaning rather than considerations drawn from his own, explicitly anti-positivist, legal theory, e.g., Dworkin (1977, 1997a). Dworkin characterized this strategy as merely, 'ad hominem against the view that "strict" [non-moralistic] construction of the Constitution provided maximum deference to the wishes of the Framers' (Dworkin 1981, 494–495). Significantly, however, Dworkin thereby identified the legal relevance of intended meaning as the common ground between those who hold that the Eight Amendment's interpretation should, respectively, pursue and eschew moral inquiry.
4. The latter possibility is tacitly acknowledged in the judicial opinion that defended Elmer's statutory right to inherit, where it was admitted that statutory provisions must be, 'substantially, if not exactly, followed to insure validity and performance' (Gray J, at 516). Indeed, Brian Leiter notes that, in another decision that was delivered on the same day as Riggs, namely, Bockes v. Wemple (22 N.E. 272 (1889)), Gray J observed that, 'The intention of the legislature is undoubtedly the great principle which controls the office of interpretation' (at 273) (Leiter 2009, 1243).
5. Act of February 19, Chapter 22, Laws of the State of New York of 1869.

References

Alexander, L. (2009). Of Living Trees and Dead Hands: The Interpretation of Constitutions and Constitutional Rights. *Canadian Journal of Law and Jurisprudence*, 22(2), pp. 227–236.

Alexander, L. (2011). Simple-Minded Originalism. In: G. Huscroft & B. W. Miller (Eds.), *The Challenge of Originalism*. Cambridge: Cambridge University Press, pp. 87–98.

Alfano, M. & Loeb, D. (2014). Experimental Moral Philosophy. In: E. Zalta (Ed.), *Stanford Encyclopedia of Philosophy*. Stanford: Stanford University Metaphysics Research Lab.

Arrow, K., Sen, A. & Suzumura, K. (2011). Kenneth Arrow on Social Choice Theory. In K. Arrow, A. Sen, & K. Suzumura (Eds.), *Handbook of Social Choice and Welfare (Vol. 2)*. Amsterdam: Elsevier, pp. 3–27.

Asgeirsson, H. (2015). Expected Applications, Contextual Enrichment, and Objective Communicative Content: The Linguistic Case for Conception Textualism. *Legal Theory*, 21(3–4), pp. 115–135.

Bedau, H.A. (1996). Interpreting the Eighth Amendment: Principled vs. Populist Strategies. *Thomas M Cooley Law Review*, *13*(3), pp. 789–814.

Bratman, M.E. (2017). The Intentions of a Group. In: E. Orts & C. Smith (Eds.), *The Moral Responsibility of Firms*. Oxford: Oxford University Press, pp. 36–52.

Brest, P., (1980). The Misconceived Quest for Original Understanding. *Boston University Law Review*, 60(2), 204–238.

Coleman, J.L. (2001). Incorporationism, Conventionality and the Practical Difference Thesis. In: J.L. Coleman (Ed.), *Hart's Postscript: Essays on the Postscript to The Concept of Law*. Oxford: Oxford University Press, pp. 99–148.

Copp, D. (1995). *Morality, Normativity, and Society*. New York: Oxford University Press.

Coyle, S. (2006). Practices and the Rule of Recognition. *Law and Philosophy*, 25(4), pp. 417–452.

Dahl R. (1979). Procedural Democracy. In: P Laslett & J Fishkin (Eds.), *Philosophy, Politics and Society* (Fifth Series). New Haven: Yale University Press, pp. 97–133.

Dummett, M. (1984). *Voting Procedures*. Oxford: Clarendon Press.

Dworkin, R. (1977). Constitutional Cases. In: R. Dworkin (Author), *Taking Rights Seriously*. Cambridge: Harvard University Press: pp. 131–150 (first published in 1972 in *The New York Review of Books* as "The Jurisprudence of Richard Nixon").

Dworkin, R. (1981). The Forum of Principle. *New York University Law Review*, 56, pp. 469–518.

Dworkin, R. (1986). *Law's Empire*. Cambridge: Belknap Press.

Dworkin, R. (1997a). Comment In: A. Gutman (Ed.), *A Matter of Interpretation: Federal Courts and the Law*. Princeton: Princeton University Press, pp. 116–120.

Dworkin, R. (1997b). Reflections on Fidelity. *Fordham Law Review*, 65(4), pp. 1799–1818.

Dworkin, R. (2006). *Justice in Robes*. Cambridge: Harvard University Press.

Easterbrook, F. (1983). Statute's Domains. *University of Chicago Law Review*, 50(2), pp. 533–552.

Ekins, R. (2012). *The Nature of Legislative Intent*. Oxford: Oxford University Press.

Epstein, L. & King, G. (2002). The Rules of Inference. *University of Chicago Law Review*, 69(1), pp. 1–133.

Finnis, J. (1980). *Natural Law and Natural Rights*. Oxford: Oxford University Press.

Finnis, J. (2015). Natural Law Theories. In: E. Zalta (Ed.), *Stanford Encyclopedia of Philosophy*. Stanford: Stanford University Metaphysics Research Lab.

Fish, S. (1989). *Doing What Comes Naturally: Change, Rhetoric, and the Practice of Theory in Literary and Legal Studies*. Durham: Duke University Press.

Flanagan, B. & Hannikainen, I. (2020). The Folk Concept of Law: Law Is Intrinsically Moral, *Australasian Journal of Philosophy*. Latest Articles <10.1080/00048402.2020.1833953>.

Gardner, J. (2001). Legal Positivism: 5½ Myths. *American Journal of Jurisprudence*, 46(1), pp. 199–227.

Gardner, J. (2010). Justification under Authority. *Canadian Journal of Law and Jurisprudence*, 23(1), pp. 71–98.

Goldsworthy, J. (2005). Legislative Intentions, Legislative Supremacy, and Legal Positivism. *San Diego Law Review*, 42(1), pp. 493–518.

Green, L. (2010). Law as a Means. In: P. Cane (Ed.), *The Hart-Fuller Debate in the Twenty-First Century*. Oxford: Hart Publishing, pp. 169–189.

Greenberg, M. (2011). The Standard Picture and Its Discontents. *Oxford Studies in Philosophy of Law*, 1, pp. 39–106.

Hart, H.L.A. (1961). *The Concept of Law*. Oxford: Clarendon Press.

Hart, H.L.A. (1994). *The Concept of Law*. 2nd ed. Oxford: Oxford University Press.

Hart, H.L.A. (2016) The New Challenge to Legal Positivism. *Oxford Journal of Legal Studies*, 36(3), pp. 459–475 (1979 lecture translated by A Grabowski).

Hart, H.M., and Sacks, A.M. (1994) [1958]. *The Legal Process: Basic Problems in the Making and Application of Law*. (W.N. Eskridge & P.P. Frickey, Eds.). Westbury: Foundation Press.

Himma, K. (2002). Ambiguously Stung: Dworkin's Semantic Sting Reconfigured. *Legal Theory*, 8(2), pp. 145–183.

Hindriks, F. (2014). How Autonomous Are Collective Agents? Corporate Rights and Normative Individualism. *Erkenntnis*, 79(9), pp. 1565–1585.

Kavanagh, A. (2002). Original Intention, Enacted Text and Constitutional Interpretation. *American Journal of Jurisprudence*, 47(1), pp. 255–298.

Knapp, S. & Michaels, W.B. (2005). Not a Matter of Interpretation. *San Diego Law Review*, 42(2), pp. 651–668.

Kramer, M.H. (2008). Is Law's Conventionality Consistent with Law's Objectivity?. *Res Publica*, 14(4), pp. 241–252.

Lakin, S. (2008). Debunking the Idea of Parliamentary Sovereignty: The Controlling Factor of Legality in the British Constitution. *Oxford Journal of Legal Studies*, 28(1), pp. 709–734.

Ledewitz, B. (1993). Could the Death Penalty be a Cruel Punishment?. *Widener Journal of Public Law*, 3(1), pp. 121–160.

Leiter, B. (2009). Explaining Theoretical Disagreement. *University of Chicago Law Review*, 76, pp. 1215–1250.

Levine, M.E. & Plott, C.R. (1977). Agenda Influence and Its Implications. *Virginia Law Review*, 63(4), pp. 561–604.

List C. (2016). What Is It Like to Be a Group Agent?. *Noûs*, 50(3), pp. 295–319.

List, C. & Pettit, P. (2011). *Group Agency: The Possibility, Design, and Status of Corporate Agents*. Oxford: Oxford University Press.

Ludwig, K. (2007). Collective Intentional Behavior from the Standpoint of Semantics. *Noûs*, 41(3), pp. 355–393.

Lyons, D. (1993). *Moral Aspects of Legal Theory*. Cambridge: Cambridge University Press.

MacCormick, N. (1978). *Legal Reasoning and Legal Theory*. Oxford: Clarendon Press.

MacCormick, N. & Summers R. (1991) *Interpreting Statutes*. Aldershot: Dartmouth.

Marmor, A. (2009). *Social Conventions: From Language to Law*. Princeton: Princeton University Press.

Murphy, L. (2008). Better To See Law This Way. *NYU Law Review*, 83, pp. 1088–1108.

Patterson, D. (2011). Methodology and Theoretical Disagreement. In: U. Neergaard, R. Nielsen, & L. Roseberry (Eds.), *European Legal Method: Paradoxes and Revitalisation*. Copenhagen: DJØF Publishing, pp. 227–241.

Plunkett, D. (2013). Legal Positivism and the Moral Aim Thesis. *Oxford Journal of Legal Studies*, 33(3), pp. 563–605.

Plunkett, D. & Sundell, T. (2013). Dworkin's Interpretivism and the Pragmatics of Legal Disputes. *Legal Theory*, 19(3), pp. 242–281.

Posner, R.A. (1998). The Problematics of Moral and Legal Theory. *Harvard Law Review*, 111(7), pp. 1637–1717.

Posner, R.A. (2008). *How Judges Think*. Cambridge: Harvard University Press.

Pound, R. (1907). Spurious Interpretation. *Columbia Law Review*, 7(6), pp. 379–386.

Raz, J. (1994). *Ethics in the Public Domain: Essays in the Morality of Law and Politics*. Oxford: Clarendon Press.

Raz, J. (2003). About Morality and the Nature of Law. *American Journal of Jurisprudence*, 48(1), pp. 1–15.

Riker, W.H. (1980). Implications from the Disequilibrium of Majority Rule for the Study of Institutions. *American Political Science Review*, 74(2), pp. 432–446.

Rodriguez-Blanco, V. (2003). A Defence of Hart's Semantics as Nonambitious Conceptual Analysis. *Legal Theory*, 9(2), pp. 99–121.

Saari, D.G. (2006). Which Is Better: The Condorcet or Borda Winner?. *Social Choice and Welfare*, 26(1), pp. 107–130.

Scalia, A. (1997). Common-Law Courts in a Civil-law System: The Role of United States Federal Courts in Interpreting the Constitution and Laws. In: A. Gutman (Ed.),

A Matter of Interpretation: Federal Courts and the Law. Princeton: Princeton University Press, pp. 3–47.

Schauer, F. (2009). Institutions and the Concept of Law: A Reply to Ronald Dworkin (with some help from Neil MacCormick). In: M. del Mar & Z. Bankowski (Eds.), *Law as Institutional Normative Order*. London: Routledge, pp. 35–45.

Scheppele, K.L. (1990). Facing Facts in Legal Interpretation. *Representations*, 30, pp. 42–77.

Searle, J. (1990). Collective Intentions and Actions. In: P. Cohen, J. Morgan, & M. Pollack (Eds.), *Intentions in Communications*. Cambridge: MIT Press, pp. 401–415.

Segal, J.A., & Spaeth, H.J. (1994). The Attitudinal Model: The Authors Respond. *Law and Courts Newsletter*, 4(1), pp. 10–12.

Shapiro, S.J. (2007). The "Hart-Dworkin" Debate: A Short Guide for the Perplexed. In A. Ripstein (Ed.), *Ronald Dworkin*, Cambridge: Cambridge University Press, pp. 22–55.

Shapiro, S.J. (2011). *Legality*. Cambridge: Harvard University Press.

Shepsle, K. (1992). Congress is a "they," not an "it": Legislative intent as oxymoron. *International Review of Law and Economics*, 12(2), pp. 239–256.

Silver, C. (1987). Elmer's Case: A Legal Positivist Replies to Dworkin. *Law and Philosophy*, 6(3), pp. 381–399.

Sinclair, M.B.W. (1997). Legislative Intent: Fact or Fabrication. *New York Law School Law Review*, 47(3–4), pp. 1329–1389.

Smith, S. (2011). That Old-Time Originalism. In: G. Huscroft & B.W. Miller (Eds.), *The Challenge of Originalism*. Cambridge: Cambridge University Press, pp. 223–245.

Smith, L. (2018). The Curious Case of Ronald McDonald's Claim to Rights: An Ontological Account of Differences in Group and Individual Person Rights. *Journal of Social Ontology*, 4(1), pp. 1–28.

Toh, K. (2011). Legal Judgments as Plural Acceptances of Norms. *Oxford Studies in Philosophy of Law*, 1, pp. 107–137.

Tuomela, R. (1995). *The Importance of Us: A Philosophical Study of Basic Social Notions*. Stanford: Stanford University Press.

Tushnet, M. (1998). Defending the Indeterminacy Thesis. In B. Bix (Ed.), *Analyzing law: New Essays in Legal Theory*. Oxford: Clarendon Press, pp. 223–238.

Waldron, J. (1995). Legislators' Intentions and Unintentional Legislation. In: A. Marmor (Ed.), *Law and Interpretation: Essays in Legal Philosophy*. New York: Oxford University Press, pp. 329–356.

Waldron, J. (2009). Who Needs Rules of Recognition?. In: M. D. Adler, & K. E. Himma (Eds.), *The Rule of Recognition and the U.S. Constitution*. Oxford: Oxford University Press, pp. 327–344.

Waluchow, W. (1994). *Inclusive Legal Positivism*. Oxford: Clarendon Press.

4 The two lives of law's moral aim

*Dimitrios Kyritsis**

4.1 The institutional nature of law and the joint activity of officials

That law is an institutional system is taken by many legal theorists to be one of its essential features (Raz, 2009, ch 6). According to a strand of legal conventionalist literature exemplified in Scott Shapiro's planning theory, law's institutional nature is best cashed out in terms of a joint activity of legal officials (Shapiro, 2011). Law, it is claimed, essentially involves legal officials acting together.[1] The task of legal theory is to elucidate the characteristics of this joint activity.

It is commonly thought that this insight gives legal positivism a comparative edge over anti-positivism because it puts a social fact – official practice – at the heart of the philosophical explanation of the law. Indeed, Shapiro and most other legal conventionalists are positivists.[2] In previous work, I sought to soften the contrast between legal conventionalism and anti-positivism. I argued that the notion of a joint activity of officials can be accommodated within what I termed robust natural law theories. These are theories that accept that moral considerations are, first, essential for understanding the legal phenomenon and, second, necessarily among the truth conditions of propositions of law (Kyritsis, 2008).[3] More specifically, I contended that robust natural law can endorse a moralized understanding of institutional cooperation (MUIC). According to it, it is morally important that legal officials look over their shoulders and 'mesh' their acts with those of other officials. The moral considerations that structure their activity – the joint project of governing- and their roles in it necessarily determine (in part) the content of the law.

But it might be objected that the synthesis I advocate is a sham because it takes the wrong lesson from law's institutional nature. If law is the joint activity of officials, as legal conventionalists claim, then it is necessarily 'morally risky'.[4] Once it is set in motion, we cannot be certain that it will live up to whatever ideals we think befits it. It may take the morally appealing shape

* I thank Wibren van der Burg, Ana Cannilla, Chris Hilson and an anonymous referee for helpful comments on earlier drafts.

DOI: 10.4324/9781003242451-6

that robust natural law theorists speak of, but it need not. Hence, it cannot be true that the content of the law is necessarily determined by the considerations that should structure it. Rather, we must look for the considerations that actually do so in this or that jurisdiction, whatever their moral merit. Any overlaps between what happens and what should happen are contingent on how a particular joint activity is arranged.

In fact, so the objection goes, we can account for the moral importance of the joint project of governing without papering over the contingent character of its success. In other words, we can say that the joint activity necessarily has a moral aim but that it does not always achieve it. This is an old strategy, and it has recently been revived by Shapiro. Shapiro claims that ascribing an essential moral aim to official practice does not entail that the content of the law is necessarily determined by morality. Hence, by relying on such an understanding of law's aim, he thinks we can inject just the right amount of moralized theorizing into a basically legal positivist framework.

In this chapter, I want to challenge Shapiro's strategy. However, I shall not do this by arguing directly against his conception of law's moral aim. Instead, I want to sketch a different one vindicating robust natural law theory and defend it from a number of criticisms. My goal is primarily constructive rather than critical, to clarify the ambition and main thrust of the MUIC I espouse and to compare it more fully to its positivistic counterparts. I shall argue that the idea of a joint activity plays a very different role in moralized and positivist accounts. In the latter, this role is explanatory: It is meant to capture the main characteristics of a more or less stable practice that emerges from the intentions and actions of a multiplicity of institutional actors; thanks to (some of) those characteristics, the law can achieve its moral aim, but they do not guarantee that it will. In the former, joint activity plays a justificatory role: It is meant to identify a dimension of moral worth that inheres in legal officials' being under a duty to be responsive to and rely on what other officials say and do. This dimension underpins a cluster of factors that bear on the legitimacy of state power.

What is the theoretical payoff of this analytical exercise? I shall suggest that it is not a defect of MUIC that it dismisses political systems which fail its moral test. Importantly, this dismissal does not signal a conflation of what is and what ought to be. Quite the opposite, it flows from MUIC's tenet that law is a set of genuinely binding standards, which may diverge from what those exercising institutional power intend them to be. Thus, it is evidence of its fundamentally different orientation compared to legal positivism. Conversely, this analytical exercise will, if successful, also bolster the anti-positivist credentials of MUIC. It can help address the – this time – intramural objection that MUIC betrays robust natural law theory. According to this objection, MUIC gives undue weight in the determination of the law to the social fact that a political decision has been made. But this, I shall suggest, is a misunderstanding. When it goes well, the joint project of governing serves a genuine value, so it makes *moral* sense to require judges and other legal officials to defer to the decisions of their fellow participants. Such deference is not a concession to legal positivism. Ultimately, it, too, is mediated by moral considerations. Although it is not possible in this chapter to fully spell out and argue for the value of institutional cooperation, I hope to do enough to establish the plausibility of the proposal.

This chapter will be divided into three sections. In Section 4.2, I shall present Shapiro's attempt to reconcile legal positivism and the belief in the law's essential moral aim. Over the following two sections, I shall defend my alternative conception of law's moral aim. First, I shall define the justificatory ambition of robust natural law theory and contrast it to Shapiro's descriptive ambition by reference to Ronald Dworkin's theory of law. Finally, in Section 4.4, I shall defend the claim that this ambition is served by MUIC against objections from both positivists and anti-positivists.

4.2 The moral aim of law

In *Legality,* Scott Shapiro contends that the central insight of MUIC can be assimilated by positivists such as himself. Shapiro thinks that this insight boils down to the idea that the joint activity of officials necessarily has a moral aim. He means by this that we cannot adequately understand the law and distinguish it from other social practices without appreciating that it is supposed to serve a morally valuable aim. This is an essential feature of law.[5] There are many social planning organizations, and one of the things that distinguish law from them is precisely its moral aim.[6] Just like the function of telling time makes a clock the thing that it is, something is not law unless it aims to 'remedy the moral deficiencies of the circumstances of legality', namely the inadequacy of other means of organization for solving many serious social problems under conditions of social complexity and disagreement (Shapiro, 2011, p. 213).[7] As is well known, Shapiro maintains that law's remedy of those deficiencies takes the form of a joint activity on a massive scale, which makes plans for the community and communicates them through general and publicly accessible standards (Shapiro, 2011, p. 203). That activity is 'official, institutional, compulsory, self-certifying' (Shapiro, 2011, p. 225).

Shapiro insists that the ascription of this aim to law is compatible with grave iniquity. The joint activity of law may simply stray off the mark. Arguably, there is nothing metaphysically problematic about this. As Shapiro writes, 'unjust regimes are like broken clocks ... They do not do what objects of their type are supposed to do' (Shapiro, 2011, p. 391).[8] What does the moral aim thesis tell us about the controversy between positivism and anti-positivism? Since the mere fact that law has a moral aim does not preclude the possibility that it may fall short of it, determining the content of the law in this or that jurisdiction ought not to focus on what it would look like if the joint activity achieved its aim because that would result in air-brushing the law in those jurisdictions where it does not. This, arguably, is the mistake of robust natural law theory, and it blocks from view important lessons, for instance, about the risks that inhere in law's operation and the special evils that law's presence makes possible and, under certain circumstances, augments. Legal positivists are particularly alert to those risks and evils, which are commonly associated with some of the characteristics of legal systems that Shapiro also stresses. Thus, for instance, the fact that being subject to law is not voluntary and that legal regulation is streamlined by formal procedures can make a tyrannical program more oppressive.

This does not mean that the moral aim thesis is without philosophical consequences. Solving serious moral problems is not a beneficial side-effect of the operation of law. It is what you get when law works as it is supposed to. As Green has put it, '[l]aw is the kind of thing that is apt for inspection and appraisal in light of justice; we might say, then, that it is justice-apt' (Green, 2008, p. 1050). Thus, we should expect that law's justice-aptness reveals itself in and helps us understand (at least some of) its essential characteristics. In addition, since telling the time is what clocks 'are supposed to do', it makes sense to fault them for not telling the right time. Likewise, it makes sense to criticize law when it fails to solve a serious moral problem. In these respects, then, the moral aim thesis appears to offer us the best of both worlds. It delivers a clear-eyed vision of law, warts and all, as is the self-proclaimed ambition of legal positivism, while at the same time preserving the moral aspiration on which anti-positivists insist.[9] Nonetheless, it keeps the two separate. It is thus better able to account for the law's successes as well as its failures.

It could be objected at this point that we should not exaggerate the separateness of reality and aspiration in functional explanations of the law. Inevitably, the aspiration bleeds into the way we perceive reality. For one thing, it pushes us to say more about how an object might fail to fulfil its function. Even a broken clock must possess certain features for it to count as a clock. Presumably, an object without a mechanism for measuring time would not be a clock, even if it looked like one. Doesn't the same apply to law? It is an unresolved question in Shapiro's analysis whether law's moral aim sets limits to the range of failures that a legal system can commit while still being a legal system or the range of deficiencies that a legal norm may suffer from while still counting as a legal norm. Arguably, though, if it is an essential feature of the law that it has a moral aim, then we should be able to draw such a line.[10] For instance, Jonathan Crowe has argued that, in order for something to qualify as a legal norm, it is necessary – though not sufficient – that it be constitutively capable of performing law's function, which he defines as that of serving as a deontic marker by creating a sense of social obligation (Crowe, 2014, pp. 750ff).[11] Crowe contends that '[a] law that is so unjust or unreasonable that it is incapable of engaging human motivations to the extent necessary to become generally accepted as binding will therefore be incapable of performing law's function as an artifact' (Crowe, 2014, p. 753).

Even with Crowe's qualification, however, we are a far cry from robust natural law theory. To begin with, for Crowe, the inability to perform law's function may be due to a norm's formal characteristics rather than its content. An incomprehensible norm or one that contradicts itself falls in this category.

More importantly, as Crowe himself emphasizes, many unjust norms will pass the threshold of lawhood, because they are capable of fulfilling law's function, that is, they can generate a sense of social obligation despite their moral shortcomings (Green, 1998, p. 122). This, after all, is a key insight of legal positivism, which Shapiro shares. The joint activity of law may well have been set up to solve serious moral problems, but it can easily be transformed into a force of evil if the joint activity is captured by wicked groups. This is a result that robust natural law theory cannot accept without rendering itself completely toothless. For robust natural law theory, it is not sufficient that a putative law is capable of satisfying the moral criterion that it designates as essential to law; it must actually satisfy it.[12] Thus, even if we allow that a functional account excludes abysmal moral failures of the joint activity of law from the concept of law, it does not collapse Shapiro's theory into robust natural law.

4.3 Describing and justifying

In the previous section, I tried to show how you can be a positivist and still embrace the view that law necessarily serves a morally valuable function. At first blush, then, the addition of the moral aim thesis helps Shapiro paint robust natural law into a corner. Proponents of robust natural law commonly argue that their accounts are competitive with and superior to positivistic accounts: They are able to explain the law in a way that brings out rather than suppress its non-redundant moral dimension. But perhaps you do not need to embrace robust natural law to do that. If Shapiro is right, the moral aim thesis accommodates both the intuition that the law is there to do good and the fact that it does not always succeed in doing so. On this view, robust natural law theory is confined to the separate justificatory task that legal positivists have always assigned to it. It does not set out existence conditions for law but only the conditions under which law, identified in a non-moralized manner, is morally justified. It is thus 'redundant' in the sense that it relies on legal positivism to determine the object of justification.[13]

In this section, I take issue with this diagnosis. I shall argue that it ignores that Shapiro's planning theory of law and robust natural law have starkly different theoretical orientations, which are also reflected in the way they conceive of the essential moral dimension they attribute to law. I shall then show that MUIC has the same orientation as robust natural law theory and is therefore also immune to the redundancy argument.

Let's begin by considering the distinction Dworkin introduces in *Justice in Robes* between the sociological and doctrinal concept of law. The former refers to 'a particular type of institutional social structure' (Dworkin, 2008, p. 3), whereas we use the latter to state 'what the law of some jurisdiction requires or forbids or permits' (Dworkin, 2008, p. 223). When we talk about law in the former sense, it is not incoherent to claim that it was created to remedy the moral deficiencies in the circumstances of legality or that it has evolved to serve this morally valuable function, and at the same time that on occasion it fails. The way we proceed is we first identify the structure the concept refers to, and then we ask questions about its emergence, history, operation and functions. Even when we investigate the moral importance of that structure, our goal is explanatory. We want to know by virtue of which features it has this moral importance.

Nonetheless, this mode of inquiry makes little sense if our interest is with the doctrinal concept of law. The doctrinal concept of law refers not to a social institution but a set of standards. For Dworkin, these standards set a (necessary) benchmark for the legitimate use of state power. In a famous passage he writes:

> Our discussions about law by and large assume, I suggest, that the most abstract and fundamental point of legal practice is to guide and constrain the power of government in the following way. Law insists that force not be used or withheld, no matter how useful that would be to ends in view, no matter how beneficial or noble these ends, except as licensed or required by individual rights and responsibilities flowing from past political decisions about when collective force is justified.
>
> (Dworkin, 1998, p. 93)

When Dworkin says that guiding and constraining the power of government is the 'point' of legal practice, he does not merely mean that legal practice has been created with this goal in mind, which it sometimes falls short of, or that this is its accepted function, even though it sometimes malfunctions. Rather, he means that for the doctrinal legal philosopher law just is what guides and constrains the power of government by justifying the use of state coercion in the special way that law does, namely by demanding that it be in line with past political decisions.

Here, morality, not social ontology, has priority. For Dworkin, we determine the meaning of the doctrinal concept of law by interpretively identifying the moral principles that best explain and justify our past political decisions. The standards that form the extension of the doctrinal concept are grounded in or justified by these principles. Sure enough, on Dworkin's view, the doctrinal concept of law is sensitive to facts about institutional action. We ask what standards 'flow from' such facts. If the facts are different, the standards may be different, too. But these facts have this role only because and to the extent that the relevant moral principles assign it to them (Stavropoulos, 2014). An institution may be salient or powerful in a given society; its decisions may enjoy broad compliance and thus effectively order that society. But unless there is a genuine moral principle justifying that institution's enjoying such an influence, if, for instance, it acts in a morally repugnant way, then it does not contribute to the doctrinal concept of law.

It might be argued that my description of Dworkin's theory is grist to legal positivism's mill. Recall that for many positivists, Dworkin's theory has the exclusively justificatory task of sifting through the body of legal norms and identifying those that are instances of the legal system living up to its moral aim (Gardner, 2006, pp. 219–22). But this is a mistake. Dworkin does not start from identifying the institutional structure that is law, subsequently taking what standards it has produced, good or bad, as the raw material to be purified with the use of morality. As already explained, he puts moral principles, interpretively specified, at the driver's seat. *They* determine what is legally binding. The difference can be brought out if we consider that Dworkinian principles may give rise to legal standards that have no anchoring in social facts such as the decisions of institutions. Presumably, the positivistic picture can make no room for such legal standards.[14] It could perhaps allow that a well-functioning legal system should include them. However, unless they are connected in the right way with the actual operation of an existing legal system, it cannot admit them into the set of valid legal norms. Again, Shapiro's theory provides a nice illustration of this point. Since the law is for him a system of interlocking intentions to create a master plan for social organization, a legal norm does not exist unless it figures in the content of those intentions or has been 'created in accordance with, and whose application is required by, such a master plan' (Shapiro, 2011, p. 225).

The critic might insist at this point that Dworkin still gets the order of explanation wrong. Legal practice is not inert until it has been touched by interpretation. It would make no sense to interpret legal practice in light of moral principles unless it was already in an important sense geared toward, say, justifying state coercion.[15] And if it is so geared, it must be by virtue of more general features than those picked out by the moral principles; otherwise, there would be no work left for interpretation to do. These are precisely the features that a less morally demanding account like Shapiro's planning theory can capture. For instance, such a theory can help explain why law and not some other social practice is charged with regulating state coercion.

Again, the critic conflates two very different theoretical projects. It may well be that talking about the doctrinal concept of law would not make sense in a society that lacked a certain kind of social organization. It is perhaps true that, when we examine the features of that social organization, we do not need to appeal to moral principles. For example, we analyze the beliefs, intentions, claims, and/or attitudes of those who act in its name or are subject to its edicts, regardless of whether they are morally misguided. But according to Dworkin that examination will tell us nothing about the content of the law; at best, it will give us an insight into what people *take* the law to be, not what the law truly is.

4.4 Two ways of caring about institutions

It could be said that MUIC occupies an uneasy middle ground between Dworkin's justificatory jurisprudence and the explanatory jurisprudence that aims to explicate the sociological concept of law. Recall, for MUIC, the law – at least in a subset of legal systems[16] – is also essentially determined by the interaction of institutions such as courts and the legislature. MUIC states that under certain circumstances, this interaction enhances the legitimacy of a political order. In other words, the use of state force is *pro tanto* legitimate when it is produced by the right sort of institutional interaction. MUIC also maintains that this legitimacy-enhancing effect is distinctly 'legal'; it is part of what it means for the use of state force to be governed by law. To this extent, MUIC shares Dworkin's justificatory ambition. However, on the suggestion we are considering MUIC is simultaneously beholden to the sociological outlook on the law that Dworkin thought unsuited for the doctrinal concept of law. The worry is not simply that MUIC allows that the content of the law may be morally sub-optimal. Any robust natural lawyer must countenance this possibility. For instance, Dworkin distinguishes between the grounds of law, 'circumstances in which particular propositions of law should be taken to be sound or true' (Dworkin, 1998, p. 110), and the force of law, 'the relative power of any true proposition of law to justify coercion in different sort of exceptional circumstances' (ibid), as he thinks that, although normally the law on his conception comes with a moral warrant, there may be cases where, exceptionally, this warrant is defeated by overriding moral considerations. Even more pertinently, he contends that integrity, which he argues is the best articulation of the value of legality, demands that the state act in accordance with a 'plausible conception of equal concern' (ibid, p. 201), not the optimal one. So, occasional deviation from the demands of ideal justice is in principle compatible with robust natural law. Why, then, should we think of MUIC as 'turncoat natural law'? Here I shall examine two arguments to this effect. The first one is that MUIC makes a major concession to the sociological concept of law because it cannot but take as a value-free given which body is a court and which a legislature. The second is that MUIC is not really a form of robust natural law because it allows that certain facts, decisions issued by competent institutions, make a contribution to the content of the law without the proper mediation of moral considerations. Let me take each of these arguments in turn.

4.4.1 The social dimension of the joint project of governing

The first argument puts forward a variant of the criticism against Dworkin that we considered earlier, whereby interpretivism presupposes a positivist account of law. This criticism seems to have more bite against MUIC, which, after all, talks about courts and the legislature working together in the joint project of governing. Surely it must rely on a prior identification of those bodies. Remember, the planning theory of law has the resources to make that identification without reliance on political morality. What makes a body one whose decisions feed into the content of the law is that others have an intention to mesh their acts with those decisions, follow them, heed them, etc. and vice versa. That is simply a (complex) social fact. So, if MUIC is helping itself to such a criterion for identifying who counts as a partner in the joint project of governing, it tacitly puts social ontology before morality.

This argument is based on a misunderstanding. MUIC does not assume that membership in the joint project of governing is constituted by the intentions of legal officials (to carry on the project and mesh their acts with those of other officials).[17] That is not to say that MUIC looks at institutional cooperation through rose-tinted glasses, whereas planning theorists take a more realistic approach. Rather, the difference reflects the underlying disagreement between the two views on what determines the content of the law. Planning theorists take the law to consist in whatever plan a group of officials intend to pursue collectively. For MUIC a set of interlocking intentions, even if they amount to a collective agent, do not by themselves give rise to legal rights and duties; coercion does not become any more legitimate simply by being carried out by this kind of collective agent. Only a joint project of governing that is internally organized in the right way *can* give rise to legal rights and duties. Hence, according to MUIC what matters for membership in the joint project of governing is, for instance, who has the requisite moral credentials to govern or stands in the requisite moral relationship with other participants in the project so as to demand their deference and support. This sort of criterion will likely pick out different institutions from the planning theory; for one thing, it will disqualify more than a few that would count as legal under that theory.

It is no accident that MUIC is far less austere than the planning theory. Inevitably the former depends on a whole host of controversial claims about the moral importance of various institutional arrangements and the contribution they make to the legitimacy of political regimes. This has repercussions on the issue of membership in the joint project of governing. For instance, MUIC assigns weight to the acts and decisions of courts and legislatures insofar as they instantiate values like impartiality and democracy, respectively. To be precise, it assigns weight to the decisions of the institutions that instantiate the relevant values, and in the legal systems with which we are familiar courts and legislatures typically fit the bill. Conversely, if an institution does not instantiate those values, it does not count as a 'court' or a 'legislature' for MUIC, regardless of what we call it or how effective it is in securing the cooperation or acquiescence of other institutions.[18] Elsewhere I have suggested that the overarching principle of political morality that should structure the joint project of governing is the separation of powers: when the joint project of governing adheres to separation of powers, it enhances the legitimacy of the political regime.[19] On this picture, separation of powers allocates government tasks to institutions that are by virtue of their composition and position in the joint project well-suited to carry them out. In other words, it is the separation of powers – a moral principle on my rendering- and not social ontology that supplies the criterion for identifying participants in the joint project of governing. Legal interpretation will then specify the bearing on the content of the law of institutional facts regarding those participants.[20]

As we have already seen in our discussion of Dworkin, upon hearing talk of moral criteria, some legal positivists immediately cry 'foul'. They lament that the line between what the law is and what it ought to be has been crossed. However, MUIC is not an exercise in ideal political theory. Legitimacy works on actual institutions that exercise more or less effective control over a territory. What MUIC asks is what it takes for an actual institution to acquire a moral warrant to direct how coercive force may be used. When it acts with such a warrant, it affects our legal rights and duties. It may be argued that this formulation gives the game away in the sense that, for an institution to exist, we must have something like a Bratmanian collective agent in place who is constituted by the interlocking intentions of a group of people. Granted, a robust natural lawyer would deny that the social fact that such an agent has planned something is sufficient for the obtaining of legal rights and duties – the agent must possess moral credentials as well. Presumably, though, all that the positivist need demonstrate is that this kind of social fact is necessary.

My response to this line of argument mirrors the more general response that I offered in Dworkin's defense in the previous section: *Some* complex set of social facts comprising, among other things, intentions and beliefs of officials and private citizens, is undoubtedly necessary for the joint project of governing to gain a foothold in society. A sociologist may well find in the same set plenty of Bratmanian agents, too. However, it is a mistake to infer from this that the Bratmanian agents as such play a constitutive role in MUIC. According to MUIC, the contribution courts and legislatures make to the content of the law depends on the moral considerations that structure the joint project of governing; these considerations will often identify as relevant to the content of the law aspects of institutional cooperation that diverge from what this or that agent, collective or otherwise, had intended. For instance, on some occasions, they will give rise to legal rights and duties that overshoot or contradict actual intentions.

4.4.2 Turncoat natural law?

The argument we have just considered is one a positivist would more likely advance, seeking to cast doubt on the status of MUIC as an alternative to legal positivism. The second objection, which we shall examine in this section, would instead be pressed by an anti-positivist. Its thrust is that, rather than vindicate robust natural law, MUIC betrays key tenets of it.

What does the alleged betrayal consist in? MUIC insists that, by virtue of its participation in the joint project of governing, one institution, say a court, must be responsive to the acts and decisions of another such as the legislature. Sure enough, institutional responsiveness sometimes takes the form of deference. But the critic cannot mean that such deference *per se* is incompatible with the robust natural law commitment that all legal rights and duties must satisfy standards of moral legitimacy. To the extent that a duty of deference to the legislature exists, it is a moral one. Its existence depends on whether this or that aspect of the joint activity of governing, say, the assignment to the legislature of the power to shape legal rights and duties, is morally justified in the right way. Only if it is, can a legislative exercise of that power affect the content of the law including the responsibilities of other officials. In my earlier defense of MUIC, I used democracy as an illustration. I suggested that this value can furnish a general basis for the duty of judicial deference to the legislature (Kyritsis, 2008 pp. 156ff). When a state body instantiates the value of democracy, other state bodies like courts have at least a pro tanto moral reason to respect and give effect to its decisions. This example illustrates a wider point, namely that the moral merit of the joint project of governing is not judged solely at the substantive or retail level, by looking at the specific rights and duties its operation gives rise to, but also at the level of institutional design. At the latter level, we focus on the institutional system that produces them. Legitimacy demands that the system, too, meet certain moral criteria.

It may be thought that deference is incompatible with robust natural law because it allows a social fact – the legislative decision – to trump an interpretive fact. For instance, so the claim goes, it sometimes instructs a judge to enforce a statute-based right or duty, even if this would be sub-optimal from the point of view of the principles that best explain and justify the rest of the law in her jurisdiction. This claim is question-begging. It assumes a premise that MUIC can plausibly deny, namely that there is a conflict between the best interpretation of legal practice and the judicial enforcement of the statutory right or duty. However, if deference is truly morally justified, then the principles that justify it will figure in the best interpretation of legal practice and will thus be balanced alongside other principles. The judge must defer only when this course of action is mandated by this more holistic exercise. But in that case, deference would flow from the best interpretation of legal practice. Of course, someone might be skeptical that any principle can be found justifying deference. There is nothing particularly troubling about this. As noted earlier, robust natural lawyers cannot afford to be parsimonious; they must advance contested moral claims about the connection between law and legitimacy. Though deference might well fall at this hurdle, its failure would be a substantive issue; it would not signal the surreptitious influence of legal positivism.

Perhaps, then, the problem lies in that deference attributes the wrong kind of attitude to legal participants. In the standard interpretivist story, the judge assumes a Protestant attitude toward legal practice (Dworkin, 1998, p. 413). She must, we are told, exercise her independent judgment in order to figure out which principles best explain and justify it; once she has identified those, legality requires that she enforce any rights and duties that flow from them; she should not refrain from doing so out of deference to the decision of another institution, even if it is the legislature.

Understood a certain way, this objection merely repeats the one examined in the previous paragraph and fails for the same reason: For the judge to show the right attitude, she would need to take into account principles counting in favor of deference just as much as any other principle that explains and justifies legal practice. But understood in a different way, the objection makes a mistake that highlights the relative strengths of MUIC vis-à-vis other variants of robust natural law. To wit, the objection could be construed to rest on the thought that the judge must take it upon herself to second-guess every other participant in the joint project of governing in the name of the law.[21] The theory of collective action shows why this is not the case. Whatever we take law's aim to be, it is one that is served by the joint project as a whole rather than by any one participant individually. Thus, the judgments, moral and otherwise, that are for courts to make depend on their – inevitably limited-role in that project. On this picture, holding a Protestant attitude means no more than honoring the responsibility of making just these judgments.[22]

Alternatively, critics might concede that deference is in theory compatible with interpretivism but insist that it will systematically give rise to a serious tension further downstream. Here's a scenario that illustrates the tension:[23] An institution that permissibly contributes to the joint project of governing decides to *disable* another institution that also has such a warrant under the moral principle of separation of powers. This seems to be a scenario where MUIC turns in on itself. Can it be avoided? The worry relies on a very static understanding of the moral principles that determine when the joint project of governing goes well. Morality does not lock political orders into a specific institutional arrangement. Separation of powers also assigns the responsibility of changing the division of labor among participants in the joint project of governing, thus allowing for it to evolve over time. What if the institution charged with this responsibility strips another institution of its powers when there are moral considerations that count against such a course of action? This situation is no different from any other situation when the joint project makes morally suboptimal decisions. Some of those decisions (say, assigning the judicial function to officials that completely lack judicial independence) will be morally beyond the pale, as far as the separation of powers is concerned, and hence cannot be legally binding. By contrast, others will have legal effects despite their moral shortcomings because those shortcomings are compensated by the value of having a joint project of governing in good (though not infallible) working order. Whether that is so will partly depend on the moral health of the rest of the joint project of governing as well. Perhaps a barely legitimate political order can ill afford a further moral deterioration, whereas more vigorous ones can get away with the occasional lapse without losing their overall legitimacy. Still, there is nothing in MUIC that counsels complacency. A legitimate political order can die of a thousand cuts.

4.5 Conclusion

Important philosophical ideas are likely to crop up in different places and enrich different viewpoints, even conflicting ones. The same goes for the idea of a joint activity as applied to the theory of law. This makes it even more pertinent to clearly distinguish the role it plays within positivist and robust natural law frameworks such as Shapiro's planning theory and MUIC, respectively. In this chapter, I have argued that the gap between these frameworks cannot be bridged by combining the moral aim thesis and the planning theory. That would be merely to add a layer of moral aspiration to a social structure identified in a non-moral way. For MUIC, by contrast, the idea of a joint activity is thoroughly moralized. It develops a crucial moral insight, namely that under certain conditions, the fact that law is administered by institutions acting *jointly* makes an important moral difference; that fact bolsters the legitimacy of state power. The goal of a theory of law is to spell out these conditions and specify how, when these conditions are met, legal institutions contribute to the content of the law.

Notes

1. One of the abiding themes of modern legal positivism is that it draws a sharp distinction between legal officials and citizens in its account of the social practice that provides the ultimate basis of the legal system. Positivists argue that, for there to be law, such a practice must hold among legal officials but need not include citizens (Coleman, 1996, 298). For different criticisms of this distinction see Kyritsis (2015, ch 5), Postema (1982) and Taekema (2008). In what follows I restrict myself to the official world so as to facilitate the comparison between the positivist account of the joint activity of law and the moralised one that I espouse. But, unlike legal positivism, I do not place a strong metaphysical emphasis on the distinction.
2. See Coleman (2001) and Marmor (1998). *Contra* see Letsas (2014).
3. Non-robust natural law theories assign only the first role to moral considerations.
4. I appropriate here Leslie Green's phrase but mean something slightly different and more modest. Green has in mind that being governed by law carries with it inherent risks. He writes: 'There are moral risks that law's subjects are guaranteed to run, and they are risks against which law itself provides no prophylactic' (Green, 2008, p. 1054).
5. Les Green distinguishes two understandings of this type of view. One takes law to have been intended to serve a particular function. The other attributes to law the function of producing a certain consequence 'if the disposition to produce the relevant consequence figures in the best explanation of the existence or persistence' of law (Green, 1998, p. 118). Shapiro maintains that law belongs to the former category. He writes: 'The law possesses the aim that it does because high-ranking officials represent the practice as having a moral aim or aims' (Shapiro, 2011, p. 217). I am not interested here to assess this position. For criticism see Plunkett (2013).
6. For instance, the moral aim distinguishes law from 'sophisticated crime syndicates like the Japanese Yakuza and the Sicilian Mafia' (Shapiro, 2011, p. 215).
7. Several commentators have suggested that the law is different from clocks because the function of clocks is determined by the intentions of those who build them, whereas arguably the same cannot be said of law, since there is law that has not been intentionally created (Green, 1998, p. 117). Jonathan Crowe has offered a modified functionalist account of law, according to which the function of functional kinds is fixed either by the intentions of a creator or by social acceptance (Crowe, 2014). It goes beyond the purpose of this chapter to adjudicate between these two views.
8. In other places Shapiro opts for a different explanation, whereby what distinguishes law is not its aim but rather its mode of operation. According to this explanation, law is essentially an instrument, which 'like all instruments, … can be used for

good or bad purposes. When the law is used for bad purposes, it is imperative not to paper over this fact by denying the identity of the instrument doing the damage. And when the law is used for good purposes, it is important not to become complacent and assume that it is guaranteed to succeed' (Shapiro, 2011, p. 399).

9. I do not address here the question whether it is possible to attribute a moral aim to law without engaging in moral reasoning. Theorists such as Kenneth Ehrenberg claim that it is (Ehrenberg, 2009).
10. This thought does not only apply to functional kinds like clocks. According to some philosophers, for instance, it is true of the concept of belief. These philosophers claim that beliefs aim for truth in the sense that they are 'regulated for truth' both descriptively and normatively (Shah and Velleman, 2005, p. 498). In his critique of Shapiro, Plunkett speculates along similar lines that the moral aim thesis may be understood to specify success conditions of legal practice. Plunkett contends that this rendition is most congenial to Shapiro's project but expresses some doubts about its plausibility (Plunkett, 2013, pp. 568ff.).
11. Crowe distinguishes putative laws that fail this condition – and thus are not real laws – from defective laws which are not minimally adapted to law's function.
12. By zeroing in on the value-laden test for legal rights and duties, robust natural law theory, as I define it, also differs from other versions of anti-positivist legal theory. Specifically, it distances itself from the view that law admits of gradations, such that a political order or norm may be more or less 'legal' depending on how closely it approximates the moral ideals that are intrinsic to law. It falls outside the scope of this chapter to evaluate this view.
13. In Kyritsis (2018), I have examined this argument at the level of the methodology of jurisprudence.
14. This, recall, is the thrust of Dworkin's original critique of legal positivism in 'The Model of Rules' (Dworkin, 1978). According to his description the principle that no man may profit from his own wrongdoing was legally binding in New York even before the Court of Appeals decided *Riggs vs Palmer*. Dworkin used this case to illustrate his claim that what makes a standard legally binding is not its pedigree, as legal positivists would have it, but its justificatory force. Tellingly, legal positivists have responded to Dworkin's critique by seeking to expand the range of ways in which a standard can be anchored in social facts. For instance, John Gardner offers the following formulation: For legal positivism 'law is made up exclusively of norms that have been announced, practiced, invoked, enforced or otherwise engaged with by human beings acting on law's behalf' (Gardner, 2001, p. 200).
15. Mark Greenberg tries to account for this with the bindingness hypothesis: '[A] legal system is supposed to operate by arranging matters in such a way as to reliably ensure that, for every legal obligation, there is an all-things-considered moral obligation with the same content' (Greenberg, 2011, p. 84). Greenberg is careful to note that the bindingness hypothesis is not necessarily a claim about law's function, though it could be cashed out in functional terms too. The bindingness hypothesis conveys the broader idea that 'it can be part of the nature of something that does not have a function that it is supposed to have a certain property or is defective to the extent that it does not' (Ibid p. 87). In subsequent work Greenberg has put the point in a weaker form. He writes: 'On the face of it, law-creating institutions try to create binding obligations' (Greenberg, 2014, p. 1288).
16. For this qualification see Kyritsis (2015, ch 1).
17. In this respect there is a crucial philosophical difference between MUIC and the understanding of institutional cooperation animating the planning theory, which follows more closely Michael Bratman's theory of collective agency.
18. It may be objected that this formulation ignores the gradated character of the concepts of a court and a legislature. These concepts capture an ideal, which actual institutions can achieve to a lesser or higher degree; consequently, it is misguided

to focus on the question what 'counts' as a court or a legislature. Be that as it may, it does not undermine the claim I am making here. For MUIC what matters is whether the values of impartiality and democracy justify giving this or that actual institution a measure of influence over the content of the law. It is possible that the answer to this moral question is gradated: the lower a legislative institution scores, say, on democracy, the less influence it ought to have. Maybe a legislature that is not fully democratic is better than none at all, but its decisions must be taken with a pinch of salt. Or maybe, lacking sufficient democratic credentials, it must fall back on a residual justification, such as predictability, for its enduring, albeit limited, influence on the content of law. Nothing I say is incompatible with this possibility. I am grateful to Wibren van der Burg for urging me to address this objection.

19. In Kyritsis (2017, ch 2), I argue that the ideal of separation of powers should not be tethered to the traditional conception that envisages a rigid tripartite distinction of organs of government, each assigned a distinct government function. Rather, on the view I propose separation of powers should be understood, more broadly, to comprise a principle of division of labour and a principle of checks and balances, both of which can be specified in different permissible ways in different jurisdictions. Despite its flexibility, though, separation of powers sets a high bar for legal orders to clear. They must be institutionally arranged (by dividing government tasks and putting in place supervisory mechanisms) in such a way that they will reliably and systematically (though not necessarily unfailingly) act in a morally justified way. To ward off a possible misunderstanding, I should add that I am not claiming separation of powers is the master-value of law (in the way that integrity is for Dworkin), solely that it is a value that underwrites the joint project of governing in the legal systems with which we are familiar. But legal interpretation will need to invoke additional values, which cannot be subsumed under separation of powers.
20. I have distinguished the question of membership from the question of determining the content of the law. But this was done for analytical purposes. In legal interpretation the two questions are intertwined. For one thing, considerations pertaining to the former question will adjust the moral significance of institutional facts. For example, a piece of primary legislation is likely to better promote legal certainty and therefore have pro tanto more weight, morally speaking, than a decision of an administrative agency.
21. I should emphasise that I do not think Dworkin makes this mistake in his account of the Protestant attitude.
22. In fact, deference can also have the function of allocating interpretive judgments among participants in the joint project of governing. See on this issue Kyritsis (2015, pp. 120ff.).
23. I am grateful to an anonymous referee for suggesting this scenario.

References

Coleman, J. (1996). Authority and Reason. In R. George ed., *The Autonomy of Law: Essays on Legal Positivism*. Oxford: Clarendon Press, pp. 287–314.

Coleman, J. (2001). *The Practice of Principle: In Defence of a Pragmatist Approach to Legal Theory*. Oxford and New York: Oxford University Press.

Crowe, J. (2014). Law as an Artifact Kind. *Monash University Law Review*, 40, pp. 737–57.

Dworkin, R. (1978). *Taking Rights Seriously*. London: Duckworth.

Dworkin, R. (1998). *Law's Empire*. Oxford: Hart Publishing.

Dworkin, R. (2008). *Justice in Robes*. Cambridge, MA: Harvard University Press.

Ehrenberg, K. (2009). Defending the Possibility of a Neutral Functional Theory of Law. *Oxford Journal Legal Studies* 29, pp. 91–113.

Gardner, J. (2001). Legal Positivism: 5½ Myths. *American Journal of Jurisprudence* 46, pp. 199–227.

Gardner, J. (2006). Law's Aims in Law's Empire. In S. Hershovitz ed., *Exploring Law's Empire: The Jurisprudence of Ronald Dworkin*. New York: Oxford University Press, pp. 208–24.

Green, L. (1998). The Functions of Law. *Cogito* 12, pp. 117–24.

Green, L. (2008). Positivism and the Inseparability of Law and Morals. *New York University Law Review* 83, pp. 1035–58.

Greenberg, M. (2011). The Standard Picture and its Discontents. In L. Green and B. Leiter eds., *Oxford Studies in Philosophy of Law*. Oxford: Oxford University Press.

Greenberg, M. (2014). The Moral Impact Theory of Law. *Yale Law Journal* 123, pp. 1288–1342.

Kyritsis, D. (2008). What Is Good about Legal Conventionalism. *Legal Theory* 14, pp. 135–66.

Kyritsis, D. (2015). *Shared Authority: Courts and Legislatures in Legal Theory*. Oxford: Hart Publishing.

Kyritsis, D. (2017). *Where Our Protection Lies: Separation of Powers and Constitutional Review*. Oxford: Oxford University Press.

Kyritsis, D. (2018). Is Moralised Jurisprudence Redundant? In K.E. Himma, M. Jovanovic and B. Spaic eds., *Unpacking Normativity: Conceptual, Normative and Descriptive Issues*. Oxford: Hart Publishing, pp. 3–15.

Letsas, G. (2014). The DNA of Conventions. *Law and Philosophy* 33, pp. 535–71.

Marmor, A. (1998). Legal Conventionalism. *Legal Theory* 4, pp. 509–31.

Plunkett, D. (2013). Legal Positivism and the Moral Aim Thesis. *Oxford Journal Legal Studies* 33, pp. 563–605.

Postema, G. (1982). Coordination and Convention at the Foundations of Law. *Journal of Legal Studies* 11, 165–203.

Raz, J. (2009). *The Authority of Law: Essays on Law and Morality*. 2nd edition. Oxford: Oxford University Press.

Shah, N. and Velleman, J.D. (2005). Doxastic Deliberation. *Philosophical Review* 114, p. 497.

Shapiro, S. (2011). *Legality*. Cambridge, MA: Harvard University Press.

Stavropoulos, N. (2021). Legal Interpretivism. In E. Zalta ed., *Stanford Encyclopedia of Philosophy*. Available at: http://plato.stanford.edu/entries/law-interpretivist/

Taekema, S. (2008). Does the Concept of Law Need Officials? *Problema: Anuario de Filosofia y Teoria de Derecho*, pp. 157–183.

Part II

Practical reasoning and duties

5 The judicial community and team reasoning

Natalie Gold

5.1 Introduction

The legal system is a constellation of different institutions, including many where individuals make decisions or take actions as members of groups. There are courts, which have juries, and law firms; in the UK, there are barristers' chambers and professional bodies, such as the UK's Law Society and Bar Association. For some legal philosophers, there is also a deeper form of sociality that underpins the legal system. Following Hart (1961), legal positivists have argued that the foundation of the law and the source of its validity is social convention, involving widely shared patterns of behavior, attitudes and beliefs. Therefore, we should not be surprised that philosophers of law have drawn on developments in social ontology to explain the validity and practice of legal systems and the groups within them. In this chapter, I show how developments in theories of rational decision-making can help legal philosophers who are grappling with these issues, applying them to reasoning in groups and reasoning of groups.

Standard theories of rational decision-making assume that agency is vested in individuals and start with the premise that individuals act on their preferences and beliefs to achieve their goals. However, the idea that teams can be agents and that there are distinct modes of reasoning that are used by members of groups has been around for a long time (Hodgson 1967; Regan, 1980; Gilbert, 1989; Hurley, 1989; Sugden, 1993; 2003; Hollis, 1998; Bacharach, 1999; 2006). Bacharach (2006) used the tools of decision theory to formalize team reasoning to show how individuals could rationally act on a group's goals and preferences (or, for those of a less collectivist cast, their 'team-directed preferences', as per Sugden, 1993). Gold and Sugden (2007a; 2007b) show how team reasoning is a mode of practical reasoning that can account for collective intentions and shared cooperative activity, thus contributing to debates in social ontology.

There are two somewhat distinct contributions that team reasoning can offer to the philosophy of law and the study of legal systems. The first is an explanation of social practice that could inform legal positivism (reasoning in groups). The second is a theory of decision-making in groups that can inform

DOI: 10.4324/9781003242451-8

our understanding of entities in the legal system (reasoning of groups). In each case, team reasoning offers the potential to refine or improve on existing suggestions. I take these two contributions in turn in each of Part I and Part II.

In Part I, I start with Shapiro's (2002; 2011; 2014) idea that the law involves 'massively shared agency'. I will present team reasoning (Section 5.2) and show how it fulfills the desiderata for a theory of massively shared agency (Section 5.3). Some authors are skeptical about whether the law really is an instance of massively shared agency (Smith, 2006; Kutz, 2001), I will not take a stand on that issue. However, there is a benefit of knowing about team reasoning, even for them. In Part 2, I examine the implications that team reasoning has for the sort of structured 'group agents' that exist within the legal system, the paradigm example of which is a court of judges deciding a case (List & Pettit, 2011). By resolving an issue for the theory of team reasoning, namely how we should understand 'reasoning' (Section 5.4), I contrast group agents with team agency and show how my account can explain the deliberations of group agents (Section 5.5). A group agent, like a court or law firm, can be considered to be doing reasoning and even team reasoning.

PART I

According to legal positivism, the law is socially constructed: its existence, content, and authority are based on conventions and norms (Hart, 1961). Therefore, it may not be surprising that contemporary legal theorists are drawing on social ontology, the philosophical study of the nature of social entities and social phenomena. Shapiro (2002; 2011; 2014) has argued that we should think of the law as a social practice, adopting Bratman's (1992; 1993) theory of 'shared cooperative activity'. For Bratman (1992), shared cooperative activity is characterized by three features: (i) *mutual responsiveness*, each participating agent attempts to be responsive to the actions and intentions of others, (ii) *commitment to the joint activity*, each participant has an appropriate commitment to the joint activity and their mutual responsiveness is in support of that commitment and (iii) *commitment to mutual support*, each agent is committed to supporting the efforts of the other to do her part in the joint activity. Bratman then analyses the interlocking web of intentions that he takes to be sufficient for the existence of shared cooperative activity.

However, many theorists have argued that the commitments involved in Bratman's account are too strong to correctly describe the judicial community (Kutz, 2001; Smith, 2006). Even Shapiro acknowledges that Bratman's (1992; 1993) account needs to be modified. Bratman seeks to understand 'modest sociality', by which he means small-scale activities carried out by non-hierarchical groups, such as singing a duet or having a conversation together (Bratman, 2009). However, Shapiro wants to explain large-scale activities, which harness the agency of multitudes. He calls this 'massively shared agency' and as examples, he gives 'business corporations, consumer cooperatives, trade unions, research universities, philanthropic organizations, professional associations, standing armies, political parties, organized religions, governments and legal systems, not to mention the collaborative ventures made possible by the internet, such as Wikipedia, MMOG's (massively multi-member on-line games), open-access software and the World Wide Web itself' (Shapiro, 2014, p. 258). Shapiro identifies two key points of difference between modest sociality and massively shared agency. First, massively shared agency often involves imbalances of power, which may be formalized in relations of authority. Second, it cannot be assumed that all individuals taking part have the same degree of shared commitment as in small-scale activities; indeed, some of the individuals taking part may simply not be committed to the activity.

In order to accommodate authority relations, Shapiro discards the mutual support and mutual responsiveness conditions (Shapiro, 2014). However, for Bratman, mutual support and mutual responsiveness are central to an activity being a shared cooperative activity. When it is possible for each participant to do their part in the activity alone, then Bratman says that we have 'prepackaged cooperation', not shared cooperative activity (Bratman, 1992, p. 239). It follows that Shapiro is using Bratman's theory to analyze a case of pre-packaged cooperation, which—according to Bratman—ought to be out of scope. Further, in order to allow for the possibility that some of the participants who are engaged in the activity are not fully committed to it, Shapiro modifies the joint commitment condition. For Bratman, the appropriate commitments of the participants involve a 'shared intention', which is a central theme in his work. However, in Shapiro's version, massively shared agency no longer involves a shared intention, he weakens the conditions: there is a shared plan to *J*, each member of the group intentionally follows her part, members of the group resolve their conflicts about *J*-ing in a peaceful and open manner; these conditions are common knowledge; and *J* takes place in virtue of them. One might wonder how much of Bratman's account is really left!

Having said that, there is one component of Bratman's theory that remains in Shapiro's solution, which looks distinctly implausible in the case of massively shared agency, namely common knowledge. The idea that every participant knows that each other participant knows that each participant is intentionally doing her part, and so on ad infinitum (Lewis, 1969; Aumann, 1976) seems implausible in some of Shapiro's examples of structured large-scale activity and downright impossible in the unstructured examples, such as Wikipedia and open-source software. In these cases, participants may not even know the identity of others who are engaging in the activity.

Luckily, there is an alternative theory of cooperative activity that explains pre-packaged cooperation, which has variants that can cover authority relations, cases where group members are not committed to the activity and cases where participants do not know each other's identity. Bratman's archetype of pre-packaged cooperation is the sort of game theoretic model where individuals make their decisions and play their parts without communication. This suggests that accounts of cooperation from game theory might be of some interest. Classical game theory, where each individual asks separately 'What should *I* do?', has trouble explaining cooperation and coordination. Team reasoning is an extension of the standard theory, which allows teams of individuals to count as agents and for players to ask the question 'What should *we* do?' (Sugden, 1993; Bacharach, 2006). This may lead to cooperative actions: team reasoning has been used to explain cooperation and coordination (Gold & Sugden, 2007a) and it retains the connection to Bratman's shared intentions (Gold & Sugden, 2007b).

5.2 Team reasoning: A theory of cooperation and coordination

The theory of team reasoning was developed separately by Sugden (1993; 2003) and Bacharach (1999; 2006) and was connected to the literature on shared cooperative activity and collective intention by Gold and Sugden (2007a; 2007b). Its development was motivated by games of cooperation and coordination that are puzzling for orthodox game theory because they have an arguably rational solution, which a substantial number of people play in real life, whose play game theory cannot explain or predict.

One of these games is the Stag Hunt, a version of which is shown in Figure 5.1. It is based on a story told by Rousseau of two hunters who have to decide whether to hunt stag or hare. A stag has more meat but takes two to catch, whereas a hare can be caught by a single hunter acting alone. So the best outcome for each player is where they both hunt stag; the worst is to choose to hunt stag, only to find that the other player has hunted hare, so the lone stag-hunter goes without food for dinner. There are two pure-strategy Nash equilibria, (*stag, stag*) and (*hare, hare*), and (*stag, stag*) is strictly better than (*hare, hare*) for both players. It seems clear that the two players should each play *stag*. However standard game theory cannot recommend that. A Nash equilibrium involves a player maximizing her payoff given what the other player is doing. Thus it can only recommend that if a player expects the other player to play *stag*, then it is rational for her to play *stag*. However, if she expects the other player to play *hare*, then it is rational for her to play hare. What it is rational for Player 1 to do is conditional on what Player 2 does, and standard game theory gives her no reason to expect Player 2 to play *stag* rather than *hare*.

		Player 2	
		stag	*hare*
Player 1	*stag*	9, 9	0, 8
	hare	8, 0	7, 7

Figure 5.1 Stag hunt.

Game theory also has a 'refinement program', which aims to introduce criteria that can select between Nash equilibria, but this does not help. Harsanyi and Selten (1988) introduce two possible criteria, but they indicate different solutions. According to 'payoff dominance', rational players should choose the Nash equilibrium where all players receive a higher payoff than other outcomes if one exists. This recommends each player to choose *stag*. According to 'risk dominance', the players should play *hare* because it is less risky—the players would sacrifice the extra payoff from catching a stag, but they would each be certain of having something for dinner no matter what the other player does. So we have two conflicting refinements. The payoff-dominance criterion solves the problem by fiat, begging the question of why it is rational to choose the strategies that lead to the payoff dominant equilibrium. Indeed, Harsanyi (1995) abandoned the payoff-dominance principle—for more details on the argument against it that he found so convincing, see Gold and Colman (2018).

Team reasoning can explain why rational players should choose *stag* (Gold, 2012; Gold & Colman, 2018). In standard game theoretic reasoning, an individual player asks, 'what should *I* do?', and the answer is a complete strategy, roughly speaking a contingency plan, which she then carries out. Team reasoning extends the syntax of game theory to allow players to ask, 'what should *we* do?', and to select the best profile of actions for the team. Then each individual can reach the conclusion that she should choose her component of that profile. There are different modes of reasoning that players may use: they may either use standard individual reasoning or team reasoning. A player team reasons when she 'identifies' with a group, which is to say that she conceives of that group as a unit of the agency, acting as a single entity in pursuit of some single objective, and considers herself a part of it.

In the Stag Hunt game, it is clear that (*stag, stag*) would be the profile of actions that is preferred by the team so, in the simplest case, if there is common knowledge that each member group identifies and common knowledge that each member aims to maximize the team payoff function (which we should just think of as a technical way of saying that they aim to achieve the team's objective, see Gold, 2018), then each can reason that she should play *stag*, as a part of playing (*stag, stag*) (Gold & Colman, 2018). In a game with a payoff dominant equilibrium, we expect the payoff dominant profile to be preferred by the team, so team reasoning can explain why it is rational to choose the strategies that lead to the payoff dominant equilibrium. In other games of cooperation, such as the prisoner's dilemma, team reasoning can recommend cooperation if the cooperative solution is known to be the team's most preferred option. (Contra Harp (2009), there does not need to be agreement on the team utility function 'all the way down'.)

It is simplest to explain how team reasoning leads to coordination and cooperation in situations with common knowledge. However, team reasoning does not rely on common knowledge assumptions. In particular, if we relax common knowledge of group identification, then a team reasoner can take into account the risk that the other player will play *hare* (or *defect* in a prisoner's dilemma), but she does so from the perspective of the team, as I will explain in Section 5.3.

Team reasoning was first proposed as a theory of rational cooperation and coordination, but Gold and Sugden (2007b) have argued that team reasoning leads to *collective intentions*, where these are understood as mental states held by individuals, which involve a plurality of participants in a joint activity, for instance, when two singers say, 'we intend to sing a duet'. They argue that collective intentions are distinguished from individual intentions by reference to the unit of agency in the reasoning that led to the formation of the intention. A team reasoner in the stag hunt plays *stag* because the team prefers (*stag*, *stag*). Gold and Sugden show how participatory intentions of the form 'I intend to do my part' can be derived from intentions of the form 'we intend', fulfilling a desideratum of Searle (1990).

Gold and Sugden (2007b) also show how a Bratman-style analysis of a shared intention as a state of affairs that obtains when people participate in a joint activity could relate to team reasoning. Bratman (1992, p. 339) differentiates shared cooperative activity from 'pre-packaged cooperation', where agents play their roles in the joint action with no further interaction. Team reasoning looks like pre-packaged cooperation. Gold and Sugden suggest that Bratman is analyzing our disposition to reason and act as a member of a group in relation to the objective of executing some broadly defined joint activity. They identify Bratman's 'shared intentions' with high-level strategic intentions, which set the framework within which subsequent tactical (team) reasoning takes place. These strategic intentions guide the practical reasoning that leads to low-level tactical intentions, which are the individual's mental states.

5.3 Team reasoning and massively shared agency

To account for massively shared agency, we need to be able to explain situations where there is an authority figure directing the activity, where some members of the group may not be committed to the activity, and where participants do not have common knowledge. There are variants of team reasoning that can explain each of these.

5.3.1 Authority (simple direction)

Massively shared agency will often require centralized control over participants' behavior, with an authority that guides individuals' conduct. Shapiro (2014) notes that, in these cases, participants may look toward the authority to coordinate their behavior rather than taking their cues from each other.

In order to understand how the theory of team reasoning can account for such authority, we can draw on Bacharach's (2006) idea of a *choice mechanism*, a causal process that determines what people do. A *team mechanism* is one is that ensures the team's common goal is achieved (at least in the usual scheme of things, since the reasoning is always ex-ante). A team mechanism consists of three steps: computing the best profile of actions for the team, identifying the component of the profile that falls to any particular individual, and telling that individual what her component is. Then the individual agents all need to follow their instructions.

Team reasoning, as presented above, is a team mechanism which has each individual team member doing the computation, identifying her own component, and following her own instructions. However, we can imagine another team mechanism, which Bacharach (2006) called *simple direction*, where the computing, identifying, and instructing is done by one individual—the *director*—and all that the other team members need do is to follow the instruction that the director communicates to them. Provided that the team members have reason to think that the director's judgment has some validity, then each of them only needs to play their part. For instance, in the Stag Hunt, if an authority figure is working out the plan and has told each player their part is to play *stag*, and they both know that the other player knows his or her part, then that is enough to make it rational to play *stag* in order to achieve the best team outcome.

In some ways, simple direction could be considered more basic than the kind of full-blown team reasoning considered above. Bacharach (2006) says that team reasoning is basically 'do-it-yourself direction'. The important core of team reasoning as a theory of collective intention and shared cooperative activity is preserved, namely the idea of doing something because it is a part of the best plan for the team. The conditions for the simple team reasoning presented in Section 5.2 (common knowledge that each member group identifies and common knowledge that each member aims to maximize the team payoff function) can be fulfilled in situations where the members do not do any of the computing themselves. Therefore, the mechanism of simple direction is well placed to model authority relationships.

5.3.2 Commitment (restricted team reasoning)

In general, Shapiro (2014) thinks that accounts of shared agency require too much in the way of commitment from participants to account for massively shared agency. He argues that, with massively shared agency, it is implausible that every individual is committed to the same goal, calling popular accounts 'hyper-committed'—even Kutz's (2000; 2007) account of participatory intentions, which is a minimalist account of shared cooperative activity that is supposed to be suitable for large groups. Shapiro gives examples of agents who are 'alienated' from a joint activity, participating without being committed. For instance, they may fulfill their part because they are being paid and not because they are committed to realizing the shared goal.

Here, we can draw on Bacharach's (2006) variant of *restricted team reasoning*. This models the case where there is a group with an objective, but some members of the group do not group identify and will not team reason (the 'remainder'). What Shapiro calls alienation, Bacharach refers to as a 'failure to function'. In this case, the active members of the team are a strict subset of the group. A team mechanism will determine the choices of those individuals who identify with the team but will have no causal influence on the choices of the remainder. Members who team reason should do the actions that best achieve the aims of the group, given the choices of those who fail to function.

It is important for Bacharach (2006) that a team reasoner decides to do her part in the team action *because* it is her part in the best possible combination for the team. There are no restrictions on what actions the remainder take, they may turn out to be a help or a hindrance. However, even if they are helpful, the actions of the remainder are not produced by team reasoning. Therefore, according to the team reasoning account, they are not a part of any collective intention or shared cooperative activity, even if their actions appear to be directed at the same ends.

5.3.3 Common knowledge (circumspect team reasoning)

Restricted team reasoning retains the feature that team reasoners know which group members will not function and what those group members will do instead. Bacharach saw these as serious limitations, which he addressed in a variant called *circumspect team reasoning*, where he makes membership of the remainder random (Bacharach, 2006). He introduces a probability ω that any individual identifies with the group and functions, which is realized independently for each individual. The team is now the set of individuals who turn out to function. Team reasoners must work out the best team plan, given the possibility that others in the group may fail to function as team members.

Bacharach (2006) illustrates circumspect team reasoning using the prisoner's dilemma. It provides an easy case study because it is clear that the individual reasoners in the remainder should choose defect. What a team reasoner should do will depend on the relative payoffs (Gold & Sugden, 2007a; 2007b). If the group ranks 'off-diagonal' outcomes (where some members cooperate and some members defect) above the outcome where all defect, then team reasoning will tell team members to cooperate regardless. If the group ranks the outcome where all defect above the off-diagonal outcomes, then whether a team reasoner should cooperate depends on the value of ω: they cooperate if ω is high and defect if it is low. It would also be possible to apply circumspect team reasoning to Stag Hunt, but you would need to say more about a potential individual reasoner's strategic reasoning in order to solve the game.

In circumspect team reasoning, there is no common knowledge of who is functioning. This variant relaxes the assumption of common knowledge of group identity and the assumption of common knowledge about what the team is trying to do. Bacharach (2006) formalized team reasoning using game theory, which assumes that the properties of the game are common knowledge among the players; Gold and Sugden (2007a; 2007b) translated it into reasoning schema, which make the role of common knowledge more explicit. In circumspect team reasoning, common knowledge conditions are replaced by what they call 'T-conditional common knowledge', whereby group members know that *if* another group member identifies, then they know the content of the proposition. They illustrate T-conditional common knowledge with an example. Imagine a member of an organization that operates via underground cells, so members' identities are unknown to each other. If all new members are inducted by oath, which they are told is common to the whole organization, then they know that *if* someone is a member of the organization, then she knows the content of the oath. If *T* is the set of members, then the content of the oath is *T*-conditional common knowledge. But there is no common knowledge about who is a member of *T*. So in circumspect team reasoning, there is *T*-conditional common knowledge that each member aims to maximize the team payoff function: those who identify know that, if other players group identify and turn out to be team members, then they will maximize the team payoff function. But they do not know who will group identify.

Circumspect team reasoners, who do their part because it is their part in the best combination, are engaged in a cooperative activity with other circumspect team reasoners even though they do not know who the other team reasoners are. Therefore, circumspect team reasoning can explain massively shared agency in the absence of common knowledge of group membership.

In many ways, we have ended up close to Shapiro's own solution: there is a group, at least some members of which (the team) have an objective or goal (the best outcome from the point of view of the group) and a plan to achieve it (the optimal team profile). The team members may work out their part in the plan, but they may also take instructions from an authority (simple direction). There may be group members who are not participating in the plan (in which case the team members engage in restricted team reasoning). However, unlike Shapiro's account, there does not need to be common knowledge of group membership (the team members can engage in circumspect team reasoning), which seems essential for analyzing some of his examples.

There is a second interesting way in which the team reasoning account diverges from Shapiro's account of massively shared agency. For Shapiro, team members who are not committed to the group still count as a part of the shared activity. But it follows from the team reasoning account that only the members of the group who are committed to the objective (the team) are a part of the web of shared intentionality; members of the group who are not committed and do not plan to contribute are not.

This will have implications for the collective responsibility of groups and how it relates to the responsibility of their individual members. When arguing that groups have collective responsibility, a common move is that groups have collective responsibility in virtue of having shared intentions. In that case, team reasoning implies that only those who are committed to the activity bear responsibility (i.e. only those who are team members, which may not be everyone whose actions contribute to the outcome or every member of the wider group). Members who contribute to the outcome, but not for the reason that they are realizing the group plan, will not be a part of the collective responsibility. However, they may still turn out to bear some individual responsibility, either because they enable the group or because they are an accessory to the outcome. In other words, they bear responsibility because of their causal role in the outcome.

An alternative move would be to ascribe collective responsibility in virtue of being a member of the group that caused the outcome rather than in virtue of being a part of the shared intention. Such an argument might start by appealing to the individual's responsibility for choosing to become a part of the group or for not exiting the group, or to the benefits that the individual derives from being a member of the group. Then, to the extent that individuals have the possibility of making those entry and exit choices or to derive benefits, the group members might be collectively responsible—even those who were not committed to the shared activity. If we go the route of ascribing collective responsibility on the basis of group membership (and not causal contribution), then we would need to say more about how we attribute group membership since a group may not have a well-defined boundary.

PART II

In the above, I have shown how team reasoning can be useful for a theory of massively shared agency. I have not addressed the question of whether the legal system actually is an instance of massively shared agency. One might wonder whether there can really be said to be a shared objective or a shared plan. In the remainder of this chapter, I show how team reasoning is of relevance when thinking about group agents, such as courts, so it has something to offer even to legal theorists who do not believe that the legal system involves massively shared agency.

Shapiro's examples of massively shared agency encompass both structured groups that have a formal organization and procedures—such as corporations, trade unions, and universities; and unstructured groups, which are looser and informal—such as many of the ventures that people engage in over the internet, such as open source software. (NB. I do not mean to claim that this is a binary distinction, there may be a spectrum of structuredness.) Many of the entities in the legal system are structured groups, such as courts or law firms. A structured group might also be a *group agent* in List and Pettit's (2011) sense: a suitably organized collective that can be an intentional agent in its own right, over and above individual members. A three-member court is the paradigm example of a group agent. Now we might doubly wonder what the usefulness of team reasoning is to philosophers of law when they already have a theory of group agency to draw on.

So far, I have presented team reasoning without defining what I mean by reasoning, relying on the reader's intuitive idea. However, it turns out that philosophers have vastly different intuitions—and theories—about what reasoning consists of. Therefore, in what follows, I reflect on how we should understand the reasoning in theory (Section 5.4). Then, in Section 5.5, I show how this has relevance to group agents, such as law courts. I compare group agency and team reasoning, and connect the two.

5.4 How should we understand the 'reasoning' in team reasoning?

Velleman (2014, Ch. 13) criticizes philosophers for their implicit conception of practical reasoning as a time-consuming process that must occur before action. Indeed, some philosophers seem to have interpreted team reasoning as conscious reasoning, leading them to argue that team reasoning requires too much reasoning to explain collective intentions (Tuomela, 2009; Schweikard & Schmid, 2013). Since many of our everyday actions occur without conscious reasoning, if team reasoning must be done consciously, then the theory would have a restricted range of application. I have explained elsewhere why team reasoning is not necessarily conscious reasoning (Gold, 2018). I won't rehash those arguments here but, as well as those arguments, we can simply note that the basic capacity for cooperation identified above, which forms the basis for collective intentions, is to carry out one's part in a team mechanism for the reason that it is one's part in reaching the team's goal.

Nevertheless, there is still a question of how we should understand the 'reasoning' in team reasoning. It is helpful to look in more detail at Velleman's critique and his proposed solution before proposing a solution of my own.

Velleman (1989, p. 106) has also argued that reasoning does not refer to an actual conscious process: 'Of course, if we wish to discuss a person's reasoning, we must state the contents of his premises and conclusions, and we must state what logical relations he believed to obtain among them. But we shouldn't be deceived by this necessity into assuming that the reasoning under discussion consisted in similar statements rehearsed in the reasoner's head'. He thinks that we can engage in some of the activities that we associate with reflective reasoning, such as making observations and inferences 'without consciously thinking them through' (Velleman, 1985, p. 52). Therefore, for Velleman, even when an agent entertains no conscious reflective thoughts, she can still be engaged in practical reflection.

Velleman (2014) presents his own account of practical reasoning. He denies that reasoning is a mental procedure of deliberation that precedes action, which leads him to make the following two moves.

Velleman (2014, Ch. 13) denies that reasoning consists of deliberation: 'deliberation is not a mode of practical reasoning: it's a procedure ancillary to practical reasoning'. Instead, he proposes a *supervisory* conception of practical reason. In his picture, most behavior is caused by sub-agential mechanisms. It is as though we are all aircraft flying on auto-pilot, which steers us according to our desires and beliefs, and corrects course in response to feedback about progress toward the desired outcome. These functions are sub-agential automatic processes. Agential-level practical reasoning is like the pilot, who perceives and supervises these automatic processes but only rarely wrests control. However, Velleman is explicit that this does not imply that we should see our behavior as automatic or rote. Perception and supervision are types of thinking—Velleman even characterizes them as being reflective thinking. So, for Velleman, practical reasoning involves thinking, it just does not necessarily involve deliberation.

Velleman (2014) also denies that reasoning must be antecedent to action: 'practical reasoning does not necessarily precede action, much less take time in advance'. He thinks that the standard conception of practical reason—as making a plan and carrying it out—is the exception rather than the rule. Velleman (2007) notes that it is a problem for Bratman's (1987) planning conception of agency that we sometimes form intentions just before acting: if intentions are plans, then there would be no point in doing this. Instead of assisting with planning, Velleman claims that one purpose of practical reasoning is to help us come to an understanding of ourselves: he gives an epistemic account of intention, whereby the way that the agent describes her action conveys information that explains the behavior to herself. For Velleman (2014), this is another function of practical reason: In the course of supervising our stream of behavior, practical reason 'places it under action concepts'. By this, Velleman seems to mean that reason describes behavior, in the Davidsonian sense of placing our actions under an intentional description. Practical reasoning can come up with these action descriptions antecedent to, simultaneous with, or retrospective to behavior. This is not supposed to be a deliberative process even though, contra Velleman, one might think that deliberation is sometimes involved in processes of self-description and self-understanding.

Thus, Velleman (2014) distinguishes practical reasoning from deliberation antecedent to action in two ways: (a) practical reasoning consists of the supervision of a process that is already ongoing, and (b) practical reasoning consists of placing our actions under an intentional description, allowing the agent to make sense of herself. These are both agent-level activities.

Velleman's (2007; 2014) idea that practical reasoning allows us to make sense of ourselves is potentially compatible with the team reasoning account of collective intentions. A team reasoner cooperates for the reason that it is her part in reaching the team's goal. In a Velleman-type picture, team reasoning would be a particular way of rationalizing behavior; collective intentions would be a way that the agent understands her behavior—that she did an action because it was a part of the best team plan. In addition, it is worth noting that Velleman (1997) has his own account of what it is to share an intention, which is consistent with Sugden's (2003) account of mutually assured team reasoning and which draws on Gilbert's (1989) idea of a conditional commitment, whereby all the agents commit to participating in the joint action if the others do too. We can explain this using the metaphor of a country signing an international treaty, which includes among its conditions that it will come into effect only if and when it has been ratified by some number of other nations; once this condition is met, the treaty is binding on all the nations that have ratified it (Gold & Sugden, 2007a; 2007b). Similarly for a shared intention, which only comes into effect if others actually participate.

However, in the team reasoning literature, team reasoning is clearly supposed to precede action. Gold and Sugden (2007b) explicitly say that an intention is interpolated between a decision and an action—precisely the view that Velleman rejects! Bacharach (2006, p. 121f.) regarded team reasoning as a 'mental activity', which is a causal process that determines, or partially determines, choice. We can square this circle by dropping a condition that Velleman implicitly places on reasoning, namely that it is an agential-level activity.

The idea that reasoning is a sub-agential activity is compatible with the way reasoning is studied in cognitive science, artificial intelligence, and machine learning. Following Marr (1982), cognitive scientists distinguish between three different levels at which one can describe a system: the *computational* level, where the goal of the system and the logic behind its output are specified, the *algorithmic* level, which specifies the representation for the input and output, and the algorithm by which inputs are transformed into outputs, and the level of *implementation*, or how the algorithm is physically realized in the brain or whatever the hardware is. Cognitive science has abandoned the idea that people use classical logic to implement reasoning at the algorithmic level since logical inference mechanisms are too slow to model the 'automatic' information processing that is antecedent to decision. However, logic or the rules of probability are still used to provide a functional model at the computational level of the task that our mental processes are designed to perform (e.g. Jaynes, 1988; Oaksford & Chater 2007; Stenning & van Lambalgen, 2008). These rules can predict what a well-operating system will do in a specified class of tasks. Then, by observing which of those tasks it performs badly, one can learn about the unobservable algorithms that the system uses (Simon, 1969).

Team reasoning—whether represented as the probability calculus of Bacharach (1999; 2006) or the manipulation of propositions of Gold and Sugden (2007a; 2007b) or the formal logic of Sugden (2003)—should be understood as a computational level model. It models the goal of the system and the logic behind the output. The goal of the individual (the 'system') is to realize the optimal group behavior, 'what should *we* do?', as computed according to the logic of team reasoning. Therefore, the claim that team reasoning leads to collective intentions should be understood as the idea that the team goal and the logic of team reasoning underpin the behavior associated with collective intentions. When we go to Barcelona together, then we both have the goal that we go to Barcelona together and our individual actions can be described by a specific logic, the logic of team reasoning. These are different goals and a different logic from individual reasoning.

However, this picture carries no implication that the formal model represents anything that is available in conscious thought or even that it provides a correct model of algorithmic processing. When Gold and Sugden (2007a;

2007b) specify team reasoning as the manipulation of conscious propositions, we should take them to be specifying a rule of inference. This might sometimes be used consciously, but it need not be. Inference still counts as reasoning if the processing is done purely at the sub-agential level. Bacharach explicitly did not assume that people have full conscious access to their reasoning:

> 'We should not expect people to be able to identify the reasoning principles that govern their conclusions even when these principles are sound: for example, most people easily and reliably reason in accordance with modus ponens, but almost no-one can tell you that it is modus ponens that sanctions their conclusions'.
>
> (Bacharach, 2006, p. 45)

We know that people may draw the conclusions that would be mandated by the rules of logic, not only without knowing those rules but also whilst they are doing something different at a conscious level. For instance, we know from research on the Wason selection task that people are not very good at making abstract inferences using the material conditional (Wason, 1966; Wason & Shapiro, 1971). However, there is plenty of evidence that people draw the conclusions that it mandates when the inferences are presented within a more concrete context (Johnson-Laird, Legrenzi & Legrenzi 1972; Griggs & Cox, 1982; Wason & Green, 1984; Cosmides & Tooby, 1992). Although subjects' answers are in accordance with the material conditional, since they don't use the material conditional in the abstract context, it is unlikely that they consciously use it in concrete contexts—or even know what rule it is that sanctions their conclusions. The idea that much reasoning may occur at a sub-agential level is consistent with a picture where people reason in accordance with a rule without being able to specify the rule that they are following, which Polanyi (1962) called tacit 'knowing'.

If reasoning can be done by any sub-agential process, then we might worry that any goal-directed system will end up being categorized as a reasoner. That could include very simple creatures or machines. Therefore we should regard the computational-level model as a necessary but not a sufficient condition for the attribution of reasoning and look for a principled way of constraining what counts as 'reasoning'. There is no space to go into that question here (instead, see Gold, 2018), but note that there are a number of ways that we could do this by putting constraints on any of Marr's (1982) three levels. We could insist that reasoners execute non-trivial computations. We could constrain the algorithm, building on the idea that rationality is a property of information processing systems (Oaksford & Chater, 2009), and insisting on a demanding notion of processing. Or we could constrain the implementation system that physically realizes the computation.

Of particular interest is Piccinini's (2007; 2015a; 2015b) mechanistic account of the implementation system. He argues that, in order to say a system performs computations, it must be possible to describe the system in terms of its spatiotemporal components, their functions, and their organization, to the effect that the system possesses its capacities because of how its components and their functions are organized. The computation itself involves an input string, a rule for transforming it given by the mechanism's function, and an output string. This account seems to place the boundaries of what counts as a computing system in the right place, excluding many systems that we might model using computations without wanting to say that they are performing computations.

Team reasoning is a computational model, but that is not a sufficient condition for reasoning. To actually count as doing reasoning a system needs to be performing computations; one way we can understand that is that there needs to be a suitable mechanistic account of the system. I take it that this can be provided at the sub-agential level for an individual and therefore that we can understand individual reasoning as a sub-agential process that occurs before action. This account is also compatible with their sometimes being conscious processes, either at the time of action or after action, when we understand ourselves by reconstructing our reasons.

5.5 Group agents as team reasoners

Courts and law firms are examples of structured groups, which have formal organization and procedures. A structured group might also be a group agent. List and Pettit's (2011) theory of group agency was inspired by the *doctrinal paradox*, where the members of a three-member court each hold positions that are individually consistent, but the aggregate of those positions is collectively inconsistent (Kornhauser & Sager, 1986; 1993). The classic example is a civil suit for breach of contract, where the judges have to find both that there is a contract and that the defendant acted in breach of it if they are to decide that damages are due to the plaintiff. It is possible for three judges to have the following consistent positions on each of these three propositions, which are individually consistent but collectively inconsistent (see Figure 5.2). Groups can hold positions that no individual within them supports.

	Is there a contract?	**Is the defendant in breach?**	**Does the defendant owe the plaintiff damages?**
Judge 1	Y	N	N
Judge 2	N	Y	N
Judge 3	Y	Y	Y
Majority opinion	Y	Y	N

Figure 5.2 The doctrinal paradox.

The fact that we can ascribe judgments to the group without them being easily reducible to the attitudes of individuals led List and Pettit (2011) to introduce the concept of a group agent. They define an agent as an entity that exhibits the following three features: (i) representational states that depict how things are in the environment, (ii) motivational states that specify how it requires things to be in the environment and (iii) the capacity to process its representational and motivational states, leading it to intervene in the environment whenever that environment fails to match a motivating specification. In other words, the group agent can be attributed belief and desire-like states, which underpin its actions. A group agent is defined by properties that are attributed to the group, not the individual members. In addition, a group agent is the sort of institution that exists over time and being an agent also involves an impetus to *rational unity*, taking steps to ensure that its intentional attitudes are consistent with each other (Pettit, 2003). Therefore, a court is a group agent because it has appropriate mechanisms for aggregating judgments in order to come to a consistent point of view.

In contrast, team reasoning allows that groups can be agents, but all the action is at the level of the individual group members. The individual must *entify* the group, conceiving of it as a unit of agency, acting as a single entity in pursuit of some single objective, and then 'identify' as a part of it. So there is a shared goal, represented by Bacharach (2006) as a group utility function, but referred to by Sugden (1993) as the individuals' 'team-directed preferences'. All beliefs are held at the level of the team members. Team reasoning is a type of reasoning that is valid for members of a team agent to use and which is similar in structure to modes of individual practical reasoning. It is done by individuals who have the individual concept *I* and a notion of grouphood (Gold & Harbour, 2012). We can use team reasoning to explain how we can reason about what 'we want to achieve' and about what 'we should choose', given that mental states are located in individual minds.

It is consistent with this that, unlike a group agent, a team agent may be ephemeral. Team reasoning can explain one-off incidents of cooperation between groups of people who may never meet again. The existence of a team agent need not imply any metaphysical claim about the status of agents in our social ontology and team agency need not be a very thick sort of agency (Gold & Sugden, 2007b). So the theory of group agency and theories of team reasoning have different targets.

The two theories may sometimes overlap since individuals within a group agent may team reason, if they take the group to be a unit of agency and ask, 'What should we do?'. However, List and Pettit's (2011) theory of group agency is neutral about the motivations or modes of reasoning used by the individuals within group agents. The whole point of the theory is that one can attribute group agency based on the structure and processes of the group, rather than on the basis of claims about the individuals within it. It seems unlikely that individuals within courts are team reasoning, since it seems more likely that they ask themselves the question 'What does the law require?'. (Indeed, one issue with accounts of the law as an instance of massively shared agency is that it seems to be stretching things to say that there is a shared objective, except maybe in the vaguest of terms like 'achieving justice'. Is that precise enough to get the shared practice story off the ground?)

However, drawing on the discussion in Section 5.4, we might think that a group agent itself is the sort of thing that can reason. As Pettit (2001, p. 210) puts it, a group agent must 'collectivize reason'. There will be internal processes that maintain the consistency of its intentional attitudes. If these are functional mechanisms for turning inputs into outputs, then we could consider a group as computing and therefore as doing reasoning. We can think of the group's internal processes as reasoning processes. Therefore, one implication is that a group agent itself may be a locus of reasoning (Gold, 2018). The reasoning of a court is the result of sub-agential processes (namely, the individual judges in the court).

It follows from this that a group agent could also be a locus of team reasoning. A group could ask itself, 'what should *we* do?', where the *we* refers to multiple group agents. For example, a number of firms in an industry could team reason to set prices or achieve other gains from cooperation. Or a number of chambers could act together. In this case, the firm or chambers would be a group agent, which can team reason and the collection of firms or chambers a team agent.

The contrast between team agency and group agents brings us back to the options for attributing collective responsibility, set out at the end of Part I. The theory of team reasoning has implications for collective responsibility if we go the route of ascribing responsibility based on the contribution of the individuals involved. However, the theory of group agency abstracts from individual processes and could provide a basis for attributing collective responsibility on the basis of group membership (on the grounds that the group itself is reasoning), irrespective of the motivations of actions of individuals.

5.6 Conclusion

Team reasoning should be of interest to legal scholars who take a social practice view of the law and, even for those who do not, it has implications for our understanding of groups and organizations that are part of the constellation of the legal system.

For scholars who believe that the law is a social practice, team reasoning provides an account of social cooperation that does not rely on mutual responsiveness and support, and there are versions that relax common knowledge conditions. All of these are necessary if we are to account for massively shared agency in large unstructured groups. More broadly, we can apply the idea that reasoning is a sub-agential process to understand how structured group agents, such as courts, law firms and barristers' chambers, can be doing reasoning in virtue of the actions of their individual members. Team reasoning *in* groups and reasoning *by* groups correspond to two ways we could attribute collective responsibility: at the microlevel, by understanding the reasoning and intentions of the individuals who participate in collective actions, or at the macro level, by focusing on the group agent and attributing collective responsibility on the basis of group membership.

Acknowledgment

Work on this chapter was supported by funding from the European Research Council under the European Union's Seventh Framework Programme (FP/2007-2013)/ERC Grant Agreement n. 283849.

References

Aumann, R. J. (1976). Agreeing to disagree. *The Annals of Statistics*, 4(6), pp. 1236–9.

Bacharach, M. (2006). *Beyond individual choice.* Princeton: Princeton University Press.

Bacharach, M. (1999). Interactive team reasoning: A contribution to the theory of cooperation. *Research in Economics*, 53, pp. 117–47.

Bratman, M. (1987). *Intention, plans, and practical reason.* Cambridge MA: Harvard University Press.

Bratman, M. (1993). Shared intention. *Ethics*, 104, pp. 97–113.

Bratman, M. E. (1992). Shared cooperative activity. *The Philosophical Review*, 101(2), pp. 327–41.

Bratman, M. E. (2009). Modest sociality and the distinctiveness of intention. *Philosophical Studies*, 144(1), pp. 149–65.

Cosmides, L., and Tooby, J. (1992). Cognitive adaptations for social exchange. In: J. Barkow, L. Cosmides and J. Tooby, ed., *The adapted mind: Evolutionary psychology and the generation of culture.* Oxford: Oxford University Press, pp. 163–228.

Gilbert, M. (1989). *On social facts.* London: Routledge.

Gold, N. (2018). Team reasoning and spontaneous collective intentions. *Revue d'économie politique*, 128(3), pp. 333–53.

Gold, N., and Colman, A. M. (2018). Team reasoning and the rational choice of payoff-dominant outcomes in games. *Topoi*, 39(2), pp. 1–12.

Gold, N., and D. Harbour. (2012). Cognitive primitives of collective intentions: Linguistic evidence of our mental ontology. *Mind and Language*, 27, pp. 111–36.

Gold, N., and R. Sugden (2007a). Theories of team agency. In: F. Peter and S. Schmidt, eds., *Rationality and commitment.* Oxford: Oxford University Press, pp. 280–312.

Gold, N., and R. Sugden. (2007b). Collective intentions and team agency, *Journal of Philosophy*, 104, pp. 109–137.

Griggs, R. A., and Cox, J. R. (1982). The elusive thematic-materials effect in Wason's selection task. *British Journal of Psychology*, 73(3), pp. 407–20.

Harp, R. (2009). Collective Goals, Collective Reasoning, Collective Action. (Unpublished doctoral dissertation). Stanford University, California.

Harsanyi, J. (1995) "A new theory of equilibrium selection for games with complete information. *Games and Economic Behavior.* vol 8, issue 1, 91-122.

Harsanyi, J. C., and Selten, R. (1988). *A general theory of equilibrium selection in games.* Cambridge, MA: MIT Press.

Hart, H. L. A. (1961). *The concept of law.* Oxford: Clarendon law series.

Hodgson, D. H. (1967). *Consequences of utilitarianism: A study in normative ethics and legal theory.* Oxford: Clarendon Press.

Hollis, M. (1998). *Trust within reason*. Cambridge: Cambridge University Press.
Hurley, S. L. (1989). *Natural reasons: Personality and polity*. Oxford: Oxford University Press.
Jaynes, E. T. (1988). How does the brain do plausible reasoning? In: G. J. Erickson and C. R. Smith, eds., *Maximum-entropy and Bayesian methods in science and engineering*. Springer: Dordrecht, pp. 1–24.
Johnson-Laird, P. N., Legrenzi, P., and Legrenzi, M. S. (1972). Reasoning and a sense of reality. *British Journal of Psychology*, 63(3), pp. 395–400.
Kornhauser, L. A., and Sager, L. G. (1986). Unpacking the court. *Yale Law Journal*, 96, pp. 82–117.
Kornhauser, L. A., and Sager, L. G. (1993). The one and the many: Adjudication in collegial courts. *California Law Review*, 81, pp. 1–59.
Kutz, C. (2000). Acting together. *Philosophical and Phenomenological Research*, 61(1), pp. 1–31.
Kutz, C. (2001). The judicial community. *Noûs*, 35(s1), pp. 442–69.
Kutz, C. (2007). *Complicity: Ethics and law for a collective age*. Cambridge: Cambridge University Press.
Lewis, D. (1969). *Convention: A philosophical study*. Cambridge: Cambridge University Press.
List, C., and Pettit, P. (2011). *Group agency: The possibility. Design, and status of corporate agents*. Oxford: Oxford University Press.
Marr, D. (1982). *Vision: A computational approach*. New York: W.H. Freeman and Company.
Oaksford, M., and Chater, N. (2007). *Bayesian rationality: The probabilistic approach to human reasoning*. Oxford: Oxford University Press.
Oaksford, M., and Chater, N. (2009). Précis of Bayesian rationality: The probabilistic approach to human reasoning. *Behavioral and Brain Sciences*, 32(01), pp. 69–84.
Pettit, P. (2001). *A theory of freedom: From the psychology to the politics of agency*. Oxford: Oxford University Press.
Pettit, P. (2003). Groups with minds of their own. In: F. Schmitt, ed., *Socializing metaphysics*. New York: Rowan and Littlefield, pp. 167–93.
Piccinini, G. (2007). Computing mechanisms. *Philosophy of Science*, 74(4), pp. 501–26.
Piccinini, G. (2015a). Computation in physical systems. In: Edward N. Zalta, ed., *The Stanford Encyclopedia of Philosophy* (Summer 2015 Edition), [online]. Available at: <http://plato.stanford.edu/archives/sum2015/entries/computation-physicalsystems/>
Piccinini, G. (2015b). *Physical computation: A mechanistic account*. Oxford: Oxford University Press.
Polanyi, M. (1962). Tacit knowing: Its bearing on some problems of philosophy. *Reviews of Modern Physics*, 34(4), pp. 601–615.
Regan, D. H. (1980). *Utilitarianism and co-operation*. Oxford: Clarendon Press.
Schweikard, D. P., and Schmid, H. B., (2013). Collective intentionality. In: Edward N. Zalta, ed., *The Stanford Encyclopedia of Philosophy* (Summer 2013 Edition), [online]. Available at: <http://plato.stanford.edu/archives/sum2013/entries/collective-intentionality/>
Searle, J. (1990). Collective intentions and actions. In: P. Cohen, J. Morgan and M. Pollack, eds., *Intentions in communication*. Cambridge: MIT Press, pp. 401–15.
Shapiro, S. J. (2002). Law, plans, and practical reason. *Legal Theory*, 8(4), pp. 387–441.
Shapiro, S. (2011). *Legality*. Cambridge, MA: Harvard University Press.
Shapiro, S. (2014). Massively shared agency. In: M. Vargas and G. Yaffe, eds., *Rational and social agency: The philosophy of Michael Bratman*. New York: Oxford University Press, pp. 257–93.

Simon, H. A. (1969). *The sciences of the artificial.* Cambridge, MA: MIT Press.

Smith, M. N. (2006). The law as a social practice: Are shared activities at the foundations of law?. *Legal Theory*, 12(03), pp. 265–92.

Sugden, R. (1993). Thinking as a team: Toward an explanation of nonselfish behavior. *Social Philosophy and Policy*, 10, pp. 69–89.

Sugden, R. (2003). The logic of team reasoning. *Philosophical Explorations*, 6, pp. 165–81.

Stenning, K., and van Lambalgen, M. (2008). *Human reasoning and cognitive science.* Cambridge, MA: MIT Press.

Tuomela, R. (2009). Collective intentions and game theory. *Journal of Philosophy*, 106, pp. 292–300.

Velleman, J. D. (1985). Practical reflection. *The Philosophical Review*, 94(1), pp. 33–61.

Velleman, J. D. (1989). *Practical reflection.* Princeton: Princeton University Press.

Velleman, J. D. (1997). How to share an intention. *Philosophy and Phenomenological Research: A Quarterly Journal*, 57(1), pp. 29–50.

Velleman, J. D. (2007). 'What good is a will?' In: A. Leist, ed., *Action in context.* Berlin/New York: Walter de Gruyter, pp. 193–215. Reprinted as Ch. 12 in Velleman (2014).

Velleman, J. D. (2014). *The possibility of practical reason.* 2nd edition. Ann Arbor, MI: Michigan Publishing, University of Michigan Library [online]. Available at: http://dx.doi.org/10.3998/maize.13240734.0001.001

Wason, P. C. (1966). Reasoning. In: B. M. Foss, ed., *New horizons in psychology.* Harmondsworth: Penguin, pp. 135–51.

Wason, P. C., and Green, D. W. (1984). Reasoning and mental representation. *The Quarterly Journal of Experimental Psychology*, 36(4), pp. 597–610.

Wason, P. C., and Shapiro, D. (1971). Natural and contrived experience in a reasoning problem. *Quarterly Journal of Experimental Psychology*, 23, pp. 63–71.

6 "I thought we were on the same team!"

Collective duties and individual moral orientation[1]

Caroline T. Arruda

The rebuke which entitles this chapter—"I thought we were on the same team"—is common in everyday life. For example, when the lawyer working pro bono on a refugee's asylum case discovers that her co-counsel has agreed to participate *largely and primarily because* he wanted to make his resumé more attractive to potential employers, she can rightfully rebuke her co-counsel in just this way. Notice that it need not be the case that her co-counsel actively (or even by omission) lied to her about his reasons; rather, it is because his reasons did not align with hers and, in particular, that there was a mismatch between the reasons that they each weighted as most significant in their respective decisions to work on the case. Hers are moral in nature (and she understands them as such), while his are putatively instrumental (and he understands them as such). She can justifiably conclude that they did not act for *relevantly similar kinds of reasons* in what was a putatively joint or collective action and use this judgment to ground the rebuke.

This import of this type of rebuke is not fully captured by pointing to when and how it is fitting to make it. To see its broader relevance for questions about collective agency, consider another example. A group of friends agrees to participate in a relay race to help a local charity. After completing the relay, they discover that one (call him Joe) of them had agreed to participate in the relay only because he needed the motivation to return to regular exercise and training for the relay provided it. Here, the others would rightfully feel that they had not acted for relevantly similar *moral* reasons. Notice that the fact that this rebuke is fitting does not necessarily entail that they have not engaged in a joint activity; rather, it suggests that the friends *may* have deliberated differently about their respective participation in the joint activity with Joe *had they each considered* that he did not have relevantly similar reasons for running the relay.

There are many reasons that the rebukes in these cases are appropriate, including reasons that draw on a Strawsonian picture of blame or fitting attitude theories of value. My interest in this rebuke, however, does not concern these issues; rather, I would like to consider whether the potential for this kind of mismatch in what I will call "moral orientation" affects how

DOI: 10.4324/9781003242451-9

individuals deliberate *about forming a group agent to fulfill their collective moral obligations*.

Collective reasoning has received a great deal of attention (e.g., Andric, 2014; Gold & Sugden, 2007; List, 2014; List & Pettit, 2002, 2011; Pettit, 2001, 2007; Rovane, 1997, 2014). In the context of debates about collective intentionality and agency, there are a number of problems for which a theory of collective reasoning is often thought to be a solution: first, how disorganized groups can become ontologically unified such that they act together; second, how groups (particularly corporate entities) can be treated as making one, representative decision on behalf of their members; third, as providing one of the necessary conditions for treating some kinds of groups (esp. corporate entities) as collectively responsible for "their" actions (or for harms that their members, together, have brought about).

Although each of these debates captures aspects of collective reasoning, it is not clear that they are applicable to the questions raised by the phenomena with which I began this chapter. These cases raised the question of whether, in cases of collective moral obligation, the fact that individuals who care about the moral orientation of each other participating agent informs and thereby affects the way in which they (should) deliberate.[2] This question is under-explored, notwithstanding its everyday familiarity, and there are few resources in the literature that provide a ready-made answer to it.

With this in mind, my aim in this chapter is to answer this question. In section 6.1, I provide an account of the phenomenon under consideration and explain why it is relevant, although not generalizable, for understanding collective moral reasoning. In sections 6.2 and 6.3, I identify two problems that affect the way in which individuals deliberate about their collective moral obligations in contexts where they each care about "being on the same team." Contrary to our intuitions about how to solve these problems, I show that none of the standard solutions—in particular, appealing to theories of judgment aggregation or team reasoning—will solve them. This is troubling, I suggest, because it looks as though, *at least when individuals care about whether others are "on the same team" as they are,* they might lack reasons to take the means to fulfill their collective moral obligations where they *also* judge those obligations to be ones that they ought to fulfill. In section 4, I propose a partial solution to these problems, drawing on Berislav Marušić's account of commitments. I show that although we cannot find the queried reasons, we can bridge the deliberative gap by appealing to the fact that whether to morally hold one's nose to fulfill one's collective moral obligations is up to us and not settled by the extant reasons. I conclude by briefly considering the implications of this argument for evaluating the claim that individual (and, by extension, group) investment in and commitment to the law is necessary for it to create obligations of the relevant sort, often associated with Hart's (1961/2012) account of what he calls the "internal perspective" on the law.

6.1 The problem

Consider the following case:

> **A STUCK DEER AND VIRTUOUS AGENTS**: Jane, Joe, and Jill are each enjoying a spring afternoon in a distant and unpopulated corner of a wooded park on the outskirts of their rural town. They do not know one another, but they are each sitting close enough to one another to each be aware of the others' presence. Also, they each take themselves (and they are mostly correct) to be deeply morally virtuous – that is, they care that they act for the right kind of moral reasons (however these might get spelled out). Nearby, a large deer crosses the wooded area. Suddenly, the deer calls out in distress. Jane, Joe, and Jill run over to the deer, who has fallen into a sink hole and will surely die if she is not pulled out. No one is sufficiently strong to pull the deer out. What's more, the deer is struggling, and none of the three knows what to do in order to pull the deer out together without being injured. None of them has cell phone service and thus cannot contact the park rangers for help. They discuss what they ought to do, and they conclude that: (1) they morally ought to help the deer; and (2) they must divide their labors in order to do so (one person should stay with the deer while the other two should each take one of the two closest trails in order to see if they encounter someone who might be able to help or to find a location where they have cellular service).

In the above case, the nature of this obligation—to form a group or a collective agent[3]—is not my direct object of concern (see, e.g., Collins, 2013; Darby & Branscombe, 2014; Held, 1970; Isaacs, 2014; Pinkert, 2014; Rovane, 2014; Wringe, 2010, 2014). Rather, it is the model of practical deliberation by which the three individuals *each* reach this conclusion *such that they, together, intend to save the deer.* This is a pressing question for three reasons: (1) the case just described is not fully captured by explaining how each individual practically deliberates; (2) it is also not, as Rovane (1997, 2014) and Townsend (2013) each argues, covered by views about collective reasoning, given that the three are not (yet) a collective agent; (3) each participating agent should be able to count on each other agent not merely to do his or her part, but also to be what I have described earlier as being "similarly morally oriented" to fulfilling their obligation to save the deer.

Taken together, these three features suggest that this case (STUCK DEER, for short) represents an important, though not necessarily generalizable, the case for theories of collective reasoning to explain. What makes it particularly distinctive, I suggest, is (3) above. While many cases of collective reasoning in the moral domain *may* very well be fully explained by the available views of collective deliberation (e.g., team reasoning), what makes this case unusual is that the participating agents *care* that each other agent is similarly morally oriented toward fulfilling their collective duty.

While this is not a necessary feature of cases of collective deliberation *simpliciter*, I suggest that this type of case represents a familiar phenomenon in our quotidian moral lives—viz., that we want others with whom we are acting to care and be oriented toward what we are doing together in roughly similar kinds of ways. This holds in many non-moral cases. If the members of a community garden discover that one of their members has been participating in beautifying their plot of land for the sole reason of increasing the praise he receives from his neighbors for his community involvement, they would rightfully feel that they were not involved in the "same" joint activity, where part of what they aimed to do together involved the assumption that others were similarly *oriented* toward said activity. The moral case is even more common. *Ex hypothesi*, when two people engage in jointly coordinated caregiving of a sick friend, they each care that the other wants to help the friend for the reason that it will contribute to her well-being. When people say things like "I thought we were on the same team" to (morally) rebuke others with whom they were engaged in a joint activity, it is precisely this interest in a similar (moral) orientation to the joint activity that the participant is underscoring.

Here, one may doubt that anything hangs on the fact that we can make this rebuke in cases of putative collective moral obligations.[4] After all, if I am right that this question of others' moral orientation is not a necessary condition for our capacity to act together, then we can clearly fulfill our collective moral obligations whether or not we have relevantly similar moral orientations toward fulfilling it. What's more, my own individual reasons do not (or need not) change even if it turns out that others may not act on (even minimally) similar moral reasons as the ones that are weighing considerations for me.

To see why being similarly morally oriented to others *matters* nonetheless (for at least some agents some of the time), even if it does not prevent us from fulfilling our obligations, consider first the parallel with how we evaluate individuals. If we discover that a close friend (call him John) has dedicated his weekends to volunteering at a local animal shelter for the reason that he wants to make friends in his new city, we would often (and, I think, rightly) judge John to have done the right thing but for the wrong reasons. Namely, he has not acted for the reason that is *relevantly moral* (whatever the relevant moral reason might be here – e.g., promoting animals' welfare, helping a charity in need, among other possibilities). One might object here that *at least one* of his reasons is plausibly moral in nature. After all, he could have joined a pick-up basketball game to make friends, but he chose to make friends *by* promoting animals' welfare. This objection does not fully respond to the claim that John has not acted for a reason that is *relevantly* moral, given that promoting animals' welfare (*ex hypothesi*, this is a moral reason in the relevant sense of 'moral') is merely a means to the end of making friends. In this regard, the only sense in which he acted in light of his moral concern for the promotion of animals' welfare is that the promotion of animals' welfare is one of a number of available means to his end, and he chose this means over others that were readily available (e.g., the pick-up basketball game). The fact that he chose this means does not entail, however, that he takes the moral weight of promoting animals' welfare to be a reason to choose these means to his end of making friends. Finally, even if John were to choose this means, for this reason, we can cast doubt on the claim that John has acted for the reason that is *relevantly* moral by pointing out that the *primary* reason for which he acted was not the *relevantly* moral one.

The fact that these kinds of evaluations track putatively morally significant, though not necessarily decisive, features of an agent's (relationship to her) actions is relevant for the cases like STUCK DEER. This is because, barring the possibility that there is an argument that conclusively shows that collective action and agency are significantly different in kind from individual action and agency, there should be a basic analogy between the individual and collective cases. This suggests that caring about others' moral orientations is not arbitrary or groundless, even if it is not necessary for collective action; rather, the reason that caring about others' moral orientation when we act together is important is precisely because we take there to be some basic parallels between individual and collective moral action. Here the relevant feature is broadly captured by the kinds of reasons we have for undertaking our actions and the ways in which we are motivated to do so. Naturally, there is significant debate about the extent to which these features of *individual* moral action matter for the action's moral worth. My argument here does not depend on any controversial assumptions in this debate; rather, I simply contend that *to the extent* that we care about *individual* agents' reasons and motivation when they act, we also might care (analogously and *mutatis mutandis*) about individual agents' reasons and motivation *when we act in concert with them.*

In the context of STUCK DEER, the relevant but underexplored question is not simply whether we learn anything about the moral worth of the group's actions by considering the moral orientation of its members. This question is surely relevant, but it is not the question that I seek to answer in this chapter. Instead, I suggest that insofar as individual's moral orientations matter when we evaluate their actions, they might also putatively matter when and affect how we deliberate about fulfilling our collective moral obligations *with them.* In this regard, moral orientation seems to matter in the strictly[5] individual case *after*, so to speak, one has performed the action, whereas in the collective case, it (also) matters when one is deliberating about performing the action.

6.2 Deliberating about saving a STUCK DEER

Before outlining the deliberative puzzles that STUCK DEER presents, a few preparatory remarks are in order. For the sake of argument, I will assume that the three indeed have an obligation to save the deer, that it is not merely supererogatory to save the deer, and that it is an obligation that they have as a group (where the way they must fulfill this obligation is to first do their parts in forming a group agent and *then* to act as a group to save the deer). With an eye toward simplicity, I will not directly engage with the question of whether this obligation is distributive or non-distributive. Even if the obligation is understood as one that applies to each doing their respective parts, it is nonetheless the case that each participant understands that they must *come to intend* to act together or jointly.

6.2.1 Saving the deer from the perspective of jane (or Joe or Jill)

STUCK DEER raises the question of *how individuals, who each recognize their collective moral obligation, reason such that they each intend to form a group to meet this obligation.*[6] While STUCK DEER is, in one sense, a case that concerns both shared intention and group deliberation, neither of these concepts explain the deliberative position of each of the individuals in STUCK DEER. Where, then, ought we look to analyze this case?

Anne Schwenkenbecher (2019: 152) has recently argued that what she identifies as "the perspective of the moral deliberating agent who faces the kind of collective action problem, that motivates the above-mentioned views, i.e., the type of reasoning she employs when deciding how to act" is a central and underexplored aspect of theories of collective moral obligation.[7] Like Schwenkenbecher, I would like to focus on this aspect of STUCK DEER.

Note, first, that the perspective of each individual agent in STUCK DEER is symmetrical to each other agent's perspective. Second, by 'perspective,' I do not mean to pick out the phenomenology of this deliberative situation; rather, I am interested in identifying the distinctive structural features of the deliberative *position* of each participating agent. These distinctive features are fixed by the following five facts:

(a) Each agent wholeheartedly embraces that she has a collective moral obligation to save the deer.
(b) Each agent recognizes that the best and only way to do her duty is to form a group with the other agents who meet condition (a).
(c) Each agent recognizes that they are not sufficiently unified to be in a position to count as collectively reasoning, notwithstanding the fact that they are in symmetrical positions regarding the end that they each aim to achieve.
(d) Each agent recognizes that they are not yet a group agent.
(e) (A)–(d) are common knowledge among the three.

Let's consider each of these facts in turn. To begin, let's assume (a) holds, *ex hypothesi*. This is an important, albeit controversial, stipulation. I make it here because I am interested in the more robust features of the deliberative situation where agents are fully invested in fulfilling their collective moral obligations *for the reason* that it is their duty or some other comparable moral reason. By contrast, (b)–(d) are relatively uncontroversial. In STUCK DEER, each agent recognizes that she alone cannot save the deer. Moreover, each recognizes that each other agent's *coordinated* help is required (and is the best or most efficient way) for them to do so. These features of the case explain (b). Similarly, (c)–(d) would seem to be undeniable, given that each of them has not *yet* formed the intention to act with each other under conditions of common knowledge.[8]

Given these facts, we can identify two distinctive features of the deliberative position of each agent in STUCK DEER:

(1) The reasoning in which each engages to form an intention to form a group agent (such that they can fulfill their collective moral obligation) is proto-collective.
(2) It matters to each agent that others are similarly oriented toward their collective moral duty when they come to act together to save the deer.

(1) captures the sense in which each agent recognizes that the reasoning in which they will each engage to reach the conclusion that they intend to save the deer is proto-collective. Here 'proto-collective' picks out three aspects of each individual's position in STUCK DEER:

(i) Each individual's reasoning is *aimed at* a goal that they each alone cannot achieve, but that they each know they are together in a position to achieve.
(ii) Each recognizes that each other agent is positively disposed to fulfilling their moral obligation by forming a group agent.
(iii) Each must deliberate about forming their individual intentions to form a group agent in a way that is attentive to (i) such that each individual agent *both* recognizes that only she alone can form *her intention* to contribute to forming a group agent *and* that she is forming this intention in the broader context of what other potential participants will intend to do.

Given this list, (1) presents a set of problems for *modeling* the kind of deliberation in which each should engage in STUCK DEER, as I will discuss in more detail insection2.1. In contrast to (1), however, (2) presents a different kind of problem. It identifies an interest that *some* agents in *some* moral contexts have–viz., they care that others with whom they are acting are similarly morally oriented toward their collective moral duty. Each agent wants all other participants to approach saving the deer in the same (or relevantly similar) way that they do. But there are a number of ways to understand what 'being similarly morally oriented' involves, including the following:[9]

(1) **REASONS**: Agents are similarly morally oriented when they approach forming an intention to do their moral duty for relevantly similar

(though not necessarily identical) reasons, where *the way in which they understand these reasons* is either explicitly moral in nature (and the way in which they understand their moral nature is *also* relevantly similar) or, when non-moral, they bear on moral deliberation in a similar fashion.

(2) **MOTIVATION**: Agents are similarly morally oriented when they are similarly motivated to form the intention to do their moral duty, where it is sufficient, but not necessary, for agents to form the intention to do their duty just because it is their duty.[10]

(3) **DELIBERATION**: Agents are similarly morally oriented when they go through a similar process of practical deliberation, both in form and content, that concludes in the intention to fulfill one's moral duty.

In addition to being non-exhaustive, this list's items are not mutually exclusive. For example, in the individual case, it is unclear whether one is more robustly morally oriented if one has more, rather than fewer, of these. In the group case, it is unclear whether someone who, say, meets only (2) and another who meets only (1) would count as being similarly morally oriented.[11] For my purposes in this chapter, it matters only that each agent in STUCK DEER acts for broadly similar moral reasons (or [1] above).[12,13] They want each other agents to wholeheartedly intend to save the deer *for the reason that it is their moral duty to do so* (or some other comparable moral reason).[14] This is because they do not want others to simply do their duty; rather, they want others to regard their duty in a similar way as they do. It is worth noting that (1) contains the phrase "*the way in which they understand these reasons.*" This phrase is important because it avoids rendering (1) in terms that are ambiguous between two notions of acting for a reason, where the reasons can be either motivating or justifying. This phrase captures the intuition that agents count as being similarly morally oriented *as long as they take themselves to be acting for a moral reason* (even if they are not or they are wrong about whether the reasons in light of which they act are the relevant kind of moral reasons).

One may be skeptical about whether moral orientation matters at all. There is a relatively intuitive sense in which we want others with whom we are fulfilling an obligation to regard their obligation seriously and for reasons that roughly match our own. To illustrate this idea, consider the following case:

> **DOG-SITTING**: Juan, Jorge, Andrea, and Julia are old friends. Julia learns that she must undergo a complicated medical procedure, which will require a six day stay in the hospital following the procedure. The doctors have advised her that this procedure's success depends on her reducing external sources of stress and anxiety prior to the procedure. Julia has a pet dog who is both blind and deaf, and requires medicine each day for a kidney problem. She does not feel comfortable leaving the dog in a kennel, given these facts. What's more, she is deeply anxious about the dog's well-being while she is away. Knowing this, Juan, Jorge, and Andrea agree that, although no single one of them can take the dog

for the entire six day period, they can each take the dog for two days. They each do so on the grounds that they care about Julia and want to help reduce the stress around her stay in the hospital.

Broadly speaking, Juan, Jorge, and Andrea are each similarly oriented toward their collective moral obligation in the sense that they have similar kinds of concerns from which they act and they are motivated by these concerns in roughly similar kinds of ways.[15] To see why it matters, although not by conceptual or logical necessity, that the three are similarly oriented toward their collective moral duty, consider a modified version of DOG-SITTING:

> **DOG-SITTING***: Everything about DOG-SITTING holds, except that Jorge agrees to help care for Julia's dog only because he does not want Andrea and Juan to judge him for failing to help out.[16]

In DOG-SITTING*, Jorge's reasons for fulfilling his part in the collective moral obligation are different in kind from Andrea's and Juan's respective reasons. In fact, they are distinctly non-moral in nature, whereas Andrea's and Juan's respective reasons cite their duty to help Julia (or, alternatively, their duty to prevent any indirect suffering Julia may suffer as a result of being anxious about her dog's well-being prior to her surgery). These differences among their reasons do not prevent them from acting together. Nonetheless, they suggest that if we were to account for the way in which each deliberates about dog-sitting, we would need to point to the differences in their reasons to fully understand their individual deliberative process.

6.3 Why it is difficult to deliberate about saving a STUCK DEER

Taking stock of what we know from the perspective of each agent in STUCK DEER, two kinds of deliberative problems arise for each agent.

6.3.1 The proto-collective problem

As I noted above, the reasoning in which Jane, Joe, and Jill each engage to form an intention to form a group is what I called 'proto-collective.' As Rovane (1997, 2014) and Townsend (2013) each argues, the deliberative position of agents in cases like STUCK DEER is unique. It is not explained by views about collective reasoning, given that the three are not (yet) a collective agent nor are they *formally* organized around the end of forming one. At the same time, their reasoning is *also* not fully individual. This raises the following deliberative puzzle:

> **The Proto-Collective Problem**: Each participating rational agent in STUCK DEER reasons about what she ought to intend to do on the

> assumption that others will also reason about what they each ought to intend such that they *each* intend to form a group agent. They each understand their reasoning as *simultaneously* concerning what they individually intend and a deliberative question for each of them only insofar as the other participating rational agents are similarly deliberatively situated. The deliberative question is thus neither wholly individual (viz., 'What should I intend?') nor wholly collective (viz., 'What should we intend?').

At first glance, it would seem that there is no genuine deliberative problem here, given that each agent must merely form a conditional intention. Namely, I intend to ψ (here, do my part in forming a group agent) in order to contribute ϕ-ing (viz., the fulfillment of our collective moral obligation to save the deer) on the condition that others intend to do their respective parts by also ψ-ing in order to contribute to ϕ-ing.

But 'intending to do her part in forming a group agent' cannot be the content of each agent's initial intention in STUCK DEER.[17] For this to be so, the conditions for the formation of the group agent would already need to be in place.[18] The relevant deliberative question that is my focus in this chapter is how each agent (Jill, Jane, and Joe) forms the relevant intention *such that they are then* in a position to do their part in forming a group agent. They cannot simply form an intention to do their part in forming a group agent because *there is no pre-existing plan* to do so on which they can each rely. To think otherwise would be analogous to the person who intends to do her part in playing on a team in a pick-up basketball game where no explicit or implicit plan for forming a team has been made. She cannot so intend; rather, she can form an intention to be ready to play on the team *should such a team come into being.*

Here one may object that, in STUCK DEER, Jill, Jane and Joe have at least implicitly agreed to the plan to form a group agent in that they discussed a plan to each play a role in helping the deer. But this agreement *piggybacks* on their respective individual intentions to form a group agent already being in place, but they are not. In this regard, the Proto-Collective Problem affects the formation of these individual intentions, not the process by which they, together, form a group agent. Agents are not in a position to form these intentions, given that they are not individually in a position to realize the formation of a group agent on their own. More important, they are also not in a position to simply form the conditional intention to do their respective parts, given that no plan for a group agent is (yet) on the table. This stands in contrast to cases of where a pre-existing structure for collective decision-making and action is already in place, such as in the case of corporate agents.

So their respective deliberations about whether to intend to form a group agent are stuck between a rock and a hard place. On the one hand, the way they reason is proto-collective insofar as it is done against the backdrop of others' reasoning in a similar fashion. At the same time, it would be irrational to form an intention to ϕ (in this case, to form a group agent) when one cannot fully realize ϕ-ing and one cannot guarantee others' participation. In this regard, it is not clear how any of the participating agents in STUCK DEER can successfully and rationally deliberate *from* the facts about the case *to* the formation of the intention to form a group agent to save the deer.

What they can each intend, however, is to *aim* to collectivize. Here, their intentions to do their respective parts in forming a group agent are subsumed under this end, which has the relevant collective flavor to capture the proto-collective way in which they deliberate. 'Aiming' is sometimes used interchangeably with 'intending.' Here, however, I am using the latter to capture the sense in which we form specific intentions in light of ends that we can realize, whereas 'aims' are general in nature and set larger ends toward which our specific intentions contribute.[19] In this regard, there seems to be a relatively straightforward solution to the Proto-Collective Problem in that agents can aim to collectivize with others without running afoul of the constraint on intention formation that whatever one intends must be something that it is within one's power to realize.[20]

6.3.2 The moral orientation problem

The solution with which I concluded the previous section is, unfortunately, incomplete. This *would* be a solution to the Proto-Collective Problem if this problem existed in isolation. There are surely cases where it does exist in isolation, and I regard this as a solution to the Proto-Collective Problem in most cases in the neighborhood of STUCK DEER. But STUCK DEER is unique (but not singular) in that it has an additional feature—namely, that each participant cares that others are similarly morally oriented as she is. When we put this fact together with her aim to collectivize, it is unclear what reasons she has to collectivize, given that she cannot be certain that others will be similarly morally oriented to fulfilling their collective duty.

So what agents need are reasons to aim to collectivize. Surprisingly, these reasons are difficult to find. The mere fact that each of the three in STUCK DEER is wholeheartedly behind fulfilling their moral obligation to save the deer does not entail that they have the same (or even roughly similar) moral reasons. The uncertainty in STUCK DEER concerns the *kinds of reasons* in light of which the other agents will act when the time comes to fulfill their moral duty. Notice that this does not mean that agents have sufficient reason to doubt that others will form an intention to do their parts in forming a group agent; rather, the problem is that agents want others to approach the formation of the intention (and their broader moral obligation) with a particular kind of moral orientation. Recall that, as I showed in section 6.1, we typically (although not by necessity) want others to be similarly morally oriented as we are to our collective duty. But none of the agents can be reasonably certain that the others will be similarly morally oriented to forming a group agent. What's more, they each have at least equally good reason to think that they may not be similarly morally oriented. Although they all seem to agree that they should save the deer, none has expressed what reasons he or she has for doing so. The fact that each wholeheartedly embraces *that she has a moral duty to save the deer* is not sufficient. In fact, one could wholeheartedly embrace this duty but act from decidedly *a* moral or even immoral reasons when it comes to time to do one's part in fulfilling it.[21]

The possibility that others will act with decidedly different (viz., not relevantly similar) moral orientations is deliberatively relevant for each agent in STUCK DEER. Jane (or Joe or Jill) judges that she might feel regret if she were to act with the others as a group *agent should it turn out that* the others are not similarly morally oriented as she is to the fulfillment of their collective moral duty. My interest here, however, is not how to account for the possibility of regret in ordering their preferences in STUCK DEER, as some decision theorists would contend;[22] rather, I am interested in whether agents' judgments that they may feel regret affects their decision to adopt the aim to collectivize.[23,24]

Each agent is stuck in the following deliberative bind regarding whether to adopt the aim of collectivizing:

> **The Moral Orientation Problem:** Each agent in STUCK DEER makes the following, incommensurable judgments: (1) They each judge that they care about others being similarly morally oriented; (2) They each judge that they cannot guarantee that others will be similarly morally oriented to fulfilling their collective moral obligation to save the deer; (3) They each judge that they may regret having acted with others should they discover, after the fact, that either or both of the other participating agents did not have relevantly similar moral orientations when doing their parts in meeting their collective moral obligation; (4) They each judge that they have a collective obligation to save the deer that is not outweighed by their possible regret as described in (3).[25]

Given these four judgments, each agent in STUCK DEER is in a deliberative bind. She lacks sufficient reasons to aim to collectivize with others, given that she cares that they are each similarly morally oriented toward the fulfillment of their collective moral duty. Moreover, the possibility for regret should she discover that others turned out not to have a similar moral orientation as she had further constrains her ability to wholeheartedly embrace the aim to collectivize. At the same time, she recognizes that she ought, all things considered, do her part to save the deer and that the possibility for regret does not override this fact.[26] Where, then, can she find a solution for her deliberative bind?

Here, one might object that (4) clearly solves the deliberative bind, both objectively and by the individual agent's own lights. It is a moral obligation to save the deer and aiming to collectivize is a necessary condition for fulfilling this obligation, so each ought to adopt this aim. To capture the deliberative import of (3) and to show why it is reasonable to grant that it has this import such that it is not overridden by (4), consider Elizabeth Harman's (2009: 193) description of the effect of the potential for regret on practical reasoning:

> The cases I have discussed all involve a reasonable *attachment* which makes a preference reasonable although it would otherwise be unreasonable. The kind of case that would exhibit the reverse phenomenon would involve a reasonable *aversion* which would make a preference reasonable although it would otherwise be unreasonable. I leave open whether such reasonable aversions exist. If reasonable aversions do exist, then there could be a case with the following features. An agent ought to perform an action A, and things would be better in all the ways the agent should care about if she performs A, but if she performs A she will reasonably regret having done so (she will have a reasonable aversion); furthermore, if she does not perform A, she will reasonably be glad she didn't (she will have a reasonable attachment), although she ought to have performed A and A would have been optimal.

STUCK DEER is just one of these latter cases. Each agent's judgment about the possibility for regret renders reasonable their respective preferences for not performing a morally required action, and yet they each ought to adopt the aim of collectivizing in order to fulfill their collective obligation to save the deer.[27] So it is possible that it is reasonable both to regret ϕ-ing *and* yet also to regard ϕ-ing as something that one ought to do.[28] Although this is beyond the purview of Harman's argument, we might add that the case of STUCK DEER establishes why this combination of claims produces a deliberative bind when agents assent to the claim that they ought nonetheless to perform the action in question.

So what solutions are there to the Moral Orientation Problem, where a 'solution' constitutes settling the deliberative bind? One possible approach to this problem is to appeal to the common knowledge condition. Here, the idea is that each agent in STUCK DEER knows that the others know (and that they know that they know, and so on) that they will each do their respective parts in forming a group agent *such that* they will fulfill their moral obligation to save the deer. Is this sufficient? Unfortunately, it is not.[29]

First, although the common knowledge condition does provide reasons (Arruda, 2015), it only provides instrumental reasons for agents to aim to collectivize. Namely, on the basis of common knowledge, agents can form the aim to collectivize were they only in need of assurance about how others will *act*. But what agents in STUCK DEER (and, I contend, many quotidian moral scenarios) need is assurance that others will be similarly morally oriented toward their actions. Common knowledge does not range over agents' moral orientation. Thus agents cannot appeal to it to aim to collectivize.

Second, individual moral agents may turn out to be motivationally apathetic or simply unmoved by the right reasons to meet their moral obligations (and instead moved by other reasons), all the while granting that they do indeed have such an obligation and ought to take the means to fulfill it.[30] Thus, pointing to the fact that they wholeheartedly embrace their moral obligation to save the deer and that this fact is common knowledge among them will not solve this problem. After all, one can wholeheartedly embrace one's moral obligation to keep one's promise to help one's friend tidy his garden, but only keep the promise out of fear about the reputational repercussions that one would suffer if one were to break it. Given that individuals in STUCK DEER might be potentially unmoved in these particular ways or they might be moved by decidedly non-moral reasons, no agent can count on the others to intend to form the group to fulfill their collective moral duty *with the same (or a relevantly similar) moral orientation as she has.*

For related reasons, appealing to team reasoning (Gold & Sugden, 2007; Petersson, 2017) will also be insufficient to solve the Moral Orientation Problem. Team reasoning is intended to explain how agents can reason (typically, about utility maximization) not with reference to their own individual interests but rather from the perspective of the group's interests (where the idea is that ranking choices from the perspective of the interests of the group *as such* will maximize individual utility in cases such as the Prisoner's Dilemma). Gold and Sugden (2007: 122) describe the goal of theories of team reasoning in just these terms: "Theories of team agency try to reformulate game theory in such a way that 'What should we do?' is a meaningful question. The basic idea is that, when an individual reasons as a member of a team, she considers which combination of actions by members of the team would best promote the team's objective, and then performs her part of that combination." The Moral Orientation Problem does not directly concern the team's objective of fulfilling their collective duty; rather, it concerns *in what way* they will go about doing so and *in light of which (kinds of) reasons* they will each perform their part. Thus, team reasoning, if it is useful in any way for cases like STUCK DEER, targets a different aspect of cases like STUCK DEER than the Moral Orientation Problem picks out.[31]

It seems, then, that the traditional places to look to solve the Moral Orientation Problem in cases like STUCK DEER have not provided the relevant reasons to aim to collectivize. If this is right, then the agents in STUCK DEER are in a deliberative bind.

6.4 A partial solution: Individual commitments to be hopeful agents

In this section, I will lay out a partial solution to the Moral Orientation Problem, but it is noteworthy that the solution requires that we take seriously the fact that there are no obvious sources of reasons to solve this deliberative bind. With this idea in mind, let us first consider two seeming solutions that require embracing the absence of reasons to solve this problem.

A natural, but ultimately unsuccessful, solution to this deliberative problem is that we often have to "hold our noses," so to speak, when fulfilling what are putatively collective moral obligations and when we cannot guarantee how others will be motivated. Of course, this is an option, and we might be willing to ignore (or significantly downgrade) the extent to which we care about others being similarly morally oriented. But this is not a solution to the problem at hand; rather, we want to know whether we can find reasons to collectivize, holding stable our care for others' moral orientations and judging that we are not willing to forgo the fulfillment of our collective moral duty to save the deer. The idea of "holding one's nose" solves the deliberative problem only if one has already decided there are reasons to ignore or bracket the fact that one cares about others' moral orientations toward saving the stuck deer.

A second possible response is that we can rely on our knowledge of others' past actions and character to mitigate the potential for regret. This does not provide reasons to aim to collectivize, but it does lower the deliberative barriers to adopting this aim. Given that Joe, Jane and Jill in STUCK DEER do not know one another, this may not directly solve the problem in STUCK DEER. Still, it solves the problem, it would seem, in many cases *similar to* STUCK DEER. Unfortunately, this solution is, at best, only partial. We are often in situations in which others' moral orientation surprises us, where their moral orientations are mixed (they involve a combination of equally weighted reasons), where others' reasons are both moral and non-moral in nature, or where their motivation is not always clear to them. Whether or not this happens more or less frequently when we know the people in question well is an empirical matter that I cannot resolve here; however, just insofar as it is not uncommon to be mistaken about or surprised by *our own* motivations or reasons, it is not uncommon to be mistaken about or surprised by others' motivations or reasons for what they do.[32] Thus, appealing to how well we know others to solve the Moral Orientation Problem is, at best, a partial solution. It cannot definitively alleviate the potential regret we might feel having discovered that others did not share our moral orientation toward doing our collective moral duty.

What, then, is left? From the perspective of the available reasons, it is entirely up to each of them whether to aim to collectivize. Given the above four judgments, however, each agent is disposed toward working to fulfill their collective moral duty, notwithstanding the potential for regret. This is because they (correctly) judge that STUCK DEER is not a case in which it is equally permissible to aim or not to aim to collectivize. What they need, however, is a way around the potential for regret that does not simply require that they simply disregard, without reason (or on a whim), their care for how others are morally oriented toward their duty.

Given the deliberative situation of each agent as well as their respective set of judgments, there is a way to provide the grounds for them to aim to collectivize. Surprisingly, however, these grounds do not come in the form of the queried *reasons* to adopt the aim of collectivizing. To see where we might find them, consider Berislav Marušić's (2015) account of the source of reasons when matters are up to us:

> The core idea [...] is that as agents, when thinking about matters that are up to us, we have a different view about what we will do than we have in thinking about matters that are not up to us. Our view of what we will do, when matters are up to us, is made rational by our practical reasons; in contrast, our view of what will happen, when matters are not up to us, is made rational by our evidence ....
>
> (2015: 123)

Marušić is interested in showing why it is rational to, for example, commit oneself to one's partner for life, notwithstanding the statistics about the likelihood of divorce. Making and keeping this commitment is "made rational" by the practical reasons we have to care about our relationship, even given the evidence that we are unlikely to be successful. This is because it is up to us what we *do in fact commit ourselves to do*, notwithstanding the evidence of what we are *likely to do*. In committing ourselves in this way, Marušić thinks, we can will to do things "against the evidence" because we can be the source of reasons for forming the aforementioned commitments. Notably, we are, on his view, doing what counts as rational (given that *we* are the source of our practical reasons). His account does not directly apply to cases like STUCK DEER, given that it is not entirely up to each agent whether reasons favor fulfilling her moral obligations. Nonetheless, aspects of his argument apply to the case at hand.[33] In STUCK DEER, what is up to each agent is whether to take seriously the possibility for regret, so much so that she is unable to do her part in fulfilling the moral obligation of saving the deer. In this regard, the question is *not* whether there are evidentiary considerations that will settle the matter for agents such that they know *when* a practical matter is up to them (as STUCK DEER is not directly analogous to the case of marriage); rather, the question is *whether* they take seriously the possibility of regret, which they take as having at least pro tanto significance, as the source of the weightier reasons.

So how does this view help us understand the agents in STUCK DEER? They cannot simply bracket the possibility of regret. This is because the object of that regret—an outcome where they have acted with others and yet they turn out not to share the same moral orientation—will *still have significance for the agent* even if it does not determine what she does. Rather, they need a way to understand what they are going to do as consistent with the possibility of regret but to license downgrading the sense in which this possibility has deliberative significance. On Marušić's view, it is the distinctive function of practical, rather than theoretical, reasons to make the formation of these commitments not only possible but also not irrational. It is clear that such reasons exist in the case of committing oneself to one's partner. After all, it is "up to us" whether we do indeed make (and, to some degree, fulfill) this commitment, in Marušić's (2015: 14) sense of the phrase. If such reasons exist in cases like STUCK DEER, Joe, Jill and Jane can each form Marušić-style commitments to adopt the aim of collectivizing.

But do such practical reasons exist in cases like STUCK DEER? At first glance, it would seem that they do not, given the fact that it is not entirely up to each agent whether to adopt the aim to collectivize. Here, however, it depends on what the sufficient conditions are for something to be "up to us" in the relevant sense. For Marušić (2015: 98), things are "up to us" for the followings sense:

> [S]ince in virtue of being agents, we enjoy the privilege of settling the question of what we will do by considering our practical reasons, it follows that we enjoy the privilege of believing that we will do something on the basis of practical reasons—and this even when we have evidence that there is a significant chance that we won't do it.

Marušić's point is a general one about agency rather than an explanation of the sufficient conditions for a particular case to be one in which specific deliberative matters are genuinely "up to us." Whether he is right about this general point is beyond the purview of this chapter; rather, my interest here is to identify a working account of the sufficient conditions for a deliberative matter to be "up to us."[34]

For a specific deliberative instance to be "up to us," it must minimally be the case that the balance of reasons does not settle the deliberative questions for us.[35] With this in mind, here is a plausible working definition:

> **UP TO US:** Whether to ϕ is up to us when, at least, the set of available agent-neutral reasons to ϕ are insufficient to override reasons against ϕ-ing but for which the agent-neutral reasons not to ϕ are not decisive and for which we have an independent (agent-relative or agent-neutral) interest in ϕ-ing.

I use the characterization of reasons as agent-neutral or -relative to emphasize what it means for agents' decisions to be fully "up to them" (in the sense that the agent-neutral reasons do not settle the matter) and yet for the agent to be responsive to some set of reasons that the agent correctly treats as deliberatively significant (though not conclusive). UP TO US has the advantage of accounting for many of the cases Marušić discusses, such as the commitment to one's partner. It also provides sufficient conditions for determining whether some *specific* deliberative matter is "up to us." Our relationship with our practical reasons, captured by our interest in ϕ-ing, makes the relevant deliberative difference when the agent-neutral reasons do not independently settle the matter.

With this working definition in place, let's return to STUCK DEER. One way of understanding the deliberative problem that the Moral

Orientation Problem presents is in terms of the available agent-neutral reasons to adopt the aim of collectivizing. Here the reasons are split between those that favor adopting it, given that it is a condition for fulfilling the collective obligation to save the deer *and* those that concern the possibility for regret. These reasons do not settle the matter at hand either for or against adopting the aim of collectivizing. Here, one might object that the fact that saving the deer is morally required *does* settle the matter of whether to do so, given that adopting this aim is instrumentally required to fulfill this collective obligation. Recall, however, that the matter at hand is whether to adopt the aim of collectivizing. This will not work to solve the problem at hand, given that agents cannot individually intend to save the deer, in that saving the deer is understood as something that they will undertake together. So the relevant intention for which adopting the aim of collectivizing *could be* instrumentally required is the intention to do one's part (in acting collectively to save the deer). But this is not instrumentally required, given that agents must first have independent reasons to adopt the aim in question.

I have suggested that the agent-neutral reasons to adopt this aim are not decisive but that agents in STUCK DEER care independently about fulfilling their moral duty to save the deer and do not regard the possibility for regret as outweighing this duty. In this regard, it is *up to each of them*, in the sense outlined above, whether to adopt this aim.

In that it is *up to each of them,* then, they can each adopt the aim to collectivize by deciding to disregard (or, at least, give less deliberative weight to) the possibility for regret. They do so by self-consciously choosing to give more deliberative weight to the importance of fulfilling their moral obligation to save the deer. This is the sense in which their practical reasons "make rational," as Marušić (2015) describes it, their judgment to downgrade the deliberative import of regret, notwithstanding the fact that they may even take it to be likely that they will suffer regret.

That this decision to adopt the aim is *rational* (or, at least, responsive to reasons) is important because it shows how: (a) each agent can come to adopt the relevant aim to collectivize such that they can then form the intention to do their parts; and (b) in adopting the aim, they are not simply acting on a whim.

6.5 Conclusion

The solution I have presented generalizes to other cases of collective moral duties where agents care about the moral orientation of other participants. This matters because, as I have contended, caring about whether others are "on the same team" is a commonplace feature of our moral lives. If what I have argued is correct, it affects the extent to which agents can settle whether to do their parts in fulfilling a collective moral obligation by appealing to extant, agent-neutral reasons alone. At the same time, my argument suggests that, in at least some cases of putative collective moral obligation, it is the will of participating agents that settles the deliberative matter at hand.

Notably, my argument has not fully addressed the question of *why* agents being "on the same team" is independently morally valuable.[36] Although my argument does not depend on doing so, the beginnings of a promising argument can be found in my claim in section 6.1 that there is a basic analogy to be drawn between the role individual agents' reasons play in determining the moral worth of their actions and the role they play in the moral worth of collective intentional action.

While much more can be said about this issue in the *moral* domain, it is often, albeit implicitly, thought to be an essential feature of the legal domain. The most (in)famous example is H.L.A. Hart's (1961/2012) account of what he calls the "internal perspective" on the law,[37] according to which one necessary condition for laws to create binding obligations is whether the individuals to whom they apply can adopt a perspective on those rules as those that rightfully apply to them. Interestingly enough, however, Hart (1961/2012: 57) denies that this "perspective" is a feeling that agents have:

> The internal aspect of rules is often misrepresented as a mere matter of "feelings" in contrast to externally observable physical behaviour [...] There is no contradiction in saying that people accept certain rules but experience no such feelings of compulsion. What is necessary is that there should be a critical reflective attitude to certain patterns of behaviour as a common standard, and that this should display itself in criticism (including self-criticism), demands for conformity, and in acknowledgements that such criticisms and demands are justified, all of which find their characteristic expression in the normative terminology of 'ought,' 'must,' and 'should,' 'right' and 'wrong.'

So, on Hart's view, the law requires as one of its necessary conditions that we are invested in, among other things, the relevant sort of *reasons* and *reasoning* in which rational agents (including ourselves) might engage when demanding conformity to the law or criticizing failures to do so. Extending this basic idea, one might think that this "perspective" allows individuals to be invested in the relevant way in the laws themselves in that it provides access to the reasons one has to adhere to them. Presumably, if such a "perspective" is unavailable to agents, then there is a question about whether the law is a good one or, at least, whether one should take there to be reasons to conform to it.

Given this gloss on Hart's account, one might be tempted to suggest that there is a rough parallel between what I have called 'moral orientation' in this chapter and the ways in which we must be invested in the law for it to have purchase on us. First, this parallel seems particularly apt given Hart's claim that part of our "internal" perspective on the law is our ability to understand and take seriously rebukes for failing to adhere to the law as well as praise for conforming to it as grounded in a pattern of good reasoning and genuinely good reasons. Second, as Joseph Raz (2009: 154–155) notes, this way of understanding the law does not require that agents do in fact act for these reasons when they act in conformity with the law; rather, they must simply be in a position to access and be relevantly invested in these reasons. This feature of the Hartian picture looks surprisingly similar to what I have said about the import of moral orientation in collective moral duty. In the latter case, while we care and are likely genuinely invested in others (and ourselves) doing our duties for the right kinds of moral reasons, this is not required for us to actually successfully realize those duties, be they collective or individual.

These parallels, however, are superficial. As noted above, Hart seemed to think that the availability of this "perspective" was *a necessary condition* for the law to have appropriate purchase on us (or to establish genuine obligations to uphold it). If this is right (or if a weaker version of the claim holds—e.g., we get a certain amount of social cohesion from agents' investment in the law or perhaps we have fewer free-riders), then this would suggest a fundamental (and surprising) *disanalogy* between the moral and the legal domains. Why? My suggestion in this chapter has been that the ways in which we care about how others act has more to do with our concern for acting for the right reasons rather than as a necessary condition for a genuinely collective enterprise (including the arguably collective enterprise that is the law). If this is right, then this suggests that we can separate the questions of *investment in* moral and legal duties from the question of how to establish the grounds for mutual conformity to them.

Notes

1. I would like to thank Teresa Marques, Chiara Valenti, and an anonymous referee for their invaluable comments, and Caitlin Fitchett, Olle Blomberg, Stephanie Collins, Katie Steele, Kimberley Brownlee, Saba Bazargan-Forward, Sara Rachel Chant, Abe Roth, Herlinde Pauer-Studer and Geoff Sayre-McCord for invaluable discussions about the core argument I make in this chapter.
2. For one view about individual reasoning about collective moral obligation, see MacMahon (2003).
3. Which one it is will depend on one's view about the metaphysics of collective agency.
4. Thanks to Katie Steele for encouraging me to draw a comparison with the individual case to determine what we gain or lose when we are not on the "same team."
5. I say 'strictly' because there is a sense in which the deliberation in STUCK DEER is individual but has a collective upshot, whereas the case of John above has no collective upshot.
6. Collins (2013) call this a "collectivisation duty."
7. Here we can see a parallel with Petersson's (2017) suggestion that neither team-reasoning nor reasoning in the "we-mode" captures what he calls the "we perspective."
8. It is worth noting, however, that many accounts of shared agency do not emphasize this feature of the deliberative situation in part because they do not think of these cases as they unfold over time. But to fully answer the question of how each agent deliberates *such that* she comes to form an intention to act with the others in STUCK DEER, we must pay careful attention to it.

9. This list applies to the case of group action or joint action under conditions of common knowledge. It does not cover cases where we form nebulous plans with others (particularly those that are long term) or cases where we are worried about own moral orientation over time.
10. This would be a judgment internalist's take on what this type of similar moral orientation is, but, as I emphasize above, this is merely sufficient for being similarly morally oriented.
11. I explore this issue in my working paper "Moral Orientation."
12. (2) is outside of the purview of this chapter, given that it is unclear whether one's motivation to form a group agent has any bearing on one's understanding of one's (collective) moral duty. This is because is unclear whether individual participants in a joint action could be similarly motivated in the kind of way that would be relevant for understanding either cases like STUCK DEER or joint action more generally. This is because the kind of similar motivation that would be relevant in these contexts would be that over which agents can exercise the relevant control. It would be too demanding a picture of the relationship between group moral orientation and collective obligation to suggest that the participants need to be motivated in roughly similar ways (e.g., Monica and Moises need to each be motivated to ϕ, à la the judgment internalist, by the mere fact that they rightly judge themselves to have a moral to ϕ). This is because it is not clear, first, that agents have the relevant kind of control over what motivates them. Second, even if they did, it is not clear what it would add to cases like STUCK DEER, given that how they are *each* motivated to act is a purely individual matter. By contrast, the question of the reasons in light of which they each act is *both* an individual matter *and* a collective, distributive matter given that their reasons bear on how they understand the collective duty in question and how they might go about fulfilling it with other members of the group. One might even be tempted to think that having roughly similar reasons for acting matters for achieving the relevant kind of deliberative unity often thought to matter, *mutatis mutandis*, for both corporate and non-corporate group agents.

    Notwithstanding this last point, (3) in the list above is also outside the purview of this chapter, albeit for different reasons. Cases like STUCK DEER are, I show below, distinct precisely because they involve agents reasoning in what I have called "proto-collective" ways. In this regard, their reasoning about their collective moral duty *is* similar in that they each take themselves to indeed have a moral duty to save the deer and they each recognize that they can fulfill it only by forming a group agent. By contrast, (3) does not concern the deliberative process that concludes in the formation of *instrumentally required* intentions to meet one's moral duty; rather, it concerns the deliberative process by which one forms the direct intention to do the action that is one's moral duty.
13. It might be that each of these forms of moral orientation matter in different moral contexts. My contention is that, in STUCK DEER, it is (1).
14. So moral orientation to their collective duty can involve how one understands one duty, one's reasons for doing one's duty, *that* one has a specific moral duty to ϕ and this is a reason to ϕ, among other options. Given space constraints, I cannot explore this issue further here, but I do so in Arruda (working paper).
15. For simplicity's sake, I assume that it is not merely supererogatory for them to care for the dog.
16. See Salomone (forthcoming) for a discussion of the possibility that agents sharing intentions might fail to cooperate in the right kind of way notwithstanding the fact that they count as sharing an intention. I am interested in a different phenomenon—namely, the kinds of reasons and orientations that agents can bring to a to-be-jointly-intended activity but for which they do not yet share an intention. Nonetheless, I think his argument highlights the role that similar orientation to what one does with others matters.

17. See Collins (2013: 232) for a related discussion that is grounded in the question of whether the duty is distributive.
18. For a competing view of how to understand the position of each agent in STUCK DEER, see Collins (2013: 244–245, 247). Collins is interested in cases where we can (and ought to) induce others to comply with their respective "collectivisation duties." More important, Collins' aim is to show how, in cases like STUCK DEER, it is appropriate to talk (however loosely) of collective moral duties. On her view, it is only appropriate when either a clear group decision-making procedure exists such that there is a collective to whom the duty applies or when the individuals have what she calls "collectivisation duties." I am interested in a conceptually nearby, but non-equivalent, phenomenon—namely, cases where we are not in a position to rely on a group decision-making procedure so we must map a clear (individual) deliberative path to fulfilling what is a collective moral duty. I take it for granted that they do have something akin to what Collins calls "collectivisation duties" in STUCK DEER.
19. See Wedgwood (2002) and Gibbard (2008) for discussions of our capacity to formulate general aims.
20. For an alternative solution, see Collins (2013: esp. Section 2).
21. See Peter (2018: 63–66) for a discussion of how a related kind of uncertainty affects our own ability to form intentions to act (where we form intentions under the guise of the good).
22. On this issue, see, e.g., Arntzenius (2008) and Joyce (2012). There is an extensive literature on regret, some of which dovetails with the potential for regret I discuss above and which, due to space constraints, I cannot discuss in detail here. See, in particular, Bagnoli (2016), Bratman (2014), Wallace (2014), and Andreou (2014).
23. For a related set of concerns, see Bagnoli (2016: 765–766), Bagnoli (2000: 174), and Wallace (2014).
24. For an account of how to explain individuals' respective moral duties to collectivize in cases where moral orientation does not matter, see Collins (2013: 233-ff, esp. 238–239).
25. The regret may be minor or significant, depending on the specific way that others turn out to be morally oriented (e.g., if one of the participants acts for particularly morally objectionable reasons) and on whether meeting the moral duty in question does outweigh the fact that they have acted in concert with others who acted for morally objectionable reasons.
26. Note that this fact is important because it distinguishes the deliberative situation in STUCK DEER from standard cases of prediction about regret. Some take it to be irrational to willfully do something we (reliably) predict we will come to regret. See, in particular, Arntzenius (2008) and Joyce (2012).
27. One might object that my account of the case of STUCK DEER requires that we take there to be reasonable aversions, given that each of the three in STUCK DEER are supposed to regard their trepidation to intend to act with one another as reasonable. There are two ways to understand this objection, and two corresponding lines of response. First, one might take this objection to amount to the claim that is putatively reasonable in that they have some *pro tanto* reason to care about others' moral orientation toward saving the deer. If this is the objection, it is simple to answer it. The agents can (and perhaps should) override this reason by favoring the weightier ones. Second, consider a stronger reading of this objection: namely, these aversions are reasonable, and it makes sense to favor them. While I think that we can show that some aversions are, on their own, reasonable in this way by, say, appealing to the weights of different kinds of reasons (viz., agent-relative and agent-neutral), space constraints prevent me from laying it out here. All that my argument in this chapter requires is that the following, more modest claim be true: viz., it is possible to have a combination of attitudes that looks

prima facie irrational—namely, to judge that one might reasonably regret ϕ-ing *and also* for ϕ-ing to be something that one ought to do–and yet for there to be no obvious logical problem in holding both at the same time. The problem in STUCK DEER is to how to decide what to do, given that one can hold both of these attitudes.

It is worth noting here that there is a difference between the following: (a) having a reasonable aversion to ϕ-ing and yet ϕ-ing being what one ought to do; and (b) having a reasonable aversion to ϕ-ing and judging that one ought to ϕ. Harman wants to show that (a) is true, but her argument also extends to the combination of attitudes in (b).

28. Harman's interest is in whether "I'll be glad I did it" reasoning is an instance of good reasoning (see, in particular, p. 187 for a discussion). In the passage above, she argues that insofar as it is not, it may also be the case that "I'll be glad I didn't do it" reasoning may also be an instance of poor reasoning.
29. As I note above, I do not take this problem to affect all (or even most) cases of deliberation about collective moral obligations. Still, it should affect any cases where what I have called agents' "orientation" to their moral duty matters to all the participating moral agents, which, I contend, captures a great many actual cases.
30. This might occur due to akrasia or motivational apathy (*accidie*) or a simple failure to be motivated by distinctly moral reasons.
31. Theories of judgment aggregation will also be unhelpful in this context (see, e.g., List & Pettit 2002). Briefly, theories of judgment aggregation focus on the question of how individuals' respective judgments become unified *such that* the decisions of a putative collective actually represent the collective as such (say, by being the output of a certain kind of unity-ensuring decision-making procedure or because they are guided by the relevant kinds of values the capture the ends the group). In this regard, they target a different phenomenon than the Moral Orientation Problem.
32. A similar response applies to the objection that we *can simply ask others* whether they will have a relevantly similar moral orientation to their collective moral duty.
33. Marušić has an account of interpersonal commitments but I adopt his account of individual commitments. The case of STUCK DEER is a deliberative puzzle for individual agents in their reasoning about intending to do their parts in forming a collective agent. In this regard, it presents a primarily individual deliberative matter.
34. Note that, for Marušić (2015: 136), this form of practical reasoning concludes in the formation of a belief (against the evidence). By contrast, I am interested in whether practical reasoning can conclude in the adoption of an intention or aim that we seem to have no overriding reason to adopt (but no overriding reason against adopting it) and yet we do not want to form the intention or adopt the aim on a whim.
35. Ruth Chang (2016) describes a related, but not identical, set of cases as "hard choices." Marušić (2015: 194) makes a related point when he writes, "the weight of our practical reasons, considered as practical reasons, does not correspond to their evidential weight, considered as predictors of what we will do if we decide to do something."
36. I am grateful to Katie Steele, as well as an anonymous referee, for emphasizing this point. On this issue, see Cullity (2018) on the value of "joining in" and Brownlee (2019) on the value of teamwork.
37. I am grateful to Chiara Valenti for drawing my attention to this parallel.

References

Andreou, C. (2014). "Temptation, resolutions, and regret." *Inquiry*, 57(3): 275–292.

Andric, V. (2014). Can Groups Be Autonomous Rational Agents? A Challenge to the List-Pettit Theory. In *Institutions, Emotions, and Group Agents*. Springer: 343–353.

Arntzenius, F. (2008). "No regrets, or: Edith Piaf revamps decision theory." *Erkenntnis*, 68(2): 277–297.

Arruda, C. T. (2015). "Shared Intention and Reasons for Action." *Philosophy of the Social Sciences*, 45(6): 596–623.

Bagnoli, C. (2000). "Value in the guise of regret." *Philosophical Explorations*, 3(2): 169–187.

Bagnoli, C. (2016). "Rooted in the past, hooked in the present: Vulnerability to contingency and immunity to regret." *Philosophy and Phenomenological Research*, 92(3): 763–770.

Bratman, M. E. (2014). "Temptation and the agent's standpoint." *Inquiry*, 57(3): 293–310.

Brownlee, K. (2019). "What's the value of teamwork?" *Jerusalem Review of Legal Studies*, 19(1): 173–186.

Chang, R. (2016). "Hard Choices." *The Journal of the American Philosophical* 92: 586–620.

Collins, S. (2013). "Collectives' duties and collectivization duties." *Australasian Journal of Philosophy*, 91(2): 231–248.

Cullity, G. (2018). *Concern, Respect, and Cooperation*. Oxford: Oxford University Press.

Darby, D. and N. R. Branscombe (2014). "Beyond the sins of the fathers: Responsibility for inequality." *Midwest Studies in Philosophy*, 38: 121–137.

Gibbard, A. (2008). *Reconciling Our Aims: In Search of Bases for Ethics*. Oxford: Oxford University Press.

Gold, N. and R. Sugden (2007). "Collective intentions and team agency." *The Journal of Philosophy*, 104(3): 109–137.

Harman, E. (2009). "'I'll be glad I did it' reasoning and the significance of future desires." *Philosophical Perspectives*, 23(1): 177–199.

Hart, H. L. A. (1961/2012). *The Concept of Law*. Eds Leslie Green, Joseph Raz, and Penelope A. Bulloch, 3rd Edition. Oxford: Oxford University Press.

Held, V. (1970). "Can a random collection of individuals be morally responsible?" *The Journal of Philosophy*, 67(14): 471–481.

Isaacs, T. (2014). "Collective responsibility and collective obligation." *Midwest Studies in Philosophy*, 38: 40–57.

Joyce, J. M. (2012). "Regret and instability in causal decision theory." *Synthese*, 187(1): 123–145.

List, C. (2014). "Three kinds of collective attitudes." *Erkenntnis*, 79(9): 1601–1622.

List, C. and P. Pettit. (2002). "Aggregating sets of judgments: an impossibility result." *Economics and Philosophy*, 18: 89–110.

List, C. and P. Pettit. (2011). *Group Agency: The Possibility, Design, and Status of Corporate Agents*. Cambridge: Cambridge University Press.

MacMahon, C. (2003). "Précis: Collective rationality and collective reasoning". *Philosophical Studies*, 116(2): 153–157.

Marušić, B. (2015). *Evidence and Agency: Norms of Belief for Promising and Resolving*. New York: Oxford University Press.

Peter, F. (2018). "The good, the bad, and the uncertain: Intentional action under normative uncertainty." *Ethical Theory and Moral Practice*, 21(1): 57–70.

Petersson, B. (2017). "Team reasoning and collective intentionality." *Review of Philosophy and Psychology*, 8(2): 199–218.

Pettit, P. (2001). "Collective Intentions." In *Intention in Law and Philosophy*, pp. 241–254. Burlington, USA: Ashgate.

Pettit, P. (2007). "Responsibility incorporated." *Ethics*, 117(2): 171–201.

Pinkert, F. (2014). "What we together can (be required to) do." *Midwest Studies in Philosophy*, 38(1): 187–202.

Raz, J. (2009) "Legal Validity." In *The Authority of Law*, 2nd Edition. Oxford: Oxford University Press.

Rovane, C. (1997). *The Bounds of Agency*. Princeton: Princeton University Press.

Rovane, C. (2014). "Group agency and individualism." *Erkenntnis*, 79(9): 1663–1684.

Salomone, Jules. Forthcoming. "Cooperation: With or Without Shared Intentions." *Ethics*.

Schwenkenbecher, A. (2019). "Collective moral obligations: 'We-Reasoning' and the perspective of the deliberating agent." *The Monist*, 102: 151–171.

Townsend, L. (2013). "Being and becoming in the theory of group agency." *Abstracta*, 7(1): 39–53.

Wallace, R. Jay. (2014). *The View from Here: On Affirmation, Attachment, and the Limits of Regret*. Oxford: Oxford University Press.

Wedgwood, R. (2002). "The aim of belief." *Noûs*, 36(16): 267–297.

Wringe, B. 2010. "Global obligations and the agency objection." *Ratio*, 23: 217–231.

Wringe, B. 2014. "Collective obligations: Their existence, their explanatory power, and their supervenience on the obligations of individuals." *European Journal of Philosophy*, 21: 472–497.

7 Directed duty, practical intimacy, and legal wronging[1]

Abraham Sesshu Roth

What is it for a duty or obligation to be *directed*? Thinking about paradigmatic cases such as the obligations generated by promises will take us only so far. We will also need to consider shared agency, where some have discerned a similar phenomenon.

I will take for granted that a duty to ϕ relates the agent to a type of action that is in some sense right or morally required. So far, this is just to speak of the duty in "monadic" terms. It just says something about the agent who is subject to the duty. Talk of directedness introduces a further relatum: some particular individual (or individuals) to whom the duty is directed, or to whom the obligation is owed. Consider a standard example of a directed duty – the obligation to keep one's promise (though the honoring of contracts and agreements might also serve as examples). Suppose I promise to look in on an elderly couple. Visiting them is not something I'm otherwise obliged to do (assume that I'm not closely related to them, and that they have friends and relations who regularly see them). Of course, I might already have some reason to visit them; it might be a good thing to do. But the promise makes the visit morally required. In this case, moreover, the obligation corresponds to a right on the part of the promisee to performance (Hohfeld 1919).[2] Promissory obligation is often regarded as a paradigmatic instance of directed or "bipolar" duty.[3] If I promise the couple, the obligation is said to be *owed* or *directed to* them. Suppose, however, that this is a promise made to their *son*. Then my obligation is to visit the couple, but it is an obligation that is owed to the son, and it is the son who has the corresponding right. What is entailed by the promissory obligation being owed or directed to the son in this way? What is it for obligations, in general, to be directed?

Why should we care about the directedness of duties? The specific aspects of directedness in duties should become clearer as we proceed, and this should help us see why they are of interest to us. But more generally, the idea of directedness suggests a distinctive way in which morality relates individuals to one another. Morality regulates our interactions with one another insofar as some actions and ways of treating one another are prohibited, others

DOI: 10.4324/9781003242451-10

required, yet others permitted or recommended, etc. But talk of directedness suggests that somehow the duties or obligations themselves, and not merely the conduct that is their subject matter, afford a way of relating us to one another. The idea is to get a better understanding of what this form of relating to one another amounts to.

This paper starts by surveying several approaches for understanding directed obligations or duties, as well as the challenges they face. It turns out that something similar to the directedness of duties is a feature of shared agency. This then suggests an account of directedness in terms of shared agency – specifically, in terms of the so-called practical intimacy that holds between individuals when they act together. The final section addresses a challenge to the shared agency approach posed by legal wronging in tort law.

7.1 Normative relationship

Progress toward an understanding of directed duties starts with the observation that at least some cases involve a special relationship between the relevant parties. For example, the act of promising (perhaps along with its uptake) links individuals normatively, relating them as promisor and promisee. Something similar happens in agreements or contracts and, as Wallace emphasizes, in friendship:

> It is built into the idea of friendship that friends have normative reasons to help each other out, so that the fact that my friend is in a bad way itself counts in favor of my doing what I can to relieve the friend's distress … Reasons of this kind, however, are not merely free-standing normative considerations … only a person who stands in a friendship relationship to you has the special claim to consideration and vulnerability to injury that is partly constitutive of friendship.
>
> (Wallace 2013, 155)[4]

When parties are related in such a way as to generate directed duties, each will have a "special claim" on or against the other; the claim is a consideration that, from the agent's perspective, would be problematic to set aside or ignore. It could be that I would do more good, for example, helping with canvassing to get out the vote than keeping the promise to look in on the elderly couple. But the relationship established with the promise structures my reasons in such a way as to have what appears to be a deontic upshot: the prospect of greater good from canvassing cannot overwhelm the requirement to fulfill the promise.[5] Similarly, there does seem to be a difference between the duties one has to a friend in need on the one hand and a stranger in similarly dire straits on the other.

Raz points out that "it would seem that duties we owe others arise in three (overlapping) ways: they may be the result of commitments or undertakings, the product of relationships, or debts of gratitude. They presuppose some kind of a personal relationship" (Raz 2003/2011, 210).

A relationship underlying directed duty is also very much a part of the picture we get from Thompson. Adapting what he says to the case of promising, when you make a promise, you and the promisee…

> … have fallen into a peculiar nexus which limits your pursuit of objectives of any kind, even the beautiful objective of charity and the love of justice. The consideration operates pairwise and the rest of the world is, at least to a certain extent, closed out.
>
> (Thompson 2004, 337)[6]

Stroud's discussion of directed duty draws on Ross and is oriented around understanding the nature of wronging another. She, too, emphasizes the importance of a substantive relationship between relevant parties:

> … some of the clearest cases of one person wronging another arise and are only possible *within certain interpersonal relationships.* I use the word "interpersonal" advisedly, for (just to state the obvious) the relationships susceptible of making dyadic wronging possible are not limited to what are usually called *personal* relationships. After all, two people can stand in the promisor-promisee relation—which, following Ross, we have taken to be a central case of the phenomenon we are after—without being in what would usually be called a "personal relationship." When, however, *R* and *S* do stand in an interpersonal relationship of an appropriate kind—a "morally significant relation," as Ross would term it—*and* *S*'s moral offence is given colour precisely *by* that interpersonal relation, this suffices to "get *R* into the picture" in the way relational wronging requires.
>
> (Stroud ms., 26–27)

Later she adds, "*already standing in a certain type of interpersonal relation* suffices to give dyadic moral concepts application" (Stroud ms., 30)

If directed duties have a special normative force, one that is in play in our practical and moral thought with respect to some individuals but not others, then perhaps there's something about the special relationships with particular individuals that accounts for the directedness of duties toward them.

The thought that there is a special relationship that underwrites the directed duty points to why we cannot simply understand such duties in terms of the idea of a correlative right. For example, the idea that I have a duty to someone not to assault them is understood in terms of their right not to be so treated. This picture ignores the *specialness* of the relationship that holds between the parties involved in directed duty, for presumably, this individual right pertains to not be assaulted by anyone. Now, we might instead think that there is a special form of right that the individual *holds specifically against the bearer* of the directed duty. But then we answer the question of what the nature of a directed duty is by invoking a special notion of what is in effect a corresponding "directed" right. And this would not seem to amount to much in the way of progress.

I think that it is important to recognize that there is some sort of underlying substantive relationship to directedness in duty. But there are a couple of reasons to think that this idea does not by itself yield an understanding of directed duties. First of all, connecting directed duties with particular special relationships does not yet tell us what exactly it is about these relationships that account for directed duties.[7] We'll want to know what it is about the relationship between promisor and promisee, or that between friends, that accounts for the directedness of any duties that might be involved. Furthermore, it may not be possible to specify adequately the relationships in question independently of directed duties; the directedness of the normativity is inextricably linked to what it is to be in that sort of relationship. Arguably, it's *with the duty* that one is related to the other. So, the concern is that we are not making progress toward understanding this directedness by invoking the relevant relationships; an understanding of those relationships presupposes the very directedness under investigation.[8]

In light of this, I want to consider several proposals for elaborating on the relationship that underwrites the directedness of the obligation. There is something of interest in each, but none is satisfactory. I will then turn to a proposal that I think is more promising.

7.2 Relational wronging[9]

The directedness of duty is often explicated in terms of the distinction between *acting wrongly* and *wronging someone* – where there is someone in particular that you are wronging (Kamm 2007, 230; Thompson 2004). Perhaps I have a duty to engage in occasional charity work. Though it might be in the interest of others that I fulfill such a duty, I don't wrong anyone in particular when I fail to live up to it. But I have acted wrongly if this obligation goes unfulfilled.[10] We might speak generally of the obligation to keep one's promises in this way; when one fails to live up to this obligation, one is acting wrongly. But failing to live up to a promise is, in addition, a wronging of someone in particular – namely, the individual promised. In neglecting to visit the elderly couple, I wrong the son whom I promised, not his parents (assume that my visit was to be a surprise, so they weren't counting on me to come by).

So, can the possibility of relational wronging – the idea of wronging someone rather than merely acting wrongly – provide an understanding of the relationship underlying directed duty? Instances of relational wronging no doubt can give us some sense or handle on the relationship. But these cases do not offer a theory or explanation of directed duty and the relationship underlying it. If anything, the proposal gets wrong what counts as explanans and what the explanandum. It's the theoretical notion of directed duty and the underlying relationship that supposedly allows us to better appreciate the nature of the various instances of relational wronging and how they all fall under a single category. We can suppose that the parents would stand to benefit most from my promised visit – certainly more so than the son. I've acted wrongly in not keeping the promise. And it is unfortunate that, as a result, the parents languish unvisited. However, it's the mildly annoyed *son* that I wrong and not the sad parents. Far from accounting for the special relationship underlying directed duty, the pattern of wronging seems to call for some explanation. If the directedness of the duty to the son explains the pattern of wronging, then the latter won't account for the former.

Another concern with seeing relational wronging as theoretical explanans is that it seems possible to wrong someone without any relationship holding between the parties, and thus without any directed duties. After all, assaulting a random stranger with whom one has no substantive relationship is not just to act wrongly. It is a *wronging of someone*, the victim. Wronging someone doesn't require some pre-existing substantive relationship. So the possibility of wronging someone is not, at least by itself, sufficient as a characterization of the relationship underlying directed duty.[11]

7.3 Accountability

Another proposal about what directedness in these relationships amounts to develops the idea mentioned above of one party having a special claim on the other (Wallace 2019 is a prominent recent example). The promisor's duty to the promisee to live up to the promise corresponds to the promisee's claim on the promisor to perform the promised ϕ-ing. The promisor is *accountable* to the promisee to perform as promised.

Accountability for fulfilling a promise entails responsibility for it. The conditions for responsibility mostly concern the agent (the promisor in this case) and the sort of control she has over the relevant action; someone is not legitimately criticized for failing to ϕ if, for example, they were under duress or coerced. But the notion of accountability, as it is often used, involves not only the responsible agent but a further party – one that has a standing to complain, to protest, and to demand explanation, apology, and conformity. The party may, in addition, modify her relationship with the responsible agent (Scanlon 2008); the agent's failure to meet the obligation would justify taking steps in response, e.g. disinviting the individual to a social gathering (May 2015, citing Darwall 2006 and Feinberg 1970; see also Feinberg 1966, 1973). Thus, the legitimacy of criticism that's grounded on accountability depends not only on what the agent did, their obligations, and the conditions under which they acted. It also depends on the standing of the further party that judges and acts in light of what the agent does. Someone who lacks the authority or standing might, when lodging a complaint, be greeted with something like *it's not your business* (Gilbert 2006, 133; Roth 2004, 384, especially n. 14). But it's very much the business of the promisee whether the promisor follows through. The promisee has the requisite standing and cannot be rebuffed. It's in this sense, the thought goes, that the promissory obligation is *owed to* or *directed to* the promisee. Unlike some uninvolved third parties, the promisee is in a special position to object if the participant does not do his part.

But the worry with this appeal to standing and accountability as an account of the directedness of obligation is that it threatens to make directed obligation so diffuse and unfocused as to no longer to be interestingly distinguished from ordinary undirected monadic obligation. Why is this? In failing to keep a promise, one fails to live up to a moral obligation. When it comes to morality, in principle, *everyone* is in a position – has standing – to object and to respond in light of the infraction (e.g. Darwall 2013, 35–36). Admittedly, the promisee is likely to be more motivated to object, assuming that she was interested enough about what was promised to want to be assured about it. And there are, of course, many reasons for third parties to leave it to the promisee to object about a broken promise; one may not want to come off as overly meddlesome. And one has one's own life to lead. Nevertheless, because it is a *moral* principle that is being violated, anyone sufficiently aware of the situation (and presumably having a general standing in the moral community) has, in principle, grounds for criticism for the failure in promise-keeping; this is no doubt related to the idea that a violation of moral norms could be grounds for third-party intervention, and punishment (if one is a retributivist). So, if we understand directed duty in terms of standing to complain or criticize, then it no longer seems to be directed specifically to the promisee (Roth 2004, 364).

This concern about the accountability approach to directedness can also be raised in the context of Strawson's influential approach to accountability and responsibility. Although Strawson himself doesn't explicitly address obligations, Darwall (2006; see also Kutz 2002) understands Strawson's treatment of accountability as key to understanding their directedness and relationality. Strawson emphasizes, in the core case, "the non-detached attitudes and reactions of people directly involved in transactions with each another, of the attitudes and reactions of offended parties and beneficiaries; of such things as gratitude, resentment, forgiveness, love and hurt feelings" (Strawson 1962, 4). If we were to apply Strawson's picture to our case, the promisor is accountable to the promisee in that failure to do as one has promised amounts to an expression of ill will (or a problematic indifference) toward the promisee. One would thus be liable to being the object of resentment or some other appropriate direct reactive attitude. Thus, Strawson's picture of participant reactive attitudes offers one way to understand accountability, and thus one sense in which the obligation to do one's part is directed toward other participants.

One obstacle to the deployment of the Strawsonian machinery of accountability for understanding directedness of obligation comes from further elements of the Strawsonian picture. As is well known, Strawson extends his story beyond these cases of participant reactive attitudes to handle blame and holding accountable in more impersonal cases that don't involve substantive relationships. In the impersonal cases, one is not oneself a target of the ill will expressed by another individual B; instead, one adopts a reactive attitude of say indignation against B, on behalf of some distinct individual C who has been targeted by B. Thus, as a subject of the reactive attitude of indignation, someone not involved in the promissory interchange might nevertheless have some standing to criticize or otherwise express their indignation regarding the failure to keep a promise.

If the Strawsonian connection between reactive attitudes and accountability holds not only for the participant attitudes but also extends as well to the impersonal, then this threatens to render all forms of accountability "second personal" in Darwall's terminology. That is, both participant reactive attitudes and impersonal reactive attitudes would be conceptually related to the interpersonal and to notions of address. (This is a point acknowledged by Darwall 2013, 36.) If we're trying to give an account of directedness in terms of accountability understood as address (as Darwall seems interested in doing), then it would be problematic if we cannot distinguish between address in cases where we have individual participatory reactive attitudes on the one hand and the impersonal cases on the other. After all, it's precisely this sort of asymmetry that offered us our first inkling of the notion of directedness. Accountability would not capture the specialness of the relationship underlying directed duty.

Darwall introduces a distinction to address this worry. Given that promissory obligation is a form of moral obligation, the promisor is accountable to everyone to follow through on the promise. Correspondingly, everyone possesses what Darwall (2013, 32–34) calls the *representative authority* to address the promisor to make a criticism and urge the promisor to respect his obligation. But no one but the promisee possesses, in addition, an *individual authority* with respect to the promisor (2013, 27–32). It's in terms of this individual authority that Darwall hopes to capture the directedness of the promisor's duty.

But the introduction of the distinction between individual as opposed to representative authority seems *ad hoc*: you cannot simply posit a special kind of authority to address in order to capture directedness (May 2015). On what grounds are we to single out individual authority? Note, after all, that the content of the individual and representative authority is the same: to address the promisor concerning the fulfillment of the obligation. If it's not the content of the authority that singles out the individual authority, then we might be tempted to say that the individual authority is that possessed by the promisee or, more generally, the obligee to whom the duty is directed. But this is viciously circular: we were trying to account for the directedness in terms of accountability, and we needed a special form of accountability to do this. We cannot then identify the special form of accountability in terms of the very notion of directedness that we were seeking to explicate.

Given Darwall's invocation of Strawson, one way to try to address this circularity might be to account for the directedness of the obligation by noting that the grounds for complaint in the case of the promisee lie in a different form of sentiment than in the third-party complaint. The promisee's complaint is connected to the *resentment* she feels when the promise is not fulfilled. Whereas a third party's standing to complain is connected with the *indignation* he might feel on behalf of the promisee. But, as May points out (2015, 528), the distinction between resentment and indignation arguably presupposes the concept of directedness and so won't serve to explicate it.

I think that the most promising response for Darwall to take at this point is to argue that resentment is more basic or fundamental than indignation. Such an asymmetry does seem to be in Strawson, who suggests that our handle on indignation stems from an empathetic or vicarious appreciation of the state of another who is in a position to feel resentment. That is, we appreciate indignation to the extent that we are able to put ourselves in the shoes of another and appreciate the resentment they would appropriately experience in such a situation. Furthermore, it is one's own relationships and the participant reactive attitudes that go with them – and not the more impartial vicarious attitudes – that for Strawson are inescapable and which render incoherent the challenge determinism is supposed to pose for our responsibility practices.

The conceptual priority of participant reactive attitudes such as resentment over the impartial or reactive attitudes such as indignation, then, might offer Darwall a way to justify singling out the individual (as opposed to representative) authority, which is what he needs to capture the exclusivity we find in directed duty. At this point, however, we might wonder whether it is accountability per se that is relevant for capturing the directedness of obligation. Mightn't it be something else about personal involvement that underwrites the directedness of the obligation? And even if accountability is important, what is it about the accountability at the participant level that is so special?

7.4 Normative power

We haven't yet properly accounted for the relation underlying directed obligation. Both relational wronging and accountability are not sufficiently restrictive to capture the exclusivity we need for directed duty. A proposal that fares better in this regard appeals to the notion of normative power. On this view, the directedness of a duty is a matter of the power exercised over the duty by the individual to whom it is directed. The promisee, for example, can release the promisor from the obligation. No other individual, not even those who might have more of an interest in the obligation being fulfilled, has this power. If my promise to look in on the couple is made to their son, then it's the son that has the power of releasing me from the obligation. It's in this sense that the promissory obligation is directed or owed to the promisee.[12]

A challenge for the normative powers view stems from the concern that sometimes a duty is directed to an individual that has no normative power

(May 2015, 525). A promise to someone on their deathbed – to complete some project of theirs or to look after their child – would involve a directed obligation, but the promisee would not be around to exercise any normative power. But perhaps a broader understanding of normative power as something not limited to the power of release, but extending to the acceptance and thus initiation of a promissory obligation, would address this worry. More troublesome, however, is the duty to care for one's young children. The duty is directed to the child even before the child is in a position to accept the relation and before they are mature enough to release the parent from it. So here, we seem to have directed duty without any normative power.[13]

Another concern is that of antecedence – similar to the concern raised about relational wronging as an account of the relationship underlying directed duty. The worry is that the normative power is explained in terms of directedness of obligation and not the other way around. In presenting this worry, May seems to be concerned that we have to have the directed obligation to ground the normative power: the promisee has the normative power of release precisely because the promisor's duty is directed to her.

If we do not or cannot appeal to directed duty to explain normative power, what alternative is there? What would explain, for example, why it is that this power holds with respect one individual and not another? It would hardly be an explanation to say that that there are bare normative powers, for then it would be quite unclear why it is that one has it with respect to some but not with respect to others. Of course, we might say in that case that the power holds with respect to everyone, but then we lose the exclusivity of the directed duty.

More generally, if there is a normative power, we'll want to know what underlies it. If it's directed duty, then the normative powers view presupposes what we're trying to account for. If it's something else, we'll need to know what it is.[14]

We've looked at wronging, normative power, and accountability; all are problematic in that they do not offer a positive, non-question-begging characterization of the normative relationship underlying directed duty. The emerging suspicion is that there isn't really anything to the idea of directed duty or an obligation owed to someone in particular. If we can't find a working model for directed duty, then we might become skeptical about duties being directed.

7.5 Shared agency

It would help at this point to turn to some recent work on shared agency. Joint or collective action exhibits a directedness or relationality in normativity similar to the duties that have been our concern here. When agents act together, they are bound to each other in a way that individual agents of a mere aggregate are not. One of the ways in which they are bound is by the distinctive obligations or commitments to do one's part in the joint activity (Gilbert has argued this in many places; see, for instance, her 2006;

see also Roth 2004). Individuals walking together, for example, are committed to keeping pace with one another. Whereas commuters – strangers to one another – are not so committed when streaming toward a station exit. The commitment of participants is mutual, not merely in the sense that a (defeasible) commitment to do one's part in the joint activity is had by *each* participating agent. There is the further thought that one's fellow participants figure not merely in the content of one's commitment, but somehow in the willing or the committing itself. My commitment to do my part in our joint activity is more properly speaking a commitment-to-you to do my part in our activity. One aim of the literature on shared agency is to show that it exhibits these "contralateral" commitments or obligations and to explicate what this amount to. If this commitment doesn't presuppose morality[15] and yet possesses a structure that is very suggestive of directedness, then it seems that a theory of shared agency might be recruited to give a non-circular account of the directedness of moral duties.

At the core of my understanding of shared agency, and these contralateral commitments in particular, is the thought that the relevant intentions of fellow participants play a particularly intimate role in one's practical reasoning (Roth 2003, 2004). The role of the intentions of fellow participants is more akin to that played by one's own intentions than that played by the intentions of third-party nonparticipants. My decisions and intentions can settle practical matters for me; if I decide (and thereby intend) to ϕ, then when it comes time to act, I simply act on the intention and ϕ. Having decided ahead of time, I don't have to consider *whether* to ϕ in this situation (unless, of course, I gain some relevant new information). Indeed, we can't make sense of deciding and settling matters ahead of time if, at the time of action, I always have to decide on whether to act on the prior decision. The prior *decision* and *intention* to ϕ can hardly merit these labels if they don't settle the matter of whether one will ϕ. And the matter would not be settled if the prior intention is held hostage to a decision and intention made anew at the time of action. What we need to say, then, is that when I make a decision and form an intention, I subsequently act *directly* on that prior intention when the time is right. Further, this prior intention imposes constraints on what other plans I make so as to ensure that I will be in a position to perform the action I intended (Bratman 1987; Harman 1986). This intention-based commitment – embodied in the immediate relevance of one's prior intention and the possibility in the normal course of events to act directly on it – is what distinguishes genuine diachronic agency from a sequence of discrete exercises of synchronic agency.

Now, just as it is possible – indeed, required if we are to make sense of deciding things ahead of time – that one be able in this sense to act directly on one's prior intention, so might it be possible to act directly on the intentions of others. And just as my own intentions constrain my practical reasoning, so might the intentions of fellow participants in joint action serve as fixed points for my practical reasoning. The immediate relevance in practical reasoning of another's intentions – and the possibility in the normal course of events to act directly on the other's intention – is what distinguishes genuinely shared agency of individuals from a set of discrete, individual exercises of agency by individuals.

Suppose that this is correct and that it's in this *practically intimate* sense that fellow participants and their relevant intentions figure in how one goes about doing one's part in genuinely shared agency. The commitment to do one's part in joint activity would be founded on just such an intention. This is how I suggest we understand contralateral commitment in shared agency. It is an intention-based commitment to do one's part in joint activity. And it is a "contralateral" commitment-*to-fellow-participants* insofar as it is subject to being set and constrained in this immediate fashion by their intentions and commitments.

I will not attempt to defend this practical intimacy picture of contralateral commitments and shared agency here (Roth 2003, 2004, 2014). What is important for my purposes now is that these contralateral commitments seem to be closely related to directed duties, so much so that it suggests a shared agency model for directed duty. Very roughly, we might understand the directedness of duties in terms of shared agency, or at least in terms of elements of a theory of shared agency. More specifically, we can see how the practical intimacy model of contralateral commitments helps us understand aspects of the relationship between relevant parties of directed duty that inspired the earlier characterizations of duty in terms of wronging, accountability, and normative power.

To illustrate, let's take the case of promising. I suggest that the acceptance of a promise involves the promisee willing what the promisor has promised to do (Roth 2016). When the promisor follows through, he is acting *directly* on the intention/will of the promisee. More specifically, the acceptance of a promise to ϕ involves the promisee willing the promisor's ϕ-ing and communicating that intention to the promisor. The promisee's agency figures in what the promisor does in a particularly intimate fashion. Part of the point of promising is to grant the promisee some element of agency over what the promisor does.[16]

This picture accounts for the elements of truth underlying the previously discussed models that invoked accountability, normative power, and relational wrongs. Thus, when the promisor's action is intimately related to promisee's intention, it's not surprising that the promisor would be accountable to the promisee, and in a way that is distinctive and does not hold between the promisor and some third party. The promisor, for example, owes some sort of explanation to the promisee of how it is that they went about acting to fulfill the promise. This is an aspect of accountability that doesn't hold between the promisor and some third party – even if the latter is in a position to criticize the promisor for failing to live up to the obligation. And given that to act to fulfill a promise is (among other things) acting on the promisee's intention, it's not surprising that it is up to the promisee to change her mind if she has reason to, and thus to exercise the normative power to release the promisor from the obligation. The normative power is based not on duty being directed to the promisee (which would lead to the circularity/antecedence problem), but on the fact that the promisor is acting on the promisee's intention. The promisee's normative power is a manifestation of the promisee's agency as exercised in the creation of the promissory obligation as well as its fulfillment. Finally, there is a special way in which the promisor can wrong the promisee: when one doesn't live up to a promise, one is letting down the promisee. Just as one lets oneself down when one fails to live up to one's own intention, so one lets down the promisee when one fails to fulfill a promise to them. This distinctive form of letting down involves frustration in the exercise of one's will. It is not something to which some third party is susceptible, who at best might suffer frustration in their expectations. It is in this sense that in failing to live up to the promise, one wrongs the promisee but not some third party who happens to be interested in the promise being fulfilled.

I am not suggesting that when the promisor acts to fulfill a promissory obligation, that the promisor and promisee are literally acting together in a way that is typical of the examples in the literature on joint action, such as walking together or painting a house together. But some element of the practical intimacy that we find in shared agency and joint action is present in promising. Specifically, if my understanding of promising is correct, the promisor acts *directly* on the promisee's intention for the promisor. The suggestion, then, is that the special relationship underlying the directedness of promissory obligation is to be understood in terms of this practical intimacy that we find in a shared agency.

I have been discussing how shared agency and practical intimacy figure in an account of the directed duty of the promisor to the promise. I have not offered a general theory of just how practical intimacy figures in different varieties of directed duty. I think that how the directed obligation is related to joint activity (or something close enough to it) will depend on the specifics of the sort of moral obligation in question. As might be gleaned from the brief account given above, how practical intimacy figures in promising depends on the details of an account of promising, such as the nature of what it is to accept a promise. Presumably, the practical intimacy in promising will differ from how it is manifest in a legal institution of contract, and there will also be important differences of detail from the practical intimacy associated with the directed duties in friendship. Directed duties in each of these cases will require its own treatment, but all will, I think, exhibit practical intimacy in one way or another.

7.6 Tort law and shared agency

A worry for the shared agency view stems from some of the duties that are the concern of private law. One might want at the outset to set aside legal duties and rest content with a theory of directedness for moral obligations.

However, foundational theorizing about private law was influential in the development of recent interest in directed duties.[17] So it would be embarrassing if a theory of directed duty cannot shed any light on the legal duties that sparked recent theorizing about directedness.[18]

In private law, a particular individual can make claims against specific other individuals; for example, in contract law, one might seek remedy against some other party for a breach of contract. Contrast public law, e.g. criminal law, which concerns whether an individual has broken a law of the state. Although criminal law can regulate behavior between individuals, the normativity in question does not lie between individuals, so to speak. Whatever interpersonal relations might be in place is incidental to one's legal duties; the relations are relevant merely as the occasion for whether the duties are met or violated; they are not constitutive of those obligations. As Thompson says,

> The verdict of the jury 'Guilty!' expresses a property of one agent; it is not a relation of agents. If another agent comes into the matter – if there is, as we say, a 'victim' – it is, so to speak, as raw material in respect of which one might do wrong. The position occupied by other agents in the associated legal facts might equally have been occupied by rare birds and old buildings.
>
> (Thompson 2004, 344)

Perhaps Thompson is being too quick here. One might consider the possibility that criminal law is also the domain of directed duty, insofar as the duty is directed or owed to the state. That this is a possibility is suggested by the thought that the state might enter into relationships with an individual in a way that individuals might relate to one another; e.g. the state might have such a relation with a contractor to build roads or supply military equipment. But whether or not the state sometimes takes on a role similar to that of a private party, it is not at all clear that the role of the state with respect to individuals in the case of criminal law is analogous to the role of one individual with respect to another in private law. For instance, in private law, the individual might have discretion as to whether to make a claim against another regarding some tort or breach of contract. The state does not, it seems, have a similar discretion in criminal law. The state might have limited resources and lack adequate evidence, and so there may be an element of triage in how it prosecutes alleged crimes. But it cannot, simply as a matter of pure discretion, fail to proceed in criminal prosecution. That would be a miscarriage of justice.

Focus, then, on private law as the domain for directed duties in the legal realm. Does the shared agency view hold promise as an account for the directedness of these duties? Some directed legal duties of private law – such as those that we find in the law of contracts – are good candidates for explication in terms of shared agency. Contracts make use of legal apparatus to secure something like an exchange of promises. It doesn't take a great leap of the imagination to think of the parties to a contract as engaging in a form of joint agency. The directed legal duties would then seem amenable to theorizing in terms of some analog of practical intimacy. I will not attempt to explore the many questions of detail surrounding this issue, but it seems that no obvious worry is raised with a shared agency approach for directed duty in the case of contracts.

However, a part of private law that does appear to pose a challenge for the shared agency model is the law of torts. Tortious interaction needn't involve a pre-existing, substantive, duty-generating relationship of the sort discussed at the outset of this paper. More to the point, tort needn't have anything to do with notions of joint action or shared agency in terms of which I am suggesting we characterize that substantive relationship. Nevertheless, the assault of a random stranger, the injury suffered by a passerby due to one's negligence – these torts suggest the violation of an underlying directed duty. The defendant is *liable to* the victim. Compensation is owed; justice demands that the defendant "make the victim whole." The challenge to the shared agency model, then, is that torts can occur completely outside the context of joint agency and without any practical intimacy. And yet, there appears to be a violation of a directed duty between the individuals.

The seriousness of this challenge depends on whether and how directed duty is manifested in tort cases. On some "functionalist" or "economic" interpretations, tort law is assimilated to a form of public law (Landes & Posner 1987). If my conduct subjects me to claims of compensation by others, this might deter me from engaging in that conduct. On this view, tort law works as punishment and deterrence; its function is to discourage behavior incompatible with the ends of the larger community or state. The rationale for tort law would be similar to whatever justification there might be for laws that criminalize certain forms of behavior. Understood this way, tort law doesn't pose any challenge for the shared agency view simply because there would not be any directed duties between individuals here. The normative force in tort law would just be grounded in instrumental or social policy considerations; tort law is simply public policy or criminal law "in disguise" (See Stone 1996, Ripstein 2002, and Zipursky 2002, for discussion).

It would, however, be problematic to invoke such a controversial interpretation of tort law to defend the shared agency approach to directed duties. It's not clear why, if the purpose is deterrence that the plaintiff receives whatever sum the defendant is liable for (Stone 1996, 238). Wouldn't a fine paid to the state serve the purpose of deterrence just as well? The liability of the defendant to the plaintiff goes unexplained on this functionalist picture. If it is suggested that directing funds to the plaintiff is a matter of a social policy to insure against the risks that come with living in society, it would seem that there could be many other more efficient insurance strategies.

Furthermore, the functionalist reading seems not to capture the backward-looking nature of tort law (Stone 1996, 239). Indeed, this reading of tort law runs roughshod over the self-presentation of tort law as a domain of private rights, where one individual is in a special position to make a claim against another on the grounds that they were wronged by that party, and that as a matter of justice some sort of compensation is called for. This functionalist or economic reading doesn't offer an understanding of what this self-presentation amounts to (Zipursky 2002, 626).

Is there a way to step away from the functionalist reading to do justice to tort law's concern with compensation and nevertheless avoid presupposing directed duties? One thought is to try to understand compensation central to tort law in monadic terms: an individual responsible for any injury of type X is subject to yielding up some appropriate amount. And an individual who suffers X is entitled to be awarded some appropriate amount. The duty itself, however, is not owed or directed between the parties on this view. If compensation can be understood in this way, then there need be no substantive normative relationship between individuals. The suffering of the plaintiff at the hands of the defendant is merely the occasion of the defendant's obligation to make a payout (and, incidentally, the occasion of the plaintiff to receive a payout). The payout can simply be regarded by the defendant as the cost of conducting business as he did. So long as the costs are met, one's legal bookkeeping is in order; one needn't engage with the victim in any substantive way. And from the point of view of the victim, the awarded payout is the sort of support one would expect in a civilized society if one suffers some mishap – like what might happen in a natural disaster or maybe some unforeseeable bear attack – except that in this case it that happens to result from the actions of another.

The monadic rendering of compensation focuses on each of the parties separately and not in relation to one another. It considers whether a just scheme for the distribution of resources across a population should take into account the misfortune that has befallen some particular individual – whether they should simply be left in their wretched state or whether something should be done to help them. And the answer, the monadic rendering suggests, is that justice demands something to be done on their behalf. Regarding the defendant, the view suggests that limited resources should not be distributed in a way that fails to impose some cost on those who have harmed others.

But once it is put this way, the proposed monadic reading of compensation seems problematic. One way of putting the concern is that the proposal seems to miss the idea of there being something like a balance *between* the parties, one that was disrupted and needs restoring. Suppose, for example, that you suffer at the hands of another, but then for some completely unrelated reason, you receive a windfall equivalent to the typical compensation for the sort one has suffered. We might feel glad for you, but it doesn't seem as if the injustice of the tort has been corrected. We might even add to the case that the tortfeasor subsequently has a stroke of pure bad luck. Then we might talk about justice. But this would be poetic, not genuine justice.[19] If this is right, the implication is that we *cannot* see issues in tort law in the global terms of *distributive* justice, where balance is understood in terms of the appropriate distribution of some benefit (whatever exactly it is that is balanced) across some population. The concern of torts has, instead, a narrow focus just on the parties involved. As Thompson (2004, 337 quoted above) says, there is a pairwise nexus between the parties and the rest of the world, and other individuals with it are closed out.

It seems, then, that the compensation we find in tort is a realization of some other notion of justice – corrective justice (Stone 1996, 246, discussing Aristotle *Nichomachean Ethics* Book V). At the heart of this picture of tort law (and private law more generally) is a norm of equality. The tort presupposes some notion of equality irrespective of the relative wealth or well-being of one party with respect to the other and irrespective of the relative merits of character. Despite any such differences, the parties are (supposedly) equal or balanced before the torts are committed, and what matters is restoring this balance afterward. In committing the tort, the tortfeasor realizes a gain equal to the sufferer's loss. Justice in the corrective sense requires repairing a past loss.

There are different understandings of how exactly to understand the abstract equality or balance invoked in tort law. But the picture most relevant (and challenging) for our purposes understands the equality in terms of reciprocal directed duties between the parties. For example, Ripstein (2002, 660) says that the basis for liability in tort law is that there is supposed to be a "sense in which plaintiff's complaint is that her injury properly belongs to the defendant because the defendant has breached a duty *that he owed to her*" (emphasis added).

Now, if the balance that is the concern of tort law is simply understood in the abstract terms of these reciprocal directed duties, or the relational normative principles that underlie them,[20] then one may wonder about the adequacy of the shared agency model of directedness. For, again, the challenge is that a tort can be committed between individuals who are strangers to one another. The abstract equality posited to make sense of the nature of tort involves a directedness of duties independent of any joint action or practical intimacy. Let me close, then, with several remarks to address this challenge to the shared agency model of directedness.

First, it should be noted that the proposed view about torts represents a significant departure from the pre-theoretic picture given at the outset – of directedness involving a special relationship, paradigms of which are promising and friendship. Since it's possible for a tort to be committed with respect to any random stranger, there is between *any two individuals* a balance that can be disrupted. The current proposal thus implies that one is subject to a pairwise relation of directed duty with respect to *every individual*.[21] Our initial characterization of directedness of duties invoked substantive relationships in friendship and promising. It is a big leap from such paradigms to a pairwise relation that holds between *any* pair of individuals.

It's quite possible that *some* abstract pairwise relationship of moral significance could hold between any two individuals. But it's implausible to think that this is what caught our attention at the outset in cases such as promising. We could very well think that the posited pairwise relationship is important –

but it would be important for something other than the phenomenon that is my concern in this paper.

The depiction of one as subject to a virtually unlimited multiplicity of directed duties misses *what it's like* to be the subject of directed duties – that *particular* others, or only certain individuals with whom one has engaged with, figure in what one is obligated to do, and in a way that third parties do not. One has a distinctive kind of duty-generating relationship for some that one doesn't have for everyone. Part of the significance of directed duties is that their value has something to do with the relations being limited or special.[22] One is not *friends with everyone*; one cannot make *promises to everyone.* No doubt it's possible for any two individuals to be involved in a tort. But maybe this is a reason to think that directed duty is not necessary for a tort to be committed. If no antecedent substantive duty generating relationship is required for A to wrong or commit a tort against B, then it could very well be that the only notion of duty required to make sense of torts and wrongings is simply the non-relational monadic duty not to commit such acts.[23]

What, apart from the idea of tort, might lead us to go beyond the paradigmatic cases that involve substantive personal relationships and lead us to posit directed duties with *everyone*? One thought stems from the idea of consent. Consent removes a barrier to forms of interaction that are otherwise prohibited. And it seems possible, for any given individual, that you could give them consent to interact with you in ways they would otherwise not be able to. The possibility of consent shows, on this suggestion, not only that there has to be a *prior* duty that forbids some forms of interaction but that this duty specifically relates the parties involved. Consent presupposes a relational normativity and cannot establish it (Ripstein 2009, Chapter 5.) In response, I would allow that in some cases, it seems that consent might release someone from a directed duty. The ability of a promisee to release a promisor would be an instance. But it's not clear that consent always involves a release from a prior *directed* duty. There are other cases involving release from monadic duty. Some forms of behavior might be prohibited as a matter of *monadic* obligation. When it comes to interaction with others, one is required to conduct oneself in a certain way *unless* some consent or arrangement is made with particular individuals; only with those individuals would one have some (limited) ability to act otherwise. So the mere possibility that someone might grant you consent is not enough to establish that you have a pre-existing directed duty toward them.[24]

So far, the picture of directedness in tort law assumes that the directed duties hold pairwise with everyone. And I've suggested that this represents a problematic departure from the idea that a substantive relationship underlies any form of directed duty. But suppose now it is suggested that the tortious interaction – the assault or harming due to negligence – *initiates* a substantive moral relationship. This would avoid some of the worries of having to invoke a non-substantive relationship for directed duties. And it would account for how one has a duty, for example, to compensate the victim, or to apologize, etc.

But the idea that the tort establishes a relationship brings problems of its own. It is an unappealing picture compared, for example, to that of individuals voluntarily coming together to form relationships that establish the duties between them.[25] Although a certain amount of teasing and harassment is a strategy some adopt to establish a substantive relationship with another, it seems, in general, to be psychologically unhealthy and morally unsavory to instigate relationships in this manner.

A further concern with the tort establishing the relationship is that sometimes third parties benefit from a wrong committed against an individual. We might think that such beneficiaries have some obligation to compensate the victim, even if they were not party to the wronging in any way.[26] If this is the case, it's not clear how the picture of the wronging directly generating a relationship would extend to explain why the third party has any sort of directed duty of compensation to the victim.

Another concern is that if the relationship and the directed duty is established by the tort, then the duty itself does not account for why one should not commit the tort in the first place. A tort might establish a relationship (and the directed duties with it) that works to account for backward looking moral responsibility and accounting. But it wouldn't underwrite the fundamental forward-looking role of duties in guiding action and proscribing those torts. What, then, would play the forward-looking role? If we are setting aside pre-existing directed duties, then presumably, what would do the work would be a non-directed, monadic duty that would proscribe the behavior.

But now we have at hand an alternative to the idea that the tort itself generates a relationship underlying directed duty. For, if we're invoking a monadic duty for this proscriptive role, why not also appeal to a monadic duty that we might specify as: be available to whomever one has harmed so as to be able to come to an understanding, make amends, and reconcile with them?[27] This proposal corresponds to the idea that the tortfeasor would be in contempt not of the plaintiff/victim but *of the court* if they don't show up to court when the plaintiff brings their case against them. This suggests that one has a public, non-directed, legal duty to enter into a court or state-sponsored procedure that would then relate one with another private party.[28]

This approach avoids the picture of something like assault or tort as a way of *securing* a substantive relationship between perpetrator and victim. It is, rather, up to the victim whether to enter into a relationship that reconciles the parties. In effect, the court facilitates a joint endeavor toward reconciliation. And it is only now, in the context of the relationship established by the victim that the defendant has a directed obligation to the victim to compensate the latter for the harm.[29] What's fundamental to the directed obligation is the joint endeavor of reconciliation; compensation should be understood in this context as an element that contributes toward the reconciliation.[30]

If tort law is understood in terms of a joint project of reconciliation facilitated by the court, then the tort case becomes more amenable to the shared agency approach to directed duty. The court sets up a forum within which plaintiff and defendant are engaged with one another. It might be adversarial, but like a boxing match or other competitive game, it is within a context of shared agency where you must reach some reconciliation (which might be facilitated by some compensation).

I think that we should think of jointness or directedness as something that comes with the shared agency involved in the civil law proceedings. Torts can occur outside the substantive relationships underlying directed duty. But the torts and wrongs can be understood in terms of monadic duties and the harming of others. Further, monadic duties can require one to be receptive to joint acts of reconciliation. And it is in terms of these joint acts that we can understand the directedness of duties for compensation. The directed duties would fall under a collective act of reconciliation, and is not something directly generated by a tort.

7.7 Conclusion

Directedness of duties involves a substantive relationship between the parties involved. The characterizations of this relationship in terms of wronging, accountability, and normative power are inadequate. But they are helpful in pointing to a similarity between directed duties and the contralateral commitments between participants in joint action. The mutual or contralateral commitments are understood in terms of the immediate practical significance of relevant states of fellow participants. The shared agency account suggests that such a practical intimacy lies at the heart of the directed duties. This was illustrated in the paradigmatic case of the directed duty between promisor and promisee. The directed duties in tort law might appear to lie beyond the ambit of the shared agency account. However, I've suggested that the directed duties associated with tort cases can be understood in terms of the collective projects of reconciliation undertaken after a tort is committed.

Notes

1. An ancestor of this chapter was presented at the Collective Action and the Law Conference at the Law Department at Pompeu Fabra University in Barcelona. I want to thank the organizers, Teresa Marquez and Chiara Valentini, as well as participants, in particular my commentator Manuel Garcia-Carpintero, and Bill Wringe and Kevin Toh who raised difficult questions. An anonymous fellow contributor to this volume provided helpful comments. Thanks also to Erasmus Mayr, Sarah Buss, Caroline Arruda, Sarah Stroud, Ariel Zylberman, Facundo Alonso, Jay Wallace, Seana Shiffrin, Lisa Downing, Herlinde Pauer-Studer, and Carla Bagnoli.
2. For discussion, see Sreenivasan (2010, 465–466). The example comes from Hart (1955).
3. The terminology of bipolar as opposed to monadic duties is prominent in recent discussion due to Thompson (2004), though he credits Weinrib (1995).
4. Wallace notes that "the most salient and familiar examples of directed duties arise from transactions and other forms of causal interaction between the parties that they link" (2019, 16). Regarding promises: "The promise creates a special relationship between the promisor and the promisee, making it the case that the new

obligation that obtains is directed specifically to the promisee" (2019, 7). However, in this more recent work Wallace has ambitions to extend this "relational normativity" in such a way as to govern our interactions with *any* individual. Thus, a pairwise normative relation holds between any two individuals, and this is quite beyond the scope of any antecedent substantive relationship. See below.

5. Wallace (2013, 157) characterizes the normative force of the special claim in terms of Razian exclusionary reasons.
6. The particular example Thompson describes is not one of promising, but it would be fair to say that he intends this characterization to apply to all instances of directed duty.
7. A worry raised by Tamar Schapiro in her talk at a conference on The Direction of Moral Duties, Simon Fraser University, 2016.
8. A further worry with invoking a substantive relationship underlying directed duty is the possibility that one might be subject to duties toward those with whom one is not so related. Arguably this is a sort of worry raised by Thompson (2004). I will consider an instance of this worry in the final section of this chapter.
9. I get this expression from the title of Sarah Stroud's "Relational Wrongs," presented at The Direction of Moral Duties, Simon Fraser University, 2016.
10. Another example: I've made mistakes and have fallen in with some crowd that seemed nice but now are bent on morally very problematic endeavor. The only way to extricate myself is to trick or otherwise manipulate them. I act wrongly in tricking them – it was my fault that I fell in with them and got myself into a situation where I had to resort to these sorts of unscrupulous tactics. But given that they are bent on involving me in their endeavors, I don't wrong *them* in doing what I have to do to get myself out of this jam. See Thompson (2004, 339–340) for a related case.
11. A point emphasized by Seana Shiffrin in conversation. A different response to the possibility of wronging strangers suggests that substantive relationships are not necessary for directed duties. I'll consider this in the final section of the paper. In arguing that wronging X needn't be correlated with a violation of X's rights, Cornell (2015) implies that wronging is not enough to capture directedness in duty.
12. Sreenivasan (2010) places this sort of view under the heading of a will theory, with Hart (1982) as a major proponent. Other relationships, such as friendship, will involve similar normative powers. (Maybe a friend has more leeway to forgive than a stranger.)
13. Another fascinating case is the duty of gratitude. This would seem to be a directed duty one has to one's benefactor. And yet, as Herman (2012) points out, it seems not to be a duty with respect to which the benefactor has a normative power, e.g. of release.
14. Another concern often raised for normative power theories involves the idea of inalienable rights. A's right to freedom is inalienable; A doesn't have the right to enslave himself. So he has no power to release B from the obligation not to enslave A. So B's directed duty to A not to enslave A cannot be understood in terms of A's normative power over B's duty (Sreenivasan 2010, 483; MacCormick 1977, 195–199). But it seems to me that the relevant duties that correspond to inalienable rights are monadic. So it's not clear that inalienability amounts to counterexample to the normative power view of directed duty.
15. Bratman (1999, 2014) has argued that *moral* obligations, though often associated with shared intention and joint action, are not necessary for them. Gilbert (2009) has argued that the mutual obligations that she takes to be essential to shared intention and action are not moral in nature.
16. For somewhat related views, see Shiffrin (2008) and Owens (2013), who see promising as granting to the promisee some control over the normative status of the action. They don't go so far as to think that promising should be understood in terms of *agency* that's shared.

17. See the references for Weinrib, Hohfeld, and Thompson. This is a point made by Stroud (ms.).
18. In any case, the challenge raised by the law of torts is similar to those posed by what Wallace refers to as the secondary obligations in our accountability practices – regarding forgiveness, apology, and moral repair (Wallace 2019, 89–95). Ignoring the legal case therefore will not eliminate this sort of concern to be raised. I will address these more specific moral issues on another occasion, but the approach I will take will be similar to what will be described below.
19. Unless one were to supply the relevant metaphysical or religious background necessary to turn the matter into one of divine or perhaps karmic justice.
20. Ripstein (2002, 660–661). The underlying principle is a conception of freedom that is relational, where one is free insofar as one is not subject to the choice of another. See Ripstein (2009, 15).
21. Weinrib (1995) and Ripstein (2009). Also Wallace (2019) extends this picture to directed duties in general, not just the legal analogues.
22. Wallace (2013, 157) does invoke the value of such relationships.
23. So it could be that theorists like Weinrib, Ripstein, and more recently, Wallace, are concerned with something that might at first pass be assimilated with the directed duties I'm concerned with here, but which in the end, is perhaps better disentangled from it. Wallace (2019), for example, argues that a normative relation must hold pairwise between any individuals that (very roughly) can affect one another. He takes this to be required for an understanding of moral obligation that does justice to the idea of equal standing fundamental to a modern cosmopolitan conception of morality. Now, it's quite possible that the notion of directedness that Wallace is working with is compatible with the more restrictive notion of directedness that is my focus here. Indeed, if Wallace is right, then the notion of monadic obligation that I am taking for granted here will turn out to be directed or bipolar in Wallace's sense. I will not attempt to address his argument for this claim. But even if he is right about this, I would want to insist on the further, more restricted sense of directedness, which I contend should be understood along the lines of the shared agency view. On the other hand, Wallace also appreciates the restrictiveness of directed duty as it is manifested in the paradigm cases, such as promising. And part of his project is to offer an account of the duties in such cases. According to Wallace (2019, Ch. 5), a normative relation – a moral nexus – holds between any pair of individuals where one can have an impact on the personal interests of the other). Wallace recognizes that the relevant understanding of personal interests needs to be spelled out, and he takes important steps toward characterizing them as they appear, for example, in the special relationship that holds between promisor and promisee. Now, if we are to capture the pattern of directedness in the case of promising, then these relations should *not* hold between the promisor and some third party whose personal interests would benefit from fulfillment of the promissory obligation. I am not as confident as Wallace is that this pattern of directedness can be captured without invoking the resources of the shared agency view, but a fuller discussion will have to wait for a separate occasion.
24. It's possible that some sort of second personal address might always be required as part of the speech act wherein one grants consent. But this observation does not, I think, entail that the duty in question is directed and not monadic. For a contrasting view, see Darwall (2011).
25. Seana Shiffrin made this clear to me in conversation.
26. The Beneficiary Pays Principle is invoked for example in Page (2012), Wenar (2006), Kukathas (2003), and Baatz (2013).
27. Compare with having babies: you cannot have this personal, directed, relationship with the child until after they come into existence. So we have some monadic duties

governing what we can do, and presumably those monadic duties will require subsequently having some special directed relationship. Likewise, there might be cases where you have to seek a relationship with those you have harmed in order to atone, reconcile, compensate, etc.

28. Stone (1996, 236) remarks that all law is public in this sense.
29. This notion of compensation would therefore not be a matter of monadic duty. It would be a duty whose directedness is a manifestation of the joint activity of reconciliation.
30. Something like this approach is an element of Barbara Herman's important discussion of the duty of gratitude. See Herman (2012).

References

Baatz, C. (2013). Responsibility for the Past? Some Thoughts on Compensating Those Vulnerable to Climate Change in Developing Countries. *Ethics, Policy and Environment*, 16(1): 94–110.

Bratman, M. (1987). *Intention, Plans, and Practical Reason*. Cambridge, MA: Harvard University Press.

Bratman, M. (1999). Shared Intention and Mutual Obligation. In: M. Bratman, ed., *Faces of Intention*. Cambridge: Cambridge University Press, pp. 130–141.

Bratman, M. (2014). *Shared Agency: A Planning Theory of Acting Together*. New York: Oxford University Press.

Cornell, N. (2015). Wrongs, Rights, and Third Parties. *Philosophy and Public Affairs*, 43(2): 109–143.

Darwall, S. (2006). *The Second-Person Standpoint: Morality, Respect, and Accountability*. Cambridge: Harvard University Press.

Darwall, S. (2011). Demystifying Promises. In: H. Sheinman, ed., *Promises and Agreements: Philosophical Essays*, 1st ed. Oxford: Oxford University Press, pp. 255–276.

Darwall, S. (2013). Bipolar Obligation. In: S. Darwall, ed., *Morality, Authority, and Law*, 1st ed. Oxford: Oxford University Press, pp. 20–39.

Feinberg, J. (1966). Duties, Rights, and Claims. *American Philosophical Quarterly*, 3(2): 137–142.

Feinberg, J. (1970). The Nature and Value of Rights. *Journal of Value Inquiry*, 4(4): 243–260.

Feinberg, J. (1973). *Social Philosophy*. Englewood Cliffs, NJ: Prentice-Hall.

Gilbert, M. (2006). *A Theory of Political Obligation*. Oxford: Clarendon Press.

Gilbert, M. (2009). Shared Intention and Personal Intentions. *Philosophical Studies*, 144(1): 167–187.

Harman, G. (1986). *Change in View*. Cambridge, MA: MIT Press.

Hart H. L. A. (1955). Are There Any Natural Rights? *Philosophical Review*, 64(2): 175–191.

Hart H. L. A. (1982). Legal Rights. In: *Essays on Bentham: Jurisprudence and Political Theory*. Oxford: Clarendon Press.

Herman, B. (2012). Being Helped and Being Grateful: Imperfect Duties, the Ethics of Possession, and the Unity of Morality. *The Journal of Philosophy*, 109(5/6): 391–411.

Hohfeld, W. N. (1919). *Fundamental Legal Conceptions, as Applied in Judicial Reasoning*, ed., W. W. Cook. New Haven: Yale University Press.

Kamm, F. M. (2007). *Intricate Ethics: Rights, Responsibilities, and Permissible Harm*. Oxford: Oxford University Press.

Kukathas C. (2003). Responsibility for Past Injustice: How to Shift the Burden. *Politics, Philosophy & Economics*, 2(2): 165–190.

Kutz, C. (2002). Responsibility. In: J. Coleman, K. Himma and S. Shapiro, eds., *Oxford Handbook of Jurisprudence and Philosophy of Law*, 1st ed. Oxford: Oxford University Press, pp. 548–587.

Landes, W. and Posner, R. (1987). *The Economic Structure of Tort Law*. Cambridge, MA: Harvard University Press.

MacCormick, N. (1977). Rights in Legislation. In: P. Hacker and J. Raz, eds., *Law, Morality, and Society*, Oxford: Clarendon.

May, S. (2015). Directed Duties. *Philosophy Compass*, 10(8): 523–532.

Owens, D. (2013). *Shaping the Normative Landscape*. Oxford: Oxford University Press.

Page, E. (2012). Give It Up for Climate Change: A Defence of the Beneficiary Pays Principle. *International Theory*, 4(2): 300–330.

Raz, J. (2003/2011). Numbers With and Without Contractualism. *Ratio*, 16(4). Reprinted in 2011 with added appendix in J. Raz, *From Normativity to Responsibility*, Oxford: Oxford University Press, pp. 193–210.

Ripstein, A. (2002). Philosophy of Tort Law. In: J. Coleman, K. Himma and S. Shapiro, eds., *Oxford Handbook of Jurisprudence and Philosophy of Law*, 1st ed. Oxford: Oxford University Press, pp. 656–686.

Ripstein, A. (2009). *Force and Freedom in Kant's Legal Philosophy*. Cambridge, MA: Harvard University Press.

Roth, A. (2003). Practical Intersubjectivity. In: F. Schmitt, ed., *Socializing Metaphysics: The Nature of Social Reality*. Lanham, MD: Rowman & Littlefield, pp. 65–91.

Roth, A. (2004). Shared Agency and Contralateral Commitments. *Philosophical Review*, 113(3): 359–410.

Roth, A. (2014). Prediction, Authority, and Entitlement in Shared Activity. *Noûs*, 48(4): 626–652.

Roth, A. (2016). Intention, Expectation, and Promissory Obligation. *Ethics*, 127(1): 88–115.

Scanlon, T. M. (2008). *Moral Dimensions: Permissibility, Meaning, Blame*. Cambridge, MA: Belknap Press of Harvard University Press.

Shiffrin, S. (2008). Promising, Intimate Relationships, and Conventionalism. *Philosophical Review*, 117(4): 481–524.

Sreenivasan, G. (2010). Duties and their direction. *Ethics*, 120(3): 465–494.

Stone, M. (1996). On the Idea of Private Law. *Canadian Journal of Law and Jurisprudence*, 9(2): 235–277.

Strawson, P. F. (1962). Freedom and Resentment. *Proceedings of the British Academy*, 48: 1–25.

Stroud, S. (ms.) Relational Wrongs.

Thompson, M. (2004). What is it to Wrong Someone? A Puzzle about Justice. In: R. J. Wallace, P. Pettit, S. Scheffler, and M. Smith, eds., *Reason and Value*, 1st. ed. Oxford: Oxford University Press, pp. 333–384.

Wallace, R. J. (2013). The Deontic Structure of Morality. In: Backhurst, Hooker and Little, eds., *Thinking about Reasons: Themes from the Philosophy of Jonathan Dancy*. Oxford: Oxford University Press.

Wallace, R. J. (2019). *The Moral Nexus*. Princeton: Princeton University Press.

Weinrib, E. (1995). *The Idea of Private Law*. Cambridge, MA: Harvard University Press.

Wenar, L. (2006). Reparations for the future. *Journal of Social Philosophy*, 37(3): 396–405.

Part III

Causality, blameworthiness and responsibility

8 Responsibility unincorporated

Group agents and corporate persons

Sara Rachel Chant

8.1 Introduction

Collective moral responsibility is unincorporated. It does not depend on group agents, embryonic group agents or groups with 'minds of their own' (Pettit 2010). The thought that it does is a consequence of a deep-seated methodological mistake in the literature. This mistake is to take the very best accounts of individual action, intention and responsibility and simply 'collectivize' them. For example, for individuals, what distinguishes actions from non-actional events or happenings is said to depend on the beliefs, desires and intentions of individual agents.[1] On the collectivizing method, what distinguishes collective actions from mere collections of actions depends on *collective* intentions, *collective* beliefs, and other 'collective mental states.' Elsewhere, I refer to the collectivizing approach as the 'wash, rinse and repeat approach' (WRR) to collective intentionality.[2]

This chapter has two aims. The first is to cast doubt on WRR and offer an alternate approach to understanding collective responsibility. We argue that a theory of collective responsibility should not be centered around the metaphysics and ontology of agents. Instead, it should focus on the internal structure of groups, with an emphasis on how that structure influences the flow of information throughout the group, as well as the group members' incentives and disincentives.

The second aim of this chapter is to generalize this argument outside of collective action theory. Our discussion of WRR shows that ontological questions about agents and agency are unproductive and that instead of focusing on ontology, we should look to the empirical facts about group structure. The same lesson applies to the legal debate in the United States about whether corporations and other associations should be considered 'persons' under the law, and if so, which rights they ought to be granted. The infamous *Citizens United* case, in which the Supreme Court granted sweeping First Amendment protections to corporations, is the basis of this discussion. We argue that the issue of 'personhood' for corporations obscures the empirical facts about corporations which ought to guide the discussion of which rights corporations and other associations ought to have.

DOI: 10.4324/9781003242451-12

8.2 Distributive and non-distributive responsibility

Collective moral responsibility may be 'distributive' or 'non-distributive.' Distributive responsibility is simply the responsibility borne by the individual members of a collective for their contribution to or complicity in a collective action. Collective responsibility, in this sense, may be apportioned among the members of the group according to each individual's causal contribution to the collective action. For example, I may be morally responsible for the causal consequences brought about by allowing my cattle to graze the commons or I may be *wholly* responsible for its ruination.[3] Distributive responsibility attaches to individuals either partially or wholly.

Non-distributive responsibility is the 'moral remainder' after all individual responsibility has been taken into account. It attaches to the group as such and not to any individual member. Cases of non-distributive moral responsibility include ones in which the group is morally responsible for a collective action, but none of its members are responsible, even for their contribution to the collective action.

Arguments for the existence of non-distributive moral responsibility are often motivated by ordinary language considerations. For example, if the New York Times reports that 'WidgetCo is responsible for its factories having polluted the river,' the subject of that sentence seems to be WidgetCo itself and not the people who compose it. The sentence leaves open the possibility that none of WidgetCo's employees bear any moral responsibility.[4] Likewise, for reports about the United States, the White House, SunTrust Bank, Germany, the Packers, and so on.

More recent arguments in favor of non-distributive moral responsibility have taken a very different approach. They deploy formal results from judgment aggregation, arguing that because the judgments of collectives sometimes come apart from the judgments of the individuals that compose them, it follows that the decisions and actions of collectives are not always reducible to the decisions and actions of the individuals in the group (List and Pettit 2004; Pettit 2010). The decisions and actions that result from such a judgment aggregation may call for an attribution of moral responsibility, and the group can bear moral responsibility only in virtue of its being an agent.[5]

Arguments from judgment aggregation may justify the existence of collective non-distributive responsibility. But in the next section, we will establish that it is an entailment of the WRR methodology.

8.3 The methodology of collective action and responsibility

Action, agency, responsibility and freedom are core interlocking notions for theories concerning individuals. Individuals may be responsible for actions, not non-actional events. Morally responsible actions are produced by free agents. Given the WRR approach to collective action theory, it follows that collective action, collective agency, collective responsibility and collective freedom would be core interlocking notions as well. Collectives may be responsible for collective actions, not non-collective-actional events. Morally responsible collective actions are produced by collective free agents.

Let us consider in more detail two theses entailed by WRR. The first is the 'collective agency thesis':

> (CA) If collective moral responsibility attaches to a collective as such, and not simply to the individuals who compose it, then the collective must be an agent distinct from the individuals who compose it.

CA is a natural consequence of WRR because it merely takes the well-appreciated 'individual agency' thesis:

> (IA) If individual responsibility attaches to an individual, then that individual must be an agent.

And 'collectivizes' it by replacing the concept of individual agency with collective agency. CA is plausible because IA is; non-agential individuals that lack agency cannot be morally responsible for what they cause. CA simply says that the same is true of groups.[6]

CA is just one consequence of WRR. It is easy to see that a similar maneuver may be made for any plausible principle surrounding the conditions necessary for individual moral responsibility. For example, consider the individual free will thesis:

> (IFW) If an individual bears individual responsibility, then the individual must have individual free will.

Just as IA leads directly to CA, so too, IFW leads directly to CFW:

> (CFW) If a collective bears collective moral responsibility, then the collective must have collective free will.

For any individual action-theoretic principle, the collectivizing approach implies a corresponding collective action-theoretic principle.

The 'collectivizing' of individual moral responsibility creates some tension, however. Agency is a difficult enough concept with respect to individuals, but it is much more difficult to make sense of when it is applied to groups, and collective free will is downright abstruse.

Having been led to the existence of collective agency and collective free will, there are two available strategies for coping with these commitments. The first is to bite the bullet and accept a heavy metaphysical commitment to the existence of collective agents and collective mental states. This is too much of a burden for many. The second is to offer accounts—usually functionalist accounts—of collective agents, collective mental states, and the like that do not commit us to the existence of such entities.

8.4 The Hollywood standoff counterexample against CA

The debate concerning collective moral responsibility is between: (1) those who reject collective responsibility because the cost of accepting collective agents and collective free will is too great and (2) those who accept collective agents and collective free will because the cost of losing collective non-distributive responsibility is too great. Proponents of either (1) or (2) accept the collectivizing methodology of WRR. They disagree only about how best to respond to its implications.

The aim of this section is to provide examples of collective responsibility without collective agency or collective free will. If it is possible to decouple collective moral responsibility from collective agency and collective free will, then WRR is unsound, it is not necessary to either reject collective responsibility or maintain a commitment to either collective agency or collective free will.

The argument against CA depends on two principles. According to 'Threat':

> (Threat) Agent S is not morally responsible for an action, A (or inaction or the consequences), if S As (or does not A and thereby brings about the consequences) only because of a credible threat of serious harm.

It is easy to come up with examples of Threat. If a person performs what ordinarily would be an immoral action only because it is the only way to avoid very severe consequences, then we do not hold that person morally responsible for the action. A clear case is when the threat of serious harm originates with another agent whose goal is to use the threat as coercion. In such cases, the moral responsibility lies not with the person who is coerced but with the agent who is the source of the threat. This is the 'Transfer' principle:

> (Transfer) If agent S is absolved of moral responsibility for doing A (or refraining from doing A or the consequences) because S did it (or refrained from doing it) only because of a credible threat of serious harm, then the moral responsibility for doing A (or refraining from doing A or the consequences), if there is any, transfers to the source of the threat.

To see how these principles operate together consider the following example:

> *The Shakedown*
> Mr. Innocent gives Mr. Guilty $1000, knowing that he will use the money to fund various criminal activities. Mr. Innocent only hands over the money to Mr. Guilty because Mr. Guilty is pointing a gun at his head, credibly threatening to shoot him if he does not.

If Mr. Innocent had simply *volunteered* to give Mr. Guilty the money, and there were no extenuating circumstances, we would attribute moral responsibility to him. But Mr. Guilty's threat does two things—it absolves Mr. Innocent of moral responsibility (by the Threat Principle), and it entails that Mr. Guilty bears the responsibility that Mr. Innocent would otherwise have borne (by the Transfer principle).

Judgments regarding the Shakedown ought to be obvious and uncontroversial, not only because the Threat and Transfer principles are well-appreciated, but because the structure of the case is so simple. When the case involves a more complex structure of threats, the Threat and Transfer principles yield more informative results. Consider the following case, which we break into two parts:

> *The Hollywood Standoff (Part I)*
> Mr. Good, Mr. Bad and Mr. Ugly find themselves in a 'Hollywood Standoff.' Each is holding a gun to the head of another member of the group such that everyone in the group has a gun pointed to his head. Everyone knows that the first to shoot will surely be shot, and everyone believes that everyone knows this. Moreover, everyone believes that if anyone were to begin to lower his gun, chaos could ensue and everyone could get shot.

This first part sets up the structure of the example in such a way as to invoke the Threat and Transfer principles. Suppose we were to accuse Mr. Good of bearing moral responsibility for the act of continuing to point his gun at Mr. Bad. In response, Mr. Good could invoke the Threat and Transfer principles by correctly claiming that he has no real choice in the matter because Mr. Ugly will surely shoot him were he to lower his gun.

Another way of understanding the predicament the three men find themselves in is that each is under threat because of the structure of the group as a whole, not because of any particular person. Therefore, if the Threat and Transfer principles hold, then those principles do not attach responsibility to any individual but to the group itself. The implication is that any moral responsibility in this scenario is attributable to the group as a whole, not to the members of the group.

However, we have not yet established that there is any moral responsibility in the Hollywood Standoff. But it is straightforward to imagine the situation having a clear moral component:

> *The Hollywood Standoff (Part II)*
> Nearby, and within clear sight of the men, a child is suffering from severe dehydration. The men see that the child is in imminent danger and could be easily saved if they were to lower their guns and give the child the last few sips of water from each of their flasks. The men neither know that no one will shoot nor do they know that they will all die if they try to help. So although they are each deeply impressed by the credible threat of serious harm, they each believe, and believe that the others believe that

> in the actual circumstances, it is possible to lower their guns and survive. In fact, if any man had begun to lower his gun, the others would have followed suit, and the child would have been saved. Nevertheless, the men maintain the standoff and the child dies.

When the child dies, are the men morally responsible? They cannot be *distributively* responsible because each man is under the credible threat of serious harm. There is also no principled way to assign moral responsibility to any of the men for being a threat to the others because each of them is a threat only because they are themselves under threat. The Transfer principle thereby rules out distributive responsibility. But it does not rule out *non-distributive* responsibility for the child's death. In fact, the case stipulates that the men together could have put down their guns and given the child the last few sips of water from each of their flasks. So even though each has an excuse that absolves him of distributive responsibility, those excuses do not clearly absolve *them* of responsibility *jointly*. The men are collectively, non-distributively morally responsible for the child's death.

The men in the Hollywood Standoff may be collectively (non-distributively) morally responsible for the child's death. But contrary to the CA thesis, the men do not constitute a collective agent. For on any reasonable criterion of collective agency, we find that the three men lack it. For example, the three are an *ad-hoc* group with no formal structure, so any criteria for the agency that depends on group structure will fail to be satisfied. *A fortiori*, there are no 'institutional roles' whatsoever. They have no decision procedures and no established methods of communication or deliberation. They do not engage in 'team reasoning' or adopt the perspective of the group in reasoning about what each of them should do.[7] In short, they are no more likely to qualify as an agent than any other *ad hoc* group or random collection. Thus, the Hollywood Standoff is a counterexample to CA.

Just as the men do not constitute an agent, they do not have a collective free will. For they do not have a decision procedure, form collective intentions, have a collective purpose, or joint goal. Thus, if the Hollywood Standoff is a counterexample to CA, it is a counterexample to CFW as well.

8.5 Arguments against the Hollywood Standoff

There are two strategies for objecting to the Hollywood Standoff counterexample. The first is to argue that the three men are non-distributively responsible for the child's death but that this is in virtue of their constituting a collective free agent. The second is to accept that the men do not constitute a collective free agent but deny that they are non-distributively responsible for the child's death.

For the reasons given above, the first argument—that the group is a collective free agent—is a non-starter because the group has none of the properties required of agency, let alone *free* agency.

The second objection accepts that the men do not constitute a collective free agent but denies that they are non-distributively responsible for the child's death. To deny that the men are non-distributively responsible, one may argue that (1) they bear moral responsibility, but it is *distributive* responsibility or that (2) they bear no moral responsibility at all. I shall respond to these two possible objections by considering what characteristics the example would have to possess in order for either (1) or (2) to be true.

On (1), the responsibility is distributed to each of the three men as individuals. Accordingly, it would have to be the case that each of the three men could reasonably have lowered his gun in order to attend to the dehydrated child. We could generate a variant of the story in which this is plausible. For instance, we might stipulate that the three men are affable colleagues who trust each other and are inclined to follow suit if any single one of them were to lower his gun. Each knows that if any of them were to take the initiative to end the standoff, the rest would have cooperated. The argument against the Hollywood Standoff would allege that if this were true, then each individual bears responsibility for not taking the initiative to end the standoff. Let's call this version of the story 'Friends.'

On the other end of the spectrum, we can come up with a variation in which (2) is plausible. For example, imagine that the three men are sworn enemies who despise and distrust each other. They know that if any of them had begun to lower his gun, the others would have taken this as an opportunity to start shooting. If this were the case, then the men could not have ended the standoff and saved the child. If the men in the standoff could not have saved the child, then the men are not responsible for the child's death, either individually or as a group. Either way, the men in the standoff are not collectively non-distributively responsible for the child's death. Let's call this version of the story 'Enemies.'

These two versions of the Hollywood Standoff define the extreme opposite ends of a spectrum of possible cases. In the former, each of the men is distributively morally responsible; in the latter, there arguably is no moral responsibility at all. Thus, the question of whether there can be any non-distributive moral responsibility in the Hollywood Standoff comes down to whether there are cases in the middle of this spectrum that 'split the difference,' so to speak, between Friends and Enemies.

Consider a scenario approximately halfway between Friends and Enemies. Each man is not *certain* that it is safe to lower his gun (as is the case in Friends), nor is he *certain* that it is unsafe (as in Enemies). But the threat is serious enough to absolve each individual responsibility, regardless of whether the threat would, in fact, be carried out.

However, despite the fact that the Threat principle absolves each man of moral responsibility, this is a case in which the group has the ability to act collectively with much more freedom than any individual in the group. Cases having this quality are very familiar. For example, a group of people can overpower a threatening individual, even if each individual would be excused for not making the attempt alone. In such a case, the group may be non-distributively morally responsible if they fail to act collectively, even though no individual is morally responsible. This sort of case has been discussed often in the literature on collective responsibility, most notably by Joel Feinberg (1968). In his example, Jesse James is holding a group of people hostage. Feinberg stipulates that no individual could safely overpower him, but that the group could. If the group permits themselves to be held hostage, then it is the group *qua* group that is morally responsible.

The only relevant difference between Feinberg's Jesse James case and the Hollywood Standoff is that the dynamics of the group play a much more prominent role in the latter. It might be possible to invoke the Transfer principle in the Jesse James case to attribute moral responsibility to Jesse James since he is the lone source of a threat. But there is clearly no such move available in the Hollywood Standoff, for it is the group itself that is the source of the coercive threat, not any external influence. The Transfer principle points back to the group, placing moral responsibility squarely on the group as a whole.

8.6 The anatomy of collective responsibility

If the arguments so far have been correct, then facts about the metaphysics of groups turn out to be far less important than previously assumed. Although agency may be central to understanding individual moral responsibility, this does not entail that collective agency is important for collective responsibility. Indeed, cases like the Hollywood Standoff suggest that collective agency—whatever it turns out to be—may be irrelevant to at least some forms of collective responsibility. This observation shows that it is a mistake to rely on the collectivizing methodology WRR when constructing a theory of collective moral responsibility.

Although we should be skeptical of the collectivizing methodology, the problem begins with making the wrong choice about *which* type of individual action to collectivize. Whilst theorists ordinarily take the most basic actions of individuals to model collective action, there is an excellent reason to think that aggregate actions—that is, actions that have other actions as parts—may be more analogous (Ginet 1990). For example, the act of 'building a doghouse' is aggregate because it consists of a number of component actions such as 'nailing two boards together,' 'sawing a plank,' and so on. Likewise, the actions of groups are normally comprised of a number of actions performed by individuals.

Questions concerning individual basic actions differ from those concerning the aggregation of action. I shall refer to the question, 'what distinguishes actions from non-actional events?' as the *first problem in action theory* (Enç 2003). Because individual intentions are crucial to understanding the difference between actions and non-actional events, discussions of the first problem in action theory are invariably centered around understanding intentions and their role in the production of action. This concern is what occupies collective action theory precisely because collective actions are modeled after basic actions. In contrast, the relevant question concerning the aggregation of action is 'when does a set of actions performed by an individual constitute a single action?' This is the *second problem in action theory*. It is a problem of composition.[8]

If we model collective actions after aggregate actions, we avoid several unproductive problems. For example, agency is no longer central to a theory of collective action in the same way that it is not central to the aggregate actions of individuals. An analysis of aggregate actions already presupposes that there is a set of actions; those actions are already produced by an agent, and so it is not important to understand how (or whether) an individual is or can be an agent over time. Likewise, having disposed of questions concerning collective agency, we refocus on a new set of questions, indicated by the Hollywood Standoff.

The most prominent feature of the Hollywood Standoff is the peculiar structure of interactions among the three men. If that structure were different, we would likely come to a different conclusion about the moral responsibility of the group and its members. For example, if Mr. Bad were the only man armed with a gun, and he was threatening the other two, the Threat and Transfer principles would simply point to him as the sole bearer of moral responsibility. This observation suggests that the structure of interactions within the group affects issues of distributive and non-distributive collective moral responsibility.

Indeed, group structure is important in at least two ways. First, as we have seen in the Hollywood Standoff, the structure of the group plays an important role in determining the structure of incentives and disincentives (including threats) that influence the group's members. In that example, there is a cascading sequence of threats that mitigate each man's moral responsibility. But groups having less dramatic structures can also create unique rewards and penalties. We see this play out, for example, in organizational 'groupthink,' when the flow of information, group cohesiveness, and the incentive structure have the effect of silencing minority views. Those with minority perspectives on important issues are often silenced for fear of falling out of favor with the group. In extremely pathological cases, it is even possible for large numbers of people with the same opinion to be silenced because of the organization's structure of incentives and disincentives. Indeed, well-known policy failures and ethical lapses in large organizations are often found to have been caused in large part by the organization having a structure that isolates and discourages people who have unpopular opinions.[9]

Second, group structure is a major factor in determining the flow of information among the members of the group. This has an impact on how we attribute moral responsibility. To illustrate this point, consider the following pair of cases:

> *Secret Bomb Factory*. An evil scientist designs a factory and hires workers to build bombs for his evil plans. However, the factory and the work

have been structured in an ingenious way such as to deceive the workers into believing that they are building harmless widgets. Although the workers all work together, nobody is ever in a position to gain an accurate understanding of their actual work. The workers each do their part of building bombs.

In *Secret Bomb Factory*, the workers perform the collective action of building bombs, which is a highly immoral thing to do. But the structure of the factory and of the relationships among the workers and their tasks prevents information from flowing among the people in the factory. For this reason, the workers are not morally responsible for what they're collectively doing.

Open Bomb Factory. An evil scientist designs a factory and hires workers to build bombs for his evil plans. For the sake of increasing efficiency, the evil scientist ensures an unimpeded flow of information among everyone in the factory through regular staff meetings, demonstrations, and so on. The workers perform the same tasks as in *Secret Bomb Factory*, but everyone understands that they are building bombs for an evil scientist.

It is clear that in *Open Bomb Factory*, the workers bear moral responsibility for their collective action of building bombs, whereas in *Secret Bomb Factory*, they do not. But in both cases, the workers perform the same individual actions, and there is no difference with respect to their agency, either as individuals or as a group. The only relevant difference is that the flow of information is free in the latter case but not in the former. And this is due, in turn, to differences in the structure of the group in each of the two cases.

8.7 Lessons learned

I believe there are two important lessons that we can learn from the preceding considerations. The first is specifically about the methodology of collective action theory as it relates to issues of agency and moral responsibility. The second is a broader lesson about the relative unimportance of ontology when studying normative questions about groups; this lesson is illuminating for the debate on the legal status of corporations as 'persons.' I will conclude this chapter by discussing each in turn.

The cases demonstrate several important lessons for the study of collective action and collective moral responsibility. The collectivizing methodology of WRR—despite seeming so reasonable—ensures that any resulting theory of collective action and responsibility will become mired in a series of false assumptions. This is because questions concerning agency loom large when considering the basic actions and moral responsibility of individuals. WRR focuses our attention on the corresponding questions in the realm of collective action and collective moral responsibility. But the Hollywood Standoff and the pair of Bomb Factory cases show us that those are the wrong questions to consider. Collective agency—whatever that turns out to be—is simply irrelevant.

The productive questions center around the structure of groups whose members act collectively. In particular, the group's structure yields important clues about the incentives and disincentives that have an impact on the group's members. Just as importantly, the structure also determines to a large extent how the information will flow through the group and which members will have access to specific pieces of information that have an impact on their choices. The philosophy of collective action has been strangely silent on those issues. But in order to make progress in understanding collective action and moral responsibility, we need to refocus our attention on the structural and epistemological features of groups.

Even in debates outside of collective action theory, the ontology of groups contributes very little to our understanding of responsibility and other attributes that we sometimes assign to them. What matters is not ontology but empirical facts about the group's structure, decision making processes, and informational dynamics. If we have a solid understanding of the structure and dynamics of the group, then the ontological categories of the group have no extra explanatory power.

In short, there are two ways of approaching the problem of collective responsibility. The first is by assigning an ontological category to groups (e.g. 'agent') and then 'reading off' the properties of agents in order to attribute those properties to groups. The second is to assign properties to groups based on their unique characteristics, group dynamics, power structure, and so on. I advocate the latter.

Although the terms of legal debates do not map cleanly onto philosophical discussions in collective action theory, we do see a strikingly similar methodological dichotomy in questions concerning the rights of certain groups, particularly corporations. I'll conclude by considering how this plays out in the majority and minority opinions in the now-infamous *Citizens United* case.

This case was brought by a non-profit corporation, Citizens United, which produced a documentary about Hillary Clinton prior to the 2008 presidential election. The group intended to make their documentary, *Hillary: The Movie*, available on cable pay-per-view within thirty days of the election and asked the court for relief from the Bipartisan Campaign Reform Act (BCRA), which prohibited corporations from express advocacy within thirty days of an election. Among the arguments offered by Citizens United was an argument that the BCRA violated the corporation's free speech rights.

In its now notorious opinion, the conservative majority of the court found that Citizens United did have the right to air their documentary in the run-up to the election, notwithstanding BCRA. Their sweeping opinion overturned the earlier *Austin* decision which had found that some laws curtailing the free speech of corporations were constitutional. *Citizens United* thereby granted broad free speech rights to corporations and opened the floodgates to virtually unlimited campaign advocacy and expenditures by large corporations.

Although the legal discussion surrounding the majority opinion in *Citizens United* is detailed and complex, the core argument is surprisingly straightforward. The court had long recognized corporations as 'persons' under the law; as such, corporations enjoy the same set of constitutional rights as other types of persons, such as ordinary human beings. Persons enjoy constitutional rights, among which is the First Amendment right to free speech, particularly free speech in the political arena. Thus, it is unconstitutional to pass a law that places an undue burden on the free speech of corporations, and so the government 'may not suppress political speech based on the speaker's corporate identity. No sufficient governmental interest justifies limits on the political speech of nonprofit or for-profit corporations' (Citizens United 2010, 913).

For the sake of the present discussion, we should note two features of this argument. First, the ontological status of the corporation as a 'person' does all the heavy lifting. Any person has the right to free speech; corporations are persons; therefore, corporations have the same right to free speech. The second feature of the argument flows naturally from the first. Because the ontological status of the corporation does all the work in establishing its free speech rights, there is little consideration of the special structures of corporations as compared to the structures of other groups. Indeed, corporations are repeatedly lumped together with arbitrary other types of groups throughout the majority opinion. For example, Anthony Scalia writes in his concurrence that:

> Surely the dissent does not believe that speech by the Republican Party or the Democratic Party can be censored because it is not the speech of 'an individual American.' It is the speech of many individual Americans, who have associated in a common cause, giving the leadership of the party the right to speak on their behalf. *The association of individuals in a business corporation is no different*—or at least it cannot be denied the right to speak on the simplistic ground that it is not 'an individual American.'
>
> (Federal Election Commission, Citizens United 2010, 928, emphasis mine)

Here, Scalia is arguing that the 'association' of individuals into a for-profit corporation is 'no different' from the association of individuals into a political party. The majority opinion also cites, with approval, grouping corporations into the much broader category of arbitrary associations of people:

> The Court has thus rejected the argument that political speech of corporations or other associations should be treated differently under the First Amendment simply because such associations are not 'natural persons.'
>
> (Federal Election Commission, Citizens United 2010, 900)

In short, the assignment of personhood to corporations and other associations of individuals is taken repeatedly throughout the opinion to establish with little to no further argument that corporations have the same rights as natural persons. In fact, the vast majority of the opinion's argument is given over to other issues, such as whether the speech of corporations has a distorting effect on political discourse.

As with the category of 'agent' in the debate about collective moral responsibility, if all parties to the dispute agree that a corporation is a person and that persons have free speech rights, then the best that a skeptic can do is argue around the margins, looking for other issues that may be relevant.

In *Citizens United*, this dynamic plays out clearly. The minority argues that despite the personhood of the corporation, the government has a compelling interest in limiting the corporation's free speech rights. One such argument is that the large financial resources of a corporation create the danger of distorting the political discourse or of capturing elected officials in a *quid pro quo* arrangement. But these tertiary arguments are found wanting. For instance, the argument alleging undue influence would equally apply to extremely wealthy individuals, and the court finds no constitutional justification for limiting the free speech of an individual, no matter how wealthy.

I think it's fair to say that once the personhood of the corporation has been granted, making an argument in favor of restricting the speech of corporations is going to be an uphill battle. For as soon as corporations and every other type of voluntary association of individuals have been lumped together into the same category, then any free speech restriction will seem inappropriately 'chilling.' For example, suppose a small number of ordinary, like-minded citizens want to pool their money in order to rent a billboard advocating for a political candidate. Surely, it would be unconstitutional to restrict their ability to do so merely because they are an association of individuals. And if corporations are grouped together with every other type of association, then we will certainly give broad constitutional rights to them. Indeed, throughout the majority's opinion, the corporate identity of an association of individuals is treated as ancillary to the discussion. A vast range of associations of individuals counts as a person, and therefore has free speech rights, regardless of the specific form that the association happens to take, including the corporate form.

If this issue follows the same general pattern as we saw with agency and collective responsibility, then it will be tempting to focus on the question of whether we really ought to consider a corporation a 'person.' However, we've already seen that such a strategy is likely to be a distraction from the most important issues at hand. The question of whether an association of individuals happens to be a 'person' is not likely to settle the issue of whether the association ought to be granted the same rights as an ordinary human person. Instead, we ought to consider the structure of the association, its information flow, power dynamics, and other characteristics in order to determine whether the association ought to have rights, side-stepping the question of personhood entirely.

To illustrate, consider two different associations. The first is a small group of individuals who pool their money to rent a billboard advocating for a political candidate. The second is a large corporation with thousands of employees and vast financial resources.

As I have mentioned, opponents of the *Citizens United* decision have focused on the power difference between large corporations and individuals or small associations of individuals. For them, the difference is that the corporation may have so much influence that it could distort the public discourse, whereas our small group of individuals does not have this power. This may be true, but it is not in virtue of the corporation being a corporation. The small group could easily decide that it would be beneficial to incorporate, and this does not automatically increase their power. The corporate structure is simply not the deciding factor, but it is relevant.

A large corporation's vast financial resources are the result of the labor of thousands of individuals, combined with the financial support of investors. But these large corporations inevitably take on a hierarchical structure which concentrates power into the hands of a relatively tiny number of managers. This is no accident; without such a concentration of power, the organization will be too unwieldy and slow to function. Information flows upwards to the managers, who make strategic and practical decisions for the corporation. Power also flows upwards, and there is rarely (if ever) any mechanism for soliciting opinions from the rank-and-file workers whose efforts sustain the corporation on a day-to-day basis. And of course, they also have no authority or power to speak on behalf of the corporation.

The justification for granting free speech rights to a corporation or other association of individuals is ultimately to protect the free speech of its members. The members 'speak through' the association, so to speak, no matter whether that association happens to take the form of a corporation, a partnership, union, or something else. Thus, the court reasons, if we place an undue burden on the free speech of the corporation, we are thereby placing a burden on individuals, which is unacceptable.

But the flaw in this line of reasoning is now clear. When only a tiny number of managers have the authority to cause the corporation to 'speak' its political opinions, then it is not the free speech of the corporation's members which is being protected. After all, it is nonsensical to argue that the court protects a worker's right to speak through the corporation if the worker had no ability to do so in the first place and never could, owing to the unique structure and power dynamics of the corporation. At best, the free speech rights of the managers are being protected; but nobody is alleging that the managers are the corporation.

The same consideration provides a compelling answer to Scalia's worry about the status of political parties. A person joins a political party precisely because she agrees with its beliefs and ideology. Thus, placing a restriction on the free speech of the political party is tantamount to denying the free speech rights of its members, just as with the small association we've just considered. The same applies to at least some religious organizations, labor unions, and political action committees. It does not ordinarily apply to large, heterogenous corporations comprising thousands of individuals with widely varying opinions and interests.

And so we are led to a conclusion very similar in spirit to what we reached with respect to collective responsibility. There, we concluded that it is not the ontological category of the group that explains why it does or does not bear collective responsibility, but the structure and dynamics of the group. Whether you decide to call the group an 'agent' is simply window-dressing. Here, we see the same pattern. It is not the ontological category of the group that explains why it does or does not deserve free speech protection but the structure and dynamics of the group.

This is as it should be. Although the philosophical literature on collective action tends to be concerned with moral responsibility and not with the rights and privileges of groups, rights and responsibilities are two sides of the same coin. So we ought not be surprised that the two issues rise or fall together with respect to the ontology of groups.

Notes

1. Following in the tradition of Donald Davidson (1963).
2. See (Chant 2015, 2017). For a positive account of collective intentions that is independent of the collectivizing approach and its metaphysical commitments, see (Chant and Ernst 2007, 2008).
3. For example, if I knew that grazing my cattle would thereby ruin the land given the amount of grazing already taken place, then I may be wholly responsible for the 'collective act.'
4. See Kirk Ludwig (2016) for a detailed analysis of the logical structure of such sentences.
5. For example, Pettit says that 'The issue of corporate responsibility gets off the ground in virtue of the argument that corporate entities do indeed count as agents in their own right …' (2009).
6. David Copp provides a particularly clear example of this approach. In his (1984), he argues for an account that paves the way for a theory of collective responsibility by providing an account in which groups can be agents. In his (2006), he argues for the existence of collective agency by arguing for (what we call) non-distributive moral responsibility because on his view, agency is clearly a necessary condition for moral responsibility. See Arruda (2017) for a survey of arguments that infer facts about agency from facts about responsibility, as well as a critique of the form of argument offered in the present chapter.
7. For an overview of theories of the agency of groups, see Gold and Sugden (2007). They take the common core of those theories to be the ability to adopt the perspective of the group so that each member does their part of the action that realizes the best available outcome.
8. Elsewhere, I have referred to this as the 'special composition question' of action theory (Chant 2006, 2010).
9. For a discussion of how this dynamic played out prior to the Challenger disaster, see Diane Vaughan (1990). She discusses in detail how the organizational structure of NASA, its contractors, and regulatory agencies created a pattern of incentives and disincentives that impeded the flow of critical safety information, which increased the probability of the disaster.

References

Arruda, Caroline, 2017. How I learned to worry about the Spaghetti Western: Collective responsibility and collective agency. *Analysis*, 77(2), pp. 249–259.

Chant, Sara Rachel, 2006. The special composition question in action. *Pacific Philosophical Quarterly*, *87*(4), pp. 422–441.

Chant, Sara Rachel, 2010. Two Composition Questions in Action. In Allan Hazlett (Ed.), *New Waves in Metaphysics* (pp. 27–53). Palgrave Macmillan, London.

Chant, Sara Rachel, 2015. Collective responsibility in a Hollywood standoff. *Thought: A Journal of Philosophy*, *4*(2), pp. 83–92.

Chant, Sara Rachel, 2017. *Collective Action and Agency.* Marija Jankovic and Kirk Ludwig (Eds.), The Routledge Handbook of Collective Intentionality, New York, NY.

Chant, Sara Rachel and Ernst, Zachary, 2007. Group intentions as equilibria. *Philosophical Studies*, *133*(1), pp. 95–109.

Chant, Sara Rachel and Ernst, Zachary, 2008. Epistemic conditions for collective action. *Mind*, *117*(467), pp. 549–573.

Citizens United v. Federal Election Commission, 2010. 130 S. Ct. 876. https://www.supremecourt.gov/opinions/09pdf/08-205.pdf

Copp, David, 1984. What collectives are: Agency, individualism and legal theory. *Dialogue: Canadian Philosophical Review/Revue canadienne de philosophie*, *23*(2), pp. 249–269.

Copp, David, 2006. On the agency of certain collective entities: An argument from. *Midwest Studies in Philosophy*, *30*, pp. 194–221.

Davidson, Donald, 1963. Actions, reasons, and causes. *The Journal of Philosophy*, *60*(23), pp. 685–700.

Enç, Berent, 2003. *How we act: Causes, reasons, and intentions.* Oxford University Press, Oxford.

Feinberg, Joel, 1968. Collective responsibility. *The Journal of Philosophy*, *65*(21), pp. 674–688.

Ginet, Carl, 1990. *On Action*. Cambridge University Press, Cambridge.

Gold, Natalie and Sugden, Robert, 2007. *Theories of Team Agency.* Oxford University Press, Oxford.

List, Christian and Pettit, Phillip, 2004. Aggregating sets of judgments: Two impossibility results compared 1. *Synthese*, *140*(1), pp. 207–235.

Ludwig, Kirk, 2016. *From Individual to Plural Agency: Collective Action: Volume 1.* Oxford University Press, Oxford.

Pettit, Philip, 2009. Corporate responsibility revisited. *Rechtsfilosofie & Rechtstyheorie*, 38(159), pp. 159–176.

Pettit, Philip, 2010. Groups with minds of their own. *Social Epistemology: Essential Readings*, 242, pp. 167–193.

Vaughan, Diane, 1990. Autonomy, interdependence, and social control: NASA and the space shuttle challenger. *Administrative Science Quarterly*, *35*(2), pp. 225–257.

9 Deviant causation and the law

Sara Bernstein

A gunman intends to shoot and kill Victim. He shoots and misses his target, but the gunshot startles a group of water buffalo, causing them to trample Victim to death. The gunman brings about the intended effect, Victim's death, but in a "deviant" way rather than the one planned. This chapter argues that such causal structures, *deviant causal chains*, demonstrate a problematic underspecification of several key legal concepts. A deviant causal chain occurs when an outcome is brought about through different or "deviant" means rather than the means intended. What the law makes of these cases, and how the law should handle them, is the focus of this chapter.

Here is the plan. After a few preliminaries (section 9.1), I show that deviant causal chains challenge the legal distinction between attempts and completed crimes and also the distinction between attempts and mere preparations (section 9.2). I then suggest that cases of deviant causation challenge existing notions of legal liability for completed crimes in terms of *actus reus* and *mens rea*, and argue that natural accounts of negligence misclassify some cases involving deviant causal chains (section 9.3). After diagnosing several conceptual vulnerabilities in the law revealed by deviant causal chains (section 9.4), I show that natural strategies for specifying or shoring up legal theories in the face of these examples are unpromising (section 9.5).

9.1 Preliminaries

Deviant causal chains share a common structure: an agent intends to bring about *x*, and *x* occurs in a different way than that intended or expected by the agent.[1] Following (Davidson, 1963), I will call *basic deviant causal chains* those deviant causal processes initiated by mere intentions. An example of basic deviance, drawn from Davidson, is the following:

> (Mountaineer) A mountaineer intends to eventually rid himself of the man below him on the rope by dropping him. Merely forming the intention so unnerves him that he loosens his grip on the rope, dropping the fellow climber.

DOI: 10.4324/9781003242451-13

Here, the mere intention to murder the fellow mountaineer initiates a causal chain leading to the murder. This and similar cases are to be contrasted with *non-basic deviant causal chains*, which stem from an intention and a particular action stemming from the intention. An example of non-basic deviance is the following:

> (Bad Shot) Assassin A is dispatched to kill Victim. Assassin A shoots at Victim, but misses. The shot wakes up Assassin B, who was independently dispatched by a different assassination agency. Assassin B shoots Victim and kills him. (Assassin B would not have shot had Assassin A not awakened him.) Had Assassin A not shot, Victim would not have died.

Here, Assassin A not only intends to kill Victim but also takes a shot in service to doing so. The shot doesn't directly kill Victim but does make it the case that Victim dies in virtue of causing Assassin B to shoot. Cases of non-basic deviance are so-called because there is an action in addition to an intention, after which the causal chain goes awry relative to the agent's plan. The extra action exemplifies non-basic deviance. I will largely focus my discussion on cases of non-basic deviance since poor intentions alone are neither criminal nor tortious.

Deviant causal chains can be further distinguished along several dimensions. There are those that contain causal processes very different in type from the one planned by the agent. One example is the one with which we began, in which a gunshot wakes up a herd of angry water buffalo. The causal process that includes stampeding water buffalo is a very different sort of causal process than the one that includes a direct gunshot. Contrast the water buffalo case with Bad Shot, in which Assassin A's shot causes Assassin B's shot, which results in Victim's death: one causal process involving a gunshot is swapped for a very similar sort of process, namely, a different gunshot. Call those deviant causal chains containing a very different sort of causal processes than the one planned *process-divergent*, and those containing a similar sort of causal processes to the one planned *process-similar*.

A parallel distinction can be drawn with respect to the nature of the outcome planned by the agent. Some deviant causal chains eventuate in an outcome unlike the one planned by the agent while still involving some shared essential planned part with the planned one, e.g., a particular victim's death. If Jane plots to kill Jacintha by gradually adding drops of slow-acting poison to her toothpaste, but Jacintha dies by choking on the same toothpaste that would have eventually killed her in any case, Jacintha dies a different sort of death than the one Jane had planned. Call this sort of event *outcome-divergent*. Contrast this sort with Bad Shot, in which Victim dies a very similar death to the one Assassin A had initially planned, i.e., death via gunshot. Call this latter sort of case *outcome-similar*. As I shall suggest, these distinctions become important when attempting to draw lessons for the law from deviant causation.

Deviant causal processes demonstrate the underspecification of legal concepts because the "ingredients" for criminal and tortious liability are present, but the cases do not easily or correctly fit into existing legal taxonomies of crimes. Such cases also reveal important ambiguities in the law involving differences between an agent's intended outcome and the actual outcome.

Problems with deviant causal chains arise in part because the standard for establishing the presence of causation in tort law and in criminal law is the simple counterfactual "but-for" test: is it the case that but for the occurrence of *x*, *y* wouldn't have occurred?[2] Since deviant causal chains are initiated by elements that pass the but-for test (i.e., if the legally relevant intention and action hadn't occurred, the deviantly caused outcome wouldn't have occurred), deviant causation becomes the vehicle for legal responsibility. So I will demonstrate in the following sections.

9.2 Deviant causal chains and attempts

Here I will suggest that deviant causal chains challenge the legal distinction between attempts and completed crimes. Intuitively, an attempt is different than a completed crime insofar as a mere attempt does not result in the intended crime, whereas a completed crime eventuates in the intended outcome. For example, if Jane attempts to injure Jacintha by taking a hammer to her toe but misses and succeeds only in scaring her, Jane would be legally culpable for an attempted crime rather than a completed one.

Roughly, a criminal attempt occurs when (i) there is specific intent to commit a crime, and (ii) the offender takes direct action toward completion of the crime. More specifically, many legal codes in the United States[3] share a definition of a criminal attempt according to which "A person commits the offense of attempt when, with intent to commit a specific offense, he or she does any act that constitutes a substantial step toward the commission of that offense" ((720 ILCS 5/8-4) (from Ch. 38, par. 8-4). According to *Model Penal Code* (USA) (Part 1, General Provisions, Article 5, Inchoate Crimes), a person is guilty of an attempt to commit a crime if, acting with the kind of culpability otherwise required for commission of the crime, s/he:

(a) purposely engages in conduct which would constitute the crime if the attendant circumstances were as he believes them to be; or
(b) when causing a particular result is an element of the crime, does or omits to do anything with the purpose of causing or with the belief that it will cause such result without further conduct on his part; or
(c) purposely does or omits to do anything which, under the circumstances as s/he believes them to be, is an act or omission constituting a substantial step in the course of conduct planned to culminate in his commission of the crime.

Satisfying the definition of a criminal attempt often depends on the establishment of *mens rea* and *actus reus*, regardless of what actually occurs as a result of these things. For example, Jane's formation of the intention to injure Jacintha, along with swinging a hammer near her toe, counts as an attempt regardless of whether the hammer landed one inch from Jacintha's toe or five inches from Jacintha's toe. What makes Jane's action an attempt rather than a completed crime is that Jane does not succeed in bringing about what she intends, i.e., injuring Jacintha.

Or so one might think. Non-basic deviant causal chains exploit this way of drawing the line between attempts and completed crimes, posing at least two specific problems. First, what would ordinarily be thought of as an attempted crime eventuates in the intended outcome, such that a deviant causal chain satisfies the definition of a completed crime rather than a mere attempt. In non-basic deviant cases, an agent both forms an intention and performs an action that counts as a substantial step toward the crime. The intended outcome is even caused by the agent's act. But the scenario does not (and should not) count as a completed crime by the agent, given that the means through which the outcome is brought about are different than those intended. In Bad Shot, Assassin A intends to cause Victim's death and takes substantial action in service to doing so. Moreover, Victim's death occurs and wouldn't have occurred had it not been for Assassin A's shot. Assassin A's shot should count only as an attempt rather than a completed crime. Because the intended outcome actually occurs, however, Assassin A counts as having initiated a completed crime rather than an attempt.[4] Exacerbating this problem is that many such cases also respect the legal concurrence requirement for *actus reus* and *mens rea*[5]: in Bad Shot, the intention and the act are concurrently timed. So the synchronicity requirement on *actus reus* and *mens rea* cannot be used to recategorize deviant causal chains.

Deviant causal chains also make trouble for the distinction between attempts and mere preparations. What one would ordinarily think of as merely preparing to attempt the crime instead counts as a full-blooded attempt or a completed crime, owing to the fortuitous occurrence of the outcome. Consider the following case:

> (Murderous Lover) Jane plots to murder Jacintha by poisoning her drink. While preparing the poison, Jane is so nervous that she breaks the bottle of poison. Very shortly thereafter, Jacintha slips on a splinter of glass from the broken poison bottle, and dies from the fall.

Intuitively, Jane was only preparing to attempt to murder Jacintha. If Jacintha's death had not occurred, Jane's actions would not have counted as anything but a mere preparation.

But because Jane's mere preparation results in the ultimately intended outcome, preparing the attempt counts (minimally) as the attempt itself. Another example:

> (Bad Driver) Jane plots to murder Jacintha with a hatchet. As she is driving to Sears to buy a hatchet, she fails to see a pedestrian in the pedestrian

walkway, and hits and kills the pedestrian. Upon rushing out of the car, she realizes the pedestrian was Jacintha.

It seems clear that Jane has merely begun to prepare to murder Jacintha rather than carry out the attempt. The law, however, is forced to view such preparations as attempts *simpliciter*, due to the collective presence of *mens rea*, *actus rea*, and the intended outcome.

Nor do existing philosophical accounts of attempts handle this problem well. According to Yaffe's (2010) proposed definition, an attempt includes a causal chain that begins with an intention that plays the proper causal role and ends with the world matching its content. But in failing to give a theory of what it is for the intention to play a proper causal role, the account classifies Murderous Lover and Bad Driver as attempts rather than mere preparations. Yaffe discloses this vulnerability in his account of attempts, admitting:

> What constraints must a causal chain that begins with the intention and ends with the world matching its content meet if it is to be an instance in which the intention plays the proper causal role? This is a very difficult question for which I do not have a complete answer, and I do not have an answer that "solves" cases of deviant causation.
>
> (2010, p. 86)

The challenge is in specifying the appropriate connection between the intention and the way the outcome occurs. The most natural answer is that outcome must be caused by the intention. In deviant causal chains, however, outcomes *are* caused by intentions, and yet the outcome does not occur in the way intended – a fact relevant to, but not accounted for, by legal treatments of these cases.

9.3 Deviant causal chains and negligence

It is tempting to think that deviant causal chains are so outré as to not warrant major concern. One might admit that these very strange cases present problems for existing legal taxonomies, yet think there is no major reason to worry about them, given their rarity. But as I shall now argue, deviant causal processes play a major role in extremely common legal scenarios, negligence torts and reveal a host of issues lurking in the background of more normal negligence cases.

Negligence occurs when there is "failure to act with a prudence that a reasonable person would have under the same circumstances," and the failure to act results in harm.

According to *Model Penal Code* (section 2.02(2) (d)), "[a] person acts negligently … when he should be aware of a substantial and unjustifiable risk that the material element exists or will result from his conduct." A negligent act that causes foreseeable harm or injury counts as liable negligence in the law. Five specific elements are required for negligence: duty (whether a defendant owed a duty to a plaintiff), breach of duty (violation of what was owed), cause-in-fact (causation as given by the but-for test), proximate causation (foreseeable causal result of negligence) and damages (harm or injury to plaintiff).

Prima facie, legal responsibility for negligent deviant causation is an unstable concept since foreseeability is required for negligence torts. Given the unexpected nature of deviant causal chains, it might seem like such cases don't involve foreseeable outcomes, and so there is no such thing as deviant negligence. In most cases of negligence, moreover, cause-in-fact and proximate causation often go together. Consider the following example:

> (Rollercoaster) Joe owns a fairground and the rollercoaster tracks have rusted away. Children are mounting the ride. One child, Jane, notices the flaw and runs off to tell someone, but trips and dies on the way. Joe's negligence caused Jane's death. But Joe is not legally responsible for Jane's death.

Here, Joe's negligence in letting the tracks rust away causes the child to trip and die. According to the law, Joe is not legally culpable: because Jane's death in that particular way was not foreseeable, Joe is not responsible for the death despite causing it.

But cause-in-fact and proximate causation do not necessarily come apart in cases involving deviant causal chains. There are foreseeable outcomes caused by negligent actions that should not necessarily be legally classified as negligence. Consider the following example:

> (Cardiac Arrest) Jacquise knows that Kaia is heart attack-prone. Jacquise jumps out from behind a pillar and scares Kaia. Kaia laughs at the dangerous prank, but in doing so, becomes distracted and trips over a planter. The surprise of tripping over the planter causes a heart attack.

This case has every element required for negligence. Jacquise has a duty to Kaia not to perform actions that might cause a heart attack, and breaches that duty by surprising her. Jacquise can foresee that Kaia might die of a heart attack if he surprises her. Had he not jumped out from behind the pillar, Kaia would not have died. And Jacquise causes injury by causing the heart attack. Intuitively, however, such a case should not count as negligence since the heart attack was deviantly caused.

Case law yields mixed results on the lesson of this latter sort of case. Generally, if an outcome is caused in an unforeseeable way, the defendant is not liable for damages. In *Bunting v. Hogsett*, however, the law ruled in the opposite direction. Hogsett, a train operator, conducted a railroad engine far above the speed limit. In an attempt to avoid a crash with plaintiff Bunting's train, Hogsett reversed the throttle, shut off the engine, and jumped from the train in the hopes that such actions would prevent a collision. The collision occurred nevertheless and did not immediately injure Bunting. However, the crash did reactivate the engine on the original train, which then struck Bunting, injuring him. The Pennsylvania Supreme Court ruled in the plaintiff's favor:

> [...] It was the engineer's negligence that caused the first collision [...] [The first collision] opened the throttle, and turned loose the destructive agency which inflicted the injuries complained of.
>
> (21 A at 32)

Even though the particular route of harm was unforeseeable, the plaintiff recovered damages.

Similarly, in *Sundquist v. Madison Railways Co.* That case concerns a victim of a negligently caused streetcar accident. Though she was physically unharmed by the accident, she was psychologically traumatized by it. Months after the traumatic accident, the victim heard a streetcar bell ring and became so frightened at the sound that she tripped, fell, and was paralyzed by the fall. Though neither the particular form of harm nor the route by which it occurred was foreseeable, the court ruled in her favor. Still, this sort of ruling is unusual.

The law is ambiguous about the role of process-divergence and outcome-divergence in legal culpability. Ideally, the law should provide as detailed principles as possible for applying rules of culpability and responsibility, rather than leaving such decisions up to individual rulings.[6] For if the law sees fit to rule on the relationship between but-for causation and liability, it should not simply leave open the relationship between deviant causation and legal responsibility. It is inconsistent to rule on one sort of causation but not another.

9.4 Diagnoses

Assuming that legal specificity is desirable, where and why does the law go wrong? It's not that the criminals or tortfeasors in these fictional and real cases are completely unaccountable. It's that their situations are either misclassified or unclassifiable under current legal treatments of the relevant concepts. Why?

First, a particular outcome's nonoccurrence or occurrence is central to the distinction between an attempt and a completed crime. In cases of both basic and non-basic deviance, however, the intended outcome actually occurs. Thus conditions for completed crimes and completed attempts are satisfied even when the cases are not good fits for existing legal categories.

Second, the law leaves open whether process-similarity or process-divergence effects legal culpability, which is to say, how closely an actual causal chain resulting from an instigator's action must adhere to the instigator's planned way of bringing about the outcome. The law leaves open, for example, whether a death brought about by instigating a water buffalo-trampling with a gunshot should result in the same culpability as an intended death by direct gunshot, where the *mens rea* and *actus rea* are the same in both cases. A causal chain diverging wildly from the planned one but with the desired result satisfies the same conditions for liability as non-deviant causal scenarios.

Third, the law leaves open how closely the nature of an outcome must hew to an instigator's plan for its occurrence—in my language, whether it is outcome-similar to or outcome-divergent from the planned event. The obvious conceptual vulnerability lies in what it is for a crime to "match" an agent's intention. In Murderous Lover, Jane's death is brought about in a very different way than the one planned. But since the law doesn't weigh in on how and whether such outcome-divergence affects criminal culpability, Jacintha can be legally responsible for Jane's death even when the outcome occurs differently than what she had intended.

Metaphysically speaking, this problem is about the modal fragility of events. An event is *modally fragile* if it couldn't have happened in a different manner without being a different event entirely. Clearly, outcomes for which people are criminally or civilly responsible are not maximally modally fragile: not even the best planner knows the precise second or spot at which the death will occur or the exact manner in which it will. But there are no implicit or explicit standards for the modal fragility of intended outcomes, leaving existing legal definitions open to intuitive counterexamples.

Fourth, the conditions for legal responsibility for completed outcomes are heavily rooted in the key elements of but-for causation and concurrent *mens rea* and *actus reus*. Since all elements are present in non-basic deviant causal chains, such cases end up satisfying definitions for more serious crimes than those committed. The most promising solutions might seem to be additions to the law that help eliminate such cases from counting as full-fledged crimes. But, as I shall suggest in section 9.5, supplementing the requirements for legal accountability does not necessarily help.

Thus far, I have focused on how the law as it is currently structured is underspecified with respect to deviant causation. But there is a more serious normative question lurking: what *should* the law say about these cases? How might the law be amended so that deviant causal chains do not pose obvious counterexamples? I do not have space to delve into this complex issue in depth, but I will conclude this section with a pessimistic observation.

Correctly and precisely classifying deviant causal chains in the law would require specific guidelines about causal process similarity and outcome similarity, i.e., how close a causal process and outcome must adhere to a criminal or tortfeasor's original intentions. The idea would be for the law to require that an outcome for which an initiator is held responsible be "the right kind" of the outcome, i.e., that the outcome must adhere fairly closely to the relevant *mens rea*. Similarly, the law would hold that a causal process be "the right kind" of causal process, i.e., that it must adhere fairly closely to the sort of causal process the initiator had planned. With these sorts of supplementary requirements, outcome-divergent and even process-divergent deviant causal scenarios would not satisfy existing legal definitions in the problematic ways detailed above. In the water buffalo case, Bad Driver, and Murderous Lover, the causal processes and particular natures of the outcomes diverge significantly from the intentions of the initiators: the outcomes occur in different ways and via different causal routes than those planned.

However, such guidelines would face major theoretical and practical barriers. First, it would be very difficult to give a precise, principled metric about process similarity and outcome similarity. Consider the following case:

> (Starry Night) Suppose that Maya plans to poison Tegan at 10pm when the storm clouds are rolling in, for extra ghoulish dramatic effect. Maya runs late attempting to mix the poison, however, and so arrives at Tegan's house at 10:45pm. Maya pushes Tegan off the balcony when the sky is starry and clear.

Exactly how much process-divergence and outcome-divergence is there in this example? A precise, detailed answer seems very hard to give. It is a mostly intuitive matter. Additionally, a law building such a metric into the standard for legal culpability would require direct epistemic access to an agent's intentions, as opposed to inferring them from what the agent said and did. Establishing *mens rea* is already a challenge, but ascertaining the contours of an agent's very specific intentions for a crime or tort seems nigh impossible in this setting.

Second, the law would need principled rules for when to emphasize process-similarity and outcome-similarity, and how much weight these should be given in legal culpability. In Bad Shot, Victim dies in very much the same way that Assassin A wanted, but the best classification of Assassin A's action is as an attempt rather than a completed crime. In the other direction, being the "right kind of outcome" should not be the major criterion for culpability or liability. Consider the following case:

> (Gang Shootout) Two rival gangs, Blue and Grey, are engaged in a standoff. Shooter A from Blue breaking the standoff by shooting at Jelena, the leader of Grey, but misses. Shooter B from Grey shoots at Shooter A from Blue, but misses and ends up killing Jelena via friendly fire.

Here, Shooter A initiates a causal chain via gunshot, intending to directly kill his rival. That the causal chain eventuates in his rival being killed by a gunshot specifically isn't enough to make Shooter A culpable for Jelena's death, however. The fact that Jelena's death is "the right kind of outcome" seems less relevant than the complicated process by which it is brought about.

9.5 Possible repairs

In this section, I consider several possible repairs to legal concepts in light of the problems posed by deviant causal chains. Though some are promising partial fixes, I suggest that none fully succeed.

9.5.1 Foreseeability

The most obvious fix is already implemented in tort law: inclusion of a foreseeability constraint on legal responsibility. Though its contours are controversial, the basic idea of foreseeability is "whether one can see a systematic relationship between the type of accident that the plaintiff suffered and … the defendant's [wrongdoing]."[7] Since some deviant causal chains involve unforeseeable process-divergent and/or outcome-divergent effects, a foreseeability constraint does solve some problems with deviant causal chains. This is particularly the case for scenarios like Rollercoaster, in which the child's tripping and dying is not a foreseeable consequence of the rusting tracks.

The foreseeability strategy faces several problems, however. The first problem is that foreseeability is presently only a constraint in tort law rather than criminal law, and generally only with respect to negligence. Thus the criminal law, as it is currently written, leaves out deviant causal chains initiated by "positive" events such as gunshots. A natural response would be to add more foreseeability conditions to other areas of the law, including criminal law and cases other than negligence. However, this strategy faces several problems as well.

First, adding foreseeability to the other conditions for legal responsibility is not always sufficient to generate the correct result. In Bad Shot, Victim's death is foreseeable, and yet Assassin A is not legally responsible for Victim's death. And in Cardiac Arrest, Kaia's potential heart attack is foreseeable and negligently caused but still shouldn't satisfy the legal definition of negligence. In both cases, the outcomes are foreseeable, but the processes by which they occurred are not. Adding foreseeability will overgenerate cases of legal responsibility.

Second and relatedly, it is very hard to construct a foreseeability constraint that is not too stringent or too lax. The law has already struggled to do so, as evidenced by several landmark negligence cases. The landmark *Palsgraf vs. Long Island Railroad Co.* exemplifies the tangle of challenges surrounding foreseeability and causation. In that case, the plaintiff Helen Palsgraf was waiting to board a train to Long Island. As the train was pulling away, two men with a package raced to jump aboard. One man made it onto the train; the other, carrying a package, stumbled to catch the train. Several train employees rushed to help the package carrier onto the train. The package, which the would-be passenger then dropped, turned out to contain fireworks. It exploded, causing injury to Palsgraf. Palsgraf sued the railroad company for negligence. The first ruling was in Palsgraf's favor: she was awarded $6000 in damages. Upon appeal, however, the decision was overturned. A judge ruled that "Here, by concession, there was nothing in the situation to suggest to the most cautious mind that the parcel wrapped in newspaper would spread wreckage throughout the station." A dissenting opinion was also issued, suggesting that "given such an explosion as here, it needed no great foresight to predict that the natural result would be to injure one on the platform at no greater distance from its scene than was the plaintiff" (1928 248 N.Y. 339, 162 N.E. 99). The lasting upshot of the case is that a defendant who is found negligent is only liable for foreseeable harm or the actual injury rather than for every injury resulting from the negligent act.

In the British case *Re Polemis & Furness, Withy & Co Ltd*, a defendant's employees loaded cargo onto a ship. Due to an employee's negligence, a plank fell into the hold of the ship. The plank then caused a spark that ignited some gas vapor in the hold. The gas vapor caused an explosion that destroyed the ship. The court ruled that "a defendant can be held liable for all consequences flowing from the wrongful conduct regardless of how unforeseeable" (1921 3 KB 560). The concept of strict liability for unforeseeable outcomes has now been stricken from British law, but its implications remain controversial even in contemporary legal thought.

Finally, in *Mauney v. Gulf Refining Co.*, an oil refinement company negligently set a fire. As people were frantically running from the refinery fire, a woman who operated a bakery across the street grabbed her child and started running. She tripped over a chair and had a miscarriage, later suing Gulf Refining Company for negligence. The court ruled in favor of Gulf Refining Company holding: "If the appellant didn't see a chair in her way in her own place of business it would impose an inadmissible burden on appellees to say that they should have seen from across the street and through the walls of a building on another corner what appellant did not see right at her feet" (1942, Supreme Court of Mississippi).

Though this seems like the correct result, legal scholars differ on what the lesson should be from this and similar sorts of cases. Of *Mauney v. Gulf Refining Co.,* Hart and Honoré (1959) lament: "Here the court not merely insists on applying the practical test of foreseeability in order to determine the limit of responsibility but also requires such detailed provision that if similar criteria were generally followed, recovery for ulterior harm would seldom be allowed." (p. 267)

A related problem is that the law is ambiguous between in-principle foreseeability and in-practice foreseeability. Moore, for example, finds the foreseeability constraint too demanding, arguing, "[The rule of foreseeability] looks as if it meant that a motorist while driving should think not merely of the children whom he sees crossing the street, but of the adults who might dash out to rescue them, and of the surgeons who might operate on them negligently should they be run over and taken to a hospital." (2009, p. 265) Exactly how much thought must be put into each ordinary action, let alone non-ordinary ones, in order to forestall liability? This explanatory obstacle is not insurmountable, but there is much more work to be done before a foreseeability condition can reliably solve problems involving deviant causation.

9.5.2 Adding a non-deviant causation requirement to legal responsibility

Another tempting solution is to include a stipulation in the law that the criminal or tortious causal relationship between the act and the outcome be non-deviant. Yaffe (2018), for example, includes a non-deviance stipulation in his definition of the correct role of the intention in guiding an action, and also in an independent account of criminal culpability. Husak (correspondence) proposes that a defendant should not be liable when the outcome "is too remote or accidental in its occurrence to have a just bearing on the actor's liability or on the gravity of his offense."

Though the devil might be in the details of such a strategy, there are several general worries about it. First, in some cases, deviant causes *should* be the subjects of legal responsibility. Consider the following case:

> (Ricochet) Jane intends to murder Jacintha. Jane shoots at Jacintha, but the bullet ricochets off of a giant slab of marble, and then strikes and kills Jacintha.

Arguably, this is a deviant causal chain. Arguably, Jane is legally culpable for Jacintha's death even though it did not occur in the way she had planned. Any blanket requirement for legal responsibility involving non-deviant causation is bound to run into similar counterexamples.

Second, philosophers (including Peacocke, 1979; Davidson, 1980; McDonnell, 2015; Blanchard and Schaffer, 2017) struggle to draw a principled distinction between deviant and non-deviant causation, and such a distinction would be essential to any legal theory based on it. Since the default/deviant distinction is irreducibly tied to norms and intentions regarding a particular causal scenario, it is extremely implausible that a principled metaphysical distinction can be drawn in such cases. There is no mind-independent, structural metaphysical difference between Assassin A's and Assassin B's shots. The difference between the shots involves Assassin A's expectation about the causal process resulting from his shot. *Mutatis mutandis* for other deviant causal chains.

Third, since the difference between a deviant and non-deviant causal chain depends on a particular agent's intentions regarding the outcome, such intentions must be evidentially accessible rather than self-reported. One can easily imagine criminal actors and tortfeasors claiming, "But I didn't intend for the death to happen in *that particular way*!" How these claims are to be legally evaluated poses an insurmountable obstacle to using such a distinction, and it's arguable, in some cases, that the particular nature of the outcome should matter so much.

9.5.3 Denying the transitivity of causation

Causation is transitive when, if *a* causes *b* and *b* causes *c*, *a* thereby causes *c*. Transitivity of causation undergirds deviant causation: the gunshot causes the water buffalo stampede that causes Victim's death; thus, the gunshot causes Victim's death. Rejecting the transitivity of causation in cases of deviant causal chains, or rejecting automatic transitivity of causation more generally, is a tempting solution. In Bad Shot, for example, one might hold that Assassin A causes Assassin B to shoot, and Assassin B causes Victim's death, but Assassin A does not thereby cause Victim's death.

This strategy is problematic for several reasons, however. Denying the transitivity of causation only in deviant cases requires a principled deviant/non-deviant causation distinction. As I suggested in section 9.5.2, the prospects for such a distinction are poor: the distinction is irreducibly mind-dependent and context sensitive, and it is poorly suited to play such a central legal role.

Denying the transitivity of causation more generally is theoretically costly. Transitivity is a central intuitive datum about the nature of causation. Setting aside well-known independent problems with transitivity (Paul, 2000; Sartorio, 2005; McDonnell, 2018), many take the transitivity of causal chains to be a theoretical desideratum of a theory of causation owing to its significant explanatory power. Such explanatory power is particularly central to legal explanations, in which causal relationships between proximate causes and their effects often have causal intermediaries. For example, an accomplice who hands his partner the gun thereby causally contributes to the crime.

Denying the transitivity of causation requires principles of demarcation for causal chains. For example, why does driving my car to the coffee shop cause me to drink coffee, but not purchase of my car a decade prior? If we are to deny that purchasing my car ten years ago caused my coffee-drinking, we must have a metaphysical or explanatory principle for ruling out the car purchase as a cause. But it is very difficult to give a principled account of when a causal chain stops and another begins. Moore (2009) holds that causation peters out as the number of events in a causal chain increases. But there are several reasons to reject this idea. Clearly, there are causal relationships between spatiotemporally distant events, like the discovery of a slate mine 300 years ago and current slate prices, or exposure to asbestos and mesothelioma 25 years after exposure. Further, it seems very unlikely that we will be able to give a principled measure of the degree to which causation "weakens" over time. (See Beebee (2013); Bernstein (2017) and Kaiserman (2017, 2018) for more on the prospects of making sense of "degrees of causation.") Such a measure would have to take a stand on the individuation conditions for events, answering questions like: was Jane's preparing the poison one event or three events? Was the commencement ceremony one event or hundreds of little ones? The law would have to take a stand on the existence and persistence conditions for causal chains, weighing in on issues like why a causal chain counterfactually dependent on, say, Jane's birth begins at *that* particular moment far after her birth and ends at *that* other moment, versus a moment before and a moment later. Such a principle must also include implausibly broad generalizations about the boundaries of causal chains: causal chains peter out after *n* number of events or *n* years or *n* meters, etc. Denying transitivity of causation guts the explanatory power of many causal claims while incurring a massive, unmanageable explanatory burden of its own.[8]

9.5.4 Modifying the type of causation required for legal responsibility

Since problems with deviant causal chains get off the ground due to the but-for test for causation, one seemingly attractive (if somewhat radical) solution is to modify the central concept of causation in the law. A natural alternative to viewing causation as counterfactual dependence is instead to view causation as a "productive" relation. According to productive accounts of causation, *c* causes *e* if *c* transfers some sort of physical energy, mark, or "oomph" to *e*. A paradigmatic case of productive causation is one domino hitting another. The legal test for causation would then be: is it the case that a physical process relates the putative cause and effect?[9] This modification is tempting because in many deviant causal chain cases, the initiator does not transfer energy to the outcome. In Bad Shot, for example, Assassin A's shot does not seem to physically interact with Victim. Thus it would not pass a modified legal test for causation.

On balance, however, such a modification wouldn't help. Productive causation isn't generally well-suited to be a legal test for causation since there are countless physical interactions with each outcome that are not legally relevant. Suppose that, in Bad Shot, a hapless intern assassin had been hoping to eliminate the target by playing a very loud boombox. (And suppose, further, that boomboxes were still in production.) Then the auditory vibrations of the boombox constitute a plethora of minute physical interactions between the hapless intern's activities and Victim's death. Even in the original Bad Shot case, the vibrations of Assassin A's shot might physically interact with Victim in minute, microscopic ways. But such interactions do not seem morally or legally relevant: the liberal, productive sense of "cause" is not alone suitable for legal use. (See Bernstein (2017) for an argument that a productive theory of causation is not well-suited to moral and legal aims.) Moreover, some deviant causal chains do contain unbroken chains of productive causation. Consider a modified version of Bad Shot:

> (Boulder) An unskilled gunman intends to shoot and kill someone. He shoots and misses his target, but the gunshot strikes a boulder, which then rolls down onto Victim, killing him.

In this case, the gunshot transfers energy to the boulder, which then transfers energy to Victim, killing him. Deviant causal chains cannot be ruled out by modifying the notion of causation into a productive one.

9.5.5 Dropping causation in favor of causal verbs

Finally, one might be tempted to drop talk of causation altogether in favor of causal verbs. For example: for A to murder B, A doesn't just make it such that B's death occurs; A *kills* B. With respect to deviant causal chains, one can then say that the initiator makes it the case that the outcome occurred but didn't cause it. In Bad Shot, for example, one might say that Assassin A made it the case that Victim died, but A didn't kill Victim. And in Murderous Lover, one might say that Jane made it the case that Jacintha died, but Jane didn't kill Jacintha.

As one might imagine, there are problems with this strategy as well. Presumably, what unites causal verbs is just that they are specific instances of causation: killing, poisoning, and shooting are just particular instantiations of the causal relation. They are determinates of a common determinable. Causal verbs cannot be explicated in non-circular, non-causal terms.

Further, unpacking the causal verbs will just bring back the problem of whether or not a causal chain is deviant. To claim that Assassin A brought about Victim's death but didn't kill Victim is just to stipulate that Assassin A initiates a deviant causal chain. As I discuss in section 9.5.2, such a distinction is irreducibly anthropocentric and difficult to produce and apply in a principled way.

9.6 Conclusions

Deviant causal chains demonstrate the ambiguity of several central legal concepts, including the legal distinction between attempts and completed crimes, attempts and mere preparations, and the joint sufficiency of *mens rea*, *actus reus*, and actual causation for legal responsibility. In addition to providing counterexamples, deviant causal chains lay bare a vulnerability in the law. Here I have focused on attempts and negligence, but similar problems can be generated for many other legal concepts and distinctions, including (e.g.) the distinction between serious and non-serious criminal attempts, proximate versus non-proximate causation, completed versus abandoned criminal attempts, and substantial vs. non-substantial steps to complete crimes. Despite the existence of a long history of legal thought on causation in the law, the relevance of non-standard causal processes to legal responsibility remains underexplored.[10]

Notes

1. Here I focus on cases of deviant causation initiated by agents, but the cases need not involve initiation by an agent. For example, a falling boulder might kill a victim by startling her to death rather than crushing her. Nor do legal contexts require that deviant causal chains be initiated by agents. For example, a jury might puzzle over whether climate change damage can occur in a peculiar way, as when a homeowner is injured while packing his bags in anticipation of an upcoming flood.

2. For more the problem of underspecification with respect to the but-for test, see Gilboa (2019).
3. This chapter uses legal codes in the United States as the main example, but similar legal codes are to be found throughout the world.
4. Cases of basic deviance sometimes generate similar puzzles. In Davidson's basic deviance case, the mountaineer's murderous intention so unnerves him that it causally results in the desired outcome. But does Mountaineer's dropping his partner count as a full-blooded criminal attempt? If we say "yes," it should be uneasily: the mountaineer did not consciously take action in service to murdering his climbing partner. A deviant causal chain resulting from a mere intention should be punished differently than a full-blooded attempt, at the very least. Even calling it a half-hearted attempt seems too strong. If we say "no," it should also be uneasily: the mountaineer was poorly intentioned and should be held legally accountable for something. Involuntary manslaughter isn't a perfect fit, either, since an intention to harm is present. Voluntary manslaughter, perhaps, is the best fit, though this might be seen as too strong on many readings of the case.
5. Husak (2017) explores the concurrence condition in detail.
6. One might wonder why the law shouldn't remain flexible with respect to cases of deviant causation—that is, why it wouldn't be better to maintain the underspecification of the law with respect to deviant causation. One reason is that many cases are settled before they reach the jury stage, and more guidance means quicker legal resolution. Another reason is that causal intuitions are notoriously malleable: leaving causal judgments to judges and other legal entities increases the chance of error and bias in the legal process.
7. "The dominant test of proximate cause in torts makes a defendant liable when but only when the harm he in fact caused was, at the time he acted, foreseeable to him ..." (Moore, 1997. p. 363).
8. McDonnell (2018) develops a strategy of using proportionality to pick out the causal relations that reliably change, without appealing to transitivity. According to his view, if an agent's intention does not match an intermediate event in the right way, then a chained causal relation cannot be safely assumed. I do not discuss such a strategy here, but I do find it promising.
9. Hart and Honoré seem to agree that such a modification is warranted in some legal cases, writing "Only by identifying causation literally with the setting in motion of a physical process which has not come to an end can the cause be said still to be contributing to the event" (1959, p. 244).
10. Many thanks to Caroline Arruda, Jessica Collins, Maytal Gilboa, Doug Husak, Neil McDonnell, Daniel Nolan, several anonymous referees, and audiences at Rutgers University, Columbia University, Bowling Green State University, and University of Barcelona for helpful feedback on this chapter.

References

Beebee, H. (2013). Legal responsibility and scalar causation. *Jurisprudence*, 4, pp. 102–108.

Bernstein, S. (2017). Causal Proportions and Moral Responsibility. In David Shoemaker (ed.), *Oxford Studies in Agency and Responsibility*, Volume 4. Oxford: Oxford University Press. pp. 165–182.

Blanchard, T. & Schaffer, J. (2017). Cause without Default. In Helen Beebee, Christopher Hitchcock & Huw Price (eds.), *Making a Difference*. Oxford: Oxford University Press. pp. 175–214.

Davidson, D. (1963). Actions, reasons, and causes. *Journal of Philosophy*, 60(23), pp. 685–700.

Davidson, D. (1980). *Essays on Actions and Events*, Oxford: Oxford University Press.

Gilboa, M. (2019). Multiple reasonable behaviors cases: The problem of legal underdetermination in Tort Law. *Legal Theory*, 25(2), pp. 77–104.

Hart, H. L. A. & Honoré, Tony. (1959). *Causation in the Law*. Oxford: Oxford University Press UK.

Husak, D. (2017). Courses of Conduct. In D. Nelkin and Sam Rickless (eds.), *The Ethics and Law of Omissions*. Oxford: Oxford University Press.

Kaiserman, A. (2017). Partial liability. *Legal Theory*, 23 (1): 1–26.

Kaiserman, A. (2018). "More of a cause": Recent work on degrees of causation and responsibility, *Philosophy Compass* 13 (7):e12498.

McDonnell, N. (2015). The deviance in deviant causal chains. *Thought: A Journal of Philosophy* 4(2):162–170.

McDonnell, N. (2018) Transitivity and proportionality in causation. *Synthese*, 195(3), pp. 1211–1229.

Moore, M. (1997). *Placing Blame: A Theory of the Criminal Law*. Oxford: Oxford University Press.

Moore, M. (2009). *Causation and Responsibility: An Essay in Law, Morals, and Metaphysics*. Oxford University Press.

Paul, L. A. (2000). Aspect causation. *Journal of Philosophy*, 97(4), pp. 235–256.

Peacocke, C. (1979). Deviant causal chains. *Midwest Studies in Philosophy*, 4(1), pp. 123–155.

Sartorio, C. (2005). Causes as difference-makers. *Philosophical Studies*, 123(1–2), pp. 71–96.

Yaffe, G. (2010). *Attempts: In the Philosophy of Action and the Criminal Law*. Oxford: Oxford University Press.

Yaffe, G. (2018). *The Age of Culpability: Children and the Nature of Criminal Responsibility*. Oxford: Oxford University Press.

10 Foreseeability, causation, and guilt

Nicholas Almendares

10.1 Introduction

The question of how to define accomplices is both a vital and vexing one. In the United States, it has spawned a series of tangled, conflicting doctrines in both federal and state[1] courts. There are rival standards, and this area of law is so muddled that courts sometimes recite conflicting standards in the same case, struggling to distinguish between them.[2] Moreover, even when courts commit to a particular definition of complicity, they fail to apply it consistently.[3] A similar story has played out on the international stage, with the institutions charged with developing international law adopting a variety of often controversial doctrines to address complicity.[4] In some sense, this widespread confusion is unsurprising because complicity is such a nebulous concept. The traditional legal definition of a crime is a combination of a mental state (the *mens rea*) and constitutive actions (the *actus reus*). The *actus reus* of a homicide is killing, the *actus reus* of a burglary is breaking into a dwelling, and so forth, while the *mens rea* often delineates the severity of a crime, such as distinguishing between gradations of homicide. This traditional formulation is a poor fit for complicity, though, as no straightforward set of actions accurately describes being an accomplice. One can help another commit a crime in innumerable ways, and case law includes examples as diverse as serving as a lookout, encouraging the principal perpetrator, and even tacit approval of the crime being committed.[5]

I want to suggest that the confusion we see in the application of complicity law stems from, or at least is parallel to, a deeper theoretical confusion about the nature of accomplice liability. The most common view in the philosophical analysis of criminal law has been to identify complicity with causal contribution. These *causal theories of complicity* essentially define aiding and abetting as causal contribution.[6] Accordingly, helping bring about the crime, i.e., acting so as to cause it, makes one into an accomplice.[7] Proponents of causal theories of complicity argue that this formulation makes complicity consistent with moral blameworthiness: just as it is morally wrong to cause some harm to come into being, it becomes legally wrong and punishable by a well-designed legal system to do the same.[8] It also has the virtue of defining

DOI: 10.4324/9781003242451-14

complicity in terms similar to other crimes. In this chapter, however, I maintain that this theoretical understanding of accomplices, despite its virtues, does not hold up to either close scrutiny or actual practice. Defining complicity purely in terms of causal contribution spreads criminal guilt implausibly broadly. The taxi driver that happens to take the killer to the site of the crime becomes an accomplice, along with arguably the mechanic who maintains the vehicle and so forth. Some limiting principle is therefore needed.

John Gardner's version of a causal theory of complicity is probably the most clear and explicit on this point: he proposes that there are limits on the amount of "rational attention" we ought to pay to how our actions affect the actions of others and that these limits should also circumscribe accomplice liability. Gardner does not elaborate much on the exact boundaries of complicity, i.e., on what analysis a court or other legal actor should engage in to determine whether someone is actually an accomplice. Jurists, confronting the same question of the proper scope of accomplice liability, have developed the foreseeability doctrine, which I argue operationalizes Gardner's rational attention idea. This doctrine, which is used in some United States jurisdictions as well as international courts through the joint criminal enterprise doctrine, limits complicity to consequences that were natural or foreseeable. All else being equal, murder is not a reasonably foreseeable result of a taxi ride, so even though the taxi driver did in fact causally contribute to the murder, she is free from guilt as an accomplice under the foreseeability doctrine. The foreseeability doctrine thus illustrates how the necessary limits on a causal theory could be implemented. However, experience with the foreseeability doctrine also illustrates that the doctrine fails to adequately limit complicity – even with the foreseeability doctrine in place, people who are not blameworthy still count as accomplices. The end result is a law of accomplices that is inconsistent and arbitrary with judges making ad hoc policy decisions in order to avoid unreasonable and unduly harsh consequences. This sort of epistemic limiting principle is therefore insufficient. It does not solve the overbreadth problem inherent in causal theories of complicity. Joint intention-based approaches to complicity show more promise because, among other reasons, they can better define its scope.[9] Intentional approaches also put foreseeability and similar epistemic concepts in their proper place. We do not have direct access to the intentions of others, so the legal system must look to actions in order to infer someone's intentions, and taking into consideration reasonably foreseeable consequences is an effective way of inferring intentions, that is, plans, from a choice or action. So, despite my criticism of the foreseeability doctrine, foreseeability still plays an important role in understanding complicity. It is simply an evidentiary one and not constitutive of complicity.

The rest of this chapter is organized as follows. The next section describes the basic features of causal theories of complicity and the need for some limiting principles. I then continue with an examination and critique of casual theories of complicity based on the foreseeability doctrine. The third section concludes with a sketch of an alternative approach to complicity, one grounded in an account of joint intention and the proper role for foreseeability.

10.2 Causal theories of complicity require limits

Causal theories define complicity in terms of causal contribution. An accomplice, therefore, is someone who causally contributes to the principal offense, answering, at least in an abstract way, the question of what *actus reus* constitutes complicity. This causal definition of complicity makes complicity just like other crimes.[10] An accomplice to crime *K* causally contributes to *K*, i.e., somehow helps bring it about or increases the probability that it will occur.[11] The manner of causal contribution differs; the principal perpetrator causally contributes through their own actions, whereas the accomplice's causal contribution involves another person.[12] But, under a causal theory of complicity, all the crimes share this causal element.[13] Providing the crowbar used to break into a home or soliciting an assassin are straightforward examples of casual contribution; these actions either help enable the crime (the crowbar makes the burglary easier to commit) or are necessary for it to have come about (the victim would not have been killed but for the solicitation).[14]

What becomes immediately apparently, though, is that this barebones causal definition of complicity is too broad. The taxi driver that transports the murderer to the site of the crime causally contributes to it. More counterintuitively, the taxi driver who transports the *victim* to that site also causally contributes to the murder, and so under a basic causal theory, would also be an accomplice to a murder. Causal contribution actually extends even further – the workers who maintain the roads used to transport both perpetrator and victim, the utility that maintains the street lights, and so on could all, depending on the circumstances, causally contribute to the crime. A common example in the literature and the law[15] is a shopkeeper who sells the primary perpetrator a tool used in the crime such as a weapon in a murder. Should the shopkeeper be considered an accomplice? Under a basic causal theory, they would be: the tool provided, let us assume, significantly aided in the commission of the crime, i.e., it increased the probability that the acts or results that define the crime would occur. Further, as above, complicity might extend to the other employees at the store or even all the way through the supply chain that brought the product to the store that eventually placed it in the principal perpetrator's hands.

Causal theories of complicity thus have a problem of overbreadth.[16] One possible response is to establish a threshold for the causal contributions, requiring them to be substantial or not de minimis.[17] This, in turn, demands a theory of causation that is both quantifiable, admitting of a range of causation, and measurable. If the causal contribution is insufficient, then the individual is not an accomplice. That would screen out situations like the famous *Wilcox v. Jeffrey*,[18] where a single concertgoer was considered an accomplice in an unlawful performance because a musician cannot perform for money if nobody buys tickets. At a certain point, perhaps when the audience numbers in the thousands, the causal contribution may be too small to count as complicity. The magnitude of the casual contribution should not conceal circumstances where the contribution is pivotal, however.

That does little to address cases like the shopkeeper, though. By construction, the causal contribution was significant, not de minimis. Likewise, it does not affect the taxi drivers mentioned above; their causal contributions transporting both principal perpetrator and victim are much more substantial than a single customer among thousands. In articulating his causal theory of complicity, John Gardner addresses this issue head on. First, he lays out the groundwork for complicity, i.e., for (legal) responsibility for the acts of another:

> there are two parts of morality. There is what I should do *simpliciter* (the morality of principalship), and then there is what I should do by way of contribution to what you do (the morality of complicity). 'Contribution' here means 'causal contribution.'
>
> ...
>
> The distinction between principals and accomplices, as we discovered, is embedded in the structure of rational agency. As rational beings we cannot live without it ... I am responsible for my actions, and you are responsible for yours. My actions are mine to justify or excuse. And yet my actions include my actions contributing to your actions. So there is a sense in which my responsibility for my actions can extend out to your actions.
>
> (Gardner 2006, pp. 133, 136)

Gardner then presents the following limiting principle in order to avoid a massive extension of accomplice liability:

> What is contentious is the further issue of how, in thinking about which actions I should perform, I should *count* those actions of yours to which I would thereby be contributing ... by and large I am better-placed to prevent my own wrongs than I am to prevent yours ... it would *often* be an inefficient use of rational energy for me to pay the same rational attention to your wrongs as I pay to my own ... This is the main consideration that militates against a radically expanded scope for complicity.
>
> (Gardner 2006, p. 132)

Considerations of rational energy or attention could be used to circumscribe the scope of complicity. Those limits could ensure that a shopkeeper, taxi driver, road worker, utility company, and so on would not be counted as accomplices in any crime that they incidentally causally contributed to.

Unsurprisingly, courts have confronted the same question about the appropriate scope of complicity in a variety of circumstances. There are the drag race cases where the drivers agree to recklessly race in city streets and one of them kills a bystander, raising the question whether the other driver, the one who did not directly harm the bystander, is complicit in that harm.[19] There are also numerous cases that inspired the shopkeeper examples, where the potential accomplice provides the means to commit the crime. In *Ayers,*[20] the defendant sold a 15-year old a stolen gun. A few days later, the purchaser accidentally shot and killed someone. The killing could not have happened but for the sale of the gun (at least not in the way the events actually unfolded), and the court had to determine whether Ayers was guilty not only of the separate offense of illegally selling the gun in the first place but also as an accomplice to the killing. Related examples involve the potential accomplice putting into motion the events that led to the crime. In *Luparello,* the defendant paid others to get some information from the victim "at any cost," and the primary perpetrators ambushed and killed the victim.[21] The question before the court was whether the defendant should be considered an accomplice to the premeditated murder. Cases like these have also been important on the international stage. Jurists and theorists of international law have had to answer the critical question of criminal responsibility for collective action, often at the level of the state or military units.

There are competing complicity doctrines within the law.[22] One way in which courts have sketched the boundaries of accomplice liability is based on whether the results that the accomplice causally contributed to were reasonably foreseeable. The exact formulation varies, but a representative standard is: "aiders and abettors should be responsible for the criminal harms they have naturally, probably and foreseeably put in motion."[23] The United States Supreme Court endorsed a version of this standard in *Pinkerton,* which held co-conspirators responsible for each other's actions: even if the co-conspirator commits crimes that were not themselves the object of the conspiracy if those acts were foreseeable as likely consequences of the initial conspiracy or criminal endeavor, all parties to the conspiracy can be deemed complicit.[24] Similarly, courts have concluded that the use of deadly force was a reasonably foreseeable consequence of a drug sale, especially if it was known to the defendants that some of the parties were armed and had expressly contemplated the possibility of violence.[25] An analogous doctrine has been developed in international law. The doctrine of joint criminal enterprise (JCE)[26] closely follows *Pinkerton* by finding liability for "incidental crimes" – additional offenses committed in the course of working toward an agreed-upon criminal enterprise or goal – provided they were foreseeable. The core idea has been likened to an assumption of risk: while the accomplice may not necessarily intend that these crimes occur, she willingly runs the risk that one of her partners in crime will commit some additional, unrelated but foreseeable, crime.[27] Accordingly, international courts have concluded that defendants are responsible for killings, beatings, and other abuses that have taken place at detention camps or during refugee crises even though there was no showing that the specific abuses were intended by those defendants and those abuses were not the objects of the criminal enterprise they were engaged in because they were naturally foreseeable consequences of that enterprise.[28]

10.3 The foreseeability doctrine: theory and practice

I want to suggest that the foreseeability doctrine is an apt operationalization of Gardner's rational energy or attention idea. Like the limitations of rational energy, foreseeability works as a limiting principle for complicity – i.e., for criminal consequences based on the acts of another – and gives shape to Gardner's rather vague idea. What was reasonably foreseeable describes the limit of one's appropriate rational attention or expenditure of rational energy and, by virtue of that, the much-needed limits of complicity on a causal theory like Gardner's. Examining the foreseeability doctrine has the added benefit of showing what this theory looks like in practice. However, this experience demonstrates that foreseeability is not an adequate limiting principle. It still leads to implausible, worrisome applications of accomplice liability, which I will illustrate below by reference to the shopkeeper example. To avoid problematic results, courts end up adopting ad hoc policy positions, leading to a law of complicity that is muddled, unpredictable, and arbitrary. On a more theoretical level, the fact that courts find themselves in this position implies that the theory of complicity is not providing enough guidance; it is missing something important. Further, because the foreseeability doctrine and causal theories of complicity generally place little weight on the potential accomplice's mental state, it does not align with concepts like blameworthiness and proportionality: the doctrine would find accomplice liability in circumstances where a *principal* would not be held liable of the same offense, which is especially striking since principals, practically by definition, will have a greater causal impact with regards to the crime. The foreseeability doctrine thus leads to the curious situation where accomplices can both do far less to bring the crime about and be less blameworthy by virtue of not intentionally causing the harm, it being more like an accident from their perspective, yet still be guilty of the exact same crime. I will begin by explaining why the foreseeability doctrine is a good way to understand the crucial limiting principle on causal theories of complicity and then identify its problems. These problems motivate the following section, which turns to an alternative, intention-based account of complicity.

According to the foreseeability doctrine, truly unforeseeable criminal acts undertaken by the principal perpetrator do not make one into an accomplice even if the potential accomplice did in fact causally contribute to those acts or the criminal result: (greater than de minimis) causal contribution is therefore considered a necessary, but not sufficient condition for accomplice liability. Foreseeability is thus framed in the right terms for a causal theory of complicity. It hinges on causality; for the crime to be a reasonably foreseeable consequence of the accomplice's actions, it must perforce be *a consequence* of those actions.[29] Moreover, the limits on complicity imposed by the foreseeability doctrine are sensitive to both causation and rational resources: more attenuated causal claims are less apparent and therefore less foreseeable, and a consequence that is not reasonably foreseeable might still be discoverable if an inordinate amount of energy were devoted to that end. (I use Gardner's language of rational energy or efficiency here in order to maintain consistency with his writing, but what he really seems to be driving at is epistemic resources.) The foreseeability doctrine would, consistent with Gardner's arguments, screen out such a case and conclude that there was no complicity. It is worth underscoring that the foreseeability doctrine is objective, which further makes it a good fit for causal theories of complicity. Despite the language sometimes used, courts have been clear that it is not necessary that the accomplice herself actually contemplated or recognized the possibility of the crime occurring. The analysis instead parallels the reasonable person standard, asking what the person should have known rather than what they actually knew.[30] In other words, the foreseeability doctrine does not define complicity as whether the accomplice actually did foresee the consequences of her actions, but whether those consequences were, in principle, sufficiently foreseeable, i.e., natural consequences of those actions given the circumstances.

Since it is based on objectively foreseeable circumstances, the foreseeability doctrine largely unmoors accomplice liability from mental states. The potential accomplice's own mental states are basically irrelevant, bracketing for the present discussion generally applicable defenses based on mental states like insanity. As noted above, it takes very little to causally contribute to a crime, and that is all the more true even once we set aside very small causal contributions.[31] Both courts and theorists have concluded that simple words of encouragement suffice,[32] and the mere presence of an accomplice is sometimes enough on the theory that it can strengthen the principal perpetrator's position or provide tacit encouragement, a functional equivalent to the more established words of encouragement conclusion. All this is consistent with a causal theory of complicity: while there is some ambiguity as to where to draw the line regarding de minimis causal contributions, it is easy to imagine situations where encouragement, either tacit or spoken aloud, would substantially increase the probability that the crime is committed. Someone hesitant to start a fight might act differently when bolstered by a dozen allies. Since causal contribution encompasses so much and the act requirements for complicity are so minimal, neither in and of itself does much to limit accomplice liability. This is the problem the foreseeability doctrine and Gardner's rational energy proposal are meant to solve.

To summarize, the foreseeability doctrine brings a causal theory like Gardner's into the law and gives some content to the rather sparse notion of rational energy, a notion that plays an essential role by limiting the scope of complicity. Without the foreseeability doctrine or something like it, a causal theory of complicity would lead to guilt for anyone that made any non-trivial casual contribution to a crime. The taxi driver that unknowingly transports the victim would otherwise be guilty of being an accomplice to homicide by virtue of their casual contribution of bringing the victim to the site of the murder even though they seem entirely blameless. With this fuller picture of what a causal theory of complicity looks like, and the added benefit of seeing it applied, we can better evaluate it.

The foreseeability doctrine certainly does constrain the scope of accomplice liability. The taxi driver examples illustrate this well. All else being equal, the probability that any given person hailing a cab is either a murderer or a victim is thankfully quite small; the natural consequence of taking taxis is not murder. Under the foreseeability doctrine, there should be no liability for the drivers in those cases. A bizarre or unlikely series of events would insulate someone from complicity, so the foreseeability doctrine is an improvement over the barebones causal theory outlined above. But, it does not do enough. Consider the shopkeeper cases where someone sells a tool used to commit the crime yet does not care whether the crime is actually committed; they are only interested in making the sale. As with the taxi driver, the shopkeeper's causal contribution is non-trivial; let us assume that the tool significantly increases the probability that the crime will be successfully committed. In a series of cases applying the foreseeability doctrine, Judge Posner has considered scenarios like this, leading him to refine the doctrine. Posner contrasts two hypothetical (though inspired from real facts) shopkeeper cases.

> Suppose you own and operate a store that sells women's clothing. Every month the same young woman buys a red dress from your store. You happen to know that she's a prostitute and wears the dress to signal her occupation to prospective customers. By selling her the dress at your normal price you assist her illegal activity, and probably you want the activity to succeed since if it fails she'll stop buying the dress and your income will be less.[33]

Clarifying Posner's example since it seems to elide between the defendant's subjective assessment and an objective one, suppose that red dresses are typically used to signal prostitution, so the relationship between the sale and the crime is reasonably foreseeable. Application of the foreseeability doctrine would make the shopkeeper an accomplice to prostitution (the shopkeeper in Posner's example actually satisfies more demanding conditions of actual knowledge and some desire that the crime occur). Following this logic, anyone who operates a store open to the public is potentially susceptible to accomplice liability. While this might make sense for inherently dangerous products like explosives, even innocuous products like a hammer, kitchen knife, or, indeed, a dress can be used in crimes.

Posner would not consider this shopkeeper an accomplice, though, explaining: "Little would be gained by imposing criminal liability in such a case. Prostitution, anyway a minor crime, would be but trivially deterred, since the prostitute could easily get her clothes from a shopkeeper ignorant of her occupation."[34] In contrast, Posner's second scenario involves someone purchasing a firearm after informing the dealer that she plans to use it to kill someone. Assuming the purchaser goes through with the murder, Posner concludes that the shopkeeper, in that case, would be guilty as an accomplice. "This liability would help to deter—and perhaps not trivially given public regulation of the sale of guns—a most serious crime. We hold that aiding and abetting murder is established by proof beyond a reasonable doubt that the supplier of the murder weapon knew the purpose for which it would be used."[35]

Posner's refinement of the foreseeability doctrine has two parts. If the crime is not a serious one, then casual contribution with actual knowledge of the principal perpetrator's plans, a standard considerably higher than reasonable foreseeability, does not necessarily lead to guilt, especially if the aid offered can be readily acquired elsewhere. Absolving someone because their contribution could have been supplied elsewhere conflicts with the core tenets of causal theories of complicity, however, and has been widely rejected by criminal law theorists, including Gardner.[36] The seller is, in fact, causally contributing to the crime. The more important part is Posner's distinction between complicity for serious and non-serious offenses. As illustrated by Posner, the foreseeability doctrine is not in and of itself a sufficient limit on complicity. We have already seen that the act requirements for complicity are too minimal to appropriately circumscribe accomplice liability, meaning that the only practical limit on it under a causal theory would be something like the foreseeability doctrine. But, on its own, that rule still defines complicity in a problematic way, making accomplices out of ordinary shopkeepers and the like. The way judges have avoided the consequences of the foreseeability doctrine is to make ad hoc policy decisions: the shopkeeper who sells the dress is not an accomplice, the argument goes, because it would be a bad idea to make them one, it would be inefficient or something similar. The actual policy effects of this way of proceeding are debatable. The definition of an accomplice ends up turning not on the legal rule – in this instance, the foreseeability doctrine – but on each judge's own assessment of policy, made with little structure or guidance. The law of complicity, therefore, becomes a confused muddle with ill-defined standards. While not the only consideration, clarity in the law is important. More critically, the foreseeability doctrine makes the law unpredictable and arbitrary. Identical cases can have different consequences depending on the judge's policy conclusions: Posner might consider prostitution to be a minor crime, but that opinion need not be universal, and there will be an array of intermediate cases like fraud. Likewise, the people living under such a legal regime cannot be sure about the law's content and cannot structure their lives accordingly.[37] The shopkeeper who sells women's clothing would not know at the time of the sale whether his actions were criminal or not. While some ambiguity is often unavoidable, the law should aspire to be more consistent and transparent than this, especially before imposing serious criminal sanctions.

Along with being arbitrary, the foreseeability doctrine is also disproportionate – the punishments it dictates do not accurately track the accomplice's blameworthiness. It creates a strange mismatch. Consider what is required for a principal perpetrator. They must have the requisite mental state (*mens rea*), perform the acts that constitute the crime (*actus reus*), and, depending on the offense, achieve certain results. For example, depending on how things are labeled in the jurisdiction, to be guilty of murder the perpetrator must purposefully kill someone. As an objective standard, the foreseeability doctrine ignores mental states and the required constitutive acts for being an accomplice are minimal. All that is needed is sufficient causal contribution toward a reasonably foreseeable end. So, for an accomplice very little is required. Not only does this lead to an implausibly broad complicity doctrine,[38] it means that the law ends up with more demanding standards for principal perpetrators than it does for accomplices. In nearly all cases, we require something more than the negligence-type standard embodied in Gardner's theory and the foreseeability doctrine before potentially depriving someone of their freedom. This difference is striking because the principal perpetrators frequently do more and have greater causal impacts than the accomplices. Put another way, under the foreseeability doctrine, an accomplice can both do less and intend less than a principal perpetrator and be guilty of the same crime. Mere negligence – which is what the foreseeability doctrine amounts to – combined with a small or even potential causal impact is enough to be guilty of a crime as an accomplice.

Sometimes an accomplice could be as blameworthy as a principal perpetrator, such as when the accomplice puts the chain of events that leads to the crime into motion.[39] This might even be true in some instances with an accomplice who meets a relatively low standard for *mens rea*. In *Luparello*, for instance, the defendant's mental state could be aptly described as recklessness or possibly gross negligence – there was a fairly obvious risk of violence given his orders to a group of armed people – and recklessness is a lesser degree of *mens rea* than the purpose requirement usually applied for murder. But, there is a credible argument that Luparello is as blameworthy as the principal perpetrators.[40] So, perhaps the result is correct in this instance. The critique of the foreseeability doctrine and the causal theories of complicity that it instantiates is that they do not distinguish between a case like *Luparello* and one where the accomplice is far less blameworthy. Compare *Luparello* to a case where a group of people hails a taxi and it would be clear to a reasonable person that they plan to commit a crime, perhaps based on their conversation while riding in the taxi to the site of the crime or some other outward signs. In this example, the taxi driver would be considered an accomplice according to the foreseeability doctrine, but she seems far less blameworthy than Luparello. Indeed, this taxi driver example is essentially the same as Posner's dress seller. The foreseeability doctrine has little bite here; the criteria it stakes out do not lead judges, prosecutors, and the whole apparatus of the law to treat more or less blameworthy cases any differently. We would need some other criteria along with it to hone in on blameworthiness. One way to read Posner's policy judgments is as an attempt to fill this gap, but they do not suffice; if the crime involved in my taxi driver example was a serious one, however that is defined, then the driver is still an accomplice even with Posner's refinements to the foreseeability doctrine. Yet it is far from obvious that she should be. That in and of itself would require substantial justification. In the next section, I will propose an alternative intention-based approach to the concept of complicity that avoids the problems in both theory and practice that confront a causal theory.

10.4 A joint intention approach to complicity

Causal theories of complicity define an accomplice as one who makes a causal contribution to the crime. Causing a crime, i.e., a societal wrong implies blameworthiness and makes the accomplice worthy of punishment. The key asset of causal theories of complicity is that they make this special sort of crime similar to other crimes: if one causes a crime to come about, then one is guilty of the crime, and complicity formulated this way is simply a distinctive kind of causation, one that runs through the actions of others rather than direct physical processes. Simple causal contribution cannot be the right definition for complicity, though, because it would mean that in our everyday lives, we could easily – and inadvertently – be accomplices to any number of crimes. As proponents of causal theories have recognized, there needs to be some limit placed on it lest the theory radically and questionably expands the scope of complicity. Gardner argues that efficient use of rational energy is the right limiting principle, and I added that the foreseeability doctrine in U.S. law, which has analogs in other countries and in international law, operationalizes his proposal. Even with these refinements in place, though, causal theories of complicity remain overinclusive. Courts applying the foreseeability doctrine have tried to mitigate its problems by supplementing the rule with ad hoc policy judgments, but that leads the law to be unpredictable and arbitrary. Furthermore, focusing on causation and foreseeability loses track of blameworthiness and proportionality. Overall, even these refined causal theories would make some people into accomplices when they should not be, and they fail to account for important gradations in blameworthiness.

By adopting this kind of definition for complicity, causal theories also make the mental state of the accomplice largely irrelevant[41] – guilt depends on the causal contribution, subject to limiting principles like the foreseeability doctrine, which leads to the problems outlined in this chapter. The project here has been primarily critical, highlighting a difficulty with some of the most influential accounts of accomplice liability. This difficulty exposes the need for an alternative account. Instead of casual contribution, complicity should depend on the accomplice's mental state, focusing on the thing that causal theories place little weight on someone should count as an accomplice to a crime if they have the right kind of intention with respect to it. Given that complicity is an inherently joint offense, an accomplice should be defined as someone with the proper *joint intention* in relation to the substantive offense. This approach can yield an account of complicity with the proper scope and that better captures the critical assessments of blameworthiness and proportionality. Defining complicity this way requires a well-defined concept of joint intention. Despite the central importance of intention in law and morality, there is confusion around the concept, and joint intention is a related but distinct idea that requires considerable elaboration. Elsewhere, Dimitri Landa and I have taken up the project of developing a theory of joint intention that can address complex cases because a simple theory that cannot account for mixed motives or complicated hierarchical relationships (such as those where the hierarchy is not entirely clear) will not be much use to the law and society, and will especially not help in defining the nebulous idea of complicity.[42] Joint intention offers a more promising approach for distinguishing people like shopkeepers, taxi drivers, and even simple bystanders from those that are truly complicit in a crime and deserving of punishment. Furthermore, it is sensitive to the same considerations of rational agency that motivated Gardner's arguments and the foreseeability doctrine. The joint intention approach is also consistent with the law's commitment to *mens rea* and the values of blameworthiness and individual responsibility that underscore it.

There is some terminological confusion, however, as the law and the philosophy of action give the term "intention" a central role but mean different things by it. In the law, calling an action intentional typically distinguishes it from an accidental one or something non-voluntary like a spasm. Philosophically, an intention indicates a plan related to a goal or project ϕ. Moreover, to have a bona fide intention to ϕ means that intention affects other plans and intentions; it means to be committed (subject to later revision) to a set of plans to bringing ϕ about.[43] This characteristic distinguishes intentions from hopes, desires, and other pro-attitudes. Philosophically speaking, if one intends to ϕ, "one is already in progress towards doing it."[44] There is not much difference between having an intention in this sense and taking at least some steps toward carrying it out.

All that being said, causal contribution and foreseeability are not irrelevant. They simply should not *define* complicity. A theorist can stipulate an agent's intentions. But we have no direct access to another agent's intentions; in practice, we can only infer them from their actions. An externally observable event will frequently be consistent with multiple intentions – the bystander and the lookout might, to outward appearances, be doing the same exact thing.[45] Examining the reasonably foreseeable consequences of an action is a useful and common way to infer intentions. A glass falling to the floor and breaking is such a naturally foreseeable consequence of dropping it that we readily infer that if one intentionally does the former, then they intended the latter. Foreseeability thus plays an important evidentiary role. Causal contribution is similar: if someone actively works to bring the crime about, then that is good evidence of their intentions toward it. But, the causal contribution or reasonably foreseeable consequences should not be taken to be constitutive of complicity. They are only means to help uncover the existence of the relevant intentions. To illustrate the difference in these treatments of foreseeability, consider a variation of *Luparello*. Suppose that the defendant again told his criminal partners to get the information "at any costs" while handing them $10,000. It was foreseeable, based on the circumstances, that his agents would have interpreted that as a solicitation to do violence, but the defendant's actual intentions were for them to use the money to hire investigators, pay bribes, and so forth. Under a simple causal theory as well as a causal theory limited by the foreseeability doctrine, the defendant would be an accomplice to the murder or whatever other violence committed by his agents. He would be held just as liable as they were. However, under a joint intention analysis, he would not because he lacks the relevant joint intention toward that crime. In practice, this means that the joint intention approach would offer the defendant the opportunity to present evidence rebutting the inference that he had a joint intention with respect to violence done to the victim, evidence that would be explicitly irrelevant to determining his guilt according to the foreseeability doctrine and a causal theory of complicity. The foreseeability doctrine and analogous causal theories of complicity are thus mistaken about the role that foreseeability plays in determining accomplice liability; it is a level of analysis mistake. As I have briefly sketched, viewing complicity through the lens of intention, especially joint intention, better circumscribes it, preventing complicity from running amok while also drawing the lines between bystander and accomplice in the right way, based on normatively relevant criteria like blameworthiness rather than potential happenstance or impromptu policymaking.

Notes

1. At the federal level, see Weiss (2002, p. 1352). At the state level, see Decker (2008, p. 237): "Due to the inconsistency between the plain language of states' accomplice liability legislation and its respective interpretation in the state courts, many states' accomplice laws present a confused picture in terms of the law's stance on accomplice liability. No aspect of this law is more complex than that relating to the mental state requirement for accomplice liability."
2. E.g., *United States v. Clayborne* (1974) 509 F.2d 473 at 480–481; see also *United States v. Fountain* (1985), 768 F.2d 790 at 798.
3. E.g., Weiss (2002 pp. 1351–1352), Decker (2008).
4. E.g., Ohlin (2007, pp. 75–76).
5. *Hicks v. United States* (1893) 150 U.S. 442; *Veney v. State* (1961) 170 A.2d 171; *United States v. Garguilo* (1962) 310 F.2d 249 at 253; *People v. Villa* (1957) 318 P.2d 828 at 833–834 ("They aided and abetted by their actual presence … At the time of the rape by each of the men the other three stood nearby and abetted the perpetrator by presenting a show of force and by keeping watch against intrusions."); *People v. Mummert* (1943) 135 P.2d 665 at 668; *People v. Hill* (1968) 233 N.E.2d 367.
6. There are some exceptions and nuances orthogonal to the arguments presented here. The defining characteristic of a causal theory of complicity, for my purposes, is that causal contribution marks out at least the paradigmatic cases of complicity.

7. Kutz (2000, pp. 220–221), Gardner (2006), and Moore (2007).
8. See, e.g., Moore (2007, p. 407).
9. Both law and philosophy of action refer to intent and intention, but they use the terms differently, an issue I untangle below.
10. Or, alternatively, like some other crimes, namely "result crimes" that are defined in terms of bringing about some particular state of affairs. These are contrasted with "conduct crimes" where the act itself, regardless of its consequences, is an offense. There is debate amongst causal theorists as to whether this distinction is meaningful and its implications for causal theories of crime in general.
11. See, e.g., Moore (2009).
12. Gardner (2006, p. 141); Moore (2007, pp. 422–423).
13. This fact motivates Moore's error theory of complicity. See Moore (2007).
14. See, e.g., Gardner (2006, p. 137) and Moore (2007, pp. 422–423).
15. E.g., *State v. Ayers* (1991) 478 N.W.2d 606; *State v. Travis* (1993) 497 N.W.2d 905.
16. It is not the only problem to be answered by this family of theories. Another common issue for these theories is overdetermination cases, where no single accomplice's causal contribution made any actual difference in the crime coming about. See Moore (2007).
17. Moore (2007, pp. 421–424).
18. *Wilcox v. Jeffrey,* (1951) 1 All E.R. 464 (K.B.).
19. E.g., *State v. McFadden* (1982) 320 N.W.2d 608; *People v. Abbott* (1981) 445 N.Y.S.2d 344; *Commonwealth v. Root* (1961) 170 A.2d 310.
20. *State v. Ayers* (1991) 478 N.W.2d 606. See also *Nash v.* Israel (1983) 707 F.2d 298.
21. *People v. Luparello* (1986) 187 Cal. App. 3d 410 at 419.
22. See, e.g., *United States v. Hill* (1995) 55 F.3d 1197 at 1200; *United States v. Otero-Mendez* (2001) 273 F.3d 46, 52; *State v. Burney* (2003) 82 P.3d 164 at 169.
23. People v. Luparello (1986), 187 Cal. App. 3d 410 at 439. See also *United States v. Fountain* (1985) 768 F.2d 790 at 798.
24. *Pinkerton v. United States* (1946) 328 U.S. 640.
25. See, e.g., *United States v. Alvarez* (1985) 755 F.2d 380; *United States v. Perez* (1981) 648 F.2d 219 at 224; see also United States v. Lippner (1982) 676 F.2d 456 at 463.
26. JCE is actually a complex doctrine with different categories of liability. The one mentioned here is usually referred to as "JCE III" and is the most expansive version.
27. See Prosecutor v Duško Tadić (1999) Case No IT-94-1-A, Judgment at ¶ 228.
28. "The Trial Chamber is not, however, convinced beyond reasonable doubt that the murders, rapes, beatings and abuses committed against the refugees at Potocari were also an agreed upon objective among the members of the joint criminal enterprise. However, there is no doubt that these crimes were natural and foreseeable consequences of the ethnic cleansing campaign." *Prosecutor v Radislav Krstic* (2001) Case No IT-98-33-T, Judgment at ¶ 616.
29. See also Gardner (2007, p. 441).
30. "[T]he issue does not turn on the defendant's subjective state of mind, but depends upon whether, under all of the circumstances presented, a reasonable person in the defendant's position would have or should have known that the charged offense was a reasonably foreseeable consequence of the act aided and abetted by the defendant." *People v. Nguyen* (1993) 26 Cal. Rptr. 2d 323 at 331. See also *People v. Woods* (1992) 11 Cal. Rptr. 2d 231 at 240 ("liability is based on an 'objective analysis of causation'"); *People v. Montano* (1979) 158 Cal. Rptr. 47 at 50–51; Heyman (2010, p. 402); Kreit (2008, pp. 612–613).
31. *United States v. Garguilo* (1962) 310 F.2d 249 at 253 ("evidence of an act of relatively small moment may warrant a jury's finding of participation in a crime"); *Hicks v. United States* (1893) 150 U.S. 442; Mueller (1988).
32. Gardner (2006, pp. 137–138).

33. *United States v. Colon* (2008) 549 F.3d 565 at 571.
34. *United States v. Fountain* (1985) 768 F.2d 790 at 798.
35. Id.
36. Gardner (2006, p. 138), Kutz (2000).
37. Kadish (1997).
38. I am hardly the first to make this point. See, e.g., Kaish (1997, p. 375).
39. Almendares and Landa (2015, p. 750).
40. But see, Kadish (1997).
41. The accomplice might still have defenses based on mental states like insanity or duress, but those are generally applicable and not part of the theory of complicity.
42. Almendares and Landa (2016).
43. Stanford Encyclopedia of Philosophy (2014); Bratman (1987, pp. 18–20).
44. Stanford Encyclopedia of Philosophy (2014).
45. The most difficult cases are those where someone like a lookout ends up being not necessary, i.e., where the accomplice's actions are superfluous or they do not even have to actively contribute to the crime. Under some circumstances, I argue these actors should count as parties to a joint intention, and therefore, accomplices. See Almendares & Landa (2015, pp. 744–753).

References

Almendares, N. and Landa, D. (2015). Mixed motives in the equilibrium view of joint intention. *Philosophical Studies, 173(3)*, pp. 733–755.

Bratman, M. (1987). *Intention, plans, and practical reason.* Cambridge, MA: SCLI Publications.

Decker, J. F. (2008). The mental state requirement for accomplice liability in American criminal law. *South Carolina Law Review, 60(2)*, pp. 237–382.

Gardner, J. (2006). Complicity and causality. *Criminal Law and Philosophy, 1*, pp. 127–141.

Gardner, J. (2007). Moore on complicity and causality. *University of Pennsylvania Law Review PENNumbra, 156*, pp. 432–443.

Heyman, M. G. (2010). The natural and probable consequences doctrine: case study in failed law reform. *Berkeley Journal of Criminal Law, 15(2)*, pp. 388–414.

Kadish, S. H. (1997). Reckless complicity. *Journal of Criminal Law and Criminology, 87(2)*, pp. 369–394.

Kreit, A. (2008). Vicarious criminal liability and the constitutional dimensions of *Pinkerton. American University Law Review, 57(3)*, pp. 585–640.

Kutz, C. (2000). *Complicity: Ethics and law for a collective age.* Cambridge: Cambridge University Press.

Moore, M. S. (2007). Causing, aiding, and the superfluity of accomplice liability. *University of Pennsylvania Law Review, 156(2)*, pp. 395–452.

Moore, M. S. (2009). *Causation and responsibility: An essay in law, morals, and metaphysics.* Oxford: Oxford University Press.

Mueller, G. E. (1988). The mens rea of accomplice liability. *Southern California Law Review, 61(6)*, pp. 2169–2192.

Ohlin, J. (2007). Three conceptual problems with the doctrine of joint criminal enterprise. *Journal of International Criminal Justice, 5(1)*, pp. 69–90.

Stanford Encyclopedia of Philosophy. (2014). *Intention.*

Weiss, B. (2002). What were they thinking? The mental states of the aider and abettor and the causer under federal law. *Fordham Law Review, 70(4)*, pp. 1341–1490.

Cases

Commonwealth v. Root (1961) 170 A.2d 310.
Hicks v. United States (1893) 150 U.S. 442.
Nash v. Israel (1983) 707 F.2d 298.
People v. Abbott (1981) 445 N.Y.S.2d 344.
People v. Hill (1968) 233 N.E.2d 367.
People v. Luparello (1986) 187 Cal. App. 3d 410.
People v. Montano (1979) 158 Cal. Rptr. 47.
People v. Mummert (1943) 135 P.2d 665.
People v. Nguyen (1993) 26 Cal. Rptr. 2d 323.
People v. Villa (1957) 318 P.2d 828.
People v. Woods (1992) 11 Cal. Rptr. 2d 231.
Pinkerton v. United States (1946) 328 U.S. 640.
Prosecutor v Duško Tadić (1999) Case No IT-94-1-A, Judgment.
Prosecutor v Radislav Krstic (2001) Case No IT-98-33-T, Judgment.
State v. Ayers (1991) 478 N.W.2d 606.
State v. Burney (2003) 82 P.3d 164.
State v. McFadden (1982) 320 N.W.2d 608.
State v. Travis (1993) 497 N.W.2d 905.
United States v. Alvarez (1985) 755 F.2d 380.
United States v. Clayborne (1974) 509 F.2d 473.
United States v. Colon (2008) 549 F.3d 565.
United States v. Fountain (1985) 768 F.2d 790.
United States v. Garguilo (1962) 310 F.2d 249.
United States v. Hill (1995) 55 F.3d 1197.
United States v. Lippner (1982) 676 F.2d 456.
United States v. Otero-Mendez (2001) 273 F.3d 46.
United States v. Perez (1981) 648 F.2d 219 at 224.
Veney v. State (1961) 170 A.2d 171.
Wilcox v. Jeffrey, (1951) 1 All E.R. 464 (K.B.).

Part IV

Citizens, states and institutions

11 Expressive theories of punishment

Who says what to whom?

Bill Wringe

11.1 Introduction

Many philosophers hold that legal punishment has an expressive dimension.[1] Advocates of this view have discussed a wide range of issues: the ways that attention to the expressive features of punishment can help us to distinguish between punishments proper and non-punitive ways of deterring undesirable behavior; the conditions punishment must meet to have a particular expressive content; the role which expressive aspects of punishment can play in justifying penal institutions; the intended audience of penal communication, and so on.[2]

Expressive theorists disagree about many issues. Two are especially significant. First, what exactly does punishment express? Second, how does it do so? Here I shall argue that we can advance our understanding of these questions by considering a further issue about which expressivists have said comparatively little: the question of *whose* attitudes punishment expresses. Who, we might ask, is the subject of penal expression?

The most plausible answer to this question, I shall argue, is that it is the state, conceived of as a collective agent, that is the subject of penal expression. This view has significant consequences for the other two questions about expression that I have raised. It makes it natural for us to see the kind of expression involved as being linguistic expression and to see the attitudes expressed as being ones that have a fairly determinate form of propositional content.

These conclusions have significant implications for a further view on which expressivists have differed: the audience of punishment's expressive message. Some, including Antony Duff, have understood that audience to be – at least in the first instance – the individual punished. I shall argue that considerations about how punishment expresses its message should lead us to prefer an alternative view, on which the audience is the political community at large.

My ambitions in this chapter are limited in two respects. First, I shall not be arguing for the truth of expressivism itself (though I have done so elsewhere) but exploring how someone with expressivist sympathies should answer the questions I have raised.[3] However, I shall assume, along with

DOI: 10.4324/9781003242451-16

many other recent advocates of expressivism, that the expressive dimension of punishment plays some role in explaining how punishment is justified.[4]

Second, and perhaps more controversially, I shall be taking it for granted that suitably organized groups of individuals can be seen as collective agents and that states are among the groups that can appropriately be viewed in this way. These views about collective agency are controversial but not idiosyncratic.[5] The idea that there are collective agents has been defended by authors such as Peter French, Margaret Gilbert, Christian List and Philip Pettit, and Stephanie Collins.[6] And the idea that states are among the groups which can be seen as collective agents is one that can be traced back as far as Hobbes and has more recently been defended by Margaret Gilbert, Anna Stilz, and Holly Lawford-Smith.[7] In what follows, I shall argue that these two suggestions should seem especially attractive to expressivists.

11.2 Who is the subject of penal communication?

Expressive theorists of punishment hold that the hard treatment meted out to offenders expresses reprobatory attitudes. However, reflection suggests that these attitudes need not correspond to those of the individual jurors who convict an offender, the judge who imposes a sentence, or the individual who inflicts on the convicted offender (or supposed offender) the hardship whose imposition constitutes legal punishment.[8] Furthermore, the attitudes which the expressivist takes to be expressed in punishment may be out of step with views held by the majority of members of society – as, for example, when a law that is widely disapproved of remains on the statute books.

Feinberg speaks of 'society' expressing reprobation and resentment through the legal system.[9] This remark suggests the existence of a subject of mental states such as resentment that is distinct from any individual. Many will find this idea metaphysically dubious, but we should not dismiss it out of hand: authors such as Margaret Gilbert, Raimo Tuomela, Hans-Bernhard Schmid, and others have argued that appropriately organized groups can themselves be seen as the subjects or bearers of certain kinds of mental state.[10] (Such conditions are, typically, quite demanding.)

I shall address the question of what the appropriate form of organization might amount to in a moment. But before doing so, it will be useful to introduce a term to describe groups of individuals who do not meet these conditions. I shall use Margaret Gilbert's term 'mere aggregates' for this purpose.[11] We might understand Feinberg, in talking of what he calls 'society as a whole' to have in mind a 'mere aggregate' of this sort.

We sometimes ascribe mental states, including affective attitudes to mere aggregates: we can, for example, talk of an angry crowd, by which we typically mean a crowd of individuals many or most of whom are angry. If we interpret Feinberg's remark along these lines, his view seems implausible for a reason we have already noted: the penalties meted out by a society's legal system need not accord with the affective attitudes of individual members of that society in any particular case.

Theorists have collective action have often found it plausible to regard some kinds of groups as collective agents. Among the kinds of groups they have focused on are groups which have decision procedures, either formal or informal, which enable us to distinguish between acts of the group as a whole and acts of individual members of the group, and which permit the promotion of a consistent pattern of action, intelligible as the expression of a particular rational point of view which is not to be identified with the point of view of any individual.[12]

States can be understood as groups of precisely this sort.[13] They have formal decision procedures which enable us to distinguish between – say – acts undertaken by the British Prime Minister, which are acts of the United Kingdom (such as signing a treaty), and acts which are merely the acts of Boris Johnson.[14] And the idea that states have interests which they pursue in a more or less consistent manner across changes of administration plays a significant role both in practical diplomacy and in the study of international relations.

To conceive of states as collective agents is to see them as entities that can be the subjects of certain kinds of mental states: of beliefs, desires, and intentions, for example. Furthermore, theorists of collective agency typically take there to be room for considerable variation between the attitudes of the individuals who compose a given collective agent and the attitudes of the collective agent. This leaves room for the possibility of legal punishment being the expression of a mental state distinct from the attitudes felt by any particular member of society, or even a majority of them.[15] But as we shall see, we need to say more to justify the idea that states can express the kinds of reprobative attitudes of which Feinberg speaks.

11.3 Collective affective attitudes

In Section 11.2, I suggested that the expressivist should see the reprobatory attitudes expressed by punishment as attitudes of the state, conceived of as a kind of collective agent. However, I left open questions about the *kinds* of attitude that punishment might express. On Feinberg's account, they seem to include distinctively affective attitudes – in particular, the attitude of resentment.

Even if states are collective agents, it does not follow that we can also see them as subjects of affective attitudes, such as emotions. One might find the very idea of collective affective attitudes implausible. One might also doubt that states can be the subjects of such attitudes. Elsewhere, I have argued that we can make sense of the idea of collective agents undergoing states which at the very least have significant analogies with affective states such as remorse.[16] However, I shall now argue that expressive theorists of punishment should deny that state punishment expresses the affective attitudes of a collective agent. I shall start by giving as sympathetic a construal as possible of the idea of a collective affective state before arguing in Sections 11.4 and 11.5 that considerations about expression mean that it is not the notion best suited to expressivist purposes.

One reason for thinking might be collective affective states runs parallel to a reason that has sometimes been given for thinking there are collective mental states of other kinds: namely, that in everyday situations, we often take certain kinds of predication of emotional states of groups to be true. We say, for example, that a nation is in mourning over the death of a celebrity; that the government should be ashamed – and hence that it is capable of being ashamed – of its treatment of some of its citizens; that an academic department is excited or apprehensive about new hires; and so on.[17]

When we say something of this sort, we need not be saying something about each member of the nation, government, or department. To see this, it helps to consider cases where every individual member of the group is in some affective state but where this would not lead us to attribute that state to the group. It can be true, for example, that every single member of the government is ashamed in a particular situation. Nevertheless, in the absence of any kind of official recognition on the part of the government that this reflects an official stance, it will not be correct to say of the government that they are ashamed.[18]

Some find the possibility of collective affective attitudes less plausible than that of collective beliefs, desires, and emotions on the grounds that affective attitudes have a rich phenomenological dimension which beliefs, desires, and intentions lack.[19] The idea that there could be such a thing as collective phenomenology may seem implausible. However, Hans-Bernhard Schmid has argued that we can make sense of this idea.[20] He draws on an example discussed by Max Scheler: that of two parents grieving for a dead child. Schmid argues that we can distinguish between cases where each parent is grieving and situations where we can say that the two parents were grieving together. He also suggests that the two situations differ on a phenomenological level: that there is a difference between what it is like *for the parents* to be grieving together or separately.

Experiences of this sort seem more characteristic of small groups interacting with one another in a face-to-face manner than large-scale, organized groups such as states. So someone who wants to defend the view that states have collective affective attitudes might prefer a more cautious view on which collective affective states are states that are functionally analogous to emotions while lacking a phenomenological dimension.[21] Advocates of a view of this sort might regard certain kinds of action carried out by the state as expressions either of states which are functionally analogous to emotions. So, for example, an official apology expresses regret; a decision to fly flags at half-mast may express grief, and so on.

Some worry that phenomenology-free accounts of collective affective states leave no room for us to distinguish between sincere and insincere expressions of these states. But in fact, we should not worry about this. We typically judge the sincerity of an individual's expressions of emotion by assessing the extent to which the emotions they express are backed up by appropriate action. The same is true for collective agents: an official apology which is not backed up by appropriate reparative action or which is delivered in a self-undermining way can be judged insincere without any reference to phenomenology.[22] In what follows, I'll take this to be the most plausible account of the state's affective attitudes. I'll also argue that it doesn't give the expressivists quite what they want.

11.4 Two notions of expression

Talk of the expression of emotions is ambiguous between at least two notions of expression. One involves what Grice calls 'natural meaning.'[23] In this sense of expression, my smile can only express happiness if I am, in fact, happy. A second notion involves what Grice calls 'non-natural meaning'. It is often this second notion of expression that we have in mind when we speak of linguistic expressions of emotion: I can express happiness by saying 'I am happy' even when I am not, in fact, happy. However, expression in this second sense need not be purely or even partly linguistic: I can express anger by banging the table or impatience by tapping my fingertips without being angry or impatient.

Joshua Glasgow has put forward a version of expressivism which seems to require that the notion of expression to be understood in the first of these senses. Glasgow suggests that harsh treatment is a way of expressing an emotion or kind of emotion which he calls 'punitive hostility', whose proper object is significant wrongdoing.[24] Glasgow takes this emotion to be merited by certain kinds of wrongdoing, and he suggests that since our forms of expression are not infinitely malleable, we cannot simply substitute ways of expressing this emotion which do not involve punitive hostility for existing forms of expression that do. This suggests that he has in mind the kind of expression where what is expressed are natural meanings, analogous to the ways in which tears express grief. For there is no obvious reason for thinking that forms of expression suitable to expressing meaning in the non-natural sense should be non-malleable.

By contrast, Christopher Bennett has put forward a version of expressivism on which punishment involves a form of expression of non-natural meaning. Bennett argues that some forms of emotional expression are 'symbolically adequate' to the emotions that we attempt to express through them.[25] Thus, for example, we might think of certain aspects of ritualized mourning – especially those that involve subdued movement, dark colors, and so on as being symbolically adequate to the expression of grief. Similarly, we might see certain aspects of paradigmatic forms of punishment, such as an offender's isolation from a community, as being symbolically adequate to certain kinds of appropriate emotional responses to wrongdoing.

Glasgow's defense of the role of harsh treatment in punishment depends on the non-malleability of our expressive responses and thus on the idea of expression as involving natural meanings. One might think this gives us a reason for preferring his view to Bennett's. For symbolic expression of the sort, Bennett has in mind seems to be susceptible of being culturally shaped. While there may be some limits to the extent to which expressions of a given emotion are capable of such cultural shaping, it seems difficult to place any a priori limits on them any more than one could place a priori limits on what might count as a form of mourning, and thus difficult to argue that such expression must involve harsh treatment rather than – for example – some simulacrum of harsh treatment intended to symbolize the inflicting of suffering on an offender.

If the expressivist intends to offer an account of punishment as something which one individual inflicts on another – as for example, when a parent punishes a child – it seems clear that they should understand the notion of expression as involving the expression of non-natural meanings. For there can obviously be instances of punishment where the individual imposing hard treatment does not feel the emotion which the punishment is supposed to express: they may simply be going through the motions. However, this line of argument cannot easily be extended to cover punishments imposed by collective agents. On account of collective emotions I have suggested, it seems natural to think of hard treatment imposed by the state as being constitutive of the emotions that it expresses. This makes it difficult to argue for the possibility of the kind of 'sincerity gap' which, in the individual case, provides us with a reason for thinking of the kind of expression involved in personal punishment must be a kind of Gricean 'non-natural' meaning.

However, there is still a prima facie case for thinking that a view on which punishment expresses the affective attitudes of a collective agent is best understood as relying on a notion of expression which involves non-natural meaning. If the expressive theorist of punishment wants to offer a single account of the notion of punishment which covers both punishment by persons and punishment by collective entities, then in the absence of countervailing considerations, they ought to draw on the same notion of expression in both cases. So even if the expressivist sees punishment as expressing the attitudes of a collective agent, they should think of this expression as involving non-natural rather than natural meanings.

11.5 Saying things with walls

Robert Nozick has developed a detailed proposal as to how punishment might express an attitude with propositional content. The account draws heavily on Gricean ideas about communication. On Grice's account of meaning, someone who means by some action to communicate some proposition p must intend that some agent.

(i) Come to believe that p.
(ii) Recognize the intention involved in (i).
(iii) Have as part of their reason for believing p the recognition involved in (ii).[26]

Nozick suggests that many acts of punishment might have the structure of an act of Gricean communication: they are intended to get a wrongdoer to believe that some action is wrong, in part because of the punitive treatment they have received.[27] I shall call this account of how punishment communicates the Gricean-Nozickian account (or GNA for short).

Many existing accounts of collective agency seem compatible with the idea that collective agents have complex communicative intentions of the sort which GNA requires.[28] If states are collective agents, then presumably, they can have such intentions as well. But even if this is true in principle, it does not follow that intention of this sort play any role in states' punitive institutions. We might think, for example, that in instituting a law which criminalizes a certain kind of behavior and imposes penalties for it, a state may intend simply to prevent behavior of certain kinds and to introduce measures which will deter people from acting in that way. If an intention of this sort is sufficient to explain the existence of the law, it is unclear why we should suppose that the state has the more complex intentions that GNA requires.

However, it is not clear that intentions to deter are sufficient to explain the existence of criminal prohibitions. When states wish to deter undesirable behavior, they can and often do make use of a range of measures which do not involve the full paraphernalia of the criminal law, and many of which are both more effective and less costly than the application of criminal law. The expressivist should insist that in attributing intentions to the state, it is appropriate to take into account not simply facts about what kinds of behavior are sanctioned, but a range of further facts about how criminal law works includes such things as rules of evidence; standard forms of the criminal process; rules about circumstances under which a defendant is and is not responsible for certain actions to certain courts; the requirement that certain facts meet a particular burden of proof and so on.[29] These facts, and in particular the resources devoted to making accurate determinations as to who is to be punished together with the ritual nature of the processes surrounding punishment can make it appropriate to attribute to the state an intention to do more than merely deter certain kinds of behavior.

Sometimes, members of a state's legislature or judiciary act in ways that might be taken as showing that the state intends a piece of criminal legislation to deter rather than to communicate. Legislators can do so, for example, by using the language of deterrence in arguing for a piece of legislation or by incorporating the language of deterrence into its text; judges can do so by interpreting the law in ways that are best understood as expressing intentions to deter.

The expressivist might respond by insisting that attributing intentions to collective agents is typically a holistic matter: the intentions of a legislature are not to be identified with those of any particular legislator and the intentions implicit in a whole system of criminal law may be misstated by an individual judge. However, there are cases where this response seems implausible:

if the Supreme Court insists, unanimously, that the purpose of a particular piece of criminal legislation is to regulate traffic, rather than to communicate, it is natural to take their judgment as either authoritative on or even partially constitutive of the state's intention being as the Court takes it to be.[30]

The distinction between natural and non-natural forms of expression discussed in Section 11.4 helps us to deal with cases of this sort. Non-natural forms of expression allow for the possibility of expressing (and thereby communicating) an attitude that is distinct from the attitude that the agent actually has. They thereby make room for the possibility of miscommunication, and in particular situations where it is natural for an audience to take an agent as having intended to communicate something that they did not intend. Consider situations in which an individual's choice of words may reasonably be taken as offensive by a particular audience even though the speaker did not intend to cause offense.

Expressivists should say that where the criminal law embodies an intention to deter rather than censure, it is fraught with the possibility of miscommunication: the use of the apparatus of criminal law results in actions on the part of the state which are naturally taken as embodying communicative intentions by those individuals on whom they impact. They might also add that if expressivism is correct, a well-functioning system of criminal law will have a reason to avoid criminalizing behavior which it intends merely to deter.

11.6 Duff's communicative expressivism

Let us use the label 'communicative' for versions of expressivism on which punishment expresses a message whose intended audience is the individual on whom punishment is inflicted. It is not clear whether a communicative expressivist needs to be committed to the GNA. As many have argued, it seems possible to communicate without satisfying all of Grice's conditions. For example, a schoolchild answering an exam on a test, a prisoner confessing under torture, or a barefaced liar might all succeed in communicating linguistically without intending that their hearer come to believe what is communicated (either because they take their audience already to believe what they are being told or because they are indifferent to being believed).[31] Furthermore, Stephen Neale has suggested that Grice's third condition is undermotivated: he argues that it seems designed to exclude, as cases of non-natural meaning, examples which might intuitively regard as involving non-natural meaning.[32]

That said, any expressive theorist owes us some account of how punishment expresses what the theorist takes it to express. Furthermore, even if the Gricean conditions are not necessary for communicative expression, it is at least plausible to think that they are sufficient. So they do provide an account of one way in which punishment might communicate with an offender. Furthermore, I shall now argue that one prominent advocate of a communicative version of expressivism – namely, Antony Duff – can reasonably be taken to be committed to the view that in punishment, states meet the conditions outlined in the GNA account.[33]

Duff holds that the communicative dimension of punishment plays an important role in the justification of punitive institutions.[34] In particular, he holds that the state has a duty to punish offenders that arises out of an obligation to engage communicatively with them in ways that are intended to prompt remorse for wrongdoing.[35] By providing an occasion for remorse, punishment promotes reintegration into and reconciliation with the political community on behalf of which the state acts.[36] Duff also takes the duty to punish to be a communicative duty that the state owes *to offenders* rather than to society as a whole or to the victims of crime.[37]

This emphasis on the idea that penal communication should be aimed at eliciting remorse as a step toward (or perhaps partially constitutive of) reconciliation has a number of consequences. First, it seems to require that the content of what is communicated concerns the moral nature of the offender's acts. For remorse – or at least remorse of a kind that could plausibly thought to play a role in the offender's reconciliation – seems to require a recognition of wrongdoing. It is hard to see how something less than this – for example, a communication of the legal status of the offender's actions to the effect that they constitute a crime, or a crime falling into a particular category, could be expected to have this effect.

The role of remorse in Duff's account also seems to commit him to both the first and third of the conditions in Grice's account. Consider a possible weakening of the first condition, which Grice considers: namely, that provided that suitably modified versions of the first two conditions are met, it will be sufficient for communication that the communicating agent intends that the recipient of a communication believe that the communicator believes that p.[38] It is hard to see how, on this conception of communication, the state's communication with an offender could be expected to have the sorts of results that Duff thinks punishment should aim at.

If the state succeeds in an intention to make the offender believe that their behavior is wrong, that might – under certain conditions – prompt remorse. But if the offender only comes to believe that the state takes their behavior to be wrong, this will not be enough. For it seems plausible that genuine remorse needs to incorporate a recognition that the behavior is indeed wrong. More importantly, if the punishment of the offender is intended to prompt remorse, this recognition will need to be intended by the punishing authority. But this is precisely Grice's first condition.

An alternative modification to the Gricean conditions for communication is one on which communication aims at something less than belief. For example, we might think that it is sufficient for communication that a communicator intends their audience to *consider,* rather than believe, a given proposition and that they do so on the basis of recognizing an intention that they consider this proposition.[39] But again, it is hard to see how, on this conception, penal communication could do what Duff wants: mere consideration by the offender of the possibility that they have acted wrongly, without any kind of assent to it, seems insufficient for remorse. If remorse is what is aimed at, the state's intentions must be to elicit something like belief.

These points suggest that Duff is committed to the first of the Gricean conditions. His view about the relationship between remorse and reconciliation suggests that he is also committed to the third. For it is plausible that reconciliation of the sort Duff has in mind will require not only that the offender accept that they have acted wrongly, but also that the punitive hard treatment inflicted on them is justified. If the punishment itself is the basis on which the offender comes to believe that they have acted wrongly, then they have a rationale for regarding it as having some kind of point. It will be less obvious that this is the case if they come to believe that their action is wrong on some other basis, or at least on some basis which does not, at least in part, involve reflection on what the purpose of punishing them might be. So even if communication as such does not require anything like Grice's third condition, penal communication justified along Duffian lines may well do so.

11.7 A problem for communicative expressivism

I have argued that we have good reason to take Duff to commit to something like GNA. But I shall now argue that anyone who accepts a view of this sort and who also holds – as I take to Duff to – that punishment communicates something to an offender about the wrongness of their actions faces a problem when we consider the punishment of so-called *mala in se* crimes – cases where the law prohibits something which would be morally wrong even if it were not prohibited by law. The problem is that on this account, the state must prevent itself in a deceptive manner when punishing *mala in se* crimes.

Paradigmatic examples of *mala in se* crimes include murder and rape. In many cases, though not necessarily all, a mature individual's reasons for believing that such actions are wrong should not include the fact that other people take them to be wrong: a mature individual should be responsive to the wrongness of the acts themselves, rather than to other peoples' opinions about them. *A fortiori,* they should be responsive to the wrongness of the acts, rather than the fact that the state declares them to be wrong.

Grice's third condition on meaning requires that in meaning that p, I should intend that an agent recognize that I intend them to come to believe that p and have their recognition that I intend them to come to believe that p be part of their reason for believing p. In the kinds of case Grice typically focuses on, the recognition can be understood as functioning in the following way: the individual with whom I am communicating takes it to be the case that if I intend them to believe that p, then p. If so, then in order to have the third Gricean intention, I must regard it as possible for the person with whom I am trying to communicate to have as part of their reason for believing that p my intention that they should believe that p.

There are cases where this condition is easy to meet. These include situations where I can bring it about that p is true. Consider a case where I signal my intention to turn in traffic. A driver who sees my signal can take my intending them to believe that I am going to turn as a reason to believe that I will turn. A state's intention to make an offender believe that an action *malum in se* is wrong cannot work like this. The wrongness of the action is not up to the state. Furthermore, this fact should be obvious to anyone whose moral development is not so impaired as to raise questions as to whether they can be held criminally responsible at all.[40] So an offender cannot treat an agent's intention to make them believe that an action of this sort is wrong as evidence that the agent intends to make it true that it is wrong.

An agent's intention to make someone believe that something is wrong might be a reason for them to believe it is wrong in a different way. It might be evidence that the agent believes that it is wrong, and the fact that the agent believes it is wrong may be evidence that it is, in fact, wrong. Suppose I regard you as a moral authority and take myself to be morally adrift. I might then ask you what I should do in a particular situation. You might find an indirect way of answering me. Reflecting on your answer, I might come to believe that you intend me to believe that the action I am contemplating is wrong and also to believe that you would not intend me to believe this unless the action was, in fact, wrong. Your intention in giving me an indirect answer might – though it need not – be to prompt me to reflect in precisely this way.[41]

In order for this to be an example of Gricean communication, you need to be able to intend me to regard you as a reliable source of moral knowledge about whether p is wrong. Furthermore, your ability to have this intention seems to depend on your taking it to be possible that I regard you as a reliable source of knowledge on this subject. Some cases of punishment, such as the punishment of a young child by a parent, or a religious novice by the head of their order, might work in precisely this way. These are cases where it is both possible and appropriate for the punished offender to regard the person punishing them as a moral authority.

However, the idea that punishment inflicted by the state could work like this seems much more dubious. There are certainly plenty of reasons for doubting that states are, in general, reliable sources of moral knowledge. There are also many cases – perhaps a majority – where offenders will not regard the state as being a reliable source of moral knowledge. There will also be cases where we can know, of particular offenders, that they will not see the state as a source of reliable moral knowledge on a particular issue. Cases like these suggest that states that punish *malum in se* crimes may have difficulty in communicating with offenders in the way that the Nozickian view suggests.

However, I think there is a deeper problem here. In order to have the kinds of intention which this kind of communication would require, the state needs to present itself as being morally authoritative: of being, that is, an agent whose declaration that something is wrong could be part of an appropriately punishable offender's reasons for taking that action to be wrong. If we are dubious that anyone's saying that certain kinds of *mala in se* crime is wrong could be part of a mature individual's reason for believing it to be wrong, then we should doubt, in particular, that the state's saying so could be such a reason.

It follows from this that if the state is to succeed in communicating with offenders along Gricean lines, it must present itself in a distorted manner. Indeed, it seems that anyone to whom it succeeds in communicating in this way must have a distorted view of the state. In other words, the account seems to entail that punishment will only achieve the goals which it is supposed to achieve if it is seen in a distorted manner by at least some of those over whom it exercises its power.[42]

There are two problems with this. The first is a practical one: institutions and practices which rely on this kind of distortion seem to be inherently unstable. If individuals come to see that the justification of punishment requires a distorted understanding of the state, they will have good reasons for rejecting those institutions and their claims to moral authority.

But there is also a moral problem here. The Gricean conditions seem to require not only that the state function in a distorted manner but that the state must intend that these offenders see it in a distorted light. In other words, it must intend to present itself deceptively, as something it could not possibly be. However, an agent, whether individual or collective, whose dealings with other requires it to present itself in a deceptive light seems to be adopting a maxim to which those to whom it presents itself could not possibly consent. In other words, on this kind of account, the state seems to treat those whom it punishes as a mere means.[43]

11.8 Communicative expressivist responses

How might Duff respond? There seem to be two possibilities. One would be to play down the role that remorse plays within the theory. For, as I argued in Section 11.6 Duff's commitment to the problematic third clause in the Gricean account of communication seems to be a consequence of the role that remorse plays in his theory. Without it, the expressivist would not be committed to the view that the state must present itself deceptively when it punishes offenders. Dropping the commitment to the role of remorse would also allow for a different view of what punishment communicates: we could, for example, take punishment to communicate either a fact about which crime was committed or about the legal rather than the moral status of the offenders' act (that it is a crime, rather than wrong).

However, it is not clear what the interest of a theory of this sort might be. In particular, it is hard to see how an account of this sort could help us to justify punishment (as Duff thinks his account can). For even if states have a duty to communicate with offenders along these lines, it seems clear that they can communicate with them in ways which do not involve the imposition of hard treatment. (Arguably, part of the point of the criminal trial is to communicate with an offender in precisely this way.)

An alternative would be to restrict the direct application of the expressive view to crimes that are not *mala in se*. On this account, the state's punishment of *mala prohibita* crimes, such as tax evasion, would have the direct expressive purpose of communicating to an offender about their wrongdoing. But the purpose of punishing crimes that are *mala in se* would be slightly different. The point of punishing such crimes would be to avoid undermining the expressive purposes embodied in the practice of punishing *mala prohibita* crimes by giving a misleading account of their wrongness: to avoid communicating, for example, that murder was less wrong than tax evasion.

On this view, the state's punishment of *mala in se* offenders would not be grounded in a commitment to communicate with them about their own crimes but in duty to avoid undermining their communications with those who commit *mala prohibita* crimes. However, a view of this sort seems to instrumentalize those who are punished for *mala in se* crimes: it treats them as a means to communicate effectively with those who commit *mala prohibita* crimes.[44]

11.9 Denunciatory expressivism: A sketch

I have argued that considerations about the way the state may permissibly communicate with offenders seem to rule out views on which punishment communicates a message to offenders about the wrongness of their actions. I have also argued that while we might take punishment to express a message to offenders which has some other kind of content, a view of this sort is unlikely to provide for the kind of justification of punishment which an expressivist might hope to give.

There is, however, another way in which the expressivist view might be developed. This view is one on which punishment communicates not with an offender but with society as a whole. Call views of this sort 'denunciatory' views. Since my disagreements with Duff depend on claims about the way in which the message which punishment expresses represents the subject of penal attitudes to its audience, and not on facts about who the audience is, we might think that denunciatory views will fare no better than communicative views here.

One natural response is for the denunciatory theorist to give a different account of the content of penal communication from the one which is most natural for the communicative theorist. The denunciatory theorist should take the expressive content of punishment to be a claim about what we are committed to treating as wrong, rather than about what actually is wrong. I shall sketch a view of this sort before explaining why I take it to be available to the denunciatory theorist but not the communicative theorist.[45]

In Section 11.2, I argued that expressive theorists should see the attitudes expressed in punishment as attitudes expressed by the state, conceived of as a collective agent. Now consider a view of the relationship between state and society like that I suggested at the end of Section 11.2, on which the state is understood as a collective agent which is constituted out of the individuals over whom the state claims authority.[46]

Margaret Gilbert has argued for a view of this sort. On Gilbert's view, political obligations are the kinds of obligation which we are subject to when we are engaged in any kind of collective activity. While these obligations have normative force, they are not moral obligations. They are consequences of being committed to collective activity, in the same way, that a commitment (such as an intention) to engage in some individual activity may give rise to commitments to engaging in parts of that activity. Gilbert's view also allows for an attractive account of the nature of law: law-making activity can be regarded as the activity of forming and entering into collective commitments, and these commitments can be regarded as binding in the same way and for the same kinds of reasons that collective intentions can be regarded as binding.[47]

If Gilbert's view of the state and of law is viable, then denunciatory theorists have a natural response to the worries we have been considering. For on this kind of account, the reprobative message of punishment from the state to its citizens involves a message communicated from the citizens of a state (considered as a collective body) to the citizens of that same state (considered as individuals). In other words, it will involve the expression of a judgment made by a collective to the members of that collective. Furthermore, the judgment expressed is not a moral judgment. So in representing its declarations about what we are committed to as reasons for believing that we are so committed, the state does not present itself deceptively, as it would – I have argued – if it represented its declaration that a certain action is morally wrong as a reason for believing it is morally wrong.

11.10 Does denunciatory expressivism solve the problem?

I presented the communicative version of expressivism as one which purported to provide a justification of punishment and, moreover, one which avoided instrumentalizing offenders. It was a result of these commitments, and the resulting view of the role of remorse and reconciliation in punishment, that the communicative expressivist seemed committed both to the claim that punishment communicated a message about the wrongness of punishment and to a view on which the state presents itself deceptively in communicating this message.

It might seem as though the denunciatory version of expressivism succeeds only by being less ambitious than the communicative view. For in presenting the denunciatory view, I have said nothing about the question of how punishment is to be justified. In fact, though, I think this gets things wrong. For what the denunciatory theorist should say about this, in the first instance, is that there is no special question to be asked about the justification of punishment as such (as opposed to the justification of particular forms or instances of punishment). Instead, we should ask about whether the state has good reasons to make the particular kinds of commitments that are embodied in its criminal laws.

From this commitment will follow a further commitment to communicate disapproval of censure individuals who renege on that commitment: to lack a commitment of this sort is for the state to be less than fully whole-hearted in the first-order commitments it has undertaken. Further questions will then arise about what form that must take in order to be understood as sincere by those to whom it is communicated. In the kinds of political society in which we live, the answer is that in some cases, they must involve inflicting hard treatment on those who renege. This may be a contingent truth about our societies, but it is no less significant for all that.[48]

One might still wonder whether this approach to punishment can avoid instrumentalizing offenders. In principle, one might think that it can, subject to one significant limitation: for insofar as the state's commitments are collective commitments of its citizens, the hard treatment that the state inflicts in punishment will be a reflection of those commitments rather than (to borrow a phrase Duff has used in a co-authored defense of his own conception of criminal law), the 'alien imposition of a foreign will.'[49] Of course, what is true in principle may fail to be true in practice; that will be one basis on which the denunciatory approach underwrites a critique of actual practices of punishment.

But the limitation is a significant one: there is one class of offenders, which contemporary states punish and whose punishment cannot be defended along these lines: those who are not citizens of the state that punishes them. But as I have argued elsewhere, the communicative theorist is no better off than the denunciatory theorist here.[50]

Notes

1. Feinberg (1968), Nozick (1980), Hampton (1986), Duff (1986, 2001), Bennett (2008), Glasgow (2015), Wringe (2016).
2. See, respectively, Feinberg (1965); Nozick (1981), Duff (1986, 2001); Hampton (1988) and Wringe (2016).
3. Wringe (2016, 2017).
4. Feinberg (1968) is a notable exception.
5. One way in which my view might be taken to be idiosyncratic is that I take the individuals who make up the collective agent that is the state to be its citizens. For objections to this 'citizen-inclusive' understanding of states as collective agents and an alternative 'citizen-exclusive' model, see Lawford-Smith (2019).
6. French (1984), Gilbert (1989), List and Pettit (2011), Collins (2019).
7. Copp (1980), Gilbert (2006), Stilz (2011), Lawford-Smith (2019); but see also footnote 5 for one way in which Lawford-Smith's view differs from the one I advocate here.

8. The exact phrasing of this point is influenced by discussions with Lars Vinx.
9. Feinberg (1965, p. 399).
10. Gilbert (1989), Tuomela (2013), Schmid (2009).
11. Gilbert (1989).
12. French (1984), Rovane (1998), and List and Pettit (2011).
13. It doesn't follow from this that they should be so regarded, of course.
14. French (1984).
15. Thus addressing a worry articulated at length in Adler (2000).
16. Wringe (2012).
17. Collins (2017).
18. Gilbert (2001)
19. Not everyone will agree that states such as belief are phenomenologically impoverished, see Pitt (2004). I leave this aside here.
20. Schmid (2013).
21. Bjornsson and Hess (2017).
22. Bjornsson and Hess (2017).
23. Grice (1957).
24. Glasgow (2015).
25. Bennett (2016).
26. Grice (1957).
27. Nozick (1981).
28. This is true in particular of the accounts put forward by French (1984), Gilbert (1989), and List and Pettit (2011).
29. Duff (2007).
30. I'm grateful to an anonymous referee for drawing my attention to the case of Whren vs United States as one which raises considerations of this sort.
31. Neale (1992) and Rumfitt (1995).
32. Neale (1992).
33. Duff (2001).
34. Duff (2001).
35. Duff (2001).
36. Duff (2001).
37. Duff (2001).
38. Grice (1989).
39. Rumfitt (1995).
40. It may not be true for psychopaths.
41. It need not be: it may simply be I intended that you reflect on the matter in ways that give you independent reason for believing your action was wrong.
42. I am grateful to Lars Vinx for prompting me to think about this issue in more depth than I might otherwise have done, and to Jose-Luis Marti for prompting to think harder about whether, as I once thought, the problem is connected to questions about how liberal states in particular should present themselves: I now think it is not.
43. Duff takes it to be a significant point in favor of his 2001 account of punishment that it does not involve treating offenders as a means. So this point should bother him.
44. Duff takes his account of punishment to be superior to both deterrent and incapacitation-based rationales for punishment because precisely because it communicates with the offender who is punished. So I take it he would reject the suggestion considered here.
45. I develop this account in more detail in Wringe (2016).
46. Gilbert (2006).
47. Gilbert's account has something in common with what are sometimes described as 'actual consent' theories of political obligation. However, it is not part of her view that one need have explicitly consented to become part of a collective body

in order to for one to be one, and to have the kinds of obligations that follow from being one: one can, as it were become aware that one is a member of a collective 'in medias res'.

48. I develop this suggestion in more detail in Wringe (2017).
49. Duff and Marshall (2016 p. 35).
50. Wringe (2021).

References

Adler, M. (2000) 'Expressive Theories of Law: A Skeptical Overview.' *University of Pennsylvania Law Review* 148: 1363–1501.

Bennett, C. (2008) *The Apology Ritual*. Cambridge UK, Cambridge University Press.

Bennett, C. (2016) 'Expressive Acts,' in J. Smith and C. Abell (eds), *The Expression of Emotion*. Cambridge, Cambridge University Press.

Bjornsson, G. and Hess, K. (2017) 'Corporate Crocodile Tears? On the Reactive Attitudes of Corporate Agents.' *Philosophy and Phenomenological Research* 94 (2):273–298.

Collins, S. (2017) 'The Government Should Be Ashamed': On The Possibility of Organisations' Emotional Duties.' *Political Studies* 66:813–829.

Collins, S. (2019) *Group Duties: Their Existence and Their Implications for Individuals*. Oxford, Oxford University Press.

Copp, D. (1980) 'Hobbes on Artificial Persons and Collective Actions.' *Philosophical Review* 89:579–606.

Duff, R. A. (1986) *Trials and Punishments*. Cambridge, Cambridge University Press.

Duff, R. A. (2001) *Punishment, Communication and Community*. Cambridge, Cambridge University Press.

Duff, R. A. (2007) *Answering for Crime: Responsibility and Liability in the Criminal Law*. Oxford, Hart Publishing.

Duff, R. A. and Marshall, S. E. (2016) 'Civic Wrongs,' in A. Dzur, I. Loader and R. Sparks (eds), *Democratic Theory and Mass Incarceration*. Oxford, Oxford University Press.

Feinberg, J. (1965) 'The Expressive Function of Punishment.' *The Monist* 49:397–423. Reprinted in *Doing and Deserving*. Princeton, NJ, Princeton University Press.

French, P. (1984) *Collective and Corporate Responsibility*. New York, NY, Columbia University Press.

Gilbert, M. (1989) *On Social Facts*. London, Routledge.

Gilbert, M. (2001) 'Collective Remorse' in A. Jokic (ed), *War Crimes and Collective Wrongdoing: A Reader*. Malden, Blackwell.

Gilbert, M. (2006) *A Theory of Political Obligation: Membership, Commitment, and the Bonds of Society*. Oxford, Oxford University Press.

Glasgow (2015) 'The Expressive Theory of Punishment Defended.' *Law and Philosophy* 34: 601–631.

Grice, H. P (1957) 'Meaning.' *Philosophical Review* 66 (3):377–388.

Grice, H. P. (1989) *Studies in the Way of Words*. Cambridge, MA, Harvard University Press.

Hampton, J. (1988) 'The Retributive Idea' in J. Murphy and J. Hampton (eds), *Forgiveness and Mercy*. Cambridge, Cambridge University Press.

Lawford-Smith, H. (2019) *Not in Their Name: Are Citizens Culpable for Their States' Actions?* Oxford, Oxford University Press.

List, C. and Pettit, P. (2011) *Group Agency: The Possibility, Design, and Status of Corporate Agents*. Cambridge, Cambridge University Press.

Neale, S. (1992) 'Paul Grice and the Philosophy of Language.' *Linguistics and Philosophy* 15: 509–559.

Nozick, R. (1981) *Philosophical Explanations*. Cambridge, MA, Harvard University Press.

Pettit, P. (2007) 'Responsibility Incorporated.' *Ethics* 117:171–201.

Pitt, D. (2004) 'The Phenomenology of Cognition, Or, What Is It Like to Think That P?' *Philosophy and Phenomenological Research* 69 (1):1–36.

Rovane, C. (1998) *The Bounds of Agency: An Essay in Revisionary Metaphysics*. Princeton, NJ, Princeton University Press.

Rumfitt, I. (1995) 'Truth Conditions and Communication.' *Mind* 104:827–862.

Schmid, H-B (2009) *Plural Action: Essays in Philosophy and Social Science*. Dordrecht, Springer.

Schmid, H-B. (2013) 'The Feeling of Being a Group. Towards a Phenomenology of Corporate Emotions,' in Mikko Salmela (ed), *Shared Emotions*. Oxford, Oxford University Press.

Stilz, A. (2011) 'Collective Responsibility and the State.' *Journal of Political Philosophy* 19:190–208.

Tuomela, R. (2013) *Social Ontology: Collective Intentionality and Group Agents*. Oxford, Oxford University Press.

Wringe, B. (2012) 'Collective Agents and Communicative Theories of Punishment.' *Journal of Social Philosophy* 43 (4):436–456.

Wringe, B. (2016) *An Expressive Theory of Punishment*. London, Palgrave.

Wringe, B. (2017) 'Rethinking Expressive Theories of Punishment.' *Philosophical Studies* 174:681–708.

Wringe, B. (2021) 'Punishing Non-Citizens.' *Journal of Applied Philosophy* 38: 384–400.

12 There's no I in team

Judicial review and community moral agents

Maggie O'Brien

12.1 Introduction

In *Law's Empire,* Dworkin argues in favor of the 'deep personification' of communities.[1] He treats the political community as if it were a unique entity distinct from the individuals who make it up and attributes moral agency and responsibility to this entity. He suggests that we consider a corporation and asks whether or not it is possible that a corporation might act wrongfully even though none of its individual members have done so. If we are drawn to this intuition, then it seems we ought to commit ourselves to the notion that some groups or collectives of people have the potential to be 'deeply personified'. The orchestra plays the symphony, the football team wins the match, and the American citizenry elects the president of the United States. These collectives perform these actions as groups, and in this way, they can be 'deeply personified'. Arguing in favor of the deep personification of groups, however, is not without its challenges – which include explaining the notion of collective action and collective intention and solving the question of fairness in ascribing collective blameworthiness, to name a few. Dworkin, however, demurs, ignoring most of these types of worries and rejecting any impetus to tell a complicated metaphysical story. For him, there is no need to posit a 'spooky, all-embracing mind that is more real than flesh-and blood people …'.[2] He seems satisfied with general language use – noting that referring to groups as moral agents and to the groups' praise or blameworthiness is vital to our moral discussions and moral evaluations.

Although the authority of ordinary language usage demands consideration and seems enough for Dworkin, this chapter re-opens the investigation of communities as moral agents. What's more it argues that, insofar as communities are moral agents, having a bill or charter of rights[3] may make them a better moral agent (at least to the extent that their bill/charter is morally sound).[4] A charter will create a feeling of kinship and solidarity in moral principles and encourage thinking in favor of the common good instead of only individual wants. A charter will give a community a definite, if only vaguely fleshed out, reminder of the moral values that they are committed to, values never completely defined but always to be re-explored. Writings

DOI: 10.4324/9781003242451-17

on collective agency and writings on charters and judicial review have not, to be the best of my knowledge, spoken to each other before. This is a mistake. This chapter brings together the literature from these two fields and highlights at least one way they ought to inform one another. I contend that accepting that nations are moral agents has consequences for the debate around charters. Namely, I contend that doing so provides an argument in favor of enshrining charters.

This chapter aims broadly to do two main things: (1) motivate a picture that takes seriously the collective agency of nations and (2) draw out the consequences of doing so for assessing for the role of a charter. This chapter does not provide a definitive case in favor of the collective agency. Like Dworkin, I will not attempt to tell a complicated metaphysical story about the collective agency. I will, however, provide some reasons in support of the claim. The focus of the chapter is to highlight how changing our perspective from an individualistic one to one that makes space for collective agency provides novel arguments in favor of enshrining a charter. To put it another way, if we are inclined to think that there is something to be said for the collective agency of nations, then we should re-examine the case for charters. The chapter takes up that task. Namely, I argue that having a charter will make communities better moral agents.

In the final section of the chapter, I will go back for those of you that I left behind, puzzled about the collective agency. Here I will attempt to demonstrate that, even if you remain unconvinced that a community is a moral agent, you can accept that charters will help individuals be better moral agents and better members of the nation's citizenry. Charters help create and define a political morality for the community that is separable from one's individual morality or one's ideas about what the good life looks like. Insofar as citizens ought to be, as Rawls says, ideal legislators, who use public reason in public debates, a charter will help them articulate those public reasons and work towards that ideal.

But first, some preliminaries. I will be making some controversial moves in this chapter and I would like to flag them now. As I said earlier, I will give no complex metaphysical story about the collective agency or group intentions. Second, in this chapter, the group I am most concerned with is the nation's citizenry: a group that acts as a group through the governmental institutions of the legislature, the judiciary, and the executive. That is, I will assume that the nation's citizenry consisting of the citizenry and the government is the appropriate group to be discussing. The arguments of those, like Jeremy Waldron, who oppose charters and judicial review as undemocratic maintain that self-governance is properly achieved through voting and that, therefore, the legislation passed by democratically elected officials represents the peoples' desires for their community.[5] The representative's decision or vote is a stand-in vote for the citizens who elected her – she expresses and carries out the democratic will. In supporting such an understanding, my opponents seem to deny any gap or distance between the people and the government and the law-making decisions it makes. Given this, it seems that I can help myself to this assumption and maintain a strong connection between the people and the government and treat them as meaningfully connected. I am, however, sensitive to arguments that may push at that. I have two responses to this sort of worry: one is to say that any suggestion that questions just how representative government actions are of their peoples' democratic will work in favor of my main purpose which is to support the validity of charters and judicial review. Roughly, this is so because, if it is the case that voting does not always ensure self-governance, then the opposition to charters and judicial review because they are not democratic is weakened. If we accept that governing based on majority voting is not always completely democratic or not always a perfect tool for self-governance, then we seem to be accepting that self-governance can never be perfectly carried out. We accept some sacrifice of self-governance if we have good reason to. For example, arguably, direct democracy is more likely to achieve ideal self-governance, but most countries, partly for reasons of practicality, do not use a system of direct democracy. And yet, we still think of these countries as democratic. Hence, if there are strong enough arguments in favor of charters and judicial review, perhaps the potential sacrifice of self-governance may be worth it and charters and judicial review will be more obviously reconcilable with democracy. Second, even if you are resistant to thinking in terms of community responsibility, questions about government responsibility and how the government may be a moral agent that may be helped by having a charter are also important and interesting questions. I believe my arguments here will go just as far in answering questions about governments and charters as they do in answering questions about communities and charters. How far that is, we shall soon see.

12.2 Let's go team

In this section of the chapter, I present reasons in favor of endorsing the notion of collective agency. In beginning such a discussion, it is important to note that not all groups of people are apt for the collective agency – that is, not all groups of people form a collective in a relevant way. An obvious example of a group that is apt for characterization as a collective is a sports team. The New York Yankees, for example, are a team, and as a team, they play games. As the saying goes, there's no I in the team, and thus no individual member of the team wins the game on their own. They win and lose together. On the other hand, a group of people shuffling down the street is likely not a group of people that is apt for the collective agency.[6] A collective is different from a set or a bunch of people who happen to be in the same location. Dwight Newman makes use of this distinction in his book *Community and Collective Rights*.[7] He uses the term 'set' to describe a group of persons defined by the identity of the persons who make it up.[8] Therefore, a different group of people means a different set. A collective, on the other hand, is a group of people that one would still identify as the same collective even when the members change (provided other criteria were met). A team is, therefore, importantly different from a set. Another distinction that may prove useful in our discussion of the collective agency is between the commonality of purpose and teamwork.[9] The commonality of purpose occurs in cases in which several people are trying to do the same thing and everyone is aware that they are all trying to do the same thing.[10] Teamwork, on the other hand, is, as John Gardner says, '... intentional coordination in a stronger sense, and it implicates a more radical idea of collective agency'.[11] Teamwork involves intentional action that is not only known by members of the team but also an action that is intended to coordinate with the intended action of the others. The members of the team intend to act as a team and to be members of the team, as well as whatever else they intend. What's more, a team member treats her membership on that team as an extra reason to achieve what she and the other team members want to achieve.[12] This is an extra reason that does not exist in the commonality of purpose. In commonality of purpose, everyone has her own reasons to try to **Φ**. In teamwork, however, all the members may have their own individual reasons to try and **Φ**, but they have an extra reason to **Φ** on top of their own, which is their membership on the team. Being a member of a team gives one an extra reason, a reason that is absent from the simple commonality of purpose. What's more, each team member recognizes the efforts of all the other team members, and together the efforts of the team members constitute and contribute to a distinct effort, the *team* effort. The team effort is the product of an agent distinct from the team members; it is the product of the team. The team, as an agent distinct from its members, tries to do things and intends to do things that are distinct from, albeit a function of, the things that its members try to do. Furthermore, the intentions of each team member make an essential reference to the intentions of the team.[13] Recognizing that the existence of the team and the intentions of the team depend on the existence of the members and the intentions of the members does not suggest that the team is simply reducible to its members. A famous example illustrates the point clearly: the orchestra plays the symphony, but the individual musicians play their particular parts.[14] What's more, each individual musician intends to play her part, but she also intends that when all the musicians each play their parts, the orchestra as a whole will play the symphony. As Gardner says, while there may only be 105 human agents playing musical instruments, there are at least 106 agents in the orchestral performance.[15]

When we describe team member intentions and their actions more generally, we are necessarily required to refer to the group as a whole and what the group is trying to do. Let's look, for example, at a soccer team that plays a match and attempt to describe what is happening. One might try and reduce the actions of the team to the actions of individual members on the team – the keeper, the defenders, the forwards, et cetera. But even in describing the actions of, say, a forward, one cannot but refer to the collective, the team. To only talk about what the forward does makes no sense of and, in fact, distorts what she actually does. Consider Jane and Lisa. Jane and Lisa are both dribbling a soccer ball forward up a pitch. Lisa does it as a forward on her school team that's currently playing a match. Jane, on the other hand, is just practicing her skills and trying to improve the speed at which she can run up and down the pitch with a ball. Lisa and Jane are not trying to do the same thing. Jane wants to improve her skill and speed, whereas Lisa is trying to create a situation such that she or another of her teammates has a clear shot on net. Her ultimate goal is for her team to win the match. The reductionist and individualistic characterization of Lisa and Jane's actions make them virtually indistinguishable: they are both running up the pitch with a ball. To accurately capture what Lisa and Jane are doing, and for it to be obvious that they are doing different things, we need to make reference to a team. To put it simply, Lisa is playing forward for her team and Jane is practicing by herself. Notice that simply adding individuals to the reductionist picture still does not accurately capture what Lisa's doing. Saying that Lisa dribbles the ball and tries to score a goal while ten other players also try and score a goal is ambiguous.[16] From this description, Lisa could just be practicing her dribbling and shooting at the same time as ten other players do the same and practice on the same net. But this is not what Lisa is doing nor what the ten others are doing. The eleven of them are playing as a team and trying to win the match. Reference to the group is ineliminable if we are to have a meaningful understanding of what Lisa is doing.[17]

What I am suggesting so far is that when we talk about collective action and collective agency, we should have something like teamwork in mind. The team is an agent distinct from the agents who make it up and the team does things that are distinct from what its members do. The whole really is more than the sum of its parts. Further, we should think of a national community in this way: the government acts as a representative of the people, and thus as the government acts, so does the community. The community (composed of both the government and citizenry), however, is not a team or natural concerted agent strictly speaking but is to use Gardner's distinction, an artificial concerted agent. For an artificial concerted agent, such as a community, to be able to act as a concerted agent depends upon the existence of norms that empower one agent to act in the name of another.[18] Perhaps the Germanic tribes described by Tacitus were natural concerted agents but the modern national communities I am concerned with are all artificial in the sense of depending on empowering norms of representation. I am assuming that at least some of the relevant norms that make the community an artificial concerted agent (comprised of everyday citizens and government officials) are the democratic voting systems and other meaningful procedures that connect the people to their government.[19,20]

Before attending to the idea of communities as concerted collective agents, it will be helpful to look more closely at what Gardner says about legislatures: what they intend and how they act as agents. After this, we will look to see if any of Gardner's insights can be applied to communities. In his discussion of legislative law Gardner asserts that legislation is both the act of an agent and the product of intention.[21] He recognizes that in the literature on legislation, there is a lot of discussion of and concern about whether or not an institution such as parliament can have intentions. Gardner suggests that doubts surrounding parliamentary intentions come mainly from worries about using parliamentary intentions as guides in interpreting statutes.[22] Using parliamentary intentions as guides in interpretation is notoriously difficult not least because the members of parliament who passed the legislation almost certainly had diverse and conflicting intentions regarding a given bill's meaning, application and effects – intentions which varied even among the members who voted in favor of the bill. But all this shows is that parliament didn't have particular intentions as to the specifics of any given legislation. It does not show, as Gardner stresses, that when parliament legislates that it does not have intentions to change the law.[23] So, while the members of parliament may have diverse intentions at one level, at a more general level, when the members of parliament participate in voting on a specific bill they intend for the law to change. Even the individual members who voted against a specific piece of legislation still intend for the law to change. That is, they intend for the law to change if parliament intends for the law to change where what parliament intends depends on what some of its members intend. While Gardner doesn't elaborate on this point, it seems reasonable to suggest that the dissenters intend for the law to change if that is what parliament intends because the dissenters accept the voting process as representative of what parliament does and intends, and also consider the rules for deciding the outcome of the voting to be fair (rules such as whether a bare majority is enough or a 60% majority is required for the legislation to pass). Notice, however, that while they may accept the procedure that dictates how parliament acts, they may actually think the procedure should be changed. For example, some government officials may think a 'first-past-the-post' voting system is a poor one, but they will accept that until that system is officially changed that it is the system that decides which political party gets which portion of the seats in parliament. This feature highlights that collective agents are not going to be characterized by perfect harmony. A collective agent can withstand some disagreement among its members.

The actions of an institution such as parliament depend on but are not reducible to the actions of the human beings who make it up. This means that an institution with no members cannot act. But we must remember that when an institution acts, those actions are distinct from the actions of its members (this point was made earlier about musicians and orchestras). As discussed above, Gardner relies on a distinction between natural concerted agency and artificial concerted agency. The natural concerted agency is teamwork and requires no special norms to make it the case that a particular group of people becomes an agent. A paradigm case of the natural concerted agency is a team that forms spontaneously during a pick-up game of hockey or soccer. Artificial concerted agency, on the other hand, requires certain norms to empower certain collectives to have the capacity for concerted agency. Gardner proposes that the actions of legislatures are a mix of both natural concerted agency and artificial concerted agency.[24] Some of the legislature's actions can be described as the products of artificial concerted agency because there are officials whose actions are taken to be the actions of the legislature as a whole and there are norms in place that make this the case. On the other hand, some of the actions of the legislature come about through teamwork or natural concerted agency. In sum: there are two ways for a group of people to be a concerted agent – one is simply through natural concerted agency: think of a sports team. The other is through an artificial concerted agency where norms make it the case that a group is an agent represented by an individual or multiple individuals, such as in some of the actions of the legislature.

The distinction Gardner[25] draws between natural concerted agency, and the artificial concerted agency has much in common with other distinctions used in the literature on the collective agency.[26] Tracy Isaacs, for example, in her book *Moral Responsibility in Collective Contexts* stresses a distinction between organizational collectives and goal-oriented collectives.[27] Goal-oriented collectives are those collectives whose members come together around the achievement of a particular goal. The shared goal is what allows them to be 'deeply personified' to return to Dworkin's phrase. Isaacs suggests that the tens of thousands of people 'Running for the Cure' constitute a goal-oriented collective.[28] Goal-oriented collectives lack the organization and structure found in organized collectives. The notion of organized collectives has its roots in Peter French's influential article, 'The Corporation as a Moral Person'.[29] He contends that corporations are meaningful moral agents because corporations have corporate internal decision structures that delineate responsibility, designate the roles within the corporations, and define decision recognition rules.[30] A corporate internal decision structure makes it the case that the corporation itself intends to do things and does things. Thus, the corporation is the appropriate bearer of responsibility. Isaacs' description of organizational collectives is quite similar to French's characterization of corporations as moral agents. She writes that organizational collectives have internal structures that give rise to collective intentions and collective actions.[31] Organizational collectives have policies, procedures, mission statements, role definitions and structures of authority that enable the collectivity to act. Isaacs lists corporations, non-profit groups, universities, nations and professional sports teams as examples of organizational collectives.[32]

No doubt there are important subtleties between each of the authors' categories, but nothing in this chapter hangs on the nuances between them. In their writing on collective effort, Gardner, Isaacs and French each stress the differences between collectives that rely on an internal structure and norms for agency and those collectives that are animated by a shared goal. It is this rough distinction we should bear in mind: the distinction between organized and goal-directed collectives.[33]

While we should keep the differences between organized and goal collectives in mind, it would be a mistake to think that they are completely distinct in reality. Organized collectives and goal collectives are ideal models that real collectives will be more and less like. That is, in the real world we will not find pure organized collectives, on the one hand, and on the other, purely goal collectives. We will find a mix of both aspects in real-world collectives: some collectives being more organized than the goal, and others being more goal collectives than organized.[34] We also may find some collectives that are both goals and organized to nearly the same degree; that is, they have a strong internal structure, and its members also strongly unite around a common goal or purpose. It is this type of collective that I contend a nation with a charter becomes.[35] A nation with a democratic constitution and charter outlining its ideals is both an organized and a goal-directed collective.

With these distinctions in hand, I want to suggest that the government as a whole, including its various bodies, acts as a collective agent. For example, in a democratic country that uses the Westminster system and has a judiciary, legislature and executive, these branches together make up the government and the government itself is an agent.[36] The government is a collective agent made up of other agents, and some of its constitutive agents are collective agents themselves, like the legislature.

Collective agency, I contend, falls on a spectrum between organized collectives and goal-oriented collectives. It follows that some actions of collective agents may be more the product of teamwork and others more the product of artificial agency. The agency of the government and the actions of the government too fall on this spectrum. The government, given the norms, systems and officials in place that make it the case that particular people represent the government and act for the government is an apt candidate for organized or artificial agency. Therefore, just as we can say that the legislature is a concerted agent, it seems reasonable that the government, by the same reasoning, is also a concerted agent. However, there may be times when government actions or certain governments themselves are animated around a collective goal.

Some may object that I have made this move too quickly. They may claim that the different bodies of government cannot form a concerted agent because at least some of those bodies seem in conflict with one another. The suggestion that a government could ever form an agent or act on the basis of a collective goal seems especially wrongheaded. For example, it may seem that the judiciary is out to thwart the efforts of parliament, especially in countries with strong judicial reviews where the judiciary can strike down legislation. Given this, what sense does it make for to talk about them as forming a concerted agent when their aims are in conflict?

To return to the example of parliament and the judiciary – both governmental bodies are trying to ensure that only constitutionally valid laws are enacted. Sometimes the judiciary declares that an enacted law is unconstitutional or strikes down a law as unconstitutional, and in these cases, presumably, the parliament thought the law was constitutionally valid.[37] But even in these cases, I think we should see both bodies as trying to ensure that constitutionally valid law is enacted. Given that the judiciary and parliament have different focuses and approaches, it is not surprising that they may come to different answers about the constitutionality of some laws. Given their different approaches, it is understandable that the court may think a law is unconstitutional even though parliament thought it to be constitutional when enacted.[38]

Also, even if it does seem that at times the different bodies of government want different things, they still accept the governmental structure and rules and they accept the process of governmental decision. Dissenting members of parliament and the dissenting governmental bodies still, in an important way, intend for parliament and the government, respectively, to act in a prescribed way even if the particular result is different from what they want. The collective agency can withstand some disagreement.[39] What's more, the government has clear hierarchical roles, policies, decision procedures, and mission statements that dictate how the government acts. So the government can form a concerted agent.

I have argued above that a community is an artificial agent, to use Gardner's term, or an organizational agent to use Isaacs. The citizens participate in the democratic system, and it is by virtue of the system that they support that their representatives have the role and authority that they do and can act the way that they can. I want, however, to resist making too strong an analogy between a community and a corporation. I want to avoid such a comparison, in part, because I think when we 'deeply personify' a community we mean to capture the genuine idea of community and a community has a positive valence. Being part of a community is a good thing and indicates certain types of bonds and feelings shared among its members.[40] Given these positive characteristics associated with community and communities, one might argue that artificial or organizational agency is too low a threshold for something to achieve the status of a community.[41] That is, we may think that it is not appropriate to call a nation a community if there is little civility or respect among its members and if there is ongoing civil unrest. And yet, it may have a well enough working democracy to satisfy the requirements for the artificial agency. I think that this worry is warranted and ultimately right. That is to say, that I do not think that every nation with minimally functioning representative norms forms a community. This means that bare artificial or organizational agency is, in fact, too low a threshold for community status.

In acknowledging that artificial agency or organizational agency is too low a threshold to animate an entire nation, government and citizenry included, I depart from Gardner, Isaacs and French. While none of the authors explicitly spells out what features of a nation, not merely the state or the government, make it an organized collective agent all claim that it is an example of one. Gardner suggests that artificial agency could make a nation a team, and both Isaacs and French list nations as an example of an organized collective agent.[42]

This chapter attempts to be explicit about what features of a nation make it a collective agent and, in doing so concludes that a whole nation cannot be animated by organizational agency alone. Communities should be at least partly animated by a goal or natural agency.[43] Another way to think about this might be captured by the idea that we think a community is similar to a team in that the description implies a certain emotional connection among the members. Being part of a community means something similar to what being on a team means. But most nations are simply too large, and their members are separated by such great distances that they will never meet everyone or come to know everyone. Thus, they couldn't possibly have the same feelings that teams' members have for one another. Moreover, most nations have serious class, ethnic, and religious differences and antagonisms. They seem, therefore, precluded from forming a team.

It seems I face the following problem: on the one hand, I acknowledge that bare artificial agency is not enough for a group of people to actually form a community and have all the positive associations that come with it. On the other hand, I recognize that most modern nation-states, for many reasons and most obviously because of their sheer size, are unable to be natural or goal-oriented concerted agents – they can only be artificial agents.[44]

Before replying – imagine the case of two best friends – Alex and Samir. Alex and Samir have a long-standing tradition of celebrating their birthdays together (their birthdays fall in the same week). But this year they are on different continents, and neither can afford the money or the time to visit the other.[45] Thus, they are forced to celebrate their birthdays apart. The only thing they can do by way of celebrating together is video chat with each other on the chosen day. The problem Alex and Samir face is that they can only celebrate together virtually with the power of the internet, but their tradition requires them to celebrate together. The ideal for Alex and Samir is to be together in the same city, and this is what they would do if they could. But they cannot, and being together virtually is the next best thing, so that is what they will do. What's more, because they sincerely want to be together, the video chat will be meaningful, albeit not the perfect way that they can celebrate their birthdays together and continue their tradition. Celebrating virtually was the next best thing for Alex and Samir given various obstacles in their way. A similar solution is available for modern nation-states and agencies – artificial or organized concerted agency is the next best thing short of the natural concerted agency. A careful reader will notice that I have stacked the deck slightly in the case of Alex and Samir. That is, I stipulated that they wanted to be together and that this feeling is part of what made video chatting a meaningful compromise and a way for them to celebrate together. Something like this feeling of wishing for the ideal will also need to be part of the story for nations to be communities. In other words, for nations to be communities through an artificial agency, there has to be some desire for the kind of emotional bond characteristic of a natural or goal group. It has to be because of a lack of opportunity that they are united only in artificial concerted agency rather than because they wouldn't want to form a natural agent. Being a team or a goal-oriented agent must be seen as the ideal but given obstacles like space, being an artificial or organized agent is the best option available. There is a sort of sincerity involved in the artificial agency that makes a modern nation-state a community. My idea of sincere artificial agency is, in some ways, an echo of David Miller's characterization of national identity.[46] He asks, 'What does it mean for people to have a common national identity, to share their nationality?'.[47] He answers that it is about '… their shared beliefs: a belief that each belongs together with the rest …' and these beliefs come from '… a long history of living together which (it is hoped and expected) will continue into the future'.[48] It is true that most Western countries tend to have diverse populations who do not all have a long history of living together, who do not share all the same beliefs, or the same mother tongue. But charters can help provide a meaningful substitute for historically shared beliefs. Charters which emphasize justice and equal rights can help create an environment in which all can reasonably give loyalty to a nation which while not perfect is moving towards the good and the humane and continually remembering its commitments towards the rights of everyone. And in giving loyalty to a nation and its ideals, citizens also give loyalty to their fellow citizens. Charters appeal to values that are part of all traditions and offer protections to peoples of all traditions. Charters can create bonds of loyalty to a shared future together even if citizens do not share a past.

I suggest in the coming paragraphs that a major function of charters is to state the ideals which form the emotional bonds between members of the community beyond any of the differences which separate them. Members of modern communities will have very different, even contradictory views on the good life, on what it means to be human. Nor will they have a homogeneous historical background. They are not a natural agent in the sense of having all grown up together. Unless these societies can find some core values that they can agree on and celebrate some truths that they all take to be self-evident, it will be impossible for them to become a community. These are the values that will be enshrined in their constitution and charter. A sincere artificial agent is one that is goal oriented; in a nation, this goal manifests itself in a desire to live together well.

The preceding discussion has outlined what I have mind when I say that the community is an agent. In what follows, I want to look briefly at some reasons why we would want to talk about collective agency. We can begin by looking again to Dworkin in his discussion of the 'deep personification' of a community.[49] Here he asks us to imagine that an automobile manufacturer has produced defective cars that have caused tragic accidents in which hundreds of people are severely injured and killed. Further, imagine that none of the employees of the company have acted wrongly or negligently. In this case, if we do not deeply personify the car company – that is, treat it as a collective agent – our moral criticism and explanation are silenced.[50] That is to say; our moral language requires the invocation of a group. Thus, many people advocating in favor of collective agency assert that if we gave it up, we would lose a large and important part of our moral vocabulary.

The preceding has emphasized that discussion of and reference to groups is common and useful in our lives and I contend that this is not a trivial fact. What's more, the examples discussed previously give us serious reason to reconsider, if not reject entirely, the idea that when we talk about groups, we do so because such talk works merely as a shorthand for discussion about individuals. There are times when the reductionist picture (that falls out of the shorthand idea) fails to accurately capture what's going on – such as in the case of the distinction between solitary practice and taking part in a match which we looked at earlier in the case of Lisa and Jane. Further, by using and adapting the broad distinction between organized groups and goal groups articulated in different forms by Gardner, Isaacs and French, I have provided reasons to think that the government as a whole as well as the people they represent form a concerted agent. This means that we can talk about what, for example, the United Kingdom did, what it tried to do, and whether or not its actions were praise or blameworthy. All of these questions are interesting and valuable. In the following section, however, I want to ask a different question. Namely, I want to ask what will make communities better collective agents. My suggestion is that enshrining a bill or charter of rights will make communities better moral agents insofar as the rights that it enshrines are morally sound.

12.3 Play as a team, win as a team

This section tries to answer the question: what would help make a community a better moral agent. A large number of the motivating arguments of this chapter have begun by looking to teams or other groups of people that seem like obvious examples of concerted agents. This portion will take that same approach. Thus, we will begin by asking what would make a team (in the traditional sense, for example, a sports team) a better one – I believe this discussion will be illuminating for our thoughts on communities as agents.

What makes a team, like a football team, better is not necessarily limited to just what improves the skill set of its individual players. To make a good team, it is not enough to just stick the eleven best players on the field. As any team athlete or coach can attest, a good team amounts to more than the aggregate of the skill of the individual players. That is why a team that has played together longer has a strong chance of beating a new team that hasn't played together before, even if the new team's players are more skilled. There is something true, albeit trite, in the saying shouted by coaches 'play as a team, win as a team'.

Playing as a team means trusting fellow team members, relying on them, and working together with them. Teammates have to trust that when they pass the ball ahead, the right player will be there to accept the pass. Players must be confident that their teammates will play their individual positions and not interfere with their fellow teammates' ability to play their own positions. Thus, even if I could make an exaggerated leap to possibly catch a tricky ball, I should refrain from doing so because I trust that my teammate is playing her position correctly and that she is therefore well placed to receive the ball. I can confidently play my position because I trust that my teammates are playing theirs. Trusting in teammates and sincerely playing with them, that is, not trying to win the match by oneself, helps make a team a good one, and this feeling of trust needs to be cultivated among a teams' players.

In some of Gardner's writings on teamwork, he makes a similar point about what occurs when a bunch of people become a team: their doing so can help overcome what he calls the 'problem of instability'.[51] Instability occurs when one agent comes to doubt whether or not the other agents that she is trying to work with will continue trying, and then, because of this doubt, she begins to stop trying. These doubts create a feedback loop and as such are escalating and self-fulfilling. Therefore, we need to do something to undercut these doubts and work to solve the problem of instability. In these types of cases, where achieving the goal requires all the agents to work co-dependently, forming a team will benefit the group because doing so will help solve the problem of instability. Being on a team will lessen the number of these doubts and reduce the strength of the remaining ones. A charter and the judicial review it inspires is a very public way of recalling the team, the nation, to the values that it is committed to. Charter decisions are group declarations of faith which remind everyone of what they are committed to and so fight against civic instability. Being a team member gives each person a new status, a new identity and a new relation to the other members of the team. This is so because being on a team gives team members one extra reason to try to Φ. If before being on a team one had five reasons to Φ after one is on a team, one now has six reasons to Φ. Of course, there are still going to be some doubts even after a team has been established – perhaps one will worry about how committed to the team the other members are or whether or not some members have been bribed to, as the expressions go, take a dive or throw the game.[52] But once a team has been formed, these types of doubts are mitigated by feelings of camaraderie, loyalty and cohesion. Ideally, team members will think of their fellow teammates in a particular way – as people with whom you try to succeed and on whose efforts your success or failure depends.[53] The more the members feel this way about their team, the better they will be as a team and the less likely it is for the problem of instability to occur. Feeling like a team and acting like a team make a team better. Similarly, feelings of camaraderie and trust will make a concerted agent work better, even if it does not have the full emotional cohesion of a team.

This aspect of a team may seem true for groups of people that are, in fact, teams like the Jamaican 4 × 100 m relay team or Arsenal F.C. Some may worry, however, that these characteristics are less applicable, if at all, to the kind of group we are primarily talking about here – communities. I suggest that this worry is off base. Granted, feelings of team bonding are not going to help a community win many sporting matches. But encouraging and engendering feelings of teamwork in a community will make it a better community. It will discourage thinking that pits sub-communities against each other and prevent thinking in terms of 'us versus them' generally. Thinking of others as fellow team members in a common venture will promote thoughtful and respectful dialogue even when people disagree. And a charter will help make the nation a team and its citizens team members. As well, it will encourage making decisions in favor of the common good instead of only one's own good and encourage concern for others on issues that may not necessarily directly affect one's life – for example, the legalization of same-sex marriage. In this way, a community becomes more than an organizational collective agent animated around procedures and policies only – it becomes goal-oriented as well. In wanting to live together well, in making that its goal, a community takes steps to live together well. There is a sense in which acting like a team makes you a team; this is also true of communities.

Engendering feelings of community and an attitude of kinship will make a team a better one. In a similar fashion, creating a feeling of togetherness and shared purpose and goals will make a community a better moral agent. I contend that entrenching a charter or bill of rights will do just this for a nation's citizenry. For example, the *Canadian Charter of Rights and Freedoms* is often heralded as a document that speaks to the Canadian people's fundamental moral beliefs and commitments. And insofar as it is an embodiment of the Canadian people's commitments, it helps create and maintain a feeling of being Canadian. Despite differences in religion, race, culture, sexual orientation, gender, sex, socioeconomic status – Canadians are all in an important way united as citizens who stand for acceptance and justice and equality as they are entrenched in their Charter. The Charter creates and captures the Canadian ethos and makes Canadians think about what would be best for Canadians as a whole, not just about what would be best for themselves as individuals. When the Charter was enshrined in Canada, the Prime Minister at the time and one of the biggest supporters of the Charter, Pierre Elliot Trudeau, said, 'We must now establish the basic principles, the basic values and beliefs which hold us together as Canadians, so that beyond our regional loyalties there is a way of life and a system of values which make us proud of the country that has given us such freedom and such immeasurable joy'.[54] The Charter embodies what holds Canadians together and helps keep them bound to each other. Interestingly, it is not clear how exactly a charter does this. That is, does a charter help create a feeling of community by reflecting the moral commitments or ethos of the population or does a charter by its very existence create such an ethos for the population or does it work by way of some mixture of the two? The older the charter gets, the more likely it is to be the latter, or at least more the latter than the former. Most countries' laws reflect, to a substantial degree, the people's moral commitments. Obvious examples of this include legal prohibitions on murder, rape, and assault. But we must not forget or underestimate the law's influence on morality. Wil Waluchow, in a discussion of charters and their connection to morality, stresses this point.[55] He quotes Tony Honoré from Honoré's 'Hart Memorial Lecture' on morality and law: 'The picture of morality as a blueprint and law as a structure put up according to or in disregard of it is … misleading. Morality is more like an outline from which details are missing. Laws, along with conventions, fill many of these in'.[56] The law of a community and the morality of that community intersect and interact in complex and significant ways. Changes in the law can effect changes in behavior and attitudes. In Canada, the dominant attitude towards things as various as drinking and driving, smoking, women in the workforce, and gay rights, have all changed drastically in large part because of legislation, some of it inspired by the Charter. Legislation changes attitudes towards particular issues: charters can help establish the overall commitments and help citizens see that a country must strive to embody basic values. Law both reflects and creates a community's morality, and insofar as a charter does this, it also helps create a feeling of community and makes it the case that the artificial agency of a nation is sincere.

While I have suggested that building on a feeling of team camaraderie will make both actual teams and communities better concerted agents, I recognize that communities are importantly different from sports teams. That is, national communities, by virtue of the types of concerted agents they are, can do and intend to do different things than a team. National communities have lives that average sports teams do not have. Communities regulate the way people within them live; they control what's legal and illegal and influence what is conventionally approved of and disapproved of, and as a result, help determine which of its members feel safe and accepted within the community and which do not. Additionally, a community affects those outside its borders – when it makes decisions about going to war, about whether or not to send foreign aid, about enforcing restrictive immigration policies, and about enacting effective climate control procedures– and in many other ways. Given the primary importance of what it means to be a nation's citizenry, we need to ensure that our questions about what will make a community a better moral agent take this power of communities into account.

Above, I advanced the claim that charters that foster a feeling of kinship and camaraderie are helpful in doing away with prejudices that manifest themselves in thoughts like 'us versus them'. As well, feeling connected to fellow community members motivates us to think of their interests when we are considering political questions, when we are deciding which political candidates to vote for or when we are appraising various legislative bills. Charters are helpful because they unite members of a community around shared values. Similarly, a charter can help a community be a good moral agent by specifying the rights of minority groups within the community. As a concerted agent – that is an agent made up of other agents – what the community intends to do and what it does is, as I have stressed throughout, a function of what its members do. This, in large part, means that what a community intends and does is dependent on what the majority of its members intend to do and what they do. Given this, there is reason to worry about what Mill famously called 'the tyranny of the majority'. It seems to me that a charter can help mitigate fears of the tyranny of the majority in at least two ways. One has already been discussed: a charter which enshrines equality beyond differences in gender, sexual identity, religion and ethnicity works to undermine the thinking that is likely behind problematic divides in the community, divisions that are often oppressive and hierarchical.[57] The worst side of communities can show when part of the community, animated by hatred or fear, turns against another part of the community in a situation of crisis. Democratic institutions tend to meliorate but not eliminate such situations. Charters with clear appeals to the values of justice and equality and liberty help associate patriotism and emotional loyalty to these values, making it more difficult for a demagogue to link love of country to hatred and contempt for those seen as other. This can help prevent the kind of grotesque emotional communities, often spawned from distortions of ethnic or religious differences, that have so often devastated human history.

Second, by entrenching rights in charters, we place those rights beyond the easy reach of the population. We thereby limit what the majority can do. For example, if a charter declares that people cannot be discriminated against based on their sexual orientation, a law that disallowed same-sex couples from receiving the same spousal benefits that heterosexual couples were allowed would clearly contravene the charter. But we could imagine that the majority of citizens and, in turn, the legislators might support such legislation because they do not think that a marriage between two people of the same sex is the same type of union or marriage as one between a man and a woman. Alternatively, we could explain the legislation's passing because gay people are a minority of the population, and those who are not gay may feel unaffected by such legislation and be generally uninterested in whether or not it is passed. A charter would be useful in both situations. It would remind everyone of her commitment to equality and fundamental justice for all. It would help to do away with the attitude of 'its not my problem' by encouraging instead a feeling of camaraderie and kinship – thus, members of the community, irrespective of whether or not they were gay, would not be uninterested and, in fact, would be opposed to the legislation. As well, a charter would make it the case that such a law could not be passed easily because it contravened the charter (or that such legislation could be struck down or deemed incompatible with the constitution depending on the type of judicial review – strong or weak – the nation has). By having a charter, a community reminds itself of what belonging to the community means and places moral and political limits on how the agent, that is, the community, can behave and what it can do to sub-groups within it.

So far, I have advanced the idea that entrenching a charter can make a community a better moral agent by creating and sustaining feelings of solidarity among its members and by placing limits on how the community can act. This discussion has focused on thinking about the community as a concerted agent (an agent made-up of other agents) and what this fact about it implies for making it a better moral agent. That is, how does a community's 'team-ness' effect what it means for it to be a moral agent. One of these implications calls us to recognize that the community agent is made up of other agents whom the community agent as a whole may harm or oppress. This is the 'tyranny of the majority' worry discussed above. That a concerted agent can harm agents who make it up is a concern distinct to the concerted agency. When we think of individual agents, we think about how the individual agent can harm others and itself. The concern about agents harming themselves is important but different from the worry about a concerted agent harming groups of agents who make it up. Thus when thinking about agents, it matters whether or not the agent is a concerted one or an individual one. We, therefore, ought to be attentive to the fact that a community is a concerted agent. But we should not ignore that the community as a concerted agent acts as a single agent – a single agent in some important way similar to an individual agent. Therefore, we should not neglect what would make an individual agent, like a person, a better one. That is, what do we expect of and require of an individual moral agent and thus of the community in its role as an agent?

One basic expectation that we might have is that an individual ought to be thoughtful and conscientious; that she reflects on her actions and thinks about her reasons for her actions.[58] For example, we would likely want someone to distinguish their knee-jerk reactions from their well-considered and reflective commitments and to form a relatively coherent set of commitments that are genuine and based on sincere belief. What's more, we would want her to act on those commitments rather than her knee-jerk reactions because her knee-jerk reactions are likely to be problematically influenced by prejudice or hatred rooted in fear (especially fear of the unknown or different), inadequate evidence or information, or severe emotional hardship (for example, depression). For example, someone with a green thumb's knee-jerk reaction to a local government imposing restrictions on outdoor water use may be that it is wrong for the government to do so. Upon reflection, however, she would likely see that, given her thoughts about the importance of recycling and composting and her commitments to energy saving, her genuine moral commitment is actually in favor of limits on the use of water outdoors. This example illustrates the perhaps obvious point that our knee-jerk reactions can conflict with our actual commitments. Because they can conflict with one another, a responsible moral agent ought to continuously reflect on both her knee-jerk reactions and her commitments and bring them in line with each other. Thus, we require that an individual moral agent reflect on her immediate reactions and act so as to remain consistent with her real commitments. Given that a community is a moral agent, it, too, ought to maintain a consistent set of moral commitments and do its best to act according to them.

In fact, the consequences of a community acting on its knee-jerk reactions rather than its commitments may be worse than those involved in an individual doing so, because the community can, in most cases, affect more people. Consider the decision of Canada to order the internment of Japanese Canadians during World War II. This decision was motivated by fear and prejudice that led to suspicion against Japanese Canadians. This decision ran contrary to the community's commitments to equality and freedom of the person. Canada acted according to its knee-jerk response of fear and prejudice, and as a result, hundreds were oppressed and unjustly vilified.

Imagine a community whose knee-jerk reaction to the legalization of same-sex marriage is negative. That is, popular opinion is against its legalization. However, further, imagine that the community reflects on this immediate reaction and considers it in light of its other commitments. Some of these commitments include those that ensure spousal benefits to same-sex couples: commitments to equality and to the rejection of sexism, racism, and the oppression of minority groups. These commitments suggest that the community should reject its hasty reaction and actually support the legalization of same-sex marriage. If the community in this example acted on this realization and legalized gay marriage, they would do tremendous good.

With these two cases in mind, we can see that it is important for a community to act so that it may remain consistent with its commitments. I contend that enshrining a charter or bill of rights will, in fact, help a community act according to its commitments. Charters can ensure that a community's moral short-sightedness does not lead to questionable decisions and actions. The moral terms enshrined in charters, although not precisely defined, are acknowledgements that the government should take seriously concerns about the values of equality and justice and should not pass legislation that violates the right to equality. Charters are central aspects of a community's morality because they represent sincere community commitments. Charters help bring communities and individuals to consider what they are really committed to. The community in enshrining those rights is committed to thoughtfully and rigorously reflecting on what those commitments require and consistently trying to uphold those commitments.

It is worth pausing here and highlighting how what I have just put forward fits into and adds to the standard debate around charters and judicial review. Judicial review is the process by which judges review legislation for consistency with a nation's constitution, bill of rights, or charter. Opponents of the judicial review claim that it is undemocratic.[59] The standard democratic objection goes something like this: judicial review is a process in which unelected judges determine the legal validity of legislation passed by the peoples' elected representatives and hence cannot be reconciled with democracy and the principle of self-governance. Such an objection, however, overlooks the fact that a nation itself is an agent. A nation, like an individual, can act and do things, and its actions, like an individual's, can be more or less in line with its commitments. Thus, claims that charters and judicial review thwart democracy fail to attend to the agency of nations. Attempts at self-governance must be made based on the sincere commitments of the agent. Consider self-governance and autonomy at the individual level. Imagine someone, let's call her Liz, who has too much to drink at the local watering hole. Liz's friends all know that she is vehemently opposed to drinking and driving, as she has expressly said so on many occasions and has also volunteered with MADD.[60] Tonight, however, after having one too many, Liz drunkenly declares that she is perfectly capable of driving herself home. Liz's friends *do not* respect her autonomy by letting her drive because her desire to drive drunk is inauthentic insofar as it is fueled by gin. Rather, in order to respect Liz's autonomy, her friends ought to prevent her from driving drunk and ensure that her actions remain consistent with her commitment to not drinking and driving. In this example, Liz's inauthentic wish is driven by alcohol, but prejudice and hatred rooted in fear (especially fear of the unknown or different), inadequate evidence or information can make agents, individuals and communities alike act in ways that are in contradiction of their commitments. I suggested above that this is what happened in the case of the Canadian internment of Japanese Canadians in WWII. Charters provide a bulwark against this moral wrongheadedness.

Acknowledging that nations are moral agents adds a new complexity for understanding the democratic nature of charters and judicial review. Charters and the judicial review of legislation should be seen as more democratic than previously recognized because they attempt to hold communities to their own most deeply held moral beliefs.[61] A charter reminds the nations of what it really is as a moral agent and reminds the citizens of who they are and of what they owe their fellows. The judiciary calls foul when they do not play by the rules.

I am arguing for a shift in perspective. I contend that we ought to think about the agency of nations, not just the agency of individuals, and about what nations are committed to. If we move away from focusing on individual laws and individual citizens and begin to focus on citizens as citizens of a nation and on the agency of nations and the legal commitments of nations, we are provided with a new perspective on the nature of judicial review: a new perspective with which to judge whether or not judicial review is democratic. This new perspective supports the democratic nature of judicial review as a means of keeping a nation true to its authentic commitments.[62] Judges in judicial review who attempt to rule in accord with a community's constitution, charter, and laws, and thus the community's commitments as expressed by its legislators, attempt to hold a community true to its fundamental beliefs. The judicial review helps prevent temporary majority decisions from going against the nation's authentic moral commitments.

In this portion of the chapter, I have suggested various ways that a charter may make a community a better moral agent and demonstrated how this adds to the debate around charters and judicial review. This discussion relied on thinking about the community as a concerted agent. In the following section, I say something briefly to those readers who are unconvinced about collective agency, about how a charter can make individuals better political citizens.

12.4 A one-woman team

This section will say something about what role a charter can play in an individual's life and in her understanding of her responsibilities as a political citizen. My suggestion is that entrenching a charter will help a citizen live up to the standard of Rawls' ideal legislator. My discussion of this point will be limited, but I hope, fruitful.

In most Western liberal democracies, there is wide and deep disagreement about what the good life consists in. That is, different people have different comprehensive doctrines[63] that form around religion, philosophy, morality, and economics. In some cases, these differences appear to be irreconcilable, and when the disagreement is deep enough, people seem unable to reach an agreement based on their comprehensive doctrines. But even in these cases, decisions about fundamental political morality have to be made – for example, about how the law will, if it will at all, regulate abortion. In such cases, Rawls argues that people need to move away from their own conceptions of the good and the good life and engage with and use what Rawls calls public reasons.[64] Public reasons are those that people cannot only be expected to understand but that people can also reasonably be expected to accept. Public reasons make reference to public values and public standards rather than idiosyncratic or religious beliefs. In a representative democracy in which citizens are asked to vote for their representatives and sometimes, although less often, to vote on particular laws in the case of referendums – Rawls calls on citizens to vote as though they were ideal legislators.[65] For Rawls, an ideal legislator is not a Platonic guardian but rather someone who uses public reason to guide their voting for both officials and for legislation in the case of referendums: someone who asks herself which potential officials seem to best represent the ideal of public reason and which laws seem best supported by public reason?

Charters help provide the framework in which engagement in public reason can best be done. They help formulate the issues of the debate in terms of public reason and help move people away from their comprehensive doctrines. In the public forum, people can argue for the same conclusions as their comprehensive doctrine would lead them to but must do so in terms and with reasons that their interlocutors can accept. This will mean, for example, abandoning arguments for the legal prohibition of acts that rest on claims that the act is sinful. By including a commitment to equality, charters remind everyone that others, who are non-Christians or non-Muslims, or non–post-modernists also have rights. Everyone has the right to advocate for her opinions as long as those opinions do not support suppressing the charter protected rights of others. Charters provide the appropriate terms and the basic values of the community, terms that citizens can use to deliberate, debate, and exchange views with each other, all the while respecting each other as free and equal citizens. Rawls stresses that 'public reasoning aims for public justification' and it is not reasoning that is simply logically valid but is reasoning that is sincerely addressed to others, that takes account of the background and beliefs of others and that proceeds in consideration of the context in which these arguments happen.[66] A charter is a statement of a society's most important public reasons. Charters provide the grounds upon which citizens can respectfully and sincerely engage with and address others.

What I have suggested in this section has taken for granted the soundness of Rawls' argument that people ought to use public reasons when engaging in debates and discussions in the political sphere. This idea is, of course, contentious and certainly not universally accepted. Some object that theories of public reason such as Rawls' are self-defeating because no such theory can be justified to all those to whom it would apply.[67] Others claim that it is unfairly exclusionary, particularly of religious arguments, and thus that it cannot maintain its claim to impartiality.[68] I am not going to defend public reasons here. My objective here is more modest. Namely, I am proposing that if we think that Rawls might be correct about public reasons or even if he merely seems on the right track, then it seems interesting to see how, if at all, charters or bills of rights could fit with and complement this aspect of Rawlsian theory.

12.5 Conclusion

In this chapter, I have attempted to demonstrate that it is reasonable and meaningful to talk about collective agency. I have suggested that our understanding of various group activities would be incomplete if we were to give up the notion of collective agency. What's more, I have advanced the idea that national communities, through a form of what I've called sincere artificial agency, form a collective moral agent. This sincerity is often manifested in a moral and intellectual commitment to ideals entrenched in a charter: ideals with which all can identify and which forge a bond uniting the members as citizens striving to make their country the embodiment of those ideals. Further, I have argued that enshrining a charter or bill of rights will make a community a better moral agent.

In acknowledging the benefits of charters, we should not mistake them for a moral panacea. Sometimes a nation may have a morally bad constitutional morality or a constitution that is ignored and flouted by the state – legislature and judiciary included. In these cases, having a charter is more than likely not going to be enough to protect minority rights or ensure equal treatment of citizens before and under the law. Sometimes a transformation of the political regime and a totally new constitution may be required.

Notes

1. Ronald Dworkin *Law's Empire* 167–175.
2. Ibid., 168.
3. For reasons of convenience, I will henceforth refer simply to charters.
4. For reasons of convenience, I will henceforth assume that the charter is morally sound. Thus, when I suggest that a charter would make a moral agent a better agent I mean that a morally sound charter would make them better.
5. For perhaps the strongest criticisms of judicial review see Waldron (1999).
6. Some, for example Virginia Held, go as far as to argue that a mob of people, in certain circumstances, can be held collectively responsibly. Virgina Held (1970).
7. Dwight Newman (2011).
8. Ibid., 4.
9. John Gardner, (2002) 500.
10. Ibid., 500.
11. Ibid., 500.
12. Ibid., 501.
13. John Gardner, 'Some Types of Law' 63.
14. Rawls, Dworkin, and Gardner all make use of the orchestra example in their respective discussions of collective action.
15. Gardner, 'Some Types of Law' 63.
16. Arguably, this isn't even accurate because normally the keeper and defense are more focussed on preventing the opposing team from scoring. Thus, in order to capture how the 11 players are united and have a shared intention we have to refer to the team. The team tries to win.
17. Tracy Isaacs (2011), in her book *Moral Responsibility in Collective Contexts*, also points out that without the notion of collectives agency we would not be able to see some acts true moral character: for example, a murder that is part of a genocide has a different moral character than an isolated murder. Genocide is aimed at eliminating a particular group of people whereas isolated murders are not.
18. Ibid., 64.
19. Interestingly, Gardner suggests that both a nation and a local community may become teams through artificial concerted agency see, ibid., 64.
20. A country's government also likely gains the power for concerted agency through norms and thus my suggestions throughout this chapter are ideally interesting to those who are not idealists about democracy.
21. Ibid., 56–65.
22. Ibid., 60.
23. Ibid., 61.
24. Ibid., 64.
25. Gardner does not explicitly refer to goals in his discussion of natural concerted agency, but rather to 'intentional coordination'.
26. Yet another, slightly different distinction is drawn by David Miller (2004) in his article 'Holding Nations Responsible'. Here he distinguishes between like-minded groups and cooperative practice group. The like-minded group is one whose members share aims and have a similar perspective and who recognise this like-mindedness in their fellow group members. Cooperative practice groups, on the other hand, involve members who participate in a system or structure and reap benefits from their participation, for example, in the form of a salary. Miller's example of a cooperative group is a manufacturing firm. On the other hand, some authors, for example Christopher Kutz (2000), deny that a distinction is necessary. He provides a uniform analysis because the individual agents in collective effort understand themselves as acting in the service of or participating in a collective goal. Tracy

Isaacs (2001), on the other hand, endorses the distinction because she thinks that the nature of the relationship between the individual and group is importantly different in the distinct types.

27. See Isaacs.
28. Ibid., 25.
29. French (1979).
30. Ibid., 212.
31. Isaacs 27.
32. Ibid., 24.
33. It is worth pointing out that acknowledging the different types of collective agents has consequences for our understanding of the formation of intentions of organized collectives and the intentions of goal collectives. The intentions of organized collectives come about through the group's internal structure, which limits and informs the intentions and actions of the collective. Isaacs uses a helpful example to illustrate the distinction between the organization's intentions and the member's intentions. Imagine that the artistic director of the Stratford Theatre Festival has carte blanche to select all the plays that the Festival will run this season. Imagine further that she does not like Broadway musicals and would not choose to include any if she were able to make the decision solely based on her preferences. The Festival, however, has a tradition of including at least two musicals each season; the shows are popular and provide a nice balance to the Shakespearean productions. The artistic director's decision is constrained by the Festival regardless of her personal tastes. The decision the director makes in selecting the productions can legitimately be described as the Festival's decision. See Isaacs (n18) 30–31. Understanding the intentions of goal collectives is slightly trickier and there is more disagreement about how to do so (See, for example Bratman *Faces of Intention: Selected Essays on Intention and Agency* (CUP, 1999); Isaacs (n18); Kutz, *Complicity* (n27); May, *Sharing Responsibility* (University of Chicago Press, 1992); Tuomela, 'Joint Intention, We-Mode and I-Mode' XXX Midwest Studies in Philosophy.). For our purposes, however the intricacies do not matter as much; we need only a basic understanding of the intentions of goal collectives. Roughly, the intentions of the individual members of the collective combine and the members meaningfully see themselves as members of the collective. They intend to be members and they stand in a relation of co-membership with the other members of the group.
34. David Miller (2004) makes a similar point in his discussion of like-minded groups and cooperative practice groups.
35. This chapter argues that charters can play a large role in creating and engendering the 'goal-oriented' aspect of collectives. I am not suggesting that enshrining a charter or bill of rights is the only way to do this.
36. I recognize that there is a narrower use of the term government in which it is just the elected officials. I am using the term in a wider sense to mean something more akin to governance. Hence why I include the judiciary, legislature and executive.
37. There are some cases where this may not be so. For example, in Canada, governments can use Section 33 of the *Charter*, often called the *Not Withstanding Clause,* to pass legislation that may be in violation of certain aspects of the *Canadian Charter.*
38. My characterization of the relationship between the different branches of government is perhaps at worst naïve and overly idealist and at the very least likely a description of things when things are going well. That is, there is surely a spectrum of the types of relationships governmental bodies can have with each other ranging from acrimonious to harmonious. What I have described falls on the more harmonious and healthy end of that spectrum. There may be, however,

relationships that fall on the more acrimonious and unhealthy end. These types of relationships are likely characterized by deep conflict and when they arise one governmental body may in fact try and thwart the plans and objectives of another body. One example of this may be when the courts ignore ouster clauses intended to shield political action from judicial review. In these cases, it may not make sense to think of the government as forming a concerted agent. This is not, however, necessarily how the different governmental bodies must interact. When governments behave as I've described and fall on the healthy end of the spectrum, I argue that it does make sense to think of the governmental bodies as forming a concerted agent. I am grateful to John Gardner and Thomas Adams for pushing me on this point.

39. Dissenters do not undermine collective agency as long as the dissenters are not revolutionaries. This is similar to what Rawls says about the difference between civil disobedience and revolution. On his picture those who engage in civil disobedience dissent from some of the laws, but they don't reject the entire legal order. See Rawls (1999) 322–323.
40. Presuming the community is not rooted in morally reprehensible beliefs.
41. I am grateful to John Gardner for discussion on this point.
42. See Gardner 'Reasons for Teamwork' 64; Isaacs; and French.
43. One might prefer a thin concept of community that does not entail any feelings of kinship. But that does not match, I contend, our everyday use of the term.
44. If my response to the objection is successful I take it that is also a response to the problem of scale – that modern nations are simply too big to form agents.
45. Or perhaps it fell during COVID lockdown 2020.
46. David Miller (1989). *Market, State, and Community: Theoretical Foundations of Market Socialism* (Oxford: Clarendon Press, 1989).
47. Ibid., 238.
48. Ibid., 238.
49. Dworkin (1986) 169–171.
50. A similar point comes out of Christopher Kutz' (2002) work.
51. Gardner, 'Reasons for Teamwork' 499.
52. White Sox fans may be reminded of the Black Sox Scandal surrounding the 1919 World Series when the Chicago White Sox lost to the Cincinnati Reds. Eight of the White Sox players were accused of deliberately losing the series in exchange for money. The eight players accused were subsequently banned from baseball.
53. This is no doubt at least part of the reason team sports encourage bonding as well as skill development in practice.
54. The Right Honourable Pierre Elliot Trudeau, 1982 (cited in *The Charter of Rights and Freedoms*), 1.
55. W.J. Waluchow (2008).
56. Waluchow quoting Honoré, see, ibid 82.
57. A community can be divided into other smaller sub-groups in ways that are not necessarily problematic; for example, the groups that people form based on religion, culture, reading, or sports teams.
58. We might articulate the thought this way: we expect individuals to act with integrity and demonstrate commitment to their principles even when under pressure.
59. Waldron *Law and Disagreement.*
60. Mothers Against Drunk Driving.
61. For a more in depth discussion of a community's commitments, see Waluchow (2007).
62. Rawls makes, I believe, a similar argument in his discussion of public reason and judicial review. He highlights the difference between the potential anti-

majoritarian nature of judicial review with respect to a particular law and the potential antimajoritarian nature of judicial review with respect to higher law. Rawls argues that judicial review is not ultimately antimajoritarian when done in keeping with the higher law. Rawls argues that when judges decide based on public reason – that is based on reasons found in higher law, in charters and constitutions – they do not thwart democracy. See Rawls, *Political Liberalism* (1993). 233–234.

63. fl. John Rawls.
64. John Rawls (1997) 766.
65. Ibid., 769.
66. Ibid., 786.
67. See, for example, Steven Wall (2002).
68. See, for example, Michael Sandel (1998).

References

Bratman, M. (1999) *Faces of Intention: Selected Essays on Intention and Agency.* Cambridge: Cambridge University Press.

Dworkin, R. (1986) *Law's Empire.* London: Belknap.

Dworkin, R. (1989) 'Liberal Community', *California Law Review* 77(3):479–504.

French, P. (1979) 'The Corporation as a Moral Person', *American Philosophical Quarterly* 16 (3): 207–215.

Gardner, J. (2002) 'Reasons for Teamwork', *Legal Theory* 8(4):495–509.

Gardner, J. (2012) 'Some Types of Law', in his *Law as a Leap of Faith: Essays on Law in General.* Oxford: Oxford University Press. p. 63.

Held, V. (1970) 'Can a Random Collection of Individuals be Responsible?', *Journal of Philosophy* 67(14):471–481.

Isaacs, T. (2011) *Moral Responsibility in Collective Contexts.* Oxford: Oxford University Press.

Kutz, C. (2000) *Complicity: Ethics and Law for a Collective Age.* Cambridge: Cambridge University Press.

Kutz, C. (2002) 'The Collective Work of Citizenship', *Legal Theory* 8(4):471–494.

May, L. (1992) *Sharing Responsibility.* Chicago: University of Chicago Press.

Miller, D. (1989) *Market, State, and Community: Theoretical Foundations of Market Socialism.* Oxford: Clarendon Press.

Miller, D. (2004) 'Holding Nations Responsible', *Ethics* 114(2): 240–268.

Newman D. (2011). *Community and Collective Rights: A Theoretical Framework for Rights Held by Groups.* Oxford and Portland, Oregon: Hart Publishing.

Rawls, J. (1993) *Political Liberalism.* New York: Columbia University Press.

Rawls, J. (1997) 'The Idea of Public Reason Revisited', *The University of Chicago Law Review,* 64:765.

Rawls, J. (1999) *Theory of Justice Revised Edition.* Cambridge, MA: The Belknap Press of Harvard University Press.

Sandel, M. (1998) *Liberalism and the Limits of Justice*: Second edition. Cambridge: Cambridge University Press.

Tuomela, R. (2006) 'Joint Intention, We-Mode and I-Mode', *Midwest Studies in Philosophy* 30(1):35–58.

Waldron, J. (1999) *Law and Disagreement.* Oxford: Oxford University Press.

Wall, S. (2002) 'Is Public Justification Self-Defeating?', *American Philosophical Quarterly* 39(4):385–394.

Waluchow, W. (2007) *The Living Tree: A Common Law Theory of Judicial Review*. Cambridge: Cambridge University Press.

Waluchow, W. (2008). 'Constitutional Morality and Bills of Rights', in Grant Huscroft (ed), *Expounding the Constitution: Essays in Constitutional Theory*. Cambridge: Cambridge University Press.

13 One among many

Self-governance and alienation in mass action

Carla Bagnoli

A widespread view is that collective agency extends or adds to individual agency via distinctive forms of normative organization.[1] These forms of normative organization by which collective agency emerges are also modes of individual empowerment in that they add to the ways in which individuals act upon the world. Collective and shared agency allow individual agents to conceive of goals that they could not conceive by themselves and achieve ends that would otherwise be out of reach for each of them individually. Current theories of collective agency have predominantly considered collective actions generated by a steady and wholehearted mutual commitment among agents with equal normative standing, which is paradigmatic of dyadic personal relations (Gilbert 2006; Bratman 2014, 2018).

The cases chosen as paradigmatic of shared agency display three features. First, all members are required to wholeheartedly endorse or fully commit to the goal or plan of action. Second, all individuals partaking in the shared action have equal normative standing so that they can exercise symmetrical authority on one another.[2] Third, it is assumed that the individuals come to an agreement on the basis of common knowledge, and hence in a context of relevant epistemic transparency.

Such requirements may not seem especially demanding in the case of dyadic interactions, but they have a significant effect on the range of cases that are taken to be paradigmatic of collective agency. For they are too onerous to be generalized to large groups interactions. A common phenomenon is that the forms of coordination characterized by the three requirements become more and more difficult in proportion to the size of groups (Shapiro 2011). Even in dyadic interactions, shared agency is likely to break down at different joints, but such failures are more likely – if not pervasive – in the case of large groups. Shared agency seems to require a level of personal commitment on the side of each of the contributing parties that is unlikely to obtain when the groups are large.

The demandingness of the requirements raises an issue about the right scope of action theory. By adopting such stringent requirements, action theory makes a choice about the kinds of cases that it takes as worthy

DOI: 10.4324/9781003242451-18

of philosophical consideration. These requirements exclude various forms of collective actions: Digital masses, flash-mobs, financial crowds, for example, are common contemporary social phenomena and yet do not have a place in the current theory of collective action. This chapter draws a contrast among different collectives, and illustrates that the relation between agency and alienation is rather complex, and affects the ways in which individuals take responsibility for collective action.

13.1 Collective action via normative self-governance

Most theories of collective action assume that collective action arises through a normative mechanism by which the collective is organized and unified, (e.g., by the formation and adoption of a shared intention), though they differ as to how they account for its emergence, structure, and modes of self-governance over time. It is commonly assumed that shared action emerges and builds upon individual agency by augmenting or adding normative devices of self-governance that warrant coordination among a plurality of subjects. The basic claim is that such normative devices not only provide for normative governance but also constitute the collective agent. Conventions and agreements represent artifices by which individual agents bind one another. Some artifices are meant to generate non-instrumental forms of coordination.

For instance, Margaret Gilbert explains the notion of agreement and intentional joint action in terms of "joint commitment", which binds each contractor when they communicate to each other their "readiness *to join with them in (jointly) committing them all to endorse plan P as a body*", in a context of common knowledge (Gilbert 2014, p. 232). Insofar as two individuals jointly commit to go for a walk, they acquire reciprocal obligations and a claim-right to the other's walking along. They bear some responsibility to one another with regard to the success of their joint venture. If one fails to respect the obligation, the other one has a claim to protest and complain, and in some cases, to blame. On this construal, an agent's defective commitment can be resented insofar as it signals a lack of reciprocity and mutuality, which undermines joint action. Supposedly, this normative apparatus revolving around joint commitment explains how people acquire obligations by agreement and can be held responsible and resented for not doing what they committed to be doing jointly.

Michael Bratman provides a similar explanation of the authority and bindingness of shared intentions, though he is concerned with more modest forms of sociality, which do not necessarily produce obligations. In his view, self-governance and agential authority can be explained in terms of a planning capacity, through which human agents organize interpersonal and diachronic action (Bratman 1999, pp. 142–165, 2014, 2018).[3] Unlike Gilbert, Bratman's theory does not ground social action on the emergence of plural subjects, but it is not dismissive or debunking of phenomena of social agency, though it builds upon the conceptual and metaphysical apparatus of individual rationality (Bratman

2014, p. 11). On this account, coordination requires that the parties intend to cooperate but also that they are "appropriately responsive to the other; each is set not to thwart the other and is at least minimally disposed to help the other if needed; there is (feasibility-based) persistence interdependence in relevant intention; there is, as a result of all this, rational pressure in the direction of social rationality; each expects all of this to issue in the joint action each intends; and all this is out in the open" (Bratman 2014, p. 95).

Aside from important differences, these models of collective agency share three requirements that restrict the scope of their pertinence: (i) the individuals are brought together by wholehearted endorsement or full commitment, (ii) they have equal normative status and symmetrical authority, and (iii) they operate on the basis of common knowledge.

13.2 Alienation as a threat to collective agency

The requirements identified at the end of the previous section play a key role: they are meant to distinguish genuine and full-fledged forms of collective agency from the causal effects of mere aggregations of individuals who happen to converge on a goal. In fact, all such requirements can be regarded as specifications of what counts as genuine agency, in stark contrast to alienation. In the individual case, it is widely agreed that agency *par excellence* is such that agents bear an undistorted, transparent, and authoritative relation to their action (Korsgaard 2014). By contrast, alienation is a defective condition of agency, marked by a lack of authority, self-control, self-understanding, and self-knowledge. In all these forms, alienated agents undertake projects half-heartedly (Frankfurt 1971), unreflectively (Korsgaard 1996), or self-deceptively (Velleman 1992; Moran 2003), and thus fail to constitute themselves as agents.[4] Alienation may not be caused by external factors or agents: it may be self-generated. It is a defective condition of agency because it undermines the distinctive relation that agents should bear to their action by compromising the normative mechanism that authorizes agents to claim responsibility for what they do. This view of the disempowering role of alienation is extended to collective forms of agency, with the interesting result that it excludes from philosophical consideration large classes of social phenomena whose protagonists are collectives affected by various forms of alienation, such as anonymous multitudes, crowds, masses and occasional mobs.

Many theories share the view that the collectives that count as agents are unified by some normative mechanism which binds them together. For instance, equilibrium-based models of coordination by convention tend to assume conformity, i.e., that individuals are motivated to conform to practice because others do (Lewis 1969; Guala and Hindriks 2015). Such models exclude that convention may tolerate alienation due to lack of conforming motivation or the presence of an independent motivation. As already noted, for Gilbert's theory of joint commitments and Bratman's planning theory of shared intention, alienation represents a serious threat to collective agency.

For all these theories, alienation is not a mere impediment to coordination but a disruptive source of instability and uncertainty. It is a fragility internal and fatal to collective agency. This is apparent both in small and large groups, though with different consequences. In the case of large groups, if individual agents act of accord on the basis of principles that they only half-heartedly, unreflectively, or submissively endorse, their adherence is conditional upon such contingencies and may easily lapse. If the covenant is made unstable by alienation, its benefits vanish, and so do its explanatory merits.[5] In the case of small groups, and in particular, those collectives unified by personal relations and fiduciary attitudes, lack of endorsement, hypocrisy, lip service, dishonesty and disloyalty do not merely threaten the capacity for collective action but represent serious distortions of the collective dynamics, which badly affect the nature and success of their shared plans and projects.

13.3 Normative robustness via externality

A general strategy to protect personal relations from the sort of failures exemplified at the end of the previous section is to reinforce the normative structure of collective agency by formalizing and institutionalizing specific forms of sociality. A formalized agreement or contract is more robust than a personal commitment or agreement because it tolerates some level of alienation from the shared project. A case in point is a longstanding marriage, in which the couple becomes emotionally estranged from one another despite the fact that their routine remains intact over the years. Their personal relation has changed significantly, and thus the nature of their intimate shared project, but one could not sense that from any performative failure of coordination. Coordination is still guaranteed by habits, routines, and other elements of their relation, which support the original plan across relational changes.[6] It would be incorrect to say that in such cases, there remains only the shell of the marriage since the institution of marriage is called into play precisely to bind couples beyond and independently of their loving and personal commitment to one another. The married couple is bound by contract, whether or not it is bound by love. Something analogous can be said about non-contractual unions, for instance, in the case of a declaration of fidelity in front of a third person. The declaration fulfills its performative function whether or not the couple truly commits to one another in the subjective and personal sense of the term. This is how a public declaration bypasses personal relations. The contract of marriage and the public declaration institute a social fact, which is strong enough to resist the corrosion of time and the waning of affect.[7] Social facts like the institution of marriage exhibit a sort of robustness that makes them resilient and invulnerable to personal affects, whims, and moods; they are not unbreakable, but they are designed so as to resist individual idiosyncrasy. Exiting is possible, but governed by norms. This robustness depends on the *externality* of the social bond, which is one form of alienation, but it is also an effective strategy for preserving a shared intention originally expressed by the couple and making it authoritative across time.

Not all dyadic or small group interactions can be formally constrained by contracts and other informal social institutions, railed by customs or organized by patterns of habits. But the point here is that the formalization and institutionalization of interactions is better viewed as constituting a distinctive form of normative organization for collective agency rather than a strategy to circumvent the problem of alienation. That is to say, the formalization and institutionalization of personal relations transform their nature and originate a distinctive kind of collective agency. This is the *second* category of collective agency, in addition to the one presented in Section 13.1, and emerges from the relaxation of requirement (i) about wholehearted endorsement as the binding force of mutual commitment and shared intentions.

13.4 Forms of local alienation in distributed agency

The *third* category of collective agency can be identified by relaxing requirement (ii), which demands that all members in the collective have equal normative standing and authority so that they hold symmetrical positions in the process of generating and carrying on action (Shapiro 2011). In the case of large groups involved in the performance of large tasks, an effective strategy of coordination is *distribution*. In distributed collective agency, the deliberative and agential activity is distributed across different individuals. While there are horizontal distributions that maintain some forms of equal normative standing across the individuals, other distributions are vertical, and rely on hierarchy. The division of deliberative and agential labor may come with a significant measure of alienation. This is especially evident in the case of vertical or hierarchical distribution, in which various forms of *local* alienation and self-abnegation are put in place.[8] Factory workers participate in the production process, but for the success of the project, there is no need that they endorse the process production, nor that they intend to produce the products that the factory intends to produce.

In fact, the workers may have no knowledge of the production process in its entirety. So, at least in some cases of distributed agency, requirement (iii) of common knowledge is relaxed. Shared knowledge of the process is not necessary at all levels of the production process. While individual ignorance does not jeopardize shared action, lack of shared knowledge may well generate specific forms of alienation. In general, lack of shared knowledge of the process in which one partakes is an impediment to self-knowledge and obstructs self-understanding of oneself as an agent. This is a problematic condition from an epistemic and a practical point of view: it undermines self-awareness of one's place in the general process, and blocks the capacity for defection and reaction to objectionable strategies employed in the pursuit of the general plan. To this extent, lack of shared knowledge amounts to a loss of individual (epistemic and normative) power over the process.

Arguably, these kinds of individual alienation are not only by-products of distributed agency, but also functional to the success of the collective process. In sum, distributed agency builds upon alienation in a systematic and substantial way. In vertical distributions of agency that are organized around hierarchical authority, alienation is a core instrumental device that ensures coordination. In contrast to forms of coordination grounded on personal commitment and wholehearted endorsement, this is a device that can be effective across large collectives and sustained for a long period of time.

Among the various forms of hierarchies, Scott Shapiro characterizes "authorization", by which members of a group "surrender their exclusive power to plan and commit to follow the plans formulated and applied by the authorized members" (Shapiro 2011, p. 142). Ignorant, unexperienced and unmotivated individuals may be brought to act together "by requiring them to hand over vast amounts of planning power to us" (Shapiro 2011, p. 149). As Shapiro remarks, "The beauty of the scheme is that the workers themselves need not care a whit about helping us; their interest can lie simply in earning enough money to make it to the next audition. Nor do they have to understand how the whole enterprise hangs together. As long as they do what they are told, our business prospers" (Shapiro 2011, p. 149). These apparent advantages are achieved at serious individual losses and can be targeted as forms of alienation which gravely affect the life of the workers and their conception of their prospects (Jaeggi 2016).

A measure of personal alienation is present also in the case of horizontal division of labor insofar as different individuals are in charge at subsequent stages of decision-making, but they have no knowledge nor control over what comes before and after their intervention. In particular, they are kept in ignorance of the way in which their work is continued at a later stage and how it contributes to the general task. In fact, the segment of the deliberative process of which individuals are in charge may be so limited that they have no sense of the entire plan. This may not be a particularly worrisome condition. At no stage in the plan, full individual commitment or wholehearted endorsement is neither necessary nor required for the success of collective action.

In the factory production case, the alienation of agential power is a normative mechanism that distinctively pertains to and creates macro-actions, that is, actions performed by large groups. Remarkably, the point is not that such deliberative processes *tolerate* a lower level of commitment in contrast to the intentionalist model of individual, dyadic and small group agency. Rather, the point is that, in these cases, collective action *thrives on* alienation, lack of commitment, and estrangement, and thus can be successfully generated in the absence of attitudes of reciprocity and trust. Thus, macro-actions are possible not merely in the face of alienation but because of it. Whether and on which grounds the costs in terms of personal alienation and estrangement are morally and politically objectionable is a further normative issue, which I have to set aside. My point here is that serious forms of practical and epistemic alienation are structural to normative systems of distributed agency; this is why such systems are irreducible to the model presented in Section 13.1.

13.5 The externality of law and conflict management

The possibility of collective actions that relax the three requirements for collective agency does not show that the theories presented in Section 13.1 fail to account for collective agency, but only that they succeed to identify a narrow range of collective actions, which is hardly generalizable to large collectives. It is a further and open question whether such theories can be adapted to adequately cover such cases.

Focusing on the importance of regulatory practices in the case of distributed agency, Scott Shapiro has recently argued that Bratman's planning theory could be expanded to cover macro-actions and, perhaps more interestingly, collective processes that aim at macro-actions by managing conflicts. That is because planning is crucial not only to the structural organization of collective action and to the maintenance of its authority over time, but more generally, to smoothing out conflicts among individual members of the group. Planning is a key resource in conflict management in that it *avoids* litigations, disputes, and fights: "Prior planning allows the community members to treat questions of fairness and what they ought to each other as settled, as matters not up for reconsideration. And in this way, they are able not only to economize on costs and increase predictability of behavior, but also to facilitate an ethic of respect among the entire community" (Shapiro 2011, p. 153).

In this perspective, the rule of law itself can be regarded as an "overarching planning" tool designed to respond to the predicaments paradigmatic of multitudes of interdependent individuals.[9] In some cases, the decision is settled on grounds similar to customs and habits; in others, the code of law relies on ethical arguments and principles that are not reducible to the patterns of habits. In either case, and differently than in the case of agreements that determine shared agency, regulatory policies work as normative constraints and generate trade-offs. In routine cases, the policy settles the matter because the trade-offs are acceptable.[10]

By and large, we can assume that conflicts can be negotiated by the law. But it is likely that in particularly trying contexts of choice, when the trade-offs are not obvious, regulatory norms become themselves a matter of deliberation. The result of this deliberation depends, again, on the specific features of the context of choice and does not merely rest on considerations about whether the risk of sub-optimal outcomes in conforming to the policy outweights the fatigue and costs of repeated deliberation and bargaining – *pace* Shapiro (Shapiro 2011, 2017).

In such cases, the appeal to policies that admit of trade-offs invite considerations about their grounds, which are normative and meta-normative. That is, they are considerations about which grounds make the policy legitimate, and meta-normative considerations about whether it makes sense to settle the matter of what to do by following the policy or by taking another route. This is to say that policies do *not* solve the problem of coordination but raise the stakes at a deeper level. At the deeper level, deliberation concerns the normative justificatory grounds of choice and the sort of reasoning that has better chances to solve the problem.

In spite of these difficulties,[11] Shapiro is right that in most cases, the law suffices for a collective to settle on a decision. In general, settling by law allows for courses of action on grounds that are independent of each of the contending parties. In this case, coordination among parties is reached not by convergence on a shared intention or plan but by handing the conflict over to a third party, i.e., a court of law.

13.6 The dynamics of law enforcement

I have argued that some forms of alienation are constitutive of some forms of collective agency. When alienation is found to be a constitutive element of the coordination strategy, how is compliance guaranteed? In place of personal commitment and endorsement, there are mechanisms of enforcement, which include sanctions and incentives.

According to Shapiro, such mechanisms are vital to the existence of large collectives, and their function is *corrective* and *compensatory*: "Planning becomes more and more important as the mass enlarges, and so do mechanisms of enforcement. They compensate for lack of trust and reciprocity and ambivalence in personal commitment. These are strategies for regulating individual actions in communal settings, e.g., institutions and dwelling. So that they do not overpower one another or undermine each other's ends" (Shapiro 2011, p. 152).[12]

Even though enforcement is corrective and compensatory, we may envision different ways in which it supports the system of law. On a mechanicanistic understanding, enforcement simply sanctions non-compliance and generates a specular incentive to non-defection. A problem of this hypothesis is that it is unlikely that a lawful arrangement may be kept in place by sanctions that punish defection and non-compliance. By contrast, it is arguable that any system of law allows for several different mechanisms of enforcement and also that such mechanisms dynamically interact with the rule of law. This hypothesis illustrates that specific modes of enforcement affect the motives and reasons for full compliance. The mechanisms of law enforcement come in different varieties, and each variety implicates personal volitions and motivations in distinctive ways. Some of these varieties are simply meant to warrant rule compliance (e.g., notices of parking fines). But other corrective measures may have larger tasks, while still compensatory, in that they are meant to encourage the defiant individual to endorse the general plan underlying the civil society (e.g., by experiencing social service). In the former case, the application of sanctions is likely to have an impact on the transgressor on the assumption of risk aversion. In the latter case, instead, it is arguable that the impact is more significant, as it is meant to foster or restore full membership in the civil society (Bennett 2008). In turn, the sense of membership may importantly affect the shape of the collective in that it is a legitimate ground for identity claims and rights.

These differences are of uttermost relevance in considering the dynamics of normative governance of agency in the case of large groups. To this extent, the collective agency organized by a system of law represents an important addition to the form of collective agency identified in Section 13.1. First, in a system of law obligations apply to individuals whether or not they endorse their content, and independently of whether such individuals consider themselves active members of the collective body. This is particularly important in accounting for duties of right and political obligations, which "apply even to members who are alienated or uncommitted to the goals of the society" (Paul 2021, p. 151).[13]

Second, the interplay between the rule of law and the mechanisms of law enforcement points out that the collective organized by law bears a dynamic structure, which exploits and tolerates different forms of alienation at different levels. The various modes of enforcement play a fundamental role, which is compensatory, but not merely backward-looking, in that they also contribute to generate a sense of membership, on which identity claims and rights can be based.

There is a strict relation between a people organized by the rule of law and issues about political identity, and this phenomenon requires at least a qualification about the scope and authority of the rule of law. The rule of law does not merely arbitrate local disagreements, nor are its effects limited to ensuring rule compliance. In addition to the management of local conflicts and disagreements, the rule of law fulfills another and more general function: it sets the background for expressing disagreements and conflicts and making them negotiable. A better approach to this overarching function requires that one pays attention to the systematic normative structure of the law. Rather than enabled by nested plans, the system of law is founded on two kinds of rules: constitutive and applicative. In the Kantian tradition, the idea of a law is best understood in terms of constitutive or "power-conferring" norms. Such norms are not general commands to be enforced, in the way discussed in the next section. This is because not all laws are coercive and such that they require individuals to perform or omit kinds of action. Rather, they are rules by which rights and duties are generated.[14] The rule of law works as a *system*, which institutes and organizes a large collective: it sets the framework within which a collective agent is constituted. To this extent, the externality of the rule of law originates a distinctive form of collective agency, which is not organized by an internal self-governance. This is a category of collective agency analogous to the one examined in Section 13.3, except for its systematic character. Ultimately, the robustness warranted by externality should be understood as justified by the normative system of law. In other words, it is the normative system of law that explains the normative authority of its obligations.

13.7 Collective agency by crowd-channeling?

The categories of collective action identified thus far are made possible by constraining normative arrangements that ensure normative self-governance. While some of these arrangements are apt to account for dyadic or small groups interactions, others bring together in action large collectives by exploiting various forms of alienation. In the next two sections, I explore the hypothesis that collective agency may occur without any form of normative organization. *If* this hypothesis is correct, then there is a *fifth* category of macro-actions, those performed by *masses*, that is, large collectives that are not internally organized around a normative core, in contrast to collectives examined thus far.

An example of macro-action performed by the masses is crowdsourcing. In marketing centered on crowdsourcing, crowds shape platform markets, thereby having positive and negative social effects. In particular, sharing economy on crowds has an impact on social welfare. Supposedly, enlightened rulers may devise strategies of governing the causal powers of crowds, with the intent to avoid the socially distorting effects of the market or in pursuit of the highest public good. In revisionary planning of new marketing strategies, the use of crowd power could be re-directed to counteract a dominant sharing platform's market power so as to become a positive political force (Gal 2019).

Is this causal power sufficient to credit *the crowd* with any agency at all? Are the effects on the market "actions" that can be imputed to crowds? That is, has the crowd agential powers, in addition to causal powers? These questions are only partly answered by remarking that the causal impact of crowds can be constrained and regulated. First, there are constraints to the causal power of crowds, which pertain to the very form of causal interactions that crowds may be likely to entertain once they make their appearance on the market. Second, the causal power of crowds can be, and generally is, also normatively constrained, e.g., regimented by strategic planning and current legislation. This is a normative operation, but it is not reducible to any of the strategies presented in the previous sections. The normative structure channels the causal power of the crowd, without shaping it into an identifiable collective.

A common view is that the examples in which the causal force of crowds is channeled do not prove that crowds have original agentive powers. The examples show, rather, that crowds can be hetero-directed and thus used strategically. The norms that channel their causal power have an external source, but we have seen that externality is not always an obstacle to the emergence of collective agency, nor an impediment to its stability. On the contrary, alienation may foster collective agency.

A stronger reason for rejecting the view that crowds are collective agents is that they are brought together by *channeling* mechanisms that do not suffice to impose on them a normative *organization*: such channelling mechanisms do not create any normative bond among the individuals constituting the crowd.

In contrast to the case of law enforcement, the individuals targeted by strategic crowdsourcing do not qualify as "members" of any community because crowdsourcing strategies do not have rules of membership. Correspondingly, there is no rule of recognition: anyone can add or depart at any time without impacting on the identity of the crowd, unless we understand identity to be fully determined by size. To be sure, the law still *applies* to crowds and masses, but it does so through the means of strategic planning. The emergence of the people through the system of law is a process of incremental normativity, which can be regarded as the opposite of the process of mass formation, e.g., in crowd-channeling.

Thus, one may conclude that masses and crowds do not count as collective agents because crowd-channeling does not suffice to provide the crowds with the normative credentials to be a collective agent. This conclusion presupposes that such credentials take the form of a distinctive normative organization, which adds, augments, or compensates for the limited agentive powers of individuals. In the next section, I consider an alternative approach.

13.8 Collective agency by radical alienation

To establish whether and under which conditions the actions of crowds count as genuine exercises of agency, I suggest that we take another route and consider the subject implicated in action. On the view pursued thus far, the mass is unorganized, and because of it, it is shapeless and *inert*. Its causal power can be appropriated by other agencies. Lacking any normative form of self-governance, the mass also lacks agential power, and its actions are explained as externally orchestrated. Like the children charmed by the Pied Piper of Hamelin, the inert crowds retain no responsibility for what they do and can be driven to act on externally imposed aims.

By contrast, on a dynamic conception, the mass has a distinctive agential power, though it lacks a coherent intentional normative structure. The emergence of masses does not involve any planning, nor does it build upon instrumental interactions. Joining the mass does not have to be an intentional step. In fact, there might not be identifiable steps by which individual agents become a mass. The formation of masses may not be initiated by any open call to join, in contrast to the case of strategic channeling. It may be the effect of interlocking, intermittent, or diluted processes of different forms of manipulation, which aim at transforming individuals into indistinguishable elements of a mass.

In fact, what confers the distinctive power to the mass is the *loss* of any internal normative structure. According to the hypothesis articulated by Elias Canetti (1960), individuals become a mass through a *transforming experience, by which they lose* individuality, and with it, any subjective goal, drive, and willpower.[15] Joining a mass entails dropping the boundaries that separate individuals. In many ways, this is a loss. However, the loss of separateness is comforting, and it is not subjectively experienced as disempowering. First, once individuals lose their *sense of being separate* they also release their distinctive willpower and, consequently, become insensitive to emotions associated with the condition of subjective vulnerability, which is a permanent feature of individual agency (such as, e.g., frustration, fear of loss, dependency, or grief), and emotions arising from comparison to others (such as, e.g., envy). This is one sense in which becoming a mass is liberating.

Second, the experience of radical alienation is described as an experience of radical equality.[16] This distinctive experience opens up the possibility of a new form of agency, and to this extent, it is felt as empowering. By losing one's individuality, one is enabled to act as a mass because anyone is functionally equivalent to any other, and not because individuals have become interchangeable, but because there is no need for discrimination on the basis of function, status, or skills. For Canetti, the experience of radical equality is a key experience that explains how various normative (moral and political) ideals of equality become subjectively authoritative: "All demands for justice and all theories of equality ultimately derive their energy from the actual experience of equality familiar to anyone who has been part of a crowd" (Canetti 1960, p. 29). I have strong reservations about the claim that this conception of radical alienation is conducive to a feasible and valuable model of equal moral standing. It is disputable that this mechanism of alienation is apt to vindicate and ground the kind of unconditional cooperation and reciprocity, which is presumed to be at work in a system of morality.[17] Furthermore, the recognition of equal moral standing does not have to be understood in stark contrast to the recognition of differences and individualities.

Why, then, should we take seriously Canetti's conjecture? What we gain is a fifth category of macro-actions by large collectives, which do not exhibit a normative organization. By relaxing the condition of the normative organization, we capture minimal forms of sociality that elude other theories. The change in focus brings to the fore considerations that otherwise remain in the background. First of all, when considering the varieties of collective agency, it emerges that alienation and agential authority stand in a complex and dynamic relation, in ways that are overshadowed and underestimated by the dominance of intentionalist accounts of agency. In particular, it is underappreciated that the various modes of alienation and externality are not merely collateral effects and byproducts of the normative arrangements which give rise to specific collective agents, but rather they are constitutive elements of the kind of coordination that is effective in the case of large groups of individuals. In some relevant cases, such as the system of law, the modes of external enforcement stand in a constructive and dynamic relation to collective agency. They can be internalized by education and thus become stabilized drives of social cohesion.

Second, the departure from the dominant intentionalist approach enables us to reconsider the range of commonalities between collective and diachronic agency on which plan-theorists have insisted (Bratman 2018). In contrast to key cases of shared agency, macro-actions performed by masses, such as flash-mob performances or orchestrated mob riots, tend to be limited in time, though they mobilize enormous groups of individuals. The fact that mass actions may not be sustainable for a long period of time does not mean that they can't be socially significant and even momentous. In fact, sometimes mass actions acquire an expressive and symbolic value precisely because of the size of the collective, rather than in view of a shared purpose or sustained activity. Such actions become themselves polarizing *foci* of new commonalities or create the opportunity to reaffirm and reinvigorate old loyalties. For instance, an infuriated mob that destroys statues commemorating values cherished by a given community signals a rupture in the civic society, and at the same time, it offers individuals the opportunity to identify themselves in relation to this divide or its reconciliation.

Another case in point – less politically charged but not altogether devoid of political value – is artistic mass performance. For instance, some mass performances by Marina Abramović originate in the artist's losing control over her embodied agency,[18] thereby forcefully implicating others into action; others openly aim at creating "new forms of interaction, and reinforcing a sense of community while fostering collective consciousness through art".[19] The resulting collective action may be occasional and unique and yet represents a distinctive bonding experience with long-lasting consequences. The artistic setting is in some ways "alienated" insofar as it is fictitious, and yet liberating and conducive to some important findings, about oneself as a responsible agent in a world of beauty and sufferance, as a member of a virtual community rather than as an alienated bystander. But the rituality of these artistic experiences enacts the possibility of representing oneself as a community member, though of a virtual kind.

Finally, and most importantly, the conjecture that the mass is dynamic introduces the idea that collective action may arise because of distinctive emotional experiences rather than around a normative core of intentions and commitments. The subjective experience of radical alienation is transforming: individuals learn to represent themselves as inseparable, unidentified elements of a whole rather than as separate identifiable deliberative units. This condition, even though entertained for a short while, becomes the normative mold for relating to one another as bare equals. This conjecture uncovers modes and functions of collective behaviors that otherwise remain unintelligible.

13.9 Alienation and responsibility

The various forms of collective agency identified in the course of this discussion show that alienation and agential authority stand in a complex relation. This finding is of some consequence for the issue of responsibility in collective action and marks a significant contrast with the sphere of individual agency.[20]

In the case of individual action, alienation is a ground for disclaiming responsibility for action. In some especially severe cases, it may be sufficient to reject the ascription of full-fledged agency and may provide an excuse that shields the agent from moral judgment and blame, though not necessarily. The relation between alienation and responsibility is not as straightforward in the case of collective action. Different forms of collective agency call for different notions of individual responsibility in group agency.

A strict relation between responsibility and lack of alienation can be defended only for the first category of collective actions presented in Section 13.1, though one may still be considered morally responsible for not being able to firmly and truly commit to shared agency. In the case in which the collective is kept together by a formal agreement, as in Section 13.3, the individuals are held responsible for entering such agreement and for the actions that fall within the domain of the agency that the agreement covers. For more complex forms of collective agency that implicate large groups in action, more differentiated concepts of distributed responsibility become necessary.

Some cases of distributed agency call into play the concept of *delegation*. Individuals composing the mass could be held (morally) responsible and blamed for having delegated their agency in full or in the relevant respects to other individuals. Delegation is an agential prerogative, and one remains responsible for its delegates, within some constraints, though may not retain full agential responsibility for the action delegated. The advantage of aligning macro-action to delegated action is to highlight that the degree of causal involvement or effective participation of individuals in macro-action is not always the criterion for the ascription of moral responsibility. Individual agents remain individually morally responsible for their participation in mass action. To forego one's individual agential responsibility for action does not excuse from the attribution of moral responsibility. On the contrary, delegation may be precisely the action under moral assessment.

In the case of distributed collective action, each person retains special responsibilities, which derive from the special role or function that they occupy. But it is arguable that not all sorts of responsibilities can be delegated, and that even in the case of collective processes that are segmented and hyper-specialized, individuals retain moral responsibility, and are entitled to demand shared knowledge of such processes. So, for instance, factory workers have the right and also the duty to know what and how they contribute to produce.

In some cases of macro-action, it might be appropriate to introduce the notion of *top-down co-responsibility*, by which the individual agents constituting the group are held accountable for the group's action as a whole because they meet the criteria of membership in the relevant group (Petersson 2008). This is a vertical form of responsibility because it transfers top-down from the group to its members. Insofar as the group is marked by membership and thus by the rule of recognition, it might seem that this notion is inapplicable to the case of crowdsourcing and radical alienation. On the basis of this consideration, it may seem that crowdsourcing is better explained as mere *convergence of individuals* in macro-action in pursuit of individual plans and interests. The resulting collective action is heterogeneous in regard to the individual ends, which indicates that action does not depend on coordination. The ordinary notion of individual responsibility is applicable here: it is a matter of tracking the relevant normative and causal relations among individual agents and establishing who did what, at what time, and why they converged on the action. But the model of convergence does not fully capture the fact that even in the example of crowdsourcing, all individuals act on the presumption that many others will do the same and that only a massive response will grant the success of collective action.

As for the case of radical alienation, it can be argued that it is the very subjective experience of radical alienation that generates "membership" in the mass. Such membership is not gained by meeting requirements that apply to individuals but by expropriating individuals of intrinsic value. By joining the mass, individuals partaking in the macro-action become top-down responsible for what the mass does.

The concept of delegation may help explain not only the emergence of the mass but also the responsibilities associated with its inception. For instance, in the case of crowdsourcing, it is arguable that crowds are not used as mere instruments by strategic channeling by mysterious forms of manipulation and driven to action in the manner of the charmed crowd following the Pied Piper of Hamelin, but they are *engaged*, openly and directly or via crowdsourcing agencies (Sheehan & Pittman 2019). Arguably, how to respond to such solicitations is and remains an individual responsibility, even though the depth and contours of specific responsibilities heavily depend on the relevant knowledge acquired.

There may be cases of macro-actions, which are thoroughly generated by manipulation, and whose generation involves no exercise of reflective agency, and at no identifiable point, individuals are openly consulted and engaged in action. In such cases, it is more difficult to determine precisely which responsibilities individuals have retained, contracted, or acquired throughout the process of mass formation. Nonetheless, it is arguable that individuals have become co-responsible with the mass, despite the fact that they cannot recount how that happened.

Conclusion

Alienation is generally considered a sign of defective agency and a threat to coordination. In Sections 13.1 and 13.2, I have argued that the latter claim is based on the widespread view that collective agency arises by adding to or augmenting normative self-governance. In Sections 13.3–13.6, I have shown that some modes of alienation serve as coordinative mechanisms, which bypass individual commitment and intention. In Sections 13.7 and 13.8, I have pointed to cases of macro-actions that build upon radical alienation. In Section 13.9, I have offered some preliminary considerations about individual responsibility in massively shared action, focusing on the moral impact of delegation.[21]

Notes

1. The former expression refers to reductivist accounts and "augmented individualism" such as Bratman's, while the latter refer to non-reductivist accounts such as Gilbert's.
2. Theorists disagree about the force and level of bindingness. For instance, some think that personal relations generate moral obligations (Korsgaard 1996), others that the obligations thereby generated are not "moral" (Gilbert 2006); and, finally, others hold that the bindingness should not be understood in terms of obligations but in terms of a "rational pressure" (Bratman 2014, 2018).
3. Bratman (2014, p. 106). It is an open question whether the features of conceptual simplicity and metaphysical parsimony provide an advantage in comparison to competing views of collective agency, such as Margaret Gilbert and John Searle, see, e.g., Petersson (2008). Simplicity and metaphysical minimalism are certainly *prima facie* theoretical virtues of any theory, unless proven inapt to adequately explain the phenomena, see Tuomela (2014). But how to construe the phenomena is precisely the main philosophical issue. Thus, theories cannot be merely tested against the phenomena. There may not be one encompassing theory that explains all modes of sociality, and so we should be open to pluralism about the theoretical accounts that fare best in accounting for radically different forms of social agency.
4. This view of the relation between agency and alienation has been seriously criticized from the perspective of the theory of rational agency (e.g., Buss 2014), the metaphysics of agency (e.g., Hornsby 2015), and also from the ethical and political perspective (e.g., Oshana 2002).
5. This reasoning is inspired by Kant's distinction between acting for the sake of duty or in conformity to it (G, Section 1), and his subsequent distinction between broad and strict duties, duties of virtue and duties of right (MM). It might be conceded that the attitude of conformity is sufficient for *some* kind of stability, though it is not stability for the right reasons. But the point is that any such stability is conditional on individual attitudes. One does not know when the rule will break down, and this is another source of uncertainty. This is why conformity to rules must be enforceable, see Section 13.4. Kant argues that compliance with some obligations (i.e., duties of right) is externally enforceable (in contrast to duties of virtue). The distinction between duties of right and duties of virtue establishes three important points. First, in the case of right, the will to conform to duty is sufficient to fulfill the obligations. Second, duties of right are applicable and enforceable independently of the state of mind of the subject to which they apply. Third, failures to conform to duty are externally sanctioned, and can be prosecuted. For a study on the nature of moral incentives as warranting the subjective authority of duty, see Bagnoli (2011).
6. On the claim that habits and customs lessen the need for repeated deliberation and bargaining, see Shapiro (2011, p. 140).
7. Importantly, this institution does not coexist with other forms of alienation, such as coercion. In fact, understood as a formalized commitment, marriage is based on consent and invalidated by coercion.
8. I talk of local alienation in contrast to radical alienation. The presence of various forms of alienation does not indicate that the agent lacks altogether agential autonomy. A self-abnegating worker lacks contact with their agency, but only under some description e.g., as a worker. For a study of self-abnegation against their will, in absence of their will, or voluntarily, see Wieland (2021).
9. Shapiro (2011, p. 17). The rules of law are grounded in the capacity that all individuals possess to adopt plans, Shapiro (2011, p. 119), Schauer (2010, p. 595, n. 33). This can be regarded as an attempt to explain how the law can provide normative

reasons for action. This is not a new idea. H. L. A. Hart's *The Concept of Law* can be regarded as a paradigm of this way of construing the function of law (Hart 1961, Shapiro 2017).

10. On a first formulation of the view that the law is to be understood in terms of planning, Shapiro holds that legal officials act together only if most intend to contribute to the creation and maintenance of a unified system of norms, Shapiro (2002, pp. 419–421). But this requirement is too strong. In order to engage in the shared intentional activity of legal regulation, it is sufficient that there be a shared plan (which does not require intentions to contribute to the goals of the plan), and the members of the group must act on that plan, see Shapiro (2009, p. 20).
11. Shapiro recognizes that a legal system's shared plan does not resolve all normative uncertainty (Shapiro 2009, p. 19). The notion of plan is typically partial: plans settle certain questions about what is to be done, but leave other issues undecided (Bratman 1987, pp. 28–30).
12. "Alienated members cooperate more easily when they can rely on precise instructions, and when the instructions are enforced", Shapiro (2011, p. 152).
13. This contradicts an objectionable claim of Gilbert's theory of political obligations, according to Paul (2021).
14. See Reath (2006, p. 177) and Bagnoli (2017). In legal theory, this distinction may be cast in reference to Hart's concept of law (1961), in contrast to John Austin's command theory of law.
15. On the loss of individuality, compare Foucault (1982), Maffesoli (1988) and Honneth (1996). For a suggestive history of crowds, see McClelland (1989).
16. "It is of fundamental importance and one might even define a crowd as a state of absolute equality. A head is a head, an arm is an arm, and the differences between individual heads and arms are irrelevant. It is for the sake of this equality that people become a crowd and they tend to overlook anything which might detract from it", Canetti (1960, p. 29).
17. It seems to me that this conception of radical alienation shares some features that are fatal to the monological view of moral obligation, which relies on an alienating divide within the reflective conscience, between the "thinking self" and the "acting self", see e.g., Korsgaard (1996, p. 104). By contrast, I favor a dialogical account in which interdependent rational agents are engaged in a shared activity constrained and driven by respect and recognition, see Bagnoli (2017). On my view, it is a moral sensibility grounded on respect that provides obligations with the required subjective authority, see Bagnoli (2011).
18. https://mai.art/; http://www.marinaabramovic.com/bio.html
19. https://mai.art/terra-comunal-content/2015/4/22/overlapping-memories
20. The claim that there is a conceptual link between agential autonomy and (moral) responsibility has been questioned also in the individual domain of agency, but with different implications than the ones I notice here. For instance, Oshana (2002) has targeted the view that there is a strong conceptual overlap between autonomy and responsibility, on the ground that it conflates the global state of being autonomous with the local condition of acting autonomously or exhibiting autonomy in respect to some act or decision. While the local phenomenon of autonomy may be closely tied to the condition of being responsible for an act, it is disputable that the global autonomy is the condition of responsibility. Oshana concludes that autonomous agency and responsible agency are logically distinct, and calls for different conceptions of rationality. I share the latter claim, though I disagree with Oshana about the conceptions of rationality that she associates with the ascription of responsibility and agency, respectively.
21. I would like to thank the editors, Damiano Canale, and an anonymous referee, for their useful comments on earlier drafts.

References

Bagnoli Carla. 2011. "Emotions and the Categorical Authority of Moral Reasons", In *Morality and the Emotions*, ed. by C. Bagnoli. Oxford: Oxford University Press, 62–81.

Bagnoli Carla. 2017. "Kant in Metaethics: The Paradox of Autonomy, Solved by Publicity", In *The Palgrave Kant Handbook/Palgrave Handbooks in German Idealism*, ed. Matthew Altman. London: Palgrave Macmillan, 355–377.

Bennett Christophe. 2008. *The Apology Ritual*. Cambridge: Cambridge University Press.

Bratman, E. Michael 1987. *Intention, Plans, and Practical Reason*. Cambridge: Harvard University Press.

Bratman, E. Michael. 1999. "I Intend that We J", In *Faces of Intention: Selected Essays on Intention and Agency*, 142–161. Cambridge: Cambridge University Press.

Bratman, E. Michael. 2006. "Planning Agency, Autonomous Agency", In *Structures of agency: Essays*, 195–222. Oxford and New York: Oxford University Press.

Bratman, E. Michael. 2014. *Shared Agency: A Planning Theory of Acting Together*. Oxford and New York: Oxford University Press.

Bratman, E. Michael. 2018. *Planning, Time and Self-Governance*. Oxford and New York: Oxford University Press.

Buss, Sarah 2014. "The Possibility of Action as the Impossibility of Certain Forms of Self-Alienation". *Oxford Studies in Agency and Responsibility* 1:12–46.

Canetti, Elias. 1960. *Crowds and Power*, translated by Carol Stewart. London: Penguin Books, 1973.

Foucault, Michel. 1982. "Subject and Power". *Critical Inquiry* 8 (4):777–795.

Frankfurt, Harry G. 1971. "Freedom of the Will and the Concept of a Person". *Journal of Philosophy* 68:5–20.

Gal, Michal S. 2019. "The Power of the Crowd in the Sharing Economy". *The Law and Ethics of Human Rights* 13 (1):29–59.

Gilbert, Margaret. 2006. *A Theory of Political Obligation: Membership, Commitment, and the Bonds of Society*. Oxford: Oxford University Press.

Gilbert, Margaret. 2014. "The Nature of Agreements: A Solution to Some Puzzles about Claim-Rights and Joint Intention", In *Rational and Social Agency: The Philosophy of Michael Bratman*, eds. Manuel Vargas and Gideon Yaffe, 190–215. New York: Oxford University Press, 215–256.

Guala, Francesco and Hindricks, Frank. 2015. "Institutions, Rules, and Equilibria: A Unified Theory", *Journal of Institutional Economics* 11: 459–480.

Hart, H. L. A. 1961. *The Concept of Law*. Oxford: Oxford University Press.

Honneth, Axel. 1996. "The Perpetuation of the State of Nature: On the Cognitive Content of Elias Canetti's Crowds and Power". *Thesis Eleven* 45 (1):69–85.

Hornsby, Jennifer 2015. "Agency and Alienation", In *Naturalism In Question*, eds. M. de Caro and D. MacArthur, 173–187. Cambridge: Harvard University Press.

Jaeggi, Rahel. 2016. *Alienation*. New York: Columbia University Press.

Lewis, David K. 1969. *Convention: A Philosophical Study*. Wiley-Blackwell.

Kant, I. 1907. *Kants gesammelte Schriften*. Berlin: Preussische Akademie der Wissenschaften (Ak).

Kant, I. (1996) Groundwork of the Metaphysics of Morals (1785), in: M. Gregor (ed.) The Cambridge Edition of the Works of Immanuel Kant: Practical Philosophy (Cambridge, Cambridge University Press), pp. 37–108. (Abbreviated G)

Kant, I. (1996) The Metaphysics of Morals (1797), in: M. Gregor (ed.) The Cambridge Edition of the Works of Immanuel Kant: Practical Philosophy (Cambridge, Cambridge University Press), pp. 353–604. (Abbreviated MM)

Korsgaard, Christine M. 1996. *The Sources of Normativity*. Cambridge: Cambridge University Press.

Korsgaard, Christine. M. 2014. The Normative Constitution of Agency. In *Rational and Social Agency: The Philosophy of Michael Bratman*, ed. Manuel Vargas and Gideon Yaffe, 190–215. New York: Oxford University Press.

Maffesoli, Michel. 1988 [1996]. *The Time of the Tribes: The Decline of Individualism in Mass Society*, translated by Don Smith. London: SAGE.

McClelland, J. 1989. *The Crowd and the Mob: From Plato to Canetti*. London: Unwin Hyman.

Moran, Richard. 2003. *Authority and Estrangement*. Princeton University Press.

Oshana, Marina A. L. 2002. "The Misguided Marriage of Responsibility and Autonomy". *The Journal of Ethics* 6 (3):261–280.

Paul, Sarah. 2021. *Philosophy of Action: A Contemporary Introduction*. New York and London: Routledge.

Petersson, Björn. 2008. "Collective Omissions and Responsibility". *Philosophical Papers* 37 (2):243–261.

Reath, Andrews. 2006. *Agency and Autonomy in Kant's Moral Theory*. New York: Oxford University Press.

Shapiro, Scott J. 2011. "Massively Shared Agency" was previously published in *Teoria e Critica della Regolazione Sociale*, 5, 2011, in a special issue on "Intenzionalità collettiva e figure della responsabilità", available online at http://mimesisedizioni.it/journals/index.php/tcrs/article/view/30/28

Shapiro, Scott J. 2002. "Law, Plans, and Practical Reason". *Legal Theory* 8 (4):387–441.

Shapiro, Scott J. 2009. "What Is the Rule of Recognition (and Does It Exist)?", In *The Rule of Recognition and the U.S. Constitution*, eds. Matthew Adler and Kenneth Himma. Oxford: Oxford University Press, 2009; *Yale Law School*, Public Law Working Paper No. 184. Available at SSRN: https://ssrn.com/abstract=1304645

Schauer, Frederick. 2010. "The Best Laid Plans", *Yale Law Journal* 120: 586–621.

Sheehan, Kim Bartel and Pittman, Matthew. 2019. "Straight from the Source? Media Framing of Creative Crowd Labor and Resultant Ethical Concerns". *Journal of Business Ethics* 154 (2):575–585.

Tuomela, Raimo. 2014. Review of Michael E. Bratman. *Shared Agency: A Planning Theory of Acting Together*. Oxford University Press. https://ndpr.nd.edu/news/shared-agency-a-planning-theory-of-acting-together/

Velleman, David. 1992. "What Happens When Someone Acts?", *Mind* 101: 461–481. Reprinted at pp. 123–143 in Velleman 2000.

Wieland, Nellie. 2021. "The Abnegated Self", In *Virtue Narrative, and Self: Explorations of Character in the Philosophy of Mind and Action*, eds. Joseph Ulatowksi and Liezl van Zyl, London and New York: Routledge, chapter 12.

Index

Note: Folios followed by "n" indicate endnotes in the text.

For Product Safety Concerns and Information please contact our EU representative GPSR@taylorandfrancis.com
Taylor & Francis Verlag GmbH, Kaufingerstraße 24, 80331 München, Germany

www.ingramcontent.com/pod-product-compliance
Lightning Source LLC
LaVergne TN
LVHW021120300926
849160LV00010B/790

* 9 7 8 1 0 3 2 1 5 0 8 3 3 *